PHILIP W. LOWN INSTITUTE
OF ADVANCED JUDAIC STUDIES

BRANDEIS UNIVERSITY

Studies and Texts

EDITED BY
Alexander Altmann

PHILIP W. LOWN INSTITUTE
OF ADVANCED JUDAIC STUDIES
BRANDEIS UNIVERSITY

Studies and Texts: Volume I

BIBLICAL AND OTHER STUDIES

EDITED BY
Alexander Altmann

HARVARD UNIVERSITY PRESS
Cambridge, Massachusetts · 1963

Distributed in Great Britain
by Oxford University Press, London
Library of Congress Catalog Card Number 62-17214
Printed in the United States of America

To

Dr. Nahum Norbert Glatzer

Michael Tuch Professor of Jewish History

Chairman, Department of Near Eastern and Judaic Studies

Brandeis University

Sexagenarian

in grateful recognition of his merits

as Scholar, Teacher, Writer

Preface

The studies gathered in this book represent the papers read at the Research Colloquia of the Philip W. Lown Institute of Advanced Judaic Studies at Brandeis University during the Institute's first academic year, 1960–61. They cover a variety of topics from widely scattered areas of Judaic research. Cyrus H. Gordon discusses Hebrew origins in the light of recent discovery; E. A. Speiser deals with the wife-sister motif in the patriarchal narratives; Nahum M. Sarna inquires into the composition of Psalm 89, and exegetical problems in Koheleth and Job are dealt with by H. L. Ginsberg and Robert Gordis respectively. Moshe Goshen-Gottstein continues his earlier investigations of the Aleppo Codex in its relation to Masoretic problems. The Biblical field thus figures prominently in this volume. Rabbinic literature likewise comes within its orbit. Taking up the challenge of I. F. Baer's bold thesis concerning a large measure of Greek influence on Rabbinic Judaism, Saul Lieberman poses the question: "How Much Greek in Jewish Palestine?" His paper has some affinity with Morton Smith's on early Rabbinic gnosis as manifested in *Hekhalot Rabbati.* Four studies are concerned with medieval subjects. Isadore Twersky evaluates the initial stages of the criticism leveled against Maimonides' *Mishneh Torah*; Arthur Hyman discusses Spinoza's "dogmas of universal faith" in the light of their medieval Jewish background; the editor analyzes the various ways in which the Delphic maxim "Know thyself" was understood in medieval Islam and Judaism, and A. S. Halkin, finally, surveys the attitude of Jewish writers to Hebrew in the Middle Ages. As in terms of numbers Biblical topics exceed the rest, the title of this volume ("Biblical and Other Studies") would seem to be justified.

It is with considerable pleasure that the Editor presents this first fruit of the Philip W. Lown Institute to the world of scholars. Founded with the primary object of promoting fundamental research in all branches of Judaic studies on the American scene, the Institute has from its inception set itself the high standard of continuing the tradition established by the founders of "Wissenschaft des Judentums" in the nineteenth century and developed since at the renowned seats of advanced Jewish learning in

Europe, America, and Israel. It is hoped to publish the results of major research projects undertaken under the Institute's auspices by its research associates as well as the Proceedings of the colloquia sessions in a series of studies and texts of which the present volume represents Number I. It is gratifying to know that the publication of this series on behalf of the Institute has been undertaken by Harvard University Press, and the Editor wishes to thank the Director and the Chief Editor for their unfailing courtesy and helpfulness.

The Editor's thanks are also offered to Dr. S. Lauer for the preparation of the Index and to Mrs. D. E. Humez for her help in proofreading.

Contents

BIBLICAL
AND OTHER
STUDIES

ABBREVIATIONS USED IN THIS BOOK

AASOR	*Annual of the American Schools of Oriental Research*
AJSL	*American Journal of Semitic Languages and Literature*
ARW	*Archiv für Religionswissenschaft*
BASOR	*Bulletin of the American Schools of Oriental Research*
BT	Babylonian Talmud
BZAW	*Beihefte der Zeitschrift für alttestamentliche Wissenschaft*
HUCA	*Hebrew Union College Annual*
JA	*Journal Asiatique*
JAOS	*Journal of the American Oriental Society*
JBL	*Journal of Biblical Literature*
JE	*Jewish Encyclopedia*
JJS	*Journal of Jewish Studies*
JQR	*Jewish Quarterly Review*
MGWJ	*Monatsschrift für die Geschichte und Wissenschaft des Judenthums*
OLZ	*Orientalistische Literaturzeitung*
PAAJR	*Proceedings of the American Academy for Jewish Research*
PT	Palestinian Talmud
REJ	*Revue des Études juives*
VT	*Vetus Testamentum*
ZAW	*Zeitschrift für alttestamentliche Wissenschaft*
ZDMG	*Zeitschrift der Deutsch-Morgenländischen Gesellschaft*
1*QS*	D. Barthélemy and J. T. Milik, *Discoveries in the Judean Desert, Qumran Cave I* (Oxford, 1953)

Hebrew Origins in the Light of Recent Discovery

By CYRUS H. GORDON

From the 1920's down to the present, excavations have yielded several groups of cuneiform tablets that have put the patriarchal narratives in a new light. In fact, the fresh collateral information is bringing us to a new understanding of many Biblical books, especially from Genesis through Samuel.[1]

Whenever we depart from accepted opinion we should exercise sound method, self-criticism, and restraint. There is little merit in deviating from standard positions merely for the sake of dissent. But we are justified in blazing new trails when factual sources compel a revaluation of an entire subject. In no case are we to play fast and loose with our primary sources: the Biblical text itself. The new discoveries often run counter to the commentaries but confirm the plain meaning of the Hebrew text.

The traditional origins of the Hebrews are embodied in the Genesis narratives. Scholars are divided as to the date of the Fathers. Some favor an early date such as around the twentieth century B.C.E.;[2] most prefer a somewhat later date such as the eighteenth century or Mari Age; a growing minority of scholars has been leaning toward the fourteenth century or Amarna Age.[3] It is important to place the Fathers in their correct historic context, as best we can with the material at our disposal.

We must start somewhere, and for several reasons the Conquest is a

1. We may term Hebrew history prior to the establishment of the United Monarchy as the "Heroic Age," characterized by movement, dislocation, and instability. Such conditions tend to evoke a heroic literature, and the Hebrew records describing the Heroic Age reflect a strong epic component. For such general considerations I refer the reader to my *The World of the Old Testament* (Garden City, N. Y.: Doubleday, 1958).

2. For example, Nelson Glueck, *Rivers in the Desert* (New York: Farrar, Straus and Cudahy, 1959), pp. 68ff.

3. For a statement of some of the pros and cons, see Martin Noth, *The History of Israel*, 2nd English ed. (London: Adam & Charles Black, 1960), pp. 123–124. Cf. also G. Ernest Wright, "Modern Issues in Biblical Studies: History and the Patriarchs," reprinted from *The Expository Times* (July 1960), pp. 3–7.

good point of departure. Though the Conquest is full of problems, the fact of the Conquest is beyond question. In order to occupy the Land, the Israelites must have invaded and conquered it. The accounts in Joshua describe a Conquest that most scholars place in the late thirteenth century. This fits the general framework of Near Eastern history rather well, because around 1200 the two great powers that shared Canaan as a sphere of influence collapsed. The Hittite Empire was destroyed for all time, and Egypt entered a period of weakness during which it lost its striking power.

There is a relationship between the patriarchal narratives and the Conquest, for the Conquest is justified as the fulfillment of the Divine Promise to the Fathers, and in keeping with the treaties and land purchases contracted by the Fathers in Genesis. The Conquest thus corresponds to the Return of the Heraclids in Greek tradition. This might suggest that the patriarchal narratives are the fictional creation of a later age—a view that still has adherents. If we judge the case by the tendentious elements in the Genesis narratives, this view might seem reasonable enough. But the internal evidence of the Genesis text is confirmed by cuneiform documents at so many points, and along so many different lines, that we are obliged to consider the patriarchal narratives as an authentic reflex of the second millennium, specifically of the fourteenth and thirteenth centuries, for the reasons given below.

There are genealogies built into the Biblical text that confirm the statement in Genesis 15:16 that the sojourn in Egypt lasted for four generations. If we collocate the genealogy of Achan in Joshua 7:1 with the genealogy of Moses, we see a double confirmation of the chronology in terms of generations:[4]

Jacob

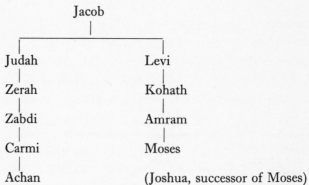

Judah	Levi
Zerah	Kohath
Zabdi	Amram
Carmi	Moses
Achan	(Joshua, successor of Moses)

4. Other genealogies tie in also. From Reuben to Dathan and Abiram (of Moses' generation) there are only four generations in Numbers 26:5ff., and from Judah to Achan (of Joshua's generation) only five in Joshua 7:1.

Genesis 15 (verses 13 and 16) tells us that the Egyptian interlude endured for four generations or four hundred years. But four hundred years are too long for four generations. As we have seen, the genealogies bear out the span of four generations. The "four hundred years" are a conventional time-span for an era, specifically then in use, and attested to in the Egyptian text of the Era of Tanis.[5]

Four generations before the late-thirteenth-century Conquest of Joshua would place the Patriarchs in the fourteenth century, with the earliest of them, Abraham, around the Amarna Age. Moving the Patriarchs back into the Mari Age is rendered difficult, not only because there are not enough generations to span the five centuries required in that case. There is simply not enough content in the patriarchal narratives to fill the gap. Abraham migrated from Paddan-Aram to Canaan, went to Egypt and returned to Canaan, fought a battle, bought some real estate, and made some treaties; Isaac moved about in Canaan, made some treaties, and tried his hand at agriculture; Jacob traveled back to Paddan-Aram and returned with the family he acquired there to Canaan, moved about in Canaan, acquired some real estate around Shechem, and eventually went to Egypt to avoid starvation during a famine in Canaan. But all such activity cannot be stretched out to account for the passing of half a millenium (from about 1800 to 1300 B.C.E.). If the study of antiquity teaches us anything, it is to avoid the assumption of "dark ages" during which nothing happened. Such dark ages sooner or later vanish like mirage.

The salient feature of the new discoveries may be epitomized thus: nearly all of the striking parallels to the patriarchal narratives come from cuneiform documents of the fourteenth and thirteenth centuries from sites well north of Babylonia.

The Nuzu tablets of the Amarna Age include extensive archives dealing with family law. The transactions tie in so closely with the patriarchal narratives that it is generally agreed that a close sociological relationship exists between the two sets of texts. The most common topic in the Nuzu contracts is adoption. Childless couples used to adopt an heir with the proviso that the adopted son would have to yield the chief heirship to a real son who might be born subsequently. The Nuzu tablets thus clarified Eliezer's relationship to Abraham. He is Abraham's adopted heir (Genesis 15:3), who gives way to Abraham's real son, born subsequent to the

5. See my *New Horizons in Old Testament Literature* (Ventnor, N. J.: Ventnor Publishers, 1960), p. 13, for this and for some other chronological data that are not repeated here.

adoption (verse 4). Similarly, the Nuzu tablets provide us with the legal background for understanding the relationship between Jacob and Laban. It was customary at Nuzu for a man with daughters but no sons to adopt his son-in-law, with the proviso that if a real son should be born, that real son (and not the son-in-law) would be the chief heir and inherit the household gods. Jacob entered Laban's household and married his daughters before the text mentions any sons of Laban. Twenty years later sons of Laban are there (Genesis 31:38, 41), and dissatisfaction on Jacob's part breaks out. Jacob runs away illegally (Genesis 31:20, 26, 43) with his family and possessions. Rachel, moreover, made off with the household gods of Laban illegally (Genesis 31:32). A study of the Nuzu contracts illuminates the details of the relation between Jacob and Laban so that the oddities of the Genesis text (such as the theft of the household gods) now fit into a well-documented context.[6]

The institutions in the patriarchal narratives are not an invention of later Israelite authors, but have been transmitted accurately from the Amarna Age. If they had been invented by later authors, they would reflect later Hebrew law and custom.

The Ugaritic tablets of the fourteenth and thirteenth centuries illuminate Hebrew culture more than any other set of discoveries. They show us the linguistic and literary heritage of the Hebrews so that our approach to the Hebrew language and literature is quite different from what it was prior to the discovery of the first Ugaritic tablets in 1929. The Hebrew contribution is distinctive in content, but the medium of expression is the pre-Hebraic heritage. To take one of many well-known illustrations, כושרות in Psalm 68:7 was misunderstood by all the interpreters until the Ugaritic cognate appeared in unequivocal contexts, showing that the word refers to songstresses comparable with the Muses. The כושרות of Ugarit are called in to gladden joyous occasions with song. Accordingly, the plain meaning of מוציא אסירים בכושרות is "He brings out prisoners with the Kosharot-songstresses," signifying that when God rescues the unfortunate, He brings them out, not into a cold world but into one of joyous song. The Hebrew psalmist probably believed in the Kosharot no more than the Christian Milton believed in the Muses, but both were creative poets who knew how to draw effectively on their ancient classical heritage.

Ugarit provides us with some of the classics that were already ancient when the Biblical authors drew on them. Ezekiel (14:14), in mentioning

6. For a comprehensive account with documentation, see my "Biblical Customs and the Nuzu Tablets," *Biblical Archaeologist* 3:1–12 (February 1940).

the Daniel who, like Noah and Job, survived with progeny a terrible catastrophe, refers to the Epic of Daniel and Aqhat, now known to us from Ugarit. Daniel lost his only son, but retrieved his body for revival, even as Job got back his seven sons and three daughters. That Noah, who survived the Deluge with his sons, belongs to the epic past is clear from his position in Genesis. Rabbinic tradition, in making Job a contemporary of the Patriarchs who lived in the Heroic Age, rightly places him in the epic past. The same holds for Daniel in Ezekiel 14:14, whose tale was already a classic in the Amarna Age.

When the Prophet Isaiah (14:12) speaks of הילל בן־שחר, we are no longer confronted with unknown quantities. Ugaritic text Number 52 tells us about the birth of שחר, sired by El, the head of the pantheon.

Palestine had a wadi named after כרית (I Kings 17:3, 5). The name is probably the same as the one written כרת in Zephaniah 2:6, designating the eponymous ancestor of the Cretans (verse 5). The Epic of Kṛet from Ugarit gives us the story of כר(י)ת in rich detail. Significantly, his quest of the fair Lady Ḥurrai took him through Palestine.

Each of the two epics from Ugarit deals with a ruler who obtained male progeny from his one and only destined wife, through divine blessing. The patriarchal narratives have the same basic features. After long waiting and frustration the Patriarchs are blessed with male offspring from the favorite wife. In the Epic of Daniel and Aqhat, Daniel's wife Dânatai is specified as the mother of the long-awaited son Aqhat (a variant of whose name is probably borne by Levi's son קְהָת). Daniel secured divine help through offerings and rituals including incubation. The Epic of Kret, too, tells how the hero was blessed with children from his destined queen, after sacrificial and incubation rites. Like Daniel and Kret, Abraham sacrifices and undergoes the sleep of incubation for the same purpose (namely, progeny through divine blessing) in Genesis 15:6–21. The emphasis on the special woman destined to be the mother of kings is present in Genesis 17:16 quite as in the Epic of Kret.

Names are an index of culture. When paganism gave way to Christianity in Italy, a change in personal names took place. Roman names like "Caesar" gave way to Biblical names like "Giuseppe." (Only with the revival of Classic interest during the Renaissance did "Cesare" come back into use.) Something comparable happened in Israel. Names like Abraham, Isaac, Jacob, or Moses were not used in subsequent Old Testament times, though they came back into use during later revivals. It is not without interest to note that the administrative texts from Ugarit tell us of two Abrams, one connected with Cyprus, the other with Egypt. Just as the Hebrew Abram moved about in accordance with East Mediterranean internationalism, so did two other Abrams of the same general period. But since the name "Abram" appears in other cuneiform sources of various periods, it is worth adding that "Israel," which has been on record as a personal name only in the Bible,[7] is now attested in another Ugaritic administrative tablet as a *maryannu* warrior.[8] So far, men called "Israel" in remote antiquity are limited to Ugarit and the Bible. Like Israel of Ugarit, the Patriarchs are also fighting men. Abraham is a victorious warrior in Genesis 14, and Israel is portrayed as a superior fighter in the same way that Homeric heroes are singled out as extraordinary: namely, by vanquishing gods as well as men.[9]

One of the noteworthy developments in the study of the patriarchal narratives is the confirmation of the repeated statement in Genesis that the Fathers had commercial interests. The wealth of the Patriarchs, including their holdings in gold and silver, is singled out several times. When Abraham is represented as paying out four hundred shekels of silver, the metal is qualified as עֹבֵר לַסֹּחֵר, "current for the merchant" (Genesis 23:16). The correctness of the text and of the usual translation is confirmed in two other passages. When the Shechemites try to induce Jacob to settle with them, they offer trading privileges.[10] And when Joseph offers his brothers the prospect of dwelling in Egypt, he too includes trading privileges.[11] All this can only mean that the Patriarchs had trading interests.

The Genesis tradition that the Patriarchs with mercantile interests migrated from Ur of the Chaldees and Harran is not isolated. The Hittite King Hattusilis III (*ca.* 1282–1250 B.C.E.) sponsored and regulated the activities of many merchants in Canaan from Ur(a).[12] It seems that Ur (of the Chaldees) was a commercial settlement in the general area of Harran. This Ur had probably been founded by the Third Dynasty of Ur

7. Otherwise it had been known only from the Mernaptah Stela, which mentions "Israel" in an ethnogeographical sense.

8. The *maryannu* warriors constituted a military elite, usually charioteers. Like so many of the guilds, the *maryannu* were international.

9. Cf. Genesis 32:29 with Iliad 5:302–351 and 855–887. Israel and Diomedes are heroes who vanquished gods and men.

10. Note וּסְחָרוּהָ in Genesis 34:10.

11. Note תסחרו in Genesis 42:34.

12. See Hattusilis' directive sent from Hattusas to Ugarit; J. Nougayrol, *Le Palais royal d'Ugarit*, IV (Paris: Imprimerie Nationale, 1957), 103–105, in the light of *Journal of Near Eastern Studies* 17:28–31 (1958). It should be noted, however, that there was more than one "Ur" in the north. The towns of this name in the Nuzu and Alalakh tablets, for example, are different places.

around 2000 B.C.E. as a trading colony. Abraham's migration to Canaan thus fits into a larger historic movement. All this is indicated on still other grounds. Harran and northern Ur, like the founding city of Sumerian Ur, were centers of the lunar cult of Sin and his consort Ningal/Nikkal. With the exception of Nikkal, who was worshipped at Ugarit and penetrated all through Canaan into Egypt, the members of the Sumero-Akkadian pantheon did not make serious inroads in Canaan and Egypt. We can now understand this development through the migration of Ur and Harran merchants of whom Abraham was one of many.

The various roles of Abraham—aristocrat, warrior, merchant—are not contrived but occur in the text. We should have to reckon with them even if we had no collateral information for putting them in context. But we have collateral information of the most convincing type. Merchants representing their sovereigns abroad often needed troops for protection. In the Amarna Age, a composition that enjoyed popularity in the outposts of the cuneiform world was the Epic of the King of Battle, dealing with the theme of merchants abroad, receiving military aid from their king.[13] Of more direct value for the study of the Patriarchs are the administrative texts from Ugarit that mention merchants supplied with troops.[14] Abraham with his three hundred and eighteen warriors (Genesis 14:14) is not fanciful embroidery; the incident was rather typical of his times in Canaan, as we learn from the most prosaic kind of document: administrative records.

The trend of archaeological discovery is to confirm the plain sense of our traditional texts. A concrete example is supplied by the mention of the camel for riding, in the patriarchal narratives. For ordinary riding in more or less cultivated areas, the donkey was used, according to the patriarchal narratives as well as the Ugaritic tablets. But the animal employed for waging war by well-equipped armies was the horse, as is attested repeatedly at Ugarit, and in Genesis 14, according to the Septuagint rendering of רכש in verses 11, 21.[15] However, for caravan travel across

13. The most accessible publication of this text is S. A. B. Mercer, *The Tell el-Amarna Tablets*, II (Toronto: Macmillan, 1939), 808–815.

14. Ugaritic text 400:III:6, VI:17, associates merchants with two kinds of troops. C. Virolleaud, *Le Palais royal d'Ugarit*, II (Paris: Imprimerie Nationale, 1957), 35, text 35:4–5: *bdl . ar . dt . inn mhr lhm*(!), "the merchants of [the town of] Ar who have no troops." "Merchants who have no troops" are the antithesis of other merchants who had troops assigned to them.

15. The Septuagint takes רכש as רֶכֶשׁ, as against Masoretic רְכֻשׁ, in verses 11, 21. I am inclined to attach weight to the Septuagint rendering (τὴν ἵππον), because it carefully distinguishes the רֶכֶשׁ of the kings in these verses from the רְכֻשׁ of the private citizen Lot in verses 12, 16.

desert stretches the camel was in full use. When Eliezer went to Aram-Naharaim to fetch a bride for Isaac, he took for the caravan ten camels (Genesis 24:10) from the extensive camel herd (verses 10, 35) of Abraham. Rebecca and her maids rode on camels (verse 61), even as Rachel did (Genesis 31:34) a generation later on the same general road.

The correctness of the text is graphically illustrated by a seal cylinder in the Walters Art Gallery, Baltimore, showing two people riding a Bactrian camel.[16] The seal is in the Mitanni style, from the northern Mesopotamian sphere of the Amarna Age. Time, place, and content link it unmistakably to our Genesis context of the Patriarchs.

In spite of the evidence, the presence of the riding camel in the Genesis narratives has been branded anachronistic by many Biblical scholars,[17] who disregard the Walters Art Gallery seal and also the mention of food for camels in the Alalakh tablets of the Mari Age.[18] Camels that are fed can only be domesticated. So, far from being an anachronism, the mention of domesticated camels in the patriarchal narratives is supported by a contemporary seal and textually in the still earlier Mari Age.

The patriarchal narratives deal with a world that we now know to have been highly literate. Canaan of the Amarna Age was the hub of a sophisticated, international order. Abraham's travels sum up the spirit of the age. He started out in Aram-Naharaim, traveled to Canaan, visited Egypt, bought real estate from Hittites, had dealings with Philistines, contracted military alliances with Amorites, and waged war against a coalition of kings who came from as far off as Elam. It is surprising in retrospect that the Patriarchs could ever have been considered unsophisticated nomadic sheikhs. Canaanite literacy during the Amarna Age is best exemplified by Ugarit, which has yielded inscriptions in many languages and scripts. One school text is a vocabulary in which words are given in Sumerian, Akkadian, and Hurrian as well as in the native Ugaritic. A school system which trains students to correlate four languages belonging to three unrelated families, and recorded in two totally different scripts, can hardly be a function of primitive or provincial society.

The only scripts from the Mediterranean that have survived in actual use to the present day are alphabetic. The more cumbersome systems using

16. See *Iraq* 6: pl. VII, no. 55 (1939).

17. For a recent, albeit brief, discussion of the date of the domestication of the camel, see Sabatino Moscati, *Rivista degli Studi Orientali* 35:116 (1960).

18. No. 269:59, published in D. J. Wiseman, *The Alalakh Tablets* (London: British Institute of Archaeology at Ankara, 1953); cf. A. Goetze, "Remarks on the Ration Lists from Alalakh, VII," *Journal of Cuneiform Studies* 13:34–38 (1959).

syllabic and logographic signs were doomed to oblivion when they came into competition with the alphabet. The Patriarchs appeared on the scene when the alphabet was already being used to record languages spoken in Canaan. The first Hebrews thus fell heir not only to a rich linguistic and literary heritage, but to an alphabet for expressing themselves in texts that would survive after all the older systems had perished.

The normal Ugaritic alphabet has thirty letters and reads from left to right. A few texts[19] in a variety of the same system are called "mirror-written" because they run in the opposite direction: from right to left, like Hebrew. Recently more texts in this script have been found at Ugarit. This "mirror ABC" is closer to the Phoenician-Hebrew system than is the normal Ugaritic script, not only in direction, but also phonetically, for in it some pairs of phonemes fall together; ḫ and ḥ fall together as ḫ,[20] and also ṯ and š fall together as a single sign.[21] Thus the "mirror ABC" of Ugarit approximates the shorter repertoire of the conventional Hebrew alphabet, which has only twenty-two letters. Two "Ugaritic" inscriptions have been found in Palestine: one at Beth-Shemesh,[22] the other on Mount Tabor.[23] Both of them are in the "mirror ABC," running from right to left. Accordingly we have reason to suspect that the pre-Hebraic cuneiform literacy of Syria-Palestine in native script was in the "mirror ABC," which was spread from at least Beth-Shemesh in the south to Ugarit in the north.

The traditional origins of the Hebrews enshrined in the patriarchal narratives are concerned with the aristocracy, not with the common people. Genesis tells us that the Fathers dealt with kings and aristocrats. The Patriarchs were men of wealth and high social status, in command of fighting men through whom they enjoyed a measure of power. We must bear in mind that the patriarchal milieu was located around the East Mediterranean at a time called the Amarna Age by orientalists and the Mycenaean Age by classicists. Numerous ethnic groups were in contact with each other: Semites, Egyptians, Hurrians, Hittites, Aegean folk, including the Philistines,[24] and many others.

Ugarit has bridged the Aegean and Canaan of the Mycenaean Age,

19. For example, texts 57 and 74.
20. Exactly like Hebrew, in which ḫ and ḥ fall together as ח. In standard Ugaritic, ḫ and ḥ are graphically as well as phonetically distinct.
21. Exactly like Hebrew, in which ṯ and š fall together as שׁ. In standard Ugaritic, ṯ and š are graphically as well as phonetically distinct.
22. Text 500 of the Ugaritic corpus.
23. Text 501.
24. The Philistines of the patriarchal narratives gravitate around Beersheba and Gerar, not around the Pentapolis like the later Philistines.

archeologically and literarily.[25] Attention was called to the site by the accidental discovery of a Mycenaean tomb at Ugarit by a peasant in 1928. The excavations have confirmed the close contacts between Ugarit and the Mycenaean world.

One of the most instructive experiences a Bible scholar can have will emerge from the perusal of a map of the Near East showing the sites at which Mycenaean pottery has been found.[26] Such sites are almost as numerous in Palestine as they are in Greece. Since the latest such map was compiled, Yigael Yadin has found at Hazor more Mycenaean pottery, which adds to but does not change the long-established character of the evidence.

We are confronted with a fact that has long been evident but yet disregarded in the annals of Biblical philology and history. During the Mycenaean Age the Greeks were part of the same complex of interpenetrating eastern Mediterranean peoples, so that we must incorporate the Homeric poems into the collateral information bearing on the Bible, in a way comparable with the texts of Egypt and of the cuneiform world in J. B. Pritchard's *Ancient Near Eastern Texts Relating to the Old Testament.*[27] The implications of this development in Biblical studies are manifold and fundamental. We will consider one implication at this time as an illustration: to wit, Hebrew leadership of the kind found in the Book of Judges.

The accepted opinion among Bible scholars is that leadership during the period of the Judges was simply charismatic. This means that inspiration was the criterion for the rise of tribal and national leaders. There is some truth to this, but it neglects an equally important factor. Like the leaders in the Homeric poems, the Hebrew Judges were members of the land-owning, military aristocracy called גבורי החיל. In peace time, a גבור חיל like Boaz (Ruth 2:1) ran a plantation. In time of war the גבור חיל would serve as an elite warrior on the battlefield or as an individual champion (compare the Book of Judges). Who were the Judges? Gideon is plainly addressed as גבור־החיל (Judges 6:12), even though he was a younger son in a lesser branch of his noble tribe (verse 15). Though Gideon became the Judge (or ruler),[28] he refused to establish any hereditary line of rulers (8:23). Abimelech, his son by a concubine (8:31), wrested

25. See my "Homer and Bible," *Hebrew Union College Annual* 43:43–108 (1955).
26. See the map in *Archaeology* 13:2–3 (Spring 1960).
27. 2nd ed. (Princeton: Princeton University Press, 1955).
28. In Ugaritic, the cognates of מלך and שופט are synonyms used to parallel each other in the poetry.

away the rule and had himself made king by his mother's townsmen, the Shechemites. Be it noted that Abimelech, as the son of a גבור חיל, belonged to the ruling class even though his mother was of lowly status.

Jephthah has been singled out as an example of charismatic leadership, raised from the dregs of society, for his mother was a harlot. But the text (11:1) clearly calls him a גבור חיל on account of his paternity. In a patriarchal society, class membership is derived from the father, not the mother.

The picture that is shaping up brings the institution of the Judges closer to Mycenaean kingship, according to which there is no guarantee that the son will succeed his father, but only that kingship is vested in the ruling class. The Judges of Israel, like the Mycenaean kings, could come from the lowest rung on the ladder of the aristocracy, but they regularly came from the aristocracy.

A special problem is raised by the divine maternity of Mycenaean rulers such as Achilles son of Thetis and Aeneas son of Aphrodite. We are to compare Shamgar, son of Anath—the goddess whose bloody exploits in the Ugaritic poems make her appropriate as the mother of the man-slaying Shamgar. Anath is not attested to as the name of any human being in the Ugaritic onomasticon, but two men in the administrative texts are, like Shamgar, "Sons of Anath."[29] Possibly there was a category of men (perhaps foundlings) dedicated to the art of war and claiming the bellicose Anath as their mother. Canaan, no less than Greece, harbored such ideas in the Mycenaean Age.

In discussing Hebrew origins in the light of recent discovery, we have constantly kept in mind the text that records the mainstream of the tradition. One might object that a tradition need have little if any historical basis. But in the case of the Bible—and indeed of Homeric epic, too—modern discovery makes it quite clear that the milieu is genuine, not invented. There is reason to believe that the lives of the Patriarchs fit into a historic framework which may be confirmed by future discoveries more specifically than is now possible. After reviewing the evidence from Nuzu, Ugarit, and Hattusas, can we despair of discovering historic texts mentioning one or more of the nine kings in Genesis 14? Cuneiform texts of the Hittite enclave around Hebron may be awaiting the excavator's spade. We cannot predict that Abraham's deed for the purchase of the real estate in Genesis 23 will be found on a clay tablet. But we can say that such a tablet was the normal medium for recording such transactions in Abraham's milieu. Abimelech, King of Gerar, with whom Abraham and Isaac

29. Virolleaud, *Le Palais royal d'Ugarit*, vol. II, p. 43, text 12; p. 61, text 6.

had dealings, probably presided over a literate court whose records may some day be found.

Hebrew origins are in the process of being revolutionized by archeological discovery. It is no exaggeration to say that the recently found texts of the Amarna-Mycenaean Age are at least as epoch-making as the Qumran Scrolls.

The Wife-Sister Motif in the Patriarchal Narratives

By E. A. SPEISER

I

The subject that I propose to take up here anew[1] is the central theme of three narratives in the Book of Genesis: namely, (a) 12:10–20, (b) 20:1–18, (c) 26:6[2]–11. Each tells essentially the same story as the others. A patriarch visits a foreign land in the company of his wife. Fearing that the woman's great beauty might prove to be a source of mortal danger to himself as the husband, he resorts to the subterfuge of passing himself off as the woman's brother.

This recurring wife-sister motif in Genesis has had a long history of abundant yet inconclusive speculation and discussion. The results have ranged from embarrassment and apologetics to expressions of gallantry, moralizing comment, and even gloating. Efforts to find mitigating circumstances in the Patriarchs' conduct are as old as the narratives themselves. Thus Genesis 20:12 has Abraham remark, "What is more, she [Sarah] is in truth my sister, my father's daughter, though not my mother's." Rabbinical sources go to great lengths in stressing Sarah's exceptional beauty, and the same holds true of the recently discovered Genesis Apocryphon.[3] But censorious notes have found their way into more than one presumably objective comment on the subject. The vast majority, however, of serious students has remained baffled. Small wonder, therefore, that scarcely a year goes by without at least one new stab at solving the problem. Yet each fresh try only points up the failure of previous solutions.

In these circumstances it would be sheer folly to rush in where so many angels have feared to tread or have gone nowhere when they did. No,

1. I made brief reference to this topic in a paper on "The Biblical Idea of History in its Common Near Eastern Setting," *Israel Exploration Journal* 5:201ff. (1955); see esp. p. 213.

2. The episode is usually listed as starting with verse 7. It is better, however, to go back to verse 6 and translate it as a temporal clause: "When Isaac stayed at Gerar," etc.

3. N. Avigad and Y. Yadin, *A Genesis Apocryphon* (Jerusalem, 1956), col. 20, 2–8.

what follows is not yet another attempted explanation of the Patriarchs' behavior, based on the data received, but rather an appeal from tradition's own version of the incidents in question. In other words, given the traditional accounts, it is hopeless to bring in a sensible verdict. The burden of the present argument is that the basic testimony contained judgments contrary to the facts and that the entire case should therefore be reopened.

It goes without saying that no such argument can be allowed, after so many intervening centuries, without new and compelling evidence. Such evidence, however, does in fact exist. It comes from pertinent extra-Biblical sources that have come to light so recently that the results have yet to be brought to bear on the case before us. It will be our task as a court of appeal to weigh the new data critically, but without prejudice, and then to decide whether the original disposition of the case can be upheld or whether it should be revised in the light of the new information.

Before the question is re-examined, it will be necessary to review the old transcript as embodied in the Book of Genesis. Very briefly, the received report consists of three separate entries, as cited above. In (a) Abraham introduces Sarah to Pharaoh as his sister, hoping to save himself by this ruse. In (b) we have a repetition of the same incident, with the identical motivation, except only that the host is this time another ruler: namely, Abimelech of Gerar. Finally, Abimelech reappears in (c), but his visitors are now Isaac and Rebekah. The excuse offered in each instance is that the wife's startling beauty might have provoked attempts on the husband's life, whereas a brother would not have been deemed to stand in the way.

Now these three incidents, which are so very alike in content in spite of differences in cast and locale, are not only repetitive in their present form; they are also mutually incompatible when analyzed side by side. Abraham's narrow escape in Egypt did not deter him from repeating the deception in Gerar. And Abimelech, for his part, was not sobered in the least by his all but fatal involvement with Sarah, for all his protestations of innocence in that affair. He would have had to be either a fool or a knave to accept Isaac's subsequent pretence at face value, yet the record depicts him as both wise and honest. In short, the accounts cannot be homogeneous. Once all three passages are attributed to a single author, we are forced to conclude that the writing is sloppy, or else that the characters do not merit our confidence.

The stories before us, however, are hardly of a piece, even on the surface. In Genesis 12:17 it is YHWH who afflicts Pharaoh and his household with severe plagues; the use of this divine name signifies in Genesis, according to the documentary hypothesis, an author whom the critics have designated as the Yahwist, or J. In Genesis 20, on the other hand, the deity is consistently indicated as Elohim (verses 3, 6, 13, 18). Moreover, God's warning to Abimelech is communicated there in a dream, and both Abraham and his host take great pains to justify their conduct. Now all these features—Elohim, dreams, emphasis on morality—recur elsewhere in passages which the critics have traced to the Elohistic source, or E. As against this, the third episode (Genesis 26:6–11) displays the same economy of thought and phrase as the first, so that it, in turn, points back to J.

As soon as our three instances of the wife-sister motif have been assigned to two individual authors, all our difficulties with the content disappear automatically. J knew of two separate occasions when a Patriarch felt it necessary to present his wife as a sister: one involved Abraham and Sarah in Egypt and the other concerned Isaac and Rebekah at Gerar. Neither the cast of characters nor the scene of action is repeated in these accounts. In E, on the other hand, the two episodes were telescoped, with the result that Abraham and Sarah were shifted from Egypt to Gerar, while Isaac and Rebekah did not figure at all; thus the E source, too, remains consistent within itself. Between the two versions, however, two original reports branched out into three.

It may be remarked in passing that the internal evidence of this trio of narratives alone, quite apart from the testimony of many other passages, would be enough to establish E as an independent document.[4] Alternative hypotheses about the composition of the Pentateuch, not to mention the traditional doctrine of its Mosaic authorship, do grave injustice to the caliber of writing involved. Nevertheless, our present argument does not hinge in any way on the acceptance of the documentary theory. If the reality of separate versions by J and E is conceded, then the circumstance that the wife-sister motif was known to both must point to a common older source. And if the argument from literary analysis is disallowed, the antiquity of tradition looms that much more prominently, since the writing would then be credited to Moses. On either view, therefore, the meaning of the incidents at issue has to be sought in the Patriarchal Age, in which these episodes have been placed. And it is precisely from that remote age that relevant extra-Biblical data have recently come to light.

I had occasion to allude to the end result of this study in several earlier

4. For a comprehensive recent summary of the documentary position see C. R. North, "Pentateuchal Criticism," in *The Old Testament and Modern Study*, ed. H. H. Rowley (Oxford, 1951), pp. 48–83. For E as an independent source, attention may be called to my forthcoming volume on Genesis, Introduction (Anchor Books).

connections.[5] Each time, however, the theme could only be stated, but not duly developed. Yet the subject is much too significant to be dismissed with casual allusions; it calls for adequate documentation. The pertinent evidence, to be sure, is diffuse and intricate enough to deserve a separate monograph. But even a minimal sampling should prove to be instructive. This will now be presented in all conciseness.

II

The data in question stem from a single society, that of the Hurrians. In the eighteenth century B.C.E. the Hurrians are known to have been thickly settled in Central Mesopotamia, in the general area of Ḫarran (Biblical Ḥārān), as we know from the Mari and Chagar Bazar texts, and in northern Syria, as shown by the tablets from Alalaḫ. By the middle of the second millennium, Hurrian settlements and influence had spread to Arrapḫa and Nuzi in the east, and all along the Mediterranean coast in the west, to judge from various sources from Nuzi, Amarna, the upper layers of Alalaḫ, and from Ḫattusas (Boghazköi).[6] On the combined evidence of this extensive documentary network it can be stated with confidence that many distinctive features of Hurrian society, especially in the field of family law, remained the same throughout, regardless of chronology, geographic location, or political influence. What was true of Nuzi, Alalaḫ, or eastern Anatolia in the fifteenth century was thus equally true of eighteenth-century Ḫarran, the approximate central area of over-all Hurrian occupation. But Ḫarran was also the home of the Patriarchs, a district where Hurrians and Western Semites lived in close cultural symbiosis, but where Hurrians constituted the dominant social element. It is for these reasons that the Nuzi texts in particular, which happen to be plentiful and rich in content, have a bearing on Ḫarran in the Patriarchal Age, and can hence contribute to the understanding of the patriarchal narratives.

Now, Hurrian family practices contain certain features which have no counterparts in any other contemporary Near Eastern society. This is true especially of the pervasive role of the brother, as a result of an underlying fratriarchal system which the encroachments of patriarchy managed to restrict but could not entirely obliterate. The pioneering work on the subject was done by the distinguished jurist and outstanding authority

5. See above, Note 1. The other occasions were oral presentations.

6. The distribution of the Hurrians is summarized, among other publications, in my "The Hurrian Participation in the Civilizations of Mesopotamia, Syria, and Palestine," *Journal of World History* 1:311ff. (Paris 1953).

on cuneiform law, Paul Koschaker.[7] Koschaker's results are basic to all subsequent study on the subject, but they can now be considerably strengthened and expanded, thanks to further work and additional material. Above all, the possibility of Biblical connections has been virtually ignored,[8] and nothing has been done as yet in regard to the wife-sister motif in Genesis.

Before the latter topic can be adduced for comparison, the pertinent evidence of the cuneiform sources may be summarized as follows.

1. The wife as sister. The Nuzi text *HSS*[9] V 80 is a contract whereby Akkulenni son of Akiya gives his sister Beltakkadummi[10] in marriage (*ana aššūti*, literally "into wifehood") to Ḫurazzi son of Ennaya.[11] But in the parallel document *HSS* V 69 the same brother gives the same girl to the same husband "as sister" (*ana aḫāti*). It follows that a wife could have simultaneously the status of sister. There can be no question in this instance of close blood ties between husband and wife, since each has a different father, nor is there any indication or likelihood that Beltakkadummi was Ḫurazzi's half-sister. The fact that a separate sistership document was deemed necessary, in addition to the usual marriage contract, points up the importance of the husband's concurrent status as brother. Interestingly enough, a third document, *HSS* V 25, carries the girl's own statement that the marriage was arranged with her personal consent (line 14), thus implying a degree of independence on the part of the woman.

2. Sistership transferred. In the sistership document cited above (*HSS* V 69), the girl is made a man's legal sister after her natural brother has ceded his own fraternal rights. The juridical basis of the transaction is thus a form of adoption. The adoptive brother may then marry the girl himself, as is the case in *HSS* V 80, or he may give her in marriage to another in return for the customary bride price.[12] The latter alternative

7. In a study entitled "Fratriarchat, Hausgemeinschaft und Mutterrecht in Keilschrifttexten," *Zeitschrift für Assyriologie* 41:1–89 (1933).

8. For an approach to the Biblical evidence, see C. H. Gordon, "Fratriarchy in the Old Testament," *Journal of Biblical Literature* 54:223–231 (1935). See also E. A. Speiser, "Of Shoes and Shekels," *BASOR* 77:15–20 (1940).

9. *Harvard Semitic Series*, vol. V, text 80. Volume V (*Excavations at Nuzi*, vol. I, *Texts* ...) was published in 1929 by E. Chiera. In the following year I presented all the family documents in that volume, in transliteration, translation, and with brief comments, in *AASOR* 10:1–73 (1930).

10. Contracted from *Bēlit-Akkadi-ummi*.

11. Koschaker, "Fratriarchat . . .," pp. 14f.

12. Amounting to forty shekels of silver.

is indicated in *JEN*[13] 78, where Zigiba son of Eḫel-Teshub gives his sister Ḫinzuri "for sistership" (*ana aḫātūti*) to Ḫudarrapḫi, who reserves the right to marry her to whomever he chooses (line 7). This is not the first time that Ḫinzuri has been the object of such a transfer. According to *JEN* 636,[14] the same woman was first given in sistership by her brother Zigiba to Inni, who then gave her back in return for the symbolic payment[15] of one cloth. The status of sister was thus negotiable, yet the woman involved was not altogether a passive party. For just as was the case with Beltakkadummi (in *HSS* V 25), Ḫinzuri, too, explicitly signifies her personal consent (*irramāniya*, "of my own free will," line 23).

3. Sistership by the woman's choice. There are indications, moreover, that the legal status of sister was beneficial to the woman, no matter whether the given brother was natural or adoptive. We learn this from instances in which the woman goes beyond formal acquiescence, as above, and becomes a principal in the transaction. Thus in *AASOR*[16] XVI 54 Kuniyashe daughter of Ḫut-Teshub states that she was previously given in marriage by Akammushni (evidently her adoptive brother) to an unnamed husband, for the full bridal payment of forty shekels of silver. Since both her guardian and her husband are now dead, Kuniyashe appoints her natural brother Akiya son of Ḫut-Teshub as her legal brother, who is given the right to marry her to another. In two other instances (*G*[17] 31; *HSS* V 26), a woman offers herself physically[18] to a prospective legal brother. In the latter document, the "sister" says this of her brother-husband: "He shall watch over me and protect me in every way, act as my brother, and be a help to me."[19] In all three cases, the woman has become a free agent by virtue of the fact that her original guardian had already given up his rights to her through a previous transaction, and the second party then divorced her or died.[20] Now she seeks a new legal relationship as sister because, as *HSS* V 26 has so strongly intimated, such a status affords her all the aid and comfort that local society obviously

13. *Joint Expedition with the Iraq Museum at Nuzi*, vols. I–V (Paris and Philadelphia), E. Chiera; vol. VI (New Haven), E. R. Lacheman. Vol. I is cited throughout.

14. For this text see H. Lewy, *Orientalia* 10:209ff. (1941).

15. Cf. my "Of Shoes and Shekels," pp. 15ff.

16. See Note 9.

17. C. J. Gadd, "Tablets from Kirkuk," *Revue d'Assyriologie* 33:49ff., and texts 1–82.

18. Cf. Koschaker, "Fratriarchat . . .," p. 28, n. 3.

19. *AASOR* 10:29 (1930); Koschaker, "Fratriarchat . . .," p. 34.

20. The Code of Hammurapi (e.g., CH 172) says of similar instances that "a man of her own choice may marry her."

associated with a brother. But the new status has to be ratified, with actual brothers no less than with adoptive ones.

4. Special safeguards for the sister. As a matter of fact, so intent was Hurrian society on protecting the favored position of a duly accredited sister that it borrowed certain safeguards from the sphere of ritual practices. This socioreligious aspect is made apparent by the solemn form of the payment involved. In ordinary marriage transactions the bride price amounted to forty shekels, payable in various commodities computed at the current rate for silver. In sistership contracts, however, the price remains the same, but thirty shekels of it must be computed as a rule in terms of animals, at the fixed rate of one ox, one ass, and ten sheep. Now this rigid mode of payment is always reserved for cases of unusual gravity,[21] and it is imposed either as a special punishment for serious offences in the past or as a deterrent against possible future violations. The animals play here a monitory part, based on the fate of sacrificial beasts. The payment, in other words, is related to the sanctions of a covenant, and the use of animals recalls the description of God's covenant with Abraham in Genesis 15:9ff.

It is highly significant, therefore, that this ominous type of payment is typical of the sistership transactions. A striking illustration is provided by *HSS* V 79, which is on the surface a case of adoption into "daughtership" as a prelude to marriage (to one of the adoptor's sons). The payment is set at the normal bride price of forty shekels of silver. The money goes, however, to the girl's brother, and the essential "sistership" aspect of the contract is further emphasized by the girl's direct statement.[22] The payment is broken down as follows: "thirty-six minas of tin in lieu of [*kīma*][23] one ox; twenty-four minas of tin in lieu of one ass; ten sheep;[24] ten shekels of . . .[25] silver." In other words, out of the total of forty shekels, thirty shekels represent the fixed "covenant" payment in the standard proportions of one ox: one ass: ten sheep. And although the animals are converted into metal currency, the record goes out of its way to show that each animal is accounted for, instead of stating simply that the

21. For the character and significance of this special type of payment, see E. A. Speiser, "Nuzi Marginalia 4: Ceremonial Payment," *Orientalia* 25:15–20 (1956).

22. Lines 27f.

23. The Biblical term in similar instances is *ᶜerkĕkā*, on which see my "Leviticus and the Cities," *Yeḥezkel Kaufmann Jubilee Volume*, ed. M. Haran (Jerusalem, 1960), pp. 30–33.

24. Sheep as currency (cf. Lat. *pecūnia*) were computed at one shekel a head.

25. The silver is qualified by the term *ḫašaḫušenni*, for which see *AASOR* 25:11, n. 1. The entire payment takes up lines 9–13.

required payment has been made in full. The monitory features are thus retained as a reminder that the implicit sanctions have not been bypassed.

In two similar instances (*HSS* V 80; *JEN* 78) the payment for a sister adds up only to twenty shekels, since the remaining half is retained for the girl as her "dowry." Hence the symbolic equation can no longer apply in full but is prorated. Thus *HSS* V 80 specifies "one ox, ten shekels of silver" (that is, twenty shekels in all), and *JEN* 78 itemizes "one ox . . .[26] sheep, one imer of barley, two minas of copper, nine minas of wool, making up [*kīma*] twenty shekels of silver." Even here, therefore, the sanction component is not eliminated but merely modified: the reduced total must still include a token entry of animals. Nothing could show more convincingly that Hurrian society went to great lengths to uphold the status of sister through the medium of brother, or the husband as brother.

5. *Practice rejected by outsiders.* That other societies found this Hurrian practice strange and unacceptable is strikingly demonstrated by a treaty between the powerful Hittite king Suppiluliumas and a certain Hukkanas, the vassal ruler of a Hurrian principality in Armenia.[27] As a political measure not uncommon in that period, the Hittite monarch gave his sister in marriage to his Hurrian vassal. By Hurrian custom, this would have made the girl her husband's sister as well. As brother, however, he would have fratriarchal authority over the woman's female siblings, since they, too, would be technically his legal sisters.[28] But such an arrangement was naturally distasteful to the Hittite overlord. He would have none of it, so he made sure to spell out in a formal treaty that the odd Hurrian practice would not be invoked in this particular case. It follows, incidentally, that fratriarchy among the Hurrians was a normal feature of the upper classes, not merely among ordinary citizens, but even in the ruling families.

6. *Evidence of personal names.* There is, finally, one other source of information that remains to be tapped in this connection: namely, the evidence of personal names. Hurrian masculine names reflect a particular liking for compounds with *šenni* "the brother"[29] (from *šena* "brother").[30]

26. The text is damaged at this point, but the figure could conceivably have been 5, which together with the ten shekels for one ox would add up to fifteen shekels, or half of the normal "covenant" payment.

27. Koschaker, "Fratriarchat . . .," pp. 1–13.

28. *Ibid.*, p. 33.

29. Cf. I. J. Gelb, P. M. Purves, and A. A. MacRae, *Nuzi Personal Names*, *Oriental Institute Publications* no. LVII (Chicago, 1943), pp. 130–131.

30. The suffix *-ne/i* (for which see E. A. Speiser, *Introduction to Hurrian* [New Haven, 1941]) serves here as a definite article.

As has already been noted by Koschaker,[31] this points suggestively to underlying fratriarchal conditions. And even though fratriarchy had been considerably weakened in the meantime under the influence of a patriarchal orientation,[32] onomastic customs remained conservative enough to echo earlier habits. We have, however, one particular type of name, in common use, which tells us more than all the compounds with *šena*. This type features the element *aḫu* "brother" together with a feminine personal pronoun: *Aḫūša*, "her brother"; *Aḫūšina*, "their [feminine] brother"; *Aḫummiša*, "her mother's brother."[33] All these forms are Akkadian, but we know from the family relations of their bearers that the persons in question were Hurrians. Moreover, while a name like Aḫūšina is known from Akkadian sources, and tells us merely that the new-born boy has older sisters (analogously, Aḫūša has one such sister), Aḫummiša is not used in Akkadian circles. There the corresponding name is *Aḫummišu* ("his mother's brother"): that is, the boy was named after his maternal uncle. Yet the seemingly paradoxical form with feminine suffix cannot be charged to peculiarities of Hurrian grammar,[34] or to scribal errors,[35] for it occurs too often (over twenty times) to be explained away.[36] In short, both the writing and the construction are correct. Accordingly, "Aḫummiša" must be understood to signify that the bearer of the name shall give his older sister the same kind of support that their mother received from her own brother.

This last example may well help to explain how the exceptional rights of the brother in Hurrian society originated in the first place. The fratriarchal system goes back ultimately to matriarchy. The mother was the dominant figure in the family, and her position was not to be usurped by an exogamous husband. But even a matriarchally governed family often has need of masculine strength and guidance; for these the mother will look to her own brother.[37] Fratriarchy is thus an extension of the part played by the maternal uncle. The name Aḫummiša, with its emphasis on the sister's maternal uncle, would be accordingly a residual witness of an antecedent matriarchal system.

31. Koschaker, "Fratriarchat . . .," p. 33.

32. *Ibid.*

33. See Gelb, Purves, and MacRae, *Nuzi Personal Names*, p. 291.

34. Which does not recognize grammatical gender, so that Hurrians writing Akkadian usually employ one form for masculine and feminine alike; but the common form is then masculine, not feminine.

35. This is immediately ruled out by the fact that this particular suffix is written either as ŠA or as ŠÁ (Gelb, Purves, and MacRae, *Nuzi Personal Names*, p. 10).

36. Gelb, Purves, and MacRae, *Nuzi Personal Names*, pp. 10, 291.

37. Koschaker, "Fratriarchat . . .," p. 80.

To sum up, the Hurrian family system contained various fratriarchal features, one of which was the wife-sister concept. Under it, a woman given in marriage by her brother, either natural or adoptive, became legally her husband's sister. Such a wife-sister had the advantage of exceptional socioreligious solicitude and protection which was not enjoyed by ordinary wives. The practice was characteristic of, though not restricted to, the top levels of Hurrian society. It was evidently a mark of superior status.

It is worth stressing again that the wife-sister customs were peculiar to the Hurrians. There is no trace of them among the Akkadians, and they were expressly stigmatized by the Hittites, who otherwise had so much culturally in common with the Hurrians. The institution of the levirate affords no parallel at all, since it operates with altogether different presuppositions[38] and is solely concerned with maintaining the line of a deceased brother. Nor can it be compared with the brother-sister marriages of the ruling houses of Egypt, Persia, and certain Hellenistic states,[39] for the Hurrian practice applied to women who were sisters by law and not by blood. The Hurrian family system in general[40] and the wife-sister feature in particular stand thus isolated within the larger social complex of the ancient Near East.

III

The foregoing review of certain marriage customs of the Hurrians can now be applied to a re-examination of the wife-sister incidents in the patriarchal account. No apology is needed for thus bringing the pertinent material from the two respective sources, the cuneiform and the Biblical, into close comparison. Abraham migrated to Canaan from the Central Mesopotamian district of Ḫarran, and it was to that same area that Isaac and Jacob eventually owed their wives. Now, Ḫarran was not only the home base of the patriarchal clan but at the same time also the central link in the far-flung chain of Hurrian settlements. In the Bible, the wife-sister theme is confined to two successive generations; elsewhere in the

38. *Ibid.*, pp. 85ff.

39. *Ibid.*, p. 82.

40. In this connection, attention may be called once again to the use of the housegods (Akk. *ilāni*, Heb. *ṭĕrāpīm* or sometimes *ʾĕlōhīm*) as a symbol of property transfer to a son-in-law, which readily explains Rachel's act as recorded in Genesis 31:19, 30; see A. E. Draffkorn, "Ilāni/Elohim," *JBL* 76:216–224 (1957). This is perhaps the outstanding example of an exclusively Hurrian custom which the patriarchal account records, but which became incomprehensible later on in Canaanite surroundings; it offers an excellent parallel to the wife-sister theme.

ancient Near East the only society that featured an analogous concept was the Hurrian. Since time, place, and opportunity point thus uniformly to one and the same quarter, it would be surprising indeed if such isolated acts of the patriarchs did not reflect a normal Hurrian practice. It remains then only to inquire how the assumption of such an interrelationship works out in detail.

In the case of Abraham, a few laconic notices about his family are found in Genesis 11:26–32. Even the critics agree that this passage includes relatively old data, since they ascribe verses 28–30 to J, the oldest documentary source in the Pentateuch. The credibility of the section is further enhanced by repeated occurrences of the name Nahor, a name shared by Abraham's grandfather and one of Abraham's brothers. The same form (written *Na-ḫu-ur*^{KI}) is now independently attested to in the approximately contemporary Mari records as the name of a city in the vicinity of Ḫarran.[41] The use of the same name for both places and persons is familiar from many sources.[42]

We are told, furthermore, that Abraham's brother Nahor married his own niece Milcah, daughter of a younger brother named Haran.[43] This agrees closely with a practice which Hurrian law recognizes by a *ṭuppi mārtūti u kallūti* ("tablet of daughtership and daughter-in-law-ship"), whereby a man adopts a girl as his daughter for the declared purpose of either marrying her himself or giving her in marriage to his son.[44] In the present instance, adoption could well have been prompted by the untimely death of Milcah's father (verse 28). Since the latter was Nahor's brother, the marriage would come simultaneously, in accordance with Hurrian law, under the classification of "brothership."

In the face of such detail regarding Nahor's wife, it would seem strange that Abraham's own wife Sarah is introduced without any notice about her parents. This omission is partially rectified in 20:12 (where the author is E!), where we are informed that Sarah was Terah's daughter, though not by Abraham's mother—in other words, she is Abraham's half-sister. Yet this particular entry only serves to bring into that much sharper relief the earlier failure to give Sarah as much genealogical attention as

41. Cf. the list of occurrences in *Archives royales de Mari* XV (Paris, 1954), 130. The town lay in the valley of the Baliḫ, a tributary of the Euphrates.

42. The practice is amply attested in the Nuzi records, where virtually any personal name could be made into a place name by the addition of the Hurrian genitive suffix *-we*.

43. Not to be confused, of course, with the city-name *Ḥārān*, which has a different initial consonant in Hebrew.

44. The status, however, of a girl acquired under such an arrangement was inferior to that of a principal in an *aḫātūtu* transaction.

was paid not only Milcah but even the wholly inconsequential Iscah. The likeliest solution under the circumstances would seem to be that Sarah was Terah's daughter by adoption, which is why the relationship was not duly recorded in Genesis 11. At all events, Sarah had adequate credentials to qualify, in one way or another, as Abraham's sister in the broader sense of the term. This would make her eligible, under the law of the land from which Abraham migrated to Canaan, for the *aḫātūtu* or "sistership" status with all its attendant safeguards and privileges.

Thus far it has been fairly clear, if roundabout, sailing. It will be readily agreed that Abraham had ample opportunity to be exposed to the distinctively Hurrian legal concept of wife-sister and to act upon it even after his arrival in Canaan. But would Isaac, born as he was in non-Hurrian surroundings, be expected to continue a Hurrian practice? Perhaps not, by himself. It was different, however, with Rebekah, a native of Hurrian-dominated Ḫarran. What is more, the details of Rebekah's assignment to Isaac, as recorded in Genesis 24:53–61, are significant enough to yield a recognizable *ṭuppi aḫātūti*, or "sistership document" in typical Nuzi style.

A composite document of that kind would embody the following specifications: (a) the principals in the case, (b) the nature of the transaction, (c) details of payment, (d) the girl's declaration of concurrence, (e) a penalty clause. It so happens that all but the last of these points are touched upon, however nontechnically, in the corresponding account in Genesis. It goes without saying that a penalty clause would be entirely out of keeping with the literary character of the narrative.

Let us go over the respective points, one by one. (a) For principals we have here, on the one hand, Abraham's servant as spokesman for the prospective bridegroom, and, on the other hand, Laban as the responsible party representing the bride. It is noteworthy that Laban is cited repeatedly (verses 53, 55) as "her brother," in which capacity he is listed both times ahead of the mother. All of this serves to bring out Laban's authority as the brother. The father was apparently dead,[45] and the mother's position was only incidental and without legal standing. (b) The transaction falls thus specifically under the heading of "sistership," since it is the girl's brother who acts on the request. (c) The emissary gives costly presents to Rebekah, but does not neglect the "gifts" for her "brother and mother"

45. Rebekah's father Bethuel could not otherwise have been ignored in this account. Significantly enough, the Nuzi documents never employ the *aḫātūtu* formula when the bride's father is still alive; cf. Koschaker, "Fratriarchat . . .," p. 31.

(verse 53), covering the bride payment. (d) Perhaps most significant of all, in view of the pertinent Nuzi evidence, is the statement that Rebekah should be consulted (verse 57). Her reply is in the affirmative: *ʾēlēk* ("I will go") (verse 58). The Nuzi texts record similarly *ramāniya u aḫūya* ("myself and my brother [agree to this marriage]"),[46] or *irramāniya* ("of my own free will [I am being given into sistership]").[47] To emphasize still further the fratriarchal aspect of the case, the Biblical narrative goes on to speak of "their sister" (*ʾăḥōtām*) (verse 59), followed by a festive parting couplet beginning with "Our sister" (*ʾăḥōtēnū*) (verse 60); the plural pronouns apply to the entire household. In short, we have here a reasonable facsimile of a standard Hurrian *aḫātūtu* document.

There are thus ample grounds for placing the marriages of Abraham and Sarah and of Isaac and Rebekah in the legal wife-sister class. We come back now to the Biblical narratives which feature the theme that a wife was introduced as sister, with admittedly ulterior motives. Something is obviously wrong there. According to Genesis 20:12, the sisterly relationship was genuine enough; moreover, it was legally correct throughout, in the light of independent evidence. At most, therefore, the statement in each case involves not an outright invention but a half-truth. To that extent, at least, the narratives themselves prove to be misleading. And since the matter at issue is one of adequate data rather than questionable morality, the error may not be irretrievable.

It should be borne in mind that the accounts before us were committed to writing several centuries after the events and hundreds of miles away from the center where the wife-sister institution was immediately understood and appreciated. The underlying concept could not have long retained its original significance on foreign soil. When the memory of an incident is preserved, but its import has been lost, a new interpretation is likely to be substituted, an interpretation in keeping with local conditions and in conformance with common human instincts. In the present instance, tradition had to deal with certain incidents the meaning of which had been lost in the course of centuries. In due time a new explanation was bound to emerge. Small wonder that the intrusive motive was just so much anachronism.

We cannot be sure, of course, what really happened on those visits to Egypt and Gerar, assuming that they actually did take place. Such back-

46. *HSS* V, 25, lines 14f.

47. *JEN* I, 78, lines 23f. In the Biblical instance Laban acts as a real *Aḫummiša*: that is, "*her* mother's brother."

ground evidence, however, as we now have may justify the following speculative reconstruction. Both Abraham and Isaac were married to women who enjoyed a privileged status by the standards of their own society. It was the kind of distinction that may well have been deemed worthy of special mention in the presence of royal hosts, since it raised the standing of the visitors. Status has always been an important consideration in international relations, as far back as available records can take us. But popular lore has seldom been internationally oriented.

One important observation remains to be made in conclusion. No matter how tradition interpreted the wife-sister theme, it clearly regarded it as significant, since it saw fit to dwell on it in three separate narratives. Why was tradition so interested in the matter? The answer is no longer far to seek, and it is fortunately free from undue speculation. In the light of the pertinent extra-Biblical evidence which this discussion has adduced, it is clear that the wife-sister status was simultaneously a mark of a cherished social status, as has repeatedly been stressed. Such an affirmation of the wife's favored position was, hence, an implicit guarantee of the purity of her children. Now the ultimate purpose of the Biblical genealogies was to establish the superior strain of the line through which the Biblical way of life was transmitted from generation to generation. In other words, the integrity of the mission had to be safeguarded in transmission, the purity of the content protected by the quality of the container. This is why the antecedents of the wife in the early stages—the mother of the next generation—were of extraordinary significance. Hence all such details, among them the wife-sister theme, were invariably emphasized, even when the appropriate background had in the meantime faded from memory. They were obligatory entries in a protocanonical body of material.

The demonstrated prestige status of the wife-sister in Hurrian society, which was normative for the Patriarchs in many ways, provides a self-evident reason for the importance of the theme to early Biblical tradition. By the same token, we have here perhaps added circumstantial encouragement that this entire discussion has not been seriously out of focus.

Psalm 89: A Study in Inner Biblical Exegesis[1]

By Nahum M. Sarna

I. The Problem

Much scholarly attention has been focused upon two aspects of Psalm 89. It has long been accepted that it is a composite of originally disparate elements[2] and it is widely agreed that verses 20–38 constitute a version of Nathan's oracle to David promising eternity to the Davidic dynasty. Little notice has been given, however, to the techniques by which the psalmist welded together the individual parts into a cohesive unity. And while the problem of the interrelationships of the several recensions of the oracle has been thoroughly explored, it has generally been overlooked that Psalm 89 verses 20–38 actually constitute, not a recension of the original oracle, but an interpretation of it.

It is the purpose of this paper to attempt to rectify both these omissions. In the course of our researches, it is hoped at the same time that we may be able to draw some new conclusions about the date and exact historical circumstances that called forth the psalm in its completed form.

II. The Integration of Disparate Elements

The combination of originally unrelated elements into an integrated unit is a literary phenomenon familiar to us from the ancient world. The classic example is the Gilgamesh epic of Babylon, many of its component parts having been formerly independent episodes borrowed from Sumerian

1. I wish to thank my colleagues, Professor H. L. Ginsberg and Professor Gerson D. Cohen, for their helpful comments on this paper. They are not, of course, responsible for the opinions expressed.

2. Cf. Martin Luther's observation, "In psalmo 89 est maxime contrariëtas," cited by H. J. Kraus, *Psalmen* (*Biblischer Kommentar* XV, Neukirchen, 1960), p. 615.

compositions,[3] while the twelfth tablet has been appended to the epic even without any attempt at integration.[4]

A similar situation obtains in the Greek epic. Without entering into the complicated "Homeric question," it may yet be noted that both the Iliad and the Odyssey exemplify the same process of literary development.[5]

The identical tendency is not lacking in Biblical literature. This is true of Psalm 19, in which an old nature hymn (verses 1–7) has been combined with a Torah hymn (verses 8–15). Psalm 70 has been incorporated into Psalm 40 (verses 14–18), and Psalm 108 is a composition of parts of Psalms 57 (verses 8–12) and 60 (verses 7–14).[6]

In these particular instances it is not always easy to distinguish the principle by which integration has been effected. However, there is an ever-growing recognition of the fact that many Biblical passages have been placed in juxtaposition solely on the basis of association of ideas, words, or phrases.[7]

III. The Psalm as a Unity

A careful study of Psalm 89 provides overwhelming evidence to prove that this same principle has been operative in the successful cohesion of the disconnected elements into a harmonious whole.

The psalm seems to fall naturally into three divisions:

(i) a hymn, verses 2–3, 6–19,

3. S. N. Kramer, *JAOS* 64:7ff. (1944), and his *History Begins at Sumer* (New York, 1959), pp. 182–199, esp. pp. 188f.; A. Heidel, *The Gilgamesh Epic* (Chicago, 1946), p. 13.

4. See E. A. Speiser's remarks in *Ancient Near Eastern Texts Relating to the Old Testament*, ed. J. B. Pritchard (Princeton, 1950).

5. See Gilbert Murray, *The Rise of the Greek Epic* (New York, 1960), esp. the remarks of Moses Hadas, p. v.

6. The Greek has combined the Hebrew Psalms 9 and 10, as also 114 and 115, into single psalms, while Masoretic text Psalms 116 and 147 have been each broken down into two separate psalms.

7. See U. M. D. Cassuto, *Ha-Kinnūs Ha-ᶜOlami Le-Madaᶜē Ha-Yahadūt*, I (Jerusalem, 1952), 165–169. Cassuto repeatedly drew attention to this phenomenon in his commentaries to Genesis and Exodus. L. J. Liebreich, *JQR* 46:259–277 (1956), 47:114–138 (1957), has made an exhaustive study of the principle of arrangement by key words in Isaiah. For the same in Ezekiel, see U. M. D. Cassuto, *Miscellanea Giovanni Mercati* (Vatican, 1946), I, 40–51. D. B. Macdonald, *The Hebrew Literary Genius* (Princeton, 1933), pp. 88f., describes the book of Amos as a "collection of fragmentary utterances arranged by a collector according to a purely mechanical principle." Franz Landsberger, "Poetic Units Within the Song of Songs," *JBL* 73:203–216 (1954), arrives at a similar conclusion about the arrangement of the poetic units of Canticles. Much the same point had previously been made by Cassuto, *Ha-Kinnūs*, p. 168, and subsequently by Otto Eissfeldt, *Einleitung in das alte Testament* (Tübingen, 1956), pp. 603f. M. H. Segal, *Mĕbō Ha-Mikraᵓ* (Jerusalem, 1955), I, 12–13, explains the present order of the Minor Prophets by this principle of juxtaposition of key words. By the same token, the Song of Hannah (I Samuel 2:1–10) and the Prayer of Jonah (2:3–10) have both acquired their present positions. For סמיכות הפרשיות as a recognized technique in Rabbinic exegesis, see W. Bacher, *Die exegetische Terminologie der jüdischen Traditionsliteratur*, I (Leipzig, 1899), 142f.

(ii) an oracle, verses 4–5,[8] 20–38,
and (iii) a lament, verses 39ff.

Now it may be noted at once that verses 4–5 have been inserted designedly after verses 2–3, on the basis of a midrash connecting God's חסד and אמונה in His sovereignty over the universe with His חסד and אמונה in His promise of eternal sovereignty to the Davidic line. It will be further observed that עולם, לדר ודר, יבנה, תכן in verses 2–3 correspond to עד עולם, לדר ודור, ובניתי, אכין in verse 5.

It is as though the psalmist, at the very outset, wanted to make this piece of exegesis perfectly clear and beyond the possiblity of misunderstanding. Having so done, he then proceeded to unite the hymn with the oracle on the basis of the juxtaposition of no less than twelve key words or phrases, as can be readily seen in Table I.

TABLE I

The Oracle	*The Hymn*
25, וחסדי; 29, חסדי; 34, וחסדי	2, חסדי; 3, 15, חסד
25, ואמונתי; 34, באמונתי	2, 3, 6, אמונתך; 9, ואמונתך
5, עד־עולם; 29, 37, לעולם; 38, עולם	2, 3, עולם
30, שמים	3, 6, שמים
5, אכין; 22, תכון: 38, יכון	3, תכן
38, בשחק	7, בשחק
26, בים	10, הים
23, אויב	11, אויביך
25, ובשמי	13, בשמך
22, זרועי	14, זרוע
25, תרום קרנו	14, תרום ימינך; 18, תרום קרננו
5, כסאך; 30, 37, וכסאו	15, כסאך

The transition between the hymn and the oracle is deftly made through the national motif of verses 16–19 being subtly superimposed upon the cosmic, while the emphasis upon the moral basis of God's rule (verse 15) serves, in turn, to accentuate the sacrosanct, inviolable nature of the Divine Promise of the Davidic rule. Finally, מלכנו as the concluding word of the hymn carries over the idea of kingship which is central to the oracle.

The consummate skill with which the psalmist handled the several elements so that they became mutually interdependent will be specially appreciated from an examination of the lament. The twin themes of the

8. That verses 4–5 undoubtedly belong to the oracle is proved by considerations of content and meter, on which see S. Mowinckel, *Psalmenstudien*, III (Kristiania, 1923), 35f., and Kraus, *Psalmen*.

hymn and the oracle, the morality of God's rule and the imprescriptible nature of His pledge, obviously encourage the psalmist to give utterance to his bitter complaint contrasting the stark reality of history with the promised ideal. But as a literary device, and to point up this contrast all the more effectively, he has made use in the lament of the key words of both the hymn and the oracle (see Table II).

TABLE II

The Lament (verses 39ff.)	*The Hymn and Oracle* (verses 2–38)
39, 52, משיחך	21, משחתיו
40, ברית	4, ברית; 29, ובריתי;
	35, בריתי
40, עבדך; 51, עבדיך	4, 21, עבדי
43, הרימות ימין	14, תרום ימינך;
	18, תרום קרננו;
	25, תרום קרנו
43, צריו	24, צריו
43, אויביו; 52, אויביך	11, אויביך; 23, אויב
45, וכסאו	5, 15, כסאך;
	30, 37, וכסאו
50, חסדיך--באמונתך	2, חסדי ה׳--אמונתך;
	3, חסד--אמונתך;
	25, ואמונתי וחסדי;
	34, וחסדי--באמונתי;
	[Cf. 15, חסד ואמת
	29, חסדי · · · נאמנת]
50, נשבעת	4, 36, נשבעתי

This repeated use of a large number of key words and phrases and the smooth transitions from one section to another constitute the techniques by which the psalmist harmoniously integrated the varied elements into a perfectly homogeneous poetic unit. The cohesive effect is heightened by fact that the pivotal words חסד and אמונה appear, each one, seven times. It is, moreover, probably not accident that ברית is used four times and its synonym שבועה three times, thus making a sevenfold mention of the covenant oath as well.[9]

9. For the significance and widespread use of the number seven in antiquity see J. and H. Lewy, *HUCA* 17:1–146 (1942–43), esp. p. 22, where reference is made to Assyro-Babylonian hymns and prayers which contain sevenfold mention of Enlil's name. For a Biblical analogy with this latter, cf. the heptad of tetragrammata to be found in Psalm 92, designated "for the Sabbath day."

All this unmistakably bears the stamp of a single creative editor-psalmist. He it is who must have composed the lament (verses 39ff.) and who has been responsible for having welded together the diverse parts that make up Psalm 89. It follows, then, that neither the hymn nor the oracular element can be dated later than the time of the composition of the lament. This problem and its implications will be dealt with hereafter. But its solution will not be possible unless the true nature of the oracular element is properly understood.

IV. The Antiquity of Exegesis

We have already noted above that verses 4–5, originally belonging to the oracle, were inserted in the hymn as a kind of exegetical note. Indeed, we shall have occasion to show that the entire oracle is a reinterpretation of Nathan's original prophecy to David. Before proceeding directly to do so, however, it will not be out of place to say a few introductory words on the history of the exegetical system involved.

The phenomenon of exegesis and exposition of a text evolves from a peculiar attitude to the written or oral word. It involves the idea of authority and immutability and, ultimately, of sanctity.[10] This notion is found for the first time in Biblical literature in Deuteronomy 4:2:

לא תספו על-הדבר אשר אנכי מצוה אתכם ולא תגרעו ממנו.

"Ye shall not add unto the word which I command you, neither shall ye diminish from it." We meet it again at the close of the prophetic age when Zechariah quotes the "earlier prophets" (הנביאים הראשונים) as authoritative (Zechariah 1:4, 7:7). But it is now clear that this Biblical concept has its roots in the more ancient Near East and was widespread, in fact, throughout the ancient world.

It is already implicit in the epilogue to the early-nineteenth-century B.C.E. laws of Lipit-Ishtar, in which the monarch curses him "who will damage my handiwork . . . who will erase its inscription, who will write his own [name] upon it."[11] A century and a half later, Hammurapi exhorts his successors not to alter his laws and invokes elaborate imprecations upon him who has not treated them as immutable, but who "has abolished the law which I enacted, has distorted my words, has altered my statutes,

10. Cf. the remarks of Louis Ginzberg, *JE*, I, 403, "Allegorical Interpretation."
11. *Ancient Near Eastern Texts*, p. 160.

effaced my name inscribed [thereon] and has then inscribed his [own] name [in its place]."[12]

Paradoxically, this very idea of authority and immutability itself engenders change. The past is drawn upon to give sanction to the present, and the ancient words, precisely because they are invested with authority, are reinterpreted to make them applicable to the contemporary scene.

This is particularly true of religious literature. An excellent example is the great Babylonian creation epic, the *Enuma elish*, which was solemnly recited by the high priest on the fourth day of the New Year's festival. It is well known that this epic, dated to the time of Hammurapi,[13] was motivated by theological and political considerations. It justified Marduk's ascendancy to a supreme position in the Babylonian pantheon and at the same time it supported Babylon's claim to political pre-eminence.[14] Now, it is of interest to note that in the Assyrian version of this epic, the name of the hero is Ashur, and his great temple is not the Esagila of Babylon but the metropolis bearing Ashur's name.[15] A striking analogy to this situation may be found in the political and theological motivations that induced the Samaritans to change the authoritative text of the Pentateuch to justify the pre-eminence of Mount Gerizim.[16]

This tendency, outside of Israel, to regard a text as authoritative and then to reinterpret it, is not restricted to Babylonian times. Thus, as Edward Meyer has pointed out, from the third century B.C.E., demotic papyri are extant which constitute midrashim on obscure prophecies about Egypt's fate.[17] Similarly, the four-monarchy theory of Daniel is but a development of an originally Achaemenian Persian doctrine, itself subjected to varying exegesis in the ancient world.[18] The history of the sibylline oracles in general and of the Jewish use of them in particular is a

12. G. R. Driver and J. C. Miles, *The Babylonian Laws* (Oxford, 1952–55), I, 39; II, 101, 107. *Ancient Near Eastern Texts*, p. 61.

13. Speiser, *Ancient Near Eastern Texts*, p. 61.

14. A. Heidel, *The Babylonian Genesis* (Chicago, 1942), p. 5.

15. *Ibid.*, p. 1. This must constitute one of the earliest examples of the kind of תקון סופרים known to us from Rabbinic literature, on which see S. Lieberman, *Hellenism in Jewish Palestine* (New York, 1950), pp. 28–37.

16. On the question of the relationship of Masoretic text Deuteronomy 27:4 to the Samaritan, see Y. Kaufmann, *Sefer Yehoshuʿa* (Jerusalem, 1959), pp. 129–132.

17. E. Meyer, *Kleine Schriften* (Halle, 1924), II (Jerusalem, 1958), 67–91. Cf. also H. L. Ginsberg, *Encyclopaedia Biblica* [Hebrew], II (Jerusalem, 1958), 689. On ancient Egyptian prophecy, see Gunter Lanczkowski, *Altägyptischer Prophetismus* (Wiesbaden, 1960).

18. Ginsberg, *Encyclopaedia Biblica*, II, 689, and *Studies in Daniel* (New York, 1948), pp. 5ff., 63ff. On the latter, cf. the remarks of Y. Kaufmann, *Tōlĕdōt Ha-Emūnah Ha-Yisraelīt* (Tel-Aviv, 1956), vol. IV (8), p. 424, n. 12.

case in point in the Hellenistic world.[19] At the same time, Virgil's Fourth Eclogue, written about the year 40 B.C.E., is a midrash on the oracles of the Sibyl of Cumae; and the early Church, in turn, reinterpreted the Fourth Eclogue as a prophetic allusion to the birth of Jesus.[20] Philo's special brand of exegesis is well known,[21] and the Dead Sea Scrolls furnish numerous examples of the use of the midrash method in adapting Scripture to their own purposes.[22] The authors of the New Testament freely reinterpreted the Jewish Bible, albeit in its Greek form,[23] as a prophecy of Christian truths,[24] a tradition earnestly pursued by the early Church Fathers.[25] In the light of all this, it is abundantly clear that the highly developed midrash system of the Rabbis was not a late innovation, but had a very long and varied history behind it.

Wilhelm Bacher has described Biblical exegesis as "the one indigenous science created and developed by Israel."[26] On the basis of the well-known passage in Ezra 7:10: "כי עזרא הכין לבבו לדרש את תורת ה׳" he attributed its foundation to Ezra the Scribe. In so far as the emphasis is upon the word "science," Bacher is no doubt correct. Yet Rabbinic tradition regarded the oral law as being conterminous with the written law. It thus actually looks for the origins of Biblical exegesis within the period of the formation of the Scriptures themselves. This Rabbinic tradition, in a generalized sense, must be upheld; for it cannot be denied that the literature of the Bible was subjected to exegesis even in pre-Exilic times.[27] The ancient Near-Eastern tradition would support such a view a priori, and the Biblical evidence itself is conclusive. A few of the more outstanding examples will suffice.

19. E. Schürer, *A History of the Jewish People in the Time of Jesus Christ* (Edinburgh, 1890), div. II, vol. III, pp. 271–292.

20. J. B. Mayor, *Virgil's Messianic Eclogue* (London, 1907), pp. 87–138, believes that the sybilline original is itself influenced by Isaiah's prophecies. Against this view, however, see the detailed objections of Kaufmann, *Tōlĕdōt*, vol. III (6), pp. 293–296.

21. On Philo's exegetical method, see the literature cited by S. W. Baron, *A Social and Religious History of the Jews* (Philadelphia, 1952), vol. I, p. 389, n. 51.

22. See F. F. Bruce, *Biblical Exegesis in the Qumran Texts* (Grand Rapids, 1959).

23. W. Dittmar, *Vetus Testamentum in Novo* (Göttingen, 1903); H. B. Swete, *Introduction to the Old Testament in Greek* (Cambridge, 1902), pp. 381–405.

24. K. Fullerton, *Prophecy and Authority* (New York, 1919).

25. Swete, *Introduction to the Old Testament in Greek*, pp. 406–432.

26. *JE*, III, 162; so I. H. Weiss, *Dōr Dōr Ve-Dōrshav* (New York–Berlin, 1924), I, 52.

27. Cf. the observation of W. F. Albright, *From the Stone Age to Christianity* (New York, 1957), p. 296, n. 27, "There was undoubtedly much more exegesis of the Hebrew text in pre-Exilic times than we often realize." See also Weiss, *Dōr Dōr*, I, 51f.; M. H. Segal, *Parshanūt Ha-Mikra*ʾ (Jerusalem, 1952), pp. 5–7; *Mĕbōʾ*, IV, 981–982, and especially the study of I. L. Seeligman, *Congress Volume* (Supplements to *VT* vol. I, Leiden, 1953), pp. 150–181.

It is universally recognized that Daniel 9:2, 24–27, is a midrash reinterpreting Jeremiah's seventy years of exile (Jeremiah 25:11–12, 29:10; compare Zechariah 1:12; 7:5). H. L. Ginsberg has recently drawn attention to the fact that Daniel chapters 10–12 also constitute a complete midrash, mainly on the Book of Isaiah.[28] Few dispute the fact that the Book of Chronicles is in large measure a midrashic reinterpretation of earlier works with a view to a paradigmatic reconstruction of the history of Israel.[29] These examples belong to the Exilic period. It is now possible, however, to trace back Biblical exegesis to a still earlier period, for Kaufmann has clearly demonstrated the existence in Israel of an ancient body of prophetic oracles upon which the literary prophets freely drew and which they adapted to their needs.[30]

V. Exegesis in Psalm 89

Now a recognition of this early phenomenon of inner Biblical exegesis holds the key to the solution of one of the problems of our psalm. Much attention has been paid to the relationship between Psalm 89:20–38 and the recensions of Nathan's oracle to David found in II Samuel 7:4–17 and I Chronicles 17:3–15. Scholarly speculation has, in fact, encompassed the entire range of possibilities. One view regards the prose version as original and our psalm as a free poetic paraphrase of it.[31] Another insists that precisely the poetic form must be the oldest version of the oracle on which the prose recensions are dependent.[32] Yet a third school of thought

28. Ginsberg, *Encyclopaedia Biblica*, II, 949–951.

29. This evaluation is not at all invalidated by recent, more positive appraisals of the chronicler's work; see, in particular, W. F. Albright, "The Judicial Reforms of Jehoshaphat," *Alexander Marx Jubilee Volume* (New York, 1950), I, 61–82, and J. Liver, *Sefer Biram* (Jerusalem, 1956), pp. 152–161.

30. Kaufmann, *Tōlĕdōt*, vol. III (6), pp. 1–55. See also the sources cited in note 27.

31. R. Duhm, *Die Psalmen* (Tübingen, 1899), p. 222; A. F. Kirkpatrick, *The Book of Psalms* (Cambridge, 1904), p. 530; Z. P. Chajes, [Hebrew] Commentary to Psalms (Kiev, 1908), p. 193; E. G. Briggs, *The Book of Psalms*, II (New York, 1917), 253; H. Gunkel, *Die Psalmen* (Göttingen, 1926), p. 392; E. A. Leslie, *The Psalms* (New York–Nashville, 1949); M. Simon, *Revue d'histoire et de philosophie religieuses*, 32:41–58 (1952); Segal, *Mĕbō*ᵓ, III, 563; *Sifrē Shĕmuel* (Jerusalem, 1956), p. 280; H. van den Bussche, *Le Texte de la prophétie de Nathan sur la dynastie Davidique* (Louvain, 1948), p. 6, n. 2, upholds the primacy of the prose version, but maintains that both II Samuel 7 and I Chronicles 17 are dependent on an older text, with the Chronicles version nearer the original.

32. Mowinckel, *He That Cometh* (New York–Nashville, 1954), p. 100, n. 3; C. R. North, *The Old Testament Interpretation of History* (London, 1946), p. 99; R. H. Pfeiffer, *Introduction to the Old Testament* (New York, 1948), p. 371f.; A. R. Johnson, *Sacral Kingship in Ancient Israel* (Cardiff, 1955), p. 23, n. 2; G. W. Ahlström, *Psalm* 89 (Lund, 1959), p. 182, also doubts the priority of II Samuel 7.

suggests that there need be no question of literary interdependence since the authors of Samuel, Chronicles, and our psalm could well have had equal and independent access to a common source, long since lost, that contained the text of the original oracle.[33]

To the present writer, a close comparison between our psalm and the texts of the oracle in Samuel and Chronicles shows that we are not dealing here with any problem of literary dependence or text transmission. The several variations from the prose versions are highly significant and can easily be otherwise explained. As a matter of fact, they add up to a pattern of deliberate and original exegesis on the part of the psalmist, who has adapted an ancient oracle to a new situation.[34] The evidence is as follows:

(i) In both versions of the oracle, the occasion of the original utterance is David's Temple project. The same is true of the quotations of Nathan's prophecy in I Chronicles 22:6ff., especially verse 10, I Chronicles 28:1ff., especially verses 6–7, II Chronicles 6:5–9, and Psalm 132:11ff. Solomon, too, quotes from the oracle in his Temple dedicatory speech (I Kings 8:25). This consistency must reflect an authentic situation. But what do we find in our psalm? Here, alone, the Temple project element is entirely lacking. The verses II Samuel 7:10–13 (I Chronicles 17:9–12) find no echo whatsoever in Psalm 89. This exclusion cannot be accidental. It accords completely with the omission of any mention of the Temple in the lament, an omission which we shall have occasion to discuss again in a different connection.[35]

(ii) The verse II Samuel 7:10 (to which compare I Chronicles 17:9) contains a promise to the people of Israel of respite from their national enemies. This is in agreement with the state of affairs toward the close of David's long reign, but it is clearly at variance with the subsequent history of Judah. A comparison with Psalm 89:23–24 shows that the psalmist has, therefore, cleverly and pointedly changed the wording so as to restrict its import to David personally.

(iii) This change is all the more forcefully emphasized by an expansion in the psalm, not to be found in either version. Verse 26 reads:

ושמתי בים ידו ובנהרות ימינו.

This is an undoubted reference to the Davidic empire,[36] and it serves a

33. J. L. McKenzie, *Theological Studies*, VIII (1947), 187–218. Cf. also the view of H. van den Bussche, cited in Note 31, and the remarks of Kraus, *Psalmen*, p. 622.

34. Segal, *Sifrē Shĕmuel*, is one of the few to observe that the psalmists have made free use of the oracle.

35. See below, Section VII.

36. This is so, even if, as A. R. Johnson, *Sacral Kingship*, p. 24, n. 2, points out, the phraseology is borrowed from mytho-cultic sources; see J. Pedersen, *Israel*, vol. III–IV (London–Copenhagen, 1959), pp. 655 and 724, n. 1.

further purpose as well. It is related to the occasion of the lament. The psalmist wishes to point up the contrast between the Davidic victories and the military humiliation of his own day.

(iv) This same tendency to oppose reality to the oracular promise is to be observed in yet another expansion original to our psalm. In II Samuel 7:14 (I Chronicles 17:13) we find:

אני אהיה־לו לאב והוא יהיה־לי לבן.

This cultic formula is also repeated, almost word for word, in the quotations in I Chronicles 22:10, 28:6. But Psalm 89:27–28 has:

הוא יקראני אבי אתה אלי וצור ישועתי: אף־אני בכור אתנהו עליון למלכי־ארץ.

This is an interpretation of the oracle stressing the implications of God's function as the father and emphasizing the benefits which the בכור (not בן!) relationship is supposed to bestow.

(v) Furthermore, it cannot fail to be noticed that, whereas in all the quotations cited above the father-son relationship refers to God's obligations to the immediate offspring of David, our psalm has applied the sonship to David himself.

(vi) In the same vein, the psalmist has transferred the threatened punishment for sin from the son of David (II Samuel 7:14) to the Davidic dynasty as a whole (Psalm 89:31). David has become the dynastic symbol.[37]

(vii) Finally, our psalmist has reinterpreted Nathan's oracle in terms of a covenant between God and David, sealed by a solemn oath (ברית, שבועה, verses 4, 35–36, 40, 50). However, in neither prose recension of the prophecy is ברית or שבועה mentioned. David, too, in his response to the oracle (II Samuel 7:18ff.; I Chronicles 17:16ff.) makes no mention of either term. The psalmist here has, for his own purposes, made use of a very early exegetical tradition in departing from the original language of the oracle. This is clear from the "last words of David," in which the old monarch says that God gave him an "eternal covenant" (ברית עולם, II Samuel 23:5). According to the chronicler (II Chronicles 13:5), King Abijah recalls to Jeroboam and to all Israel as something well known that God gave the kingdom to David "forever" (לעולם) with a "covenant of

37. A. Alt, *Kleine Schriften zur Geschichte des Volkes Israel*, II (Munich, 1953), 132f., points out the analogy with the covenant of God with Levi mentioned in Deuteronomy 33:8ff., Jeremiah 33:21, Malachi 2:4ff., and Nehemiah 13:29. Cf. also the covenant with Phineas, Numbers 25:12f. The supreme importance of the dynastic symbolism probably explains why the theme of the shepherd origins of David, mentioned in II Samuel 7:8 and I Chronicles 17:7, irrelevant to the psalmist's purposes, has been replaced in Psalm 89:21 by the simple phrase מצאתי דוד עבדי.

salt" (ברית מלח). The quotation in Psalm 132:11 also refers to the oracle in legal terms of ברית and שבועה, and Jeremiah (Jeremiah 33:17, 21) and Deutero-Isaiah (Isaiah 55:3) both have the same understanding of it.[38]

The explanation for all this lies in the fact that the author of the lament needed to adapt Nathan's oracle to his own immediate purposes. He had not the slightest interest in the original occasion of the oracle, the Temple project, and, as a matter of fact, as we shall see later, the omission of any mention of the Temple was necessary for the subject of the lament. Likewise, the problem of David's successor was quite irrelevant to his theme. His sole concern was with the Divine Pledge of perpetuity to the Davidic dynasty as such and with the glaring contrast between the promised ideal and the present reality. It is this exclusive interest that explains the expansions, selectivity, departures from, and changes of emphasis in the psalmist's citations from the text of the oracle. Psalm 89, verses 4–5, 20–38, accordingly, do not represent a different, independent recension of Nathan's oracle to David, and there is no question of deciding upon the relationship of the prose to a supposed poetic version. These verses constitute, rather, an exegetical adaptation of the oracle by the psalmist to fit a specific historic situation.

VI. The Date of Nathan's Oracle

This conclusion as to the nature of verses 4–5, 20–38, presupposes the anteriority of Nathan's oracle to the psalm. The evidence for this assumption, however, requires elucidation in view of the astonishing divergence of scholarly opinion that has been expressed.

From some comes a rather vague admission that the prophecy contains an ancient nucleus.[39] Others are certain that it is Davidic[40] or, at latest, Solomonic.[41] It has been dated pre-Deuteronomic[42] as well as post-

38. For an analogous exegetical development, cf. Genesis 8:21f. with Jeremiah 33:20, 25. This proves, incidentally, that the terms ברית and שבועה need not always have cultic significance.

39. J. Hänel, in Rothstein-Hänel, *Das erste Buch der Chronik* (Leipzig, 1927), pp. 332ff.; McKenzie, *Theological Studies*, VIII, 208; J. Bright, *A History of Israel* (Philadelphia, 1959), p. 204 and n. 94.

40. A. Klostermann, *Die Bücher Samuelis und der Könige* (Nordlingen, 1887); C. Steuernagel, *Lehrbuch der Einleitung in das Alte Testament* (Tübingen, 1912), p. 325; M. Noth, *Die Gesetze in Pentateuch* (Halle, 1940), p. 12; cf. his *The History of Israel* (New York, 1958), p. 222; Kaufmann, *Tōlĕdōt*, II, 369; A. Bentzen, *Introduction to the Old Testament* (Copenhagen, 1959), I, 161.

41. Segal, *Sifrē Shĕmuel*, p. 276.

42. E. Sellin, *Introduction to the Old Testament* (London, 1923), p. 112, gives a date *ca.* 800 B.C.E. S. R. Driver, *An Introduction to the Literature of the Old Testament* (Edinburgh, 1913), p. 183, thinks it can hardly be later than 700, in the main.

Deuteronomic,[43] and more precisely, Josianic,[44] Exilic,[45] post-Exilic, and even as late as the fourth century B.C.E.[46]

Notwithstanding the complete lack of consensus, it would appear to the present writer that the facts are overwhelmingly in favor of a Davidic date.

(i) The entire oracle is devoted to the idea of the perpetuity of the Davidic line. Now such an oracle would certainly be nonsensical in post-Exilic times unless it be Messianic or eschatological. It is true that it has been widely so interpreted in medieval and modern times, but such an understanding is possible only if the numerous other factors, hereafter described, are ignored. Furthermore, the fact that Solomon applied the oracle to himself (I Kings 8:20; II Chronicles 6:10) proves that to the Biblical writers, at least, the prophecy was well rooted in history.

(ii) The oracle makes very clear the possibility of sin on the part of David's offspring and its inevitable punishment (II Samuel 7:14). Yet the reference is entirely individual. In not one of the different recensions or quotations of the oracle is there any mention of national sin or national punishment. Subsequent to the work of the eighth-century prophets this omission would be very strange.

(iii) Still more strange is the lack of even a hint of the division of the kingdom, despite the fact that this could most conveniently be interpreted as the promised punishment. The prophecy must therefore derive, at the latest, from before the time of Solomon's death.

(iv) Several times the oracle is cited in support of the legitimacy of the Solomonic succession. Solomon himself invokes it in his Temple dedicatory speech and applies it specifically to himself (I Kings 8:20; II Chronicles 6:10). Yet his quotation agrees with all the versions of the prophecy in maintaining the anonymity of David's successor. This is explicable only on the assumption that the text of the oracle was fixed before the Solomonic succession.

(v) This conclusion is strengthened by yet another consideration. The chronicler finds himself in desperate need of legitimating the Solomonic succession.[47] To this end he omits from his narrative several inconvenient episodes leading up to it. The murder of David's first-born son, Amnon,

43. P. Dhorme, *Les Livres de Samuel* (Paris, 1910), p. 362.

44. J. Wellhausen, *Die Composition des Hexateuchs* (Berlin, 1889), p. 257.

45. H. P. Smith, *The Books of Samuel* (New York, 1909), p. 297; cf. B. Stade, *Encyclopaedia Biblica* (New York, 1903), column 4278, who feels it may even be post-Exilic.

46. Pfeiffer, *Introduction to the Old Testament*, p. 371.

47. See on this and the following, Kaufmann, *Tōlĕdōt*, vol. IV (8) (1956), pp. 460–465.

by Absalom (II Samuel 13), the murder of Absalom by Joab after the former's abortive revolt (II Samuel 15–18), Adonijah's bid for the crown with considerable and important court support (I Kings 1:5–10), the swift and successful pro-Solomonic reaction headed by Nathan and Bath-Sheba in which the decisive event is Nathan's invocation of a promise by David to Bath-Sheba (I Kings 1:11–53), the subsequent murder of Adonijah (I Kings 2:25)—on all these decisive incidents which regulated Solomon's accession to the throne, the chronicler is significantly silent, for they interfere with his notion of Solomon's natural and divine right of succession. Now in view of this situation, it is passing strange that neither in I Chronicles 17 nor in the abbreviated quotation in I Chronicles 6:5–9 is the text of Nathan's oracle tampered with in order to identify the unnamed successor of David. This, once again, can be explained only on the supposition that the text of Nathan's oracle as it appears in I Chronicles 17 and II Samuel 7 from the mouth of Nathan was substantially fixed before Solomon's accession to the throne.

(vi) The chronicler's historiosophical purposes led him on other occasions to adapt the text of the prophecy to his needs. David is made to recite it to Solomon as though Nathan had actually named Solomon in it (I Chronicles 22:7–10). This is in glaring contrast to II Samuel 12:25, in which Nathan names Solomon ידידיה but makes no mention of his own oracle in reference to the newly-born son. Likewise, in David's address to the princes, he is made paraphrastically to quote Nathan's oracle as though Solomon had actually been named in it (I Chronicles 28:1–7). Yet, in the original citation in II Samuel 7, and I Chronicles 17 (compare also II Chronicles 6:5–9), Solomon's name is not to be found. The absence of identification of David's successor must be due to the fact that the oracle indeed preceded the designation of Solomon as David's successor and that II Samuel 7 and I Chronicles 17 were not reworked in the light of subsequent events.

(vii) Biblical literature is emphatic that David was called to the throne by divine designation (compare I Samuel 25:30, II Samuel 5:2). The oracle, too, stresses this point (II Samuel 7:8, I Chronicles 17:7; compare Psalm 89:20–21). But, significantly, there is no Divine Word recorded in Samuel or Kings on the election of Solomon. He attains the throne only by order of David's decision, based upon a promise he had once made to Bath-Sheba (I Kings 1:16ff.). Moreover, Nathan, who played no minor role in the palace intrigue, strangely, does not invoke his own oracle in support of Solomon's claim to the throne. In the light of the foregoing argument, this is conceivable only if the successor to David was not designated in the original oracle. In other words, Nathan's prophecy must antedate both David's death and the designation of Solomon as his successor.

(viii) We have previously taken note of a consistent tradition linking Nathan's oracle to David's Temple project. The validity of this tradition is enhanced by the fact that it harmonizes perfectly with yet another, equally consistent, Biblical tradition. Deuteronomy 12:9ff. makes the selection of a centralized place of worship dependent upon the attainment of peace and national security. The formula is significant:

והניח לכם מכל־איביכם מסביב וישבתם־בטח.

Solomon uses it in enlisting the aid of Hiram, King of Tyre, to build his Temple (I Kings 5:18–19) and it is repeated several times in the same connection (I Kings 8:15; I Chronicles 22:7–9, 28:3). This, as Wellhausen has pointed out,[48] is due to the fact that Israelite historiosophy envisaged this stage as being first fully realized in the times of David and Solomon. Accordingly, David's Temple project would be just the appropriate time for a prophecy such as that of Nathan. National security and peace having advanced to a point that allowed for the building of the Temple, an opportune occasion presented itself for a prophecy promising eternal stability to the Davidic dynasty.

(ix) Finally, the fact that the exclusive right of the Davidic line to kingship was never challenged in Judah proves conclusively that in the popular conception the legitimacy of the dynasty must have been based upon a Divine sanction of commitment to the descendants of David.

To sum up, the converging lines of evidence are overwhelmingly conclusive in proving that the Biblical tradition about the original prophecy of Nathan to David is an authentic document, contemporaneous with the events it describes. There is, accordingly, no chronological objection to our interpretation of the second element of Psalm 89 as being an exegetical adaptation of that prophecy.

VII. The Date and Background of the Psalm

It now remains to determine, if possible, the particular historical circumstances that stirred the author of the lament to put together the psalm

48. J. Wellhausen, *Prolegomena to the History of Ancient Israel* (New York, 1957), p. 19, n. 1. Cf. Kaufmann, *Tōlĕdōt*, vol. II (4), p. 369. This is true even though Deuteronomy 25:19, which uses the same formula, was interpreted in I Samuel 15:2ff. as referring to the time of Saul.

in substantially its present form. We may, at the outset, emphatically and completely rule out the possibility that the Babylonian destruction of Jerusalem and the Temple and the subsequent Exile evoked the bitter complaints to be found in verses 39ff.[49] For one thing, the total absence of any mention of or reference to any of these cataclysmic events would be utterly inexplicable. For another, there is not the slightest suggestion of even a threat to Jerusalem or of a foreign yoke, no notion of a national sin, no hint of the dissolution of the monarchy, no prayer or hope for national and monarchical restoration. Anyone who compares this psalm with Psalms 79 or 137 will note immediately the striking contrast in historical background and treatment. There cannot be the slightest doubt that the lament must reflect some situation prior to the Babylonian invasion.

Now any attempt further to narrow down the historical circumstances that inspired the psalmist must take account of his exegetical treatment of Nathan's oracle, which, as we have shown, was adapted to the immediate purposes of the lament. It must explain why the Divine Promise of eternity for the Davidic line is there the exclusive theme and why David's Temple project, which evoked the oracle, is ignored. It has to make clear why, in turn, the lament refers only to some danger to the ruling dynasty, but passes over in silence Jerusalem, the Temple, and the people at large. We have to know why the sin mentioned in the original oracle only in reference to David's immediate successor is reinterpreted to apply to the royal descendants of David in general. Finally, we must understand the meaning of the repeated emphasis upon חסד, and the appeal to the inviolable nature of the ברית.

Bearing in mind all the foregoing, it is possible to reconstruct the nature of the events which produced the lament. This latter must reflect an invasion of Judea, but it must have been one that did not have as its primary goal the conquest of Jerusalem or the Temple. The real target was the reigning monarch, whom the invaders wished to depose and replace by an outsider, not of Davidic descent. In other words, the invasion constituted

49. *Contra* Pfeiffer, *Introduction to the Old Testament*, p. 373, whose view has recently been upheld by J. Liver, *The House of David* [Hebrew] (Jerusalem, 1959), pp. 64f., esp. n. 1. Even if his own view is mistaken, Liver's criticism of Kaufmann, *Tōlĕdōt*, vol. II (5), pp. 525–526, 663, n. 39, who sees in the lament a reference to Hezekiah, is correct. See also the criticism of this view by Segal, *Mĕbōʾ*, vol. III, p. 531, n. 23. Equally objectionable are the views of Segal himself, *ibid.*, and Chajes, [Hebrew] Commentary to Psalms, p. 97, who refer to the death of Josiah, and of Briggs, *The Book of Psalms*, II, 250, who sees in the exile of Jehoiachin the occasion of the lament. Apart from other objections, in neither instance was any attempt made to place an outsider upon the throne of David.

a mortal threat, not to the integrity of the kingdom, but to the Davidic dynasty. This alone explains the reiterated invocation of God's eternal covenant with the House of David.

At the same time, the psalmist did not have too high an opinion of the ruling king; in fact, he clearly regarded him as a sinful man who had forsaken God's law and had not walked in His judgments; who had violated the Divine Statutes and had not heeded God's precepts (verse 31f.). Very significantly, the psalmist does not mention the injustice of the situation he is lamenting. The monarch, through his personal unworthiness, would really have had no legal case were it not for the appeal to God's חסד, to the Divine "covenant-love," which promised the unbroken continuity of the Davidic line (verses 29, 34–37, 50).

From the language of the lament, it is possible to glean yet one more vital and illuminating detail. The invasion of Judea had inflicted a humiliating defeat upon the king (verses 40–45). True, he had emerged from it alive, but he was a young man and had now become prematurely aged (verse 46).[50]

Such an understanding of the historic situation alone makes the singularities of Psalm 89 intelligible. It also enables us to pinpoint the particular event. The only known threat to the Davidic dynasty in Judea is that recorded in Isaiah 7:5–6[51] when, in the year 735–34 B.C.E., an anti-Assyrian coalition led by Rezin of Damascus and Pekaḥ of Israel launched an invasion of Judea with the expressed purpose of deposing King Ahaz and of replacing him by an Aramean puppet, one ben Tabʾel.[52] Ahaz was only twenty years old at the time (II Kings 16:2; II Chronicles 28:1), having just ascended the throne. That he suffered defeat and humiliation

50. This is the only possible meaning of verse 46, "הקצרת ימי עלומיו," as may be seen from Psalm 102:24, where the speaker is the psalmist himself. Further, the preceding verses all imply that the king is still alive.

51. On Isaiah chapter 7, see H. L. Ginsberg, "Judah and Transjordan Steles from 734–582 B.C.E.," *Alexander Marx Jubilee Volume* (New York, 1950), pp. 347–368, esp. p. 348, n. 7, and his "Immanuel," *Tarbiz* 20:29–32 (1950). It is quite likely that the use of the expression בית דוד in Isaiah 7:2, 13, is intended to point up the threat to the dynasty. Note also Isaiah 9:1–6, the affirmation of the eternity of the Davidic House and cf. verse 6, "על כסא דוד ועל ממלכתו, להכין אתה . . . ועד עולם" with Psalm 89:5, 30, 37 and II Samuel 7:12–13, 16.

52. For the name ben Tabʾel, see W. F. Albright, "The Son of Tabeel," *BASOR* 140:34f. (1955). It is not necessary to presume, with Albright, that the puppet was a son of Uzziah or Jotham. Noth, *The History of Israel*, p. 259, thinks he was probably an Aramean, and B. Mazar, "The House of Tobias," *Tarbiz* 12:122f. (1941); *Encyclopaedia Biblica* [Hebrew], II, 80, makes the interesting suggestion that the imposter may have been connected with the later distinguished Tobiad family.

is related by the chronicler[53] (II Chronicles 28), and this dovetails very well into the circumstances presupposed by the lament. This invasion did not really bring with it a danger of destruction to Jerusalem or the Temple, only a threat to King Ahaz, scion of the House of David. His experience must indeed have shortened his days, for he died at the early age of thirty-six (II Kings 16:2; II Chronicles 28:1). That Ahaz was a sinful man, thoroughly deserving of God's chastisement, is clear from the Biblical evaluation of him (II Kings 16:2ff.; II Chronicles 28:1ff.; Isaiah 7:13ff.). The profound impact of the invasion and the consternation, bordering on panic, that ensued in Jerusalem can easily be imagined from the vivid account in Isaiah 7:1ff. and the more prosaic, detailed narratives in II Kings 15:37—16:5 and II Chronicles 28:5ff. A psalm such as ours would certainly have been written immediately after the humiliation of the king, when the final outcome of the Aramean-Israelite venture was still uncertain. In all probability the psalmist was a court poet, but totally out of sympathy with the pro-Assyrian policy of Ahaz and opposed to his religious perversions.

VIII. Summary

Psalm 89, in its present form, is a unity of originally diverse elements. This unity has been skillfully constructed through the reiterated use of key words and phrases, combined with a subtle interweaving of motifs and themes. The second of the three natural divisions of the psalm constitutes an exegetical adaptation, not another recension, of Nathan's oracle about the House of David, and this oracle is certainly Davidic. The writer of the lament is the real author of our present psalm, which was inspired by the Aramean-Israelite invasion of Judea in 735–34 B.C.E., when an attempt was made to depose Ahaz and to replace him by a non-Davidic king.

Postscript

My attention has been drawn to two relevant articles which have appeared too late to be referred to in the foregoing study.

J. M. Ward in *VT* 11:321–339 (1961) has independently reinforced my own conclusions as to the integrity and unity of the psalm. He has not,

53. For the general historicity of the Chronicles account, see the remark of J. Bright, *A History of Israel*, p. 256, n. 10.

however, sufficiently considered the possibility of a specific historic situation as the occasion of the psalm.

Gerald Cooke, *ZAW* 73:202–225 (1961) agrees that at least part of Nathan's prophecy stems "from near the time of David himself." He further states that there is no need to "assert the dependence of the midrashic author of II Sam. 7 upon Ps. 89." However, Cooke has failed to realize that the Psalm 89 version is itself a midrash on the original oracle of Nathan.

The Quintessence of Koheleth[1]

By H. L. Ginsberg

In "The Structure and Contents of the Book of Koheleth," after disengaging the body of the Book (1:2—12:8) from the at least partly secondary title (1:1) and the wholly secondary epilogues (12:9–14), I divided the body itself into the following four main divisions: (1) A, 1:2—2:26; (2) B, 3:1—4:3; (3) A′, 4:4—6:9 (with 4:9—5:8 constituting a block of associative digressions); (4) B′, 6:10—12:8 (with 9:17—10:14a, 15–19, constituting a block of associative digressions [and with 11:9b being the one gloss the body of the Book contains; it is from the hand of the Second Epilogist, the author of 12:12–14]).

The contents of these main divisions may be summarized as follows.

A and A′: all is futility, or zero (*hebel*); that applies even to wisdom, and still more to empty merrymaking. The only benefit a man can attain is the utilization of his wordly goods for his enjoyment. Whether or not he has both the means and the good sense to use them depends entirely on God's whim.

B and B′: in human affairs, the same, numbered activities, emotions, or experiences (*ḥepeṣ*, in this sense best rendered by "doing") are repeated over and over to the end of time. When each one is to occur is determined in advance by God; human beings have an irresistible urge to try to guess His time-table, but they are never completely successful. The moral is

1. My previous publications on Koheleth are: *Studies in Koheleth* (New York, 1950); "Supplementary Studies in Koheleth," *Proceedings of the American Academy for Jewish Research* (1952), pp. 35–62; "The Structure and Contents of the Book of Koheleth," *VT*, Supplement III (1955), pp. 138–149; "Koheleth 12:4 in the Light of Ugaritic," *Syria* 33:99–101 (1956); *Koheleth*, Tel Aviv–Jerusalem, 1961 (Hebrew, in press).

Commentaries on Koheleth are referred to in this paper simply by the names of their authors: e.g. "Podechard."

Pending publication of *Koheleth* (the last-named), the most complete statement of my position is embodied in "The Structure and Contents," which is supplemented by "Supplementary Studies," except where the former corrects the latter.

The present paper will not be rendered superfluous by the publication of *Koheleth*, since it embodies supplements, modifications, and corrections which could not be included in that book.

that the only real value a man can get out of life is the utilization of his worldly goods for his enjoyment.

It will be seen that the substance of A and A′ is included in B and B′, but not vice versa.[2] Consequently, a quick way of covering all the essentials of Koheleth's teaching is by giving a translation and a detailed exegesis of the short main division B, with several references to parallels in the other sections.

Koheleth B: 3:1—4:3

Our Doings Are Preordained; Their Appointed Hours Are God's Secret

1. *All is foreordained yet not foreseeable, 3 : 1–13.*

Summary. [1–8] Every one of our doings has its predestined hour. [9–13] God gave man the craving to discover the schedule of future events but not the ability to do so. What is possible for man is, if he is one of the lucky ones, to eat, drink, and enjoy himself for the money he earns.

Translation

(1) There is a time for everything, an hour for every doing under heaven:

(2) an hour for being born and an hour for dying,
an hour for planting and an hour for uprooting a thing planted;

2. The nearest thing to an exception is 1:4–11, where the author proves his assertion (1:2) that literally everything is futile by showing that all of creation is a Sisyphus, condemned to repeat the same phenomena over and over, never to be done with any one of them and never to perform a new one. Since *dabar* is employed only of phenomena in this "cosmic" sense (1:8, 10), whereas *ḥepeṣ* applies only to human "doings" (3:1, 17; 5:7; 8:6—in 8:6 omit *umišpaṭ* as an intrusion from 8:5), I previously ("The Structure and Contents," p. 140, and still in *Koheleth*) erred in rendering *dabar* and *ḥepeṣ* indiscriminately by "phenomenon." I am, however, as right as ever in ruling out "purpose" as a rendering of *ḥepeṣ* anywhere in Koheleth, since Koheleth certainly does not speak of purposed dying (3:1–2, 17; 8:4–8), purposed weeping (3:4), or purposed hating (3:8; 9:1; in this last verse Koheleth explicitly denies that one can plan to love or hate).

I take this opportunity to correct the interpretation of 1:11 which I was unable to alter in *Koheleth*. It actually means: the earlier ([phenomena] verses 8, 10) are forgotten; and so will the later ones be, *as surely as* those that will *happen* at the end. (The phenomena that will happen at the end will obviously not be remembered, since there will be no more potential rememberers.) I previously failed to realize that in this verse: (1) *ᶜim* means "(just) like," exactly as in 2:16 (twice); 7:11; Ps. 72:5 (where *lipne* also means "like, as," cf. I Sam. 1:16; Job 3:24); cf. the verb *ᶜamam* "to be like," Ezek. 31:8. "Like" is also the best word for rendering *ᶜm* (twice) in the Ugaritic passage 2 Aqht VI:28–29 (Gordon's system of reference). (2) The verb *haya* is to be added to the many other instances of its use in the sense of "to happen" that I have pointed out in all of my previous publications on Koheleth, and its subject must therefore be not "people" but "phenomena."

(3) an hour for ⌜wrecking⌝ and an hour for repairing,
an hour for breaching and an hour for rebuilding;
(4) an hour for weeping and an hour for laughing,
an hour of keening and an hour of dancing;
(5) an hour for throwing stones away and an hour for gathering stones,
an hour for embracing and an hour for shunning embraces;
(6) an hour for seeking and an hour for losing,
an hour for keeping and an hour for discarding;
(7) an hour for tearing and an hour for sewing;
an hour for keeping silent and an hour for speaking;
(8) an hour for loving and an hour for hating,
an hour of war and an hour of peace.

(9) What profit is there for him who gains in that which he acquires? (10) I observed the task that God made the sons of men engage in: (11) while bringing everything to pass precisely at its hour, He planted in their hearts the ⌜striving⌝ to anticipate the things that God brought to pass from beginning to end, but without man's ever succeeding. (12) Thus I know that there is no good attainable by ⌜him⌝ except enjoying himself and doing that which is worthwhile in his lifetime; (13) also, that whenever a man does eat and drink and get his fill of pleasure for all his earnings, that is a gift of God.

Commentary

(1) The rendering "doing" was justified above in Note 2.

(2) That the meaning intended by the author was, in spite of the active form *laledet*, not "for giving birth" but "for being born" is clear from the antithesis to *lamut* "for dying."

(3) I now adopt the emendation *laharos* for *laharog*. As is argued by A. B. Ehrlich, *Randglossen zur hebräischen Bibel, ad loc.*, "to wreck" is an exact antithesis of "to repair" (compare I Kings 18:30), but "to slay" is not an exact antithesis of "to heal." Besides, in most verses in this series, the first antithesis is rather closely parallel to the second (on verse 5, see below).

(4b) In Hebrew, "keening" is *sepod* and "dancing" *reqod*. In Aramaic, however, the root *rqd* can express both notions: the former in the *aphel* conjugation, the latter in the *pael*. Thus the Peshitta (Syriac) rendering of our half-verse is *wzab̲nā lmarqād̲ū wzab̲nā lamraqqād̲ū*. See further C. C. Torrey, *ZAW* 65:245–246 (1953), on Matthew 11:17, and

J. Fürst, *REJ* 19:148 (1889), 39:138 (1899), on *Ekah Rabbati*, Petiḥata, Rabbi Ḥinnana I. If, therefore, the theory that Koheleth is translated from Aramaic is correct (those of the unconvinced who are objective are requested to suspend judgment pending publication of my final statement of the case in chapter iv of the Introduction to my *Koheleth*), the Aramaic original of our half-verse probably read something like this: *ᶜiddān lharqāḏā wᶜiddān lraqqāḏā.*

(5) The Rabbinic interpretation of "throwing stones" (sexual intercourse) and "gathering stones" (continence)—*Koheleth Rabbah, ad loc.*—is probably correct, since in most of these verses the first pair of opposites is closely related in meaning to the second.

(9) Gains . . . acquires. See for the present my "The Structure and Contents," page 140, top. Abundant parallels from other writings and even other languages will appear on pages 13–15 of my *Koheleth.*

(11) Bringing . . . to pass. In this book, *maᶜaśe* means most often "happening(s)," *naᶜaśa* nearly always "to happen," and *ᶜaśa* with "God" for subject nearly always (the only exception I can think of is in 7:29) "to bring to pass."

That *hᶜlm* is corrupt for *hᶜml* (*heᶜamal*, "the striving") was seen by Macdonald, *JBL* 18:212 (1899), and Kamenetzky, *ZAW* 24:238 (1904). A correct understanding of our verse and its context on the one hand and of 8:17—9:1 (look at these closely!) and their context (which extends down to 9:10) on the other leaves no room for doubt as to the correctness of the Macdonald-Kamenetzky emendation.

For "to anticipate," compare *maṣa*, "to guess," Judges 14:18. Apparently it is still necessary to insist that Koheleth never indulges in pious or philosophical reflections on man's lack of capacity for learning to know all the *things* that God *has created*, but only regrets man's inability—whose *practical importance* he deals with at length in B′—to figure out the *happenings* that God *is going to bring to pass*. Doubters may consult for the present my two analyses of B′ in "Supplementary Studies," pages 45–57, and "The Structure and Contents," pages 142–145; or, if they are lazy as well as skeptical, let them at least look up the immediately comprehensible verses 8:17; 11:2b, 6, and then read 6:11b, 10:14b, with the help of this hint: *ʾašer yihye* (*me*)*ʾaḥaraw* means "what the future has in store for him." (Compare also 3:22b.)

(12) For *bam* read *bo*, since the reference is to the singular *ʾadam* in 11b*b*; compare *beḥayyaw* (not *beḥayyehem*) at the end of verse 12. "Doing that which is worthwhile in his lifetime" means: doing that which we

proved in main division A to be worth while to do in his lifetime; see 2:3, 24.

(13) Get his fill of. *Raʾa* is frequently equivalent to *rawa* in Koheleth. Earnings: see above on verse 9.

2. *All is foreordained—including goodness and badness and the death of both the good and the bad, 3 : 14–22.*

Summary. [14–16] The various phenomena keep recurring to the end of time (compare 1:9); goodness and badness are no exceptions. [17] And the same end, death, awaits the good man and the bad alike. [18] And there is no difference at all between the death of a man and the death of a beast. [22] So one should enjoy what one acquires, since one never knows what the future holds.

Translation

(14) I know that all the things that God ⸢has brought⸣ to pass will recur evermore—they can neither be added to nor diminished from—and God has brought to pass reverence for Him. (15) Again ⸢what is occurring⸣ ⸢occurred⸣ long ago, and what is going to occur ⸢occurred⸣ long ago; so God ⸢tolerates⸣ ⸢the oppressor⸣. (16) And in effect, I observed under the sun justice side by side with wickedness, righteousness side by side with wickedness.

(17) I reflected: God will doom the righteous and the wicked man alike, for He ⸢has set⸣ an hour for *every* doing and for *every* happening. (18) Then I resolved in my mind concerning the sons of men to dissociate them ⸢from⸣ the divine and to realize that they are but beasts. (19) For when it comes to the fate of the sons of men and the fate of the beasts, their fates are alike. As the one dies so does the other, and both have the like breath; and superiority of man over beast there is none, for both are insignificant. (20) Both go to the same place: both arose from dust, and both return to dust. (21) Who knows if the breath of sons of men does go up on high and the breath of beasts does go down into the depths of the earth? (22) So I saw that there is no greater good than a man's enjoying his possessions, since that is his portion. For who can enable him to see what the future holds for him?

Commentary

(14) I have now come to the conclusion that the sense must be "*has brought* to pass," and I surmise that our אשר יעשה resulted from a translator

taking an intended די עֲבַד (= אשר עָשָׂה) as דִּיֶעְבֵד. And in any case, ᶜ*aśa* has both in the first and in the last clause the sense of "to bring to pass"; see above on verse 11. Consequently Ezekiel 36:27b, "and I will bring it about that you follow my laws and faithfully practice my norms," is to be compared for the sense of our last clause.

Thus Koheleth explicitly negates the exception in the famous dictum of Rabbi Ḥanina (*Berakot* 33b; *Megillah* 25a), "Everything is determined by God except reverence for God" (הכל בידי שמים חוץ מיראת שמים). On the other hand, there is much agreement between Koheleth's view (see also verse 15b) and that of the Qumran sectarians. The latter, to be sure, diverge from Koheleth in positing an eschatological annihilation of evil, but as regards the Present Age, here is what they have to say: "Everything that happens and that is to happen proceeds from the God of Knowledge . . . Now, He created man to rule over Tebel and appointed for him two spirits to follow until the time appointed by Him, to wit, the spirits of truth and falsehood. . ." (1*QS*, 9:15ff.) "In these, all the stories of the sons of men run their courses, and in their divisions all their multitudes have their portions throughout the generations, and in their paths they walk. All their actions and conduct fall in those divisions, according to each man's portion (great or small), through all the ages of time. For God has set them [i.e., the two spirits] side by side until the last age." (4:15ff.)

(15a) Failure to apply consistently the observation that the word כבר is always emphatic and always means "long since," never merely "already," is none the less a sin for being very prevalent and for my having myself been guilty of it by implication in my *Koheleth ad* 3:2 (though the fact may escape the reader of my Hebrew comment on the passage concerned, and though I shall of course make atonement in my treatment of that verse below). Consequently, our Hebrew text of 15*aa* can only mean: "What has occurred is long ago"—if that can be called a meaning. What we have here is one of several instances in this Book where the ambiguity of the graph הוא in Aramaic—where it can be read הָוֵא (equivalent to Hebrew הֹוֶה) and הֲוָא (equivalent to Hebrew הָיָה), as well as הוא (identical in meaning with Hebrew הוא)—has led the translator to produce a Hebrew which might have been tailor-made for glibsters. Others have no choice but to retrovert it into Aramaic and to interpret the latter. The Aramaic of 15a which our translator had before him read as follows:

מה די הוא כבר הוא ודי למהוא כבר הוא

Unlike him, we read the first הוא *hawe* (=Heb. *howe*), the second *hawa*

(=Heb. *haya*), and only the third in the same way as was done by our predecessor (the translator of Koheleth's Aramaic book into Hebrew), namely as *hawa* (=Heb. *haya*). Hence our English rendering above. The student hardly needs to be reminded to compare 1:9–10, but it may not be superfluous to repeat in connection with 1:10 what was stressed at the beginning of this paragraph: *kebar* means "long ago."

(15b) Here again Kamenetzky (see above on verse 11) hit the nail on the head by emending *nrdp* to *hrdp* (*harodep*), "the persecutor, or oppressor." It makes of 15b exactly the right counterpart to the last clause in verse 14 (according to its only possible *peshaṭ*, of course—see above *ad loc.*—not according to any erroneous exegesis); it makes it express an opinion which Koheleth repeats in 4:1–3 (see below) and in 5:7 (above all human protectors of oppressors there is still a higher one), and it eliminates an abnormal *ʾet* before an indeterminate object (on 7:7, see for the present my "Supplementary Studies," page 50, with footnote 46). *Ybqš*, finally, seems to be transposed from *yšbq*, "lets alone." On the witness of the "original Hebrew" of Ben Sira 5:3 to the received text of our verse, all that needs to be said can be found in "Supplementary Studies," page 40, note 13.

(16) Koheleth's observation confirms the assertions of the last clauses in 14 and 15 (as interpreted above!). Perhaps those are right who emend in the last clause "the wicked man side by side with the righteous."

(17a) That is, God decrees death for both alike. Compare 8:5b–6a, where, omitting the second *umišpaṭ* as repeated mechanically after the second *ʿet* under the influence of the *umišpaṭ* which rightly follows the first (*we*)*ʿet*, render: "but the wise man will bear in mind the hour of doom. For there is an hour for every doing." (The Hebrew "hour *and* doom" is a hendiadys. For an interpretation of all of 8:1–8, see for the present my "Supplementary Studies," pages 52–55.) Koheleth never employs either the verb *šapaṭ* or the noun *mišpaṭ* with reference to a divine judgment. On 11:9b see for the present my "The Structure and Contents," page 145, with note 1: in the long run, the conclusion that it is an interpolation—the only one in the body of the book—by the same hand that wrote 12:13 is bound to impose itself.

(17b) Those who retain the Masoretic "there" make it a euphemism either for the traditional Sheol or for the world to which the soul travels to be judged after death, a belief in which is not attested in Jewry in any pre-Amoraic source. (Even the Tannaim know only of an eschatological judgment after resurrection.) But in neither of these is there "an hour for every doing." In the traditional Sheol there are no sorts of doings at all-

(9:6, 10b)—even dying takes place "under heaven" (3:1–2) and precedes the descent to Sheol—and in the other there is at least no "hour for being born" (3:2), and hardly an hour for "seeking" or "losing" (3:6) or for "war" and "peace" (8). The old solution (C. F. Houbigant, *Biblia hebraica cum notis criticis et versione latina ad notas criticas facta*, 1743–54, cited by Podechard) of simply shifting the diacritical point of the *shin* to the left (שָׂם) and obtaining the sense given in the above translation, is still the best. "*God will do* such and such *because there is* an hour for it" is not natural; "*God will do* such and such *because He has set* an hour for it" is. The inverted word order serves the same purpose as in verse 17a (and in countless other passages in both Biblical and Roman Age Hebrew): namely that of emphasis, which in this case is so strong as to require italics in the English translation ("for *every* doing," including dying).

(18) The very slight emendation of *lbrm hʾlhym* to *lbrm mhʾlhym* (haplography) yields a credible Hebrew (see Ezekiel 20:38) and excellent sense. I do not know of any other legitimate procedure that does. At the end of the verse, *hmh* seems to me to be a dittography of the last three letters of the preceding word and *lhm* to have intruded from the next verse. The sense, then, of verses 18ff. is merely a more pessimistic interpretation of the same situation that inspired Psalm 8:6ff. The optimist says that since man is lord over the beasts he is but little inferior to the angels; the pessimist says that since man is not immortal like the angels (compare Genesis 3:22), he is to be classified not with them but with the beasts.

(19) In the first two occurrences of *miqre*, the *segol* is abnormal for *ṣere*. *Hakkol* in this verse (twice) and the next (three times) means "both." So also in 2:16 and 6:6, and similarly *kullam* in 2:14. The masculine adjective *ʾeḥad* after *ruaḥ* is probably due to contamination by the word *ʾeḥad* after the second *umiqre*, for elsewhere in Koheleth *ruaḥ* in the sense of "breath (of life)" is feminine (3:21; 12:7).

(20) Our verse is probably directly dependent on Genesis 3:19, but compare Psalm 104:29 (with reference to land animals and sea creatures as well as men; see Psalm 104:19–30).

(21) The part of a man that went down to Sheol was conceived of as a sort of shadow of his body (I Samuel 28:11–14). There does not seem to have been any speculation in early times about what happened to the breath of life, of either men or beasts, when God withdrew it (Psalm 104:29). By Koheleth's time, however, some echoes of the end of the Tenth Book of Plato's *Republic* must have percolated down to wider circles

in the Hellenistic world, and Koheleth seems to be making fun of it. At any rate, the notion Koheleth here rejects, of men's life-breath going up and animals' life-breath going down, is curiously reminiscent of the scene that Plato makes Socrates describe in the name of a certain Pamphylian by the name of Er, whose soul was sent back into his still unburied and mysteriously fresh body after spending twelve days in the Beyond. He found that not, to be sure, both men's and animals' spirits, but only all men's souls traveled to an eerie place from which they were sent, according to their deserts, either down into the earth or up into heaven for a thousand years. (The returnees reported that some bad cases remained below forever.)

Of course the normal vocalization would be הַעלה...הֲירדת. Zimmermann may be right in seeing in *lemaṭṭa laʾareṣ* a dual rendering of the Aramaic *laʾaraᶜ*, which can mean both "down" and "to earth."

(22) For "possessions," see above on verse 9.

"For that is his portion." It is the only thing he can expect. The "Host" has not prepared anything else for any of his "guests." The final phrase means literally "what will happen after him"; compare above on verse 11.

3. *Oppression will also endure forever*, *4 : 1–3*.

Summary. [1] That "God ⌜tolerates⌝ the ⌜oppressor⌝" is borne out by the fact that there is no relief for the oppressed and no hinderance for the oppressor. [2–3] Which makes the lot of the long-dead seem more enviable than that of the still-living and that of the yet-unborn more enviable than that of either. (In the light of other considerations, the picture looks somewhat different, 11:7.)

Translation

(1) I further observed all the oppression that goes on under the sun. There are the tears of the oppressed, with none to comfort them, and the power ⌜in⌝ the hand of their oppressors, with none to ⌜check⌝ them. (2) Therefore I accounted those who died long since more fortunate than those who are still living; (3) and more so than either, him who has not yet come into being, because he has not seen the evil happenings that occur in the world.

Commentary

(1) The first *ᶜašuqim* is an abstract *plurale tantum*, the second the plural of the passive participle of *ᶜašaq*.—In the Hebrew, each half of the second sentence ends with the phrase "with none to comfort them," which is appropriate only at the end of the first half. At a minimum, the second

מנחם is to be emended to ממחה. The well known post-Biblical phrase מיחה ביד פ׳ ("to hinder or stop somebody") is attested even Biblically in Aramaic; see Daniel 4:32. One is tempted to go even further and to read ואין לה מוחה ("with none to wipe them away") (referring to דמעת ["the tears"], compare Isaiah 25:8) at the end of the first half of the sentence and ואין לה ממחה ("with none to check it") (with reference to יד ["the hands"]) at the end of the second half. Probably, too, וביד is to be read for ומיד.

(2) ושבח אני is hardly correct. It probably ought to read ושבחתי אני, as in 8:15, in view of Koheleth's fixed usage (1:16; 2:1, 12, 17, 18, 20; 4:1, 4, 7, and so on; compare Canticles 5:5, 6). At any rate, the Karetepe phrases that are cited as analogies to the Masoretic text are more likely to be explained according to J. Friedrich, *Phönizische Grammatik* (Rome, 1951), since *yrdm ʾnk*, for example, (1) lacks the copula, which no consecutive infinitive absolute can do in Hebrew, and (2) has a pronominal suffix, which no infinitive absolute of any kind can have in Hebrew.—When the subject of a Hebrew sentence is simply the participle of the finite verb which is its predicate, that subject is best rendered by a pronoun in English; thus in Deut. 22:8 *hannopel* means simply "somebody."

(3) I incline to take *ṭob* in the sense of Syriac *ṭāḇ*, Babylonian Aramaic *ṭūḇā* ("much"). That the rendering "but happier than either is the one that has not yet," is grammatically possible, is, however, demonstrated by Ehrlich with examples from the Mishnah.

It is not a cheerful view of the world that greets us from the foregoing verses, nor indeed from the Book of Koheleth as a whole. It is because everything else is so disappointing that the author keeps stressing that the only positive value is eating and drinking and enjoying one's worldly goods. And he repeatedly adds that even those pleasures are not given to everybody. That not everybody has a reasonable amount of wealth is obvious, but not even everybody who does have has also the good sense to apply it to his enjoyment. Yet it is so necessary, in a world where every life is full of griefs and disappointments (2:22–23, followed by 24–26; 5:16, followed by 5:17—6:9). (A sage like Koheleth has the added heartache of a better understanding of reality, 1:18!) This "sating oneself with bounty by means of one's wealth" is, then, a compensation which God grants to His lucky favorites for those griefs of life; in fact it is a distraction from them. Here is a translation of 5:14–19:

(15a) This too[3] is a grievous ill: he must go just as he came. (14) As he came out of his mother's womb naked, so must he later[4] depart—just as he came; nothing of his wealth can he take along[4] with him. (15b) Then what profit is there in his earning for naught? (16) Besides, all his days (are spent) "in darkness and mourning, abounding vexation, and sickness[5] and anger."[6]

(17) This, I have found, is a real good:[7] to eat and to drink and to get one's fill of[8] pleasure for all the wealth that one acquires under the sun for the whole number of the days that God has given him to live, for that is his portion.[9] (18) Also, that whenever God has both given a man riches and possessions and enabled him to partake of them—to take his portion and to enjoy himself for his money—that is a gift of God. (19) For little will he brood about[10] the days of his life,[11] since God will keep him occupied[12] with his enjoyment.

And necessary as material enjoyment is as a palliative for the many ills of life, Koheleth insists that it be done with restraint. It is remarkable how often he disparages revelry (2:2; 7:2, 3, 4; 10:19).

A man who speaks with so much feeling about life's griefs (2:23; 5:16, 19) must have had his share of them. One cannot help suspecting that they included family troubles, in view of 2:12b (read ʾ*aḥarai* with Podechard, and read the next word *hammolek* ["who will possess"]), 18–21; 7:26. Is that, perhaps, the reason why, as against a number of passages in which "to eat and drink and to get one's fill of enjoyment for all one's money" is stated to be the "portion" one may obtain (if one is lucky), there is only one which includes "happiness with a woman you love" in

3. In addition to the evil that wealth may be lost in one's own lifetime (verses 12–13), there is the evil that in any case one must leave it behind when one dies.

4. Both *yašub* and *šeyyolek* are equivalent to English adverbs.

5. Or perhaps rather "care"? Cf. the meaning of the verb in I Samuel 22:8; Amos 6:6.

6. Reading בְּחֹשֶׁךְ וָאֵבֶל with LXX and וְכַעַס . . . וָחֳלִי with several versions.

7. Literally, "a good which is right" (cf. *yape* in 3:11, for which see above). Others emend to *yipne*, and interpret "it is good that one should turn to eating and drinking," etc.

8. See above on 3:13.

9. See above on 3:22.

10. Literally, "be mindful of."

11. Which are depressing to think about, verse 16.

12. Vocalize with LXX and Peshitta מַעֲנֵהוּ. This is the *hiphil*, or causative, of ʿ*ana*, "to engage [intrans.], busy oneself," above 3:10.

that portion? Moreover, while it is not to be doubted that he believed in that value, one wonders whether his enthusiasm for it would have sufficed to make him formulate a commendation of it in his own words if he had not found ready-made one that he could cite or paraphrase.

The relevant passage in Koheleth reads as follows (9:7–9):

> Go, eat your food in gladness
> and drink your wine in good cheer,
> for your actions were long ago willed by God.[13]
> At all times let your clothes be fresh,[14]
> and let not oil be wanting on your head.
> Enjoy happiness with a woman you love
> all the fleeting days of life
> that God has allotted to you under the sun . . .
> For that is your portion in life
> and in the money you earn under the sun.

The resemblance of these lines to Epic of Gilgamesh, Tablet X, Old Babylonian Version, column 3, was pointed out long ago. The latter goes like this:[15]

> Gilgamesh, whither rovest thou?
> The life[16] thou pursuest thou shalt not find.
> When the gods created mankind,
> Death for mankind they set aside,
> Life in their own hand retaining.[17]
> Thou, Gilgamesh, let full be thy belly,
> Make thou merry by day and by night.
> Of each day make thou feast of rejoicing,
> Day and night dance thou and play!
> Let thy garments be sparkling fresh,
> Thy head be washed; bathe thou in water.
> Pay heed to the little one that holds on to thy hand,
> Let thy spouse delight in thy bosom!
> For that is the task of [mankind]!

13. Nobody "eats, drinks, and enjoys himself" except by God's will, 2:24–26; 3:13; 5:18.

14. *Laban* here means "washed, laundered," as does *melubban* in the Mishnah (*Bekorot* 4:7; *Ḥullin* 11:2 [Tosefta *Ḥullin* 10:5]). The active verb *libben* is also employed in the sense of "to wash [clothes]" in Roman Age Hebrew. Our interpretation of the word is presupposed by the midrashic homily on our verse which Rashi cites from *Shabbat* 153a and *Koheleth Rabbah, ad loc.*

15. *Ancient Near Eastern Texts relating to the Old Testament* (Princeton, 1950), p. 90.

16. I.e., immortality.

17. In the Biblical text too, the advice is preceded by the observation that death is the lot of all (Koheleth 9:3–6).

I owe to the author of the above translation (Professor E. A. Speiser) the oral observation that the proof that the Biblical passage must be literarily (even if not directly) dependent on the Babylonian one is the identical order in which the ideas are presented. One might add that the imperative "go" is hardly motivated by anything in the Book of Koheleth, but is entirely natural in the situation of the Babylonian parallel. (Gilgamesh, on his way to the distant region where Ut(a)napishtim, the immortalized hero of the Flood, abides, for the purpose of obtaining from him the secret of immortality, stops at the house of the alewife Siduri, tells her his tale, and asks her for directions. She advises him to give up his vain quest and go home to the good things that are attainable by man.) Also, though lifelong festivity is perhaps not quite the same thing as the carousing that Koheleth, as we have noted, views with distaste, I do not wish to repress the thought that, like life "with a woman you love," it was a thing about which Koheleth was perhaps not sufficiently enthusiastic to have gone to the trouble of commending it if not for the stimulus of an Aramaic version of "The Advice of the Alewife Siduri."

Elihu the Intruder

A Study of the Authenticity of Job (Chapters 32-33)

By ROBERT GORDIS

Great works are rarely simple, and this truth is exemplified by the Book of Job, which J. A. Froude described as "towering up alone, far above all the poetry of the world."[1] Virtually every conceivable view has been expressed with regard to the authenticity of each section in this architectonic masterpiece and the integrity of the work as a whole.[2]

The prose tale (chapters 1–2, 42) raises an entire complex of problems: (a) its relationship to the poetry, (b) the earlier history of the Job tradition, several stages of which can now be constructed, and (c) the inner unity of the prose narrative itself. The Dialogue of Job and his Friends which follows contains three cycles of speeches. While all scholars recognize that all three cycles are original,[3] virtually all are agreed that the third cycle (chapters 22–31) is incomplete and disarranged, but there is no unanimity with regard to a possible reconstruction of the material.[4] Chapter 28, the Hymn to Wisdom, which is embodied in this third cycle, is regarded

1. Cf. his *The Book of Job* (1854), p. 3.

2. The extent of the literature on the Book of Job and the problems it poses is enormous. Every study of the book necessarily seeks to deal with previous work in the field. An excellent conspectus, rich in bibliographical data, is available in R. H. Pfeiffer, *Introduction to the Old Testament* (New York, 1941), pp. 660–708. It may now be supplemented by H. H. Rowley, "The Book of Job and its Meaning," in *Bulletin of the John Ryland Library* 41:167–207 (1958).

The approach of the present writer, which he is presenting *in extenso* in a full-length study and commentary on Job on which he is now engaged, may be found in several *Vorstudien*: "All Men's Book—A New Introduction to Job," in *Menorah Journal* 37:329ff. (1949); "The Temptation of Job—Tradition vs. Experience in Religion," in *Judaism* 4:195–208 (1955), reprinted in R. M. MacIver, ed., *Great Moral Dilemmas* (New York, 1956), as well as in several studies on Wisdom literature, "The Social Background of Wisdom Literature," *HUCA* 18:77–118 (1944); "Quotations as a Literary Usage in Biblical, Oriental and Rabbinic Literature," in *HUCA* 22:157–219 (1949), especially pp. 209–210, and in a full-length work, *Koheleth—The Man and His World* (New York, 1st ed., 1951; 2nd ed., 1955), chapters i–iii.

3. See Pfeiffer, *Introduction*, p. 670.

4. See Pfeiffer, *Introduction*, p. 671, and Rowley, "The Book of Job," p. 188, n. 2, for a brief conspectus of a score of proposed reconstructions.

by most scholars, though not by all, as an independent poem, but its relationship to the Book of Job and its author is by no means certain.[5] The speeches of the Lord out of the whirlwind (38:1—40:1 and 40:6—41:26) have also been subjected to critical analysis. Some scholars have denied the authenticity of several sections in these superb major poems, notably the description of the ostrich (39:13–18), the behemoth (40:15–24) and leviathan (40:25—41:26).[6] Others have rejected the second of the God speeches *in toto*.[7] Even more fundamental is the pivotal issue as to the meaning and intent of the God speeches, how they relate to Job's position, and what solution, if any, they offer to the basic issue of the book, "why the righteous suffer and the wicked prosper."

II

Between the three cycles of speeches spoken by Job and his friends, Eliphaz, Bildad, and Zophar (chapters 3–31) and the words of the Lord out of the whirlwind (chapters 38–41), our Book of Job contains the speeches of Elihu Ben Barakhel (chapters 32–37), the authenticity of which Rowley describes as "the first of the critical problems" of the book.[8] The vast majority of critical scholars in our day have agreed in denying, on the grounds of style, structure, and substance,[9] that they belong to the original book.

A scientific question may, however, always be reopened. This will prove highly fruitful, since a re-examination of the arguments hitherto advanced, a consideration of phenomena not previously noted, and a rethinking of the relationship of these chapters to the theme and structure of the rest of the book lead to a new appreciation of the significance and

5. Cf. Rowley, "The Book of Job," p. 191, n. 2.

6. Ewald, Dillmann, Cheyne, Kuhl, Eissfeldt, Pfeiffer, and others, with variations. Cf. Pfeiffer, *Introduction*, p. 674.

7. Gray, in S. R. Driver and G. B. Gray, *A Critical and Exegetical Commentary on the Book of Job*, International Critical Commentary (New York, 1921), I, lxiii, and apparently Rowley, "The Book of Job," pp. 190f. Pfeiffer (p. 675), following earlier scholars, combines chapters 38–39 and 40:2, 8–14, into one speech for God and 40:3–5 and 42:2–5 into one reply for Job, and deletes the rest.

8. Rowley, "The Book of Job," p. 173.

9. J. G. Eichhorn, *Einleitung in das Alte Testament*, 3rd ed., III (Leipzig, 1803), 597f., and W. M. L. de Wette, *Introduction* (Boston, 1843), II, 558f.; P. Dhorme, *Le Livre de Job* (Paris, 1926), pp. lxxviiff.; J. Goettsberger, *Einleitung in das Alte Testament* (Freiburg-im-Breisgau, 1928), p. 227; E. J. Kissane, *The Book of Job* (Dublin, 1939), p. xl; E. König, *Das Buch Hiob*, 2nd ed. (Gütersloh, 1929), pp. 466ff.; N. H. Tur-Sinai, *The Book of Job* (Jerusalem, 1957), pp. xxxviiif.; S. R. Driver, *Introduction to the Literature of the Old Testament*, 9th ed. (New York, 1913), p. 429; Driver-Gray, *Commentary*, I, xlff.; M. Buttenwieser, *The Book of Job* (New York, 1922); Oesterley and Robinson, *Introduction to the Old Testament*.

form of the Book of Job as a whole. To place the Elihu chapters in context, a brief summary of the preceding chapters is called for.

In the three cycles of speeches, the friends, who have come to console Job in his suffering, present a defense of God's justice in terms of the accepted religious ideas of the times. These are the beliefs by which Job himself has hitherto lived, and which they have no reason for assuming he has since rejected. When the friends arrive, Job breaks out in a lament, cursing the day of his birth, but as yet he has uttered no complaint against his Maker.

In an effort to console him, Eliphaz, the oldest and most respected of the friends, begins a reply. With tact and consideration, he reminds Job of the universally accepted doctrine that justice prevails in God's world, and therefore no innocent man is ever destroyed, while, on the contrary, the sowers of iniquity reap the fruit of their doings. Eliphaz makes a few significant additions to the conventional doctrine of reward and punishment. Often the sinner's just penalty is visited upon his children, a view highly congenial to the ancient concept of the solidarity of the family. Moreover, suffering often acts as a discipline and is therefore a mark of God's love. Finally, all men are sinful; in fact, sin is not God's creation, but man's doing. It therefore behooves Job to be patient and wait for restoration. For all its urbanity, the address of Eliphaz contains nevertheless the implication that Job must be a sinner, since suffering is the result of sin.

The two younger friends, Bildad and Zophar, are both less incisive in their ideas and less sympathetic to Job. Bildad paints a picture of the destruction of the wicked and the ultimate restoration of the righteous, and he hymns the power of God. Job does not deny God's power; it is His justice he calls into question. Zophar, probably the youngest and least discreet of the friends, summons Job to repent of his secret sins.

Job has no theory to propose as a substitute, merely his consciousness that he is suffering without cause. He does not claim to be perfect, but insists he is not a willful sinner. The conventional ideas of his environment Job counters with the testimony of his own experience, which he will not deny, whatever the consequences. But his attacks upon the disloyalty of his friends, his pathetic description of his physical pain and mental anguish, his indignant rejection of the theology of the friends, serve all the more to convince them that he is a sinner. For do not arrogance and the assumption of innocence by man, with the implied right and capacity to pass judgment on God, constitute the height of impiety?

In the second cycle, changes are rung on the same ideas, but with greater vehemence. And a few additional ideas emerge. Eliphaz emphasizes that there is even more to the punishment of the wicked than his ultimate destruction, whether in his own person or in that of his offspring. During the very period of his ostensible prosperity he lives in trepidation, never knowing when the blow will fall. Job, on the other hand, insists that, though his unjustified suffering does arouse universal pity, righteous men will not be deflected from the good life because of his sad fate. Thus Job boldly cuts the nexus in utilitarian morality between virtue and prosperity, and makes righteousness its own justification. He calls upon the earth not to cover his blood or absorb his cry. In fact, he wants his words to be engraved permanently upon a monumental inscription to await his ultimate vindication, because he is convinced that God, his witness, is in the heavens and that his "Redeemer liveth, even though he be the last to arise upon earth."

The second cycle is concluded by Job again with a powerful refutation of the friends' arguments. As against the comfortable doctrine that the wicked are destroyed, Job paints a picture of the actual case—well-being and honor being enjoyed by the malefactors. Job then concludes by citing four of the friends' contentions and riddling them with logic.[10]

The third cycle has been gravely disarranged, and a good deal of the original material has been lost. To a large degree, though not without lacunae, the third cycle can be restored.[11] A few new notes are struck in the ever blunter argument. Now Eliphaz accuses Job of being an out-and-out sinner, who has taken refuge in God's distance from man and therefore expects to avoid retribution. Observe that the heretic in ancient Israel, like the Epicurean school in Greece, did not deny the existence of God but rather His interference in human affairs. Eliphaz relentlessly presses Job to repent, and even promises his restoration to Divine favor, so that as of yore he will be able to intercede for other sinners. Bildad somewhat academically re-emphasizes the imperfection of all men. Job insists again upon his innocence, picturing the absolute faith in God's government by which he had formerly lived. Zophar declares once more that the prosperity of the wicked is an illusion; it is but a process of garnering wealth for the enjoyment of the righteous.

This speech of Zophar's Job does not dignify by a reply. The friends and their arguments fade from his consciousness. He ends as he began,

10. Cf. my "Quotations as a Literary Usage," pp. 211–217, for a detailed analysis and interpretation of this chapter.

11. See Note 4 above.

with a soliloquy, his last great utterance. At the outset, Job recalls the high estate of dignity and honor he once occupied, and the universal esteem he once commanded. Then he moves on to his magnificent climax—his "Confession of Integrity" (chapter 31). This classic statement may be described as the code of the Jewish gentleman. It is significant that, with the exception of a brief reference to the worship of heavenly bodies, the code is exclusively moral and not ritualistic in character. Job's final words are a plea to God to answer him and thus at least compensate him for his agony. Job has paused for a reply, hoping that God will answer him.

III

The reply which is forthcoming comes from a totally unexpected quarter. A young man named Elihu, son of Barakhel, intervenes. In a long introduction, he tries to justify his interruption of the proceedings. His wrath has been kindled against Job for daring to assume a righteousness greater than that of God. He is equally indignant about the friends for their failure to answer Job adequately. Elihu is conscious of his youth and has therefore waited for the aged, who presumably possess the wisdom needed for a reply. But he has come to the conclusion that the mere passing of days is no guarantee of insight:

> I said, Days should speak,
> And multitude of years should teach wisdom.
> But there is a spirit in man:
> And the inspiration of the Almighty gives them understanding.
> Old men are not always wise:
> Neither do the aged understand judgment.
>
> (32:7–9)

This long, brash apology may strike the modern reader as prolix. It can be understood only against the background of Semitic and ancient society in general, where age and wisdom were synonymous.[12]

In the next four chapters (33–36 inclusive), Elihu proceeds to unburden himself. He addresses himself to Job's three major contentions, which he cites: (1) that he is innocent (33:8 and 9), (2) that God's persecution is therefore an act of wanton power and injustice (33:10–11), and (3) that God has ignored his suffering by refusing to answer him (33:12–13).

12. Cf., *inter alia*, Hebrew *zākēn*, Latin *senex, senator*, English *alderman*.

In accordance with Semitic usage, Elihu proceeds to answer these arguments in reverse order.[13] In chapter 33, Elihu denies that God has a lack of concern for his creatures. Job has failed to note that God actually speaks to man in many ways. One is through visions and dreams in the night, in which God reveals His will that man turn aside from evil and avoid the arrogance that all too often comes from the consciousness of virtue (33:11). When this mode of communication proves ineffective, another is available to God—He brings pain and suffering upon man. When man is brought to the very threshold of death, his virtues save him. Once restored to youthful vigor and health, he recognizes that he was indeed sinful and that the suffering he has undergone has chastened his spirit and by disciplining him, saved him from perdition (33:19–28).

This is the heart of Elihu's position. He then proceeds to refute Job's other contentions. The patriarch, he avers, is wrong in denying God's justice. Actually God plays no favorites, for He is the Creator of all and is beholden to no one. God destroys the mighty in their wickedness (chapter 34). Man has only to observe the glories of nature in order to see evidence of the creative power of God. God is so exalted over man that it is laughable to imagine that man's actions affect Him for good or ill. Only man suffers from man's inhumanity and sin (chapter 35).

Elihu then proceeds to recapitulate his views (chapter 36). Through suffering, men are warned against sin. If they take the message to heart, they are restored to well-being. If not, destruction, the inevitable consequence of sin, comes upon them. As Elihu speaks, the signs of a gathering storm are seen in the sky (36:27–33).[14] Elihu turns to describe the majesty of God as revealed in the tempest, and His power to use the rainstorm either as a rod of chastisement or an instrument of mercy (37:13). The squall passes and the sky is revealed in its golden glory. Though God's might cannot fully be grasped by man, it is certain that He will not afflict the just. The man who is righteous and wise will ultimately emerge out of the storms of adversity into the sunshine of God's favor (chapter 37).

13. Thus the Mishnah (*Aboth* 5:7) declares, "There are seven traits in a fool and seven in a wise man," and in listing then among them:

ואומר על ראשון ראשון ועל אחרון אחרון

it ignores this very principle, by describing the wise man first and the fool last. The reason is inherent in human psychology—when the second element of two is mentioned, association tends to an extension of the last-named theme. This is the basis for the rhetorical figure of chiasmus.

14. See Pfeiffer, *Introduction*, p. 666, and the commentaries.

IV

The authenticity and relevance of the Elihu speeches have long been subjects of contention in the study of the Book of Job. The Church Father, Gregory the Great (died 604), stigmatized the Elihu chapters as being of little value, a view which has been widely accepted today both with regard to the content and the literary quality of the speeches. It is fair to say that today most critical scholars regard them as a more or less clumsy effort at interpolation by a defender[15] or by several defenders[16] of the orthodox religion of the time. Only a relatively few scholars have defended the authenticity of the Elihu speeches,[17] though often on contradictory or unconvincing grounds.

Before embarking on a detailed investigation of the evidence, it is well to note the growing disfavor in which the atomization of ancient literary documents is viewed by contemporary scholarship. Increasingly, the study of ancient literatures, like that of the Homeric epics, has been focusing attention upon the unity and meaning of the whole work rather than upon the disparity of the parts. That the indiscriminate, and even accidental, lumping together of scattered literary fragments by an obtuse redactor, who often did not understand the material he was working with, will produce a masterpiece—that naive faith of nineteenth-century literary critics is no longer widely shared today.[18]

15. See Note 9 above.

16. Helen Nichols, *AJSL* 27:97ff. (1910–11); M. Jastrow, *The Book of Job* (Philadelphia, 1920), pp. 77ff.; U. A. Irwin in *Journal of Religion* 17:36ff. (1937), all assume several interpolators of the Elihu passages.

17. They include K. Budde, *Beiträge zur Kritik des Buches Hiob* (Göttingen, 1876), pp. 65ff., and *Das Buch Hiob*, pp. xxivff., and C. Cornill, *Introduction to the Canonical Books of the Old Testament*, trans. G. H. Box (New York, 1907), pp. 426ff., as well as other critics like Rosenmüller, Umbreit, Stickel, and Wildeboer. R. H. Pfeiffer, who originally maintained the authenticity of the Elihu chapters (*Le Problème du Livre de Job*, Geneva, 1915), later changed his mind on the question (*ZATW*, NF, 1926, p. 23f.); cf. his *Introduction*, pp. 673f. Rowley also cites W. S. Bruce, *The Wisdom Literature of the Old Testament* (1928), pp. 22f.; Kallen, pp. 31ff.; L. Dennefeld, *Introduction à l'Ancien Testament* (1935), p. 121, and *Revue Biblique*, 48: 163ff. (1939); P. Szczygiel, *Das Buch Job* (1931), pp. 24ff.; B. D. Eerdmans, *Studies in Job*, pp. 16f.; J. H. Kroeze, *Old Testament Studies*, II (1943), 156ff.; A. M. Dubarle, *Les Sages d'Israel* (1946), pp. 84ff.; J. E. Steinmueller, *A Companion to Scripture Studies*, 2nd ed., II (1944), 167; P. Humbert, *Vetus Testamentum Supplements*, III (*Rowley Festschrift*, 1955), p. 150, as retaining the Elihu chapters. By and large, however, these scholars content themselves largely with the mere assertion of the authenticity of chapters 32–37; a full re-examination of the problem is not undertaken.

18. Cf. the trenchant observations of H. D. F. Kitto, *The Greeks* (Harmondsworth, 1951), p. 63. "This attribution [of the *Iliad* and the *Odyssey* to Homer] was accepted quite wholeheartedly until modern times, when closer investigation showed all sorts of discrepancies of fact, style and language both between the two epics and between various

It is self-evident that this change of intellectual climate will not suffice to reverse the present widely held views on the inauthenticity of the Elihu chapters. The impressive arguments in favor of this view need to be analyzed and evaluated.

It is maintained that there are important differences in *vocabulary* between them and the rest of the poetic dialogue.[19] Thus a marked variation is noted in the use of Divine names. Elihu uses the name *El* far more frequently than the other names *Eloah* and *Shaddai*, while in the rest of the book, they are used with almost equal frequency.[20] Elihu shows a preference for *ʾanī* over *ʾanōkhī* as the first person singular pronoun, more markedly than in the earlier poetic dialogue.[21] Elihu uses less frequently the longer, archaic forms of the prepositions,[22] and avoids the archaic forms of the enclitic particles ending in *-mō*.[23]

It has been maintained that Elihu's vocabulary differs, since he uses terms like *dēᶜah* ("opinion"), *tāmīm* ("perfect") instead of *tām*, and *nōᶜar* ("youthfulness") instead of *neᶜurim*, et cetera.[24]

The style offers several divergent features. Particularly noticeable is

---

parts of each. The immediate result of this was the minute and confident division of the two poems, but especially of the *Iliad*, into separate layers of different periods, appropriately called 'strata' by critics who . . . imperfectly distinguished between artistic and geological composition. The study of the epic poetry of other races, and of the methods used by poets working in this traditional medium, has done a great deal to restore confidence in the substantial unity of each poem: that is to say, that what we have in each case is not a short poem by one original 'Homer' to which later poets have added more or less indiscriminately, but a poem conceived as a unity by a relatively later 'Homer' who worked over and incorporated much traditional material—though the present *Iliad* certainly contains some passages which were not parts of 'Homer's' design."

19. See Driver-Gray, *Commentary*, I, xli–xliv, for a painstaking statistical summary of the stylistic differences. W. E. Staples, *The Speeches of Elihu* (*University of Toronto Studies*, Philological Series, No. 8, 1925), pp. 19ff., and J. Herz, *Wissenschaftliche Zeitschrift der Karl-Marx-Universität*, III (Leipzig, 1953–54), 107ff., find the Elihu speeches to be distinct from the dialogue on stylistic grounds.

20. Elihu uses *El* nineteen times, *Eloah* six times, *Shaddai* six times. In the rest of the book, *El* appears thirty-six times, *Eloah* thirty-five times, and *Shaddai* twenty-five times.

21. In the dialogue, *ʾanī* occurs fifteen times, *ʾanōkhī* eleven times. In Elihu they occur respectively nine and twelve times. In the prose prologue, *ʾanī* occurs four times, *ʾanōkhī* not at all.

22. The prepositional forms with *yodh*, *ᶜalei* (for *ᶜal*, "on"), *ᶜadei* (for *ᶜad*, "toward"), *ʾelei* (for *ʾel*, "to") occur only twice in Elihu, nineteen times in the poetic dialogue, thirty-five times elsewhere in the Old Testament as a whole.

23. Elihu does not use the enclitics *bemō*, *kemō*, *lemō*, as well as such other poetic forms as *minnī*, *belī*, *ᶜalēmō*. They occur eighteen times in the poetic dialogue.

24. Driver-Gray, *Commentary*, p. xlv. But *tamim* occurs in 12:4, which is dismissed unjustifiably as an addition to the text.

the higher concentration of Aramaisms in Elihu.[25] There are a large number of verses that are highly obscure and which give the impression of a very labored style.

Not only the style but the structure of the book has been adduced in order to deny the authenticity of these chapters. There is no reference to Elihu in the prologue or the epilogue. While he refers to the friends and cites their statements, they do not return the courtesy. He appears without warning and disappears without a trace. Moreover, Job in his last speech (31:35ff.) has appealed for God's answer. With Elihu eliminated, such an answer would be forthcoming directly in God's speech in chapter 38. Finally, and most crucially, it has been argued that Elihu adds nothing significant to the argument and is therefore entirely superfluous.[26]

These contentions cannot be dismissed out of hand, but they are by no means conclusive. With regard to the arguments from vocabulary, it should be noted that the alleged variations are relative rather than absolute. It is principally the proportion that has shifted, not the usage, whether it be in the case of the Divine names, the pronouns, or the prepositional forms, all of which occur throughout the book. Moreover, any literary composition, particularly a short one, may turn up words lacking in another composition by the same author.

25. Thus the entire stich 36:2a: כַּתַּר־לִי זְעֵיר וַאֲחַוֶּךָּ can, with a slight revocalization of the last word, be read as Aramaic! On the other hand, *zeʿēr* occurs in Isaiah (28:10, 13), as does *mizʿār* (10:25; 16:14; 24:6; 29:17). The verb *ḥāwāh* occurs in Psalm 19:8 and Job 25:17, and the noun *ʾaḥwāh* in Job 13:17. The very *kathār* in the Aramaic–Syriac nuance of "wait, hope for," does not occur elsewhere in Biblical Hebrew, but the root is to be found in the *piel* and *hiphil* in the sense "surround," (*piel*, Judg. 20:43; Ps. 22:13; *hiphil*, Hab. 1:4) which F. Brown, S. R. Driver, C. A. Briggs, *A Hebrew and English Lexicon of the Old Testament* (Oxford, 1907), regard as basic to the meaning "wait." The use in Ps. 142:8 and Prov. 14:18 are also probably denominatives from *keter* ("crown").

It should be noted that the list of Aramaisms in Job cited by E. Kautzsch (*Die Aramäismen im alten Testament*, p. 101) was severely criticized by T. Noeldeke in his review *ZDMG* 57:412–420). Cf. Driver-Gray, *Commentary*, pp. xlvif.

A reconsideration of so-called Biblical Aramaisms is in order, not only because of new epigraphic material, but because of a basic methodological error, the failure to recognize the three categories of Biblical Aramaisms, which, incidentally, cannot always be distinguished: (a) words originally part of the Northwest Semitic vocabulary which were therefore indigenously Hebrew, but rare, while they became common in Aramaic and therefore *appear* as Aramaisms, as, e.g., *ʾātāh* ("come") (Deut. 33:2); (b) words probably borrowed from Aramaic during the period of the First Temple due to geographical proximity with Syria, as, e.g., *rāʿāh* ("chase") (Hos. 12:2); and (c) words borrowed during the hegemony of Aramaic as the *lingua franca* of the Near East, where it became the spoken tongue of the Jews, as, e.g. *sālaq* ("rise, go up") (Ps. 139:8).

26. Cf. Driver-Gray, *Commentary*, p. xli, "They are superfluous because they add nothing substantial to what the friends have said except in so far as they anticipate what Yahveh is to say."

That Elihu cites arguments from the preceding speeches, far from being an argument against his authenticity,[27] is a point in his favor. Elsewhere we have called attention to a basic element of Biblical and Semitic rhetoric, particularly common in Wisdom literature, which is especially characteristic of Job's style—the use of quotations. It is noteworthy that in each of Job's concluding addresses, at the end of the first cycle (chapter 12), at the end of the second cycle (chapter 21), and in his brief rejoinder after God's second speech (42:2–6), Job employs this same literary device. That Elihu does the same strengthens the view that his speeches emanate from the same author.[28]

Budde's original contention that Elihu's style is identical with that of the earlier dialogue is untenable, as he himself came to recognize later. *It is important not to exaggerate either the variations or the similarities, both of which are genuine.* The differences are not so extensive as to require the assumption of a different author, a view which is ruled out, as we shall see, by other considerations as well. It should be added that the Elihu speeches give evidence of having suffered a higher degree of textual corruption than other sections of the book. This phenomenon occurs in literary documents where part of the text has been exposed to poorer care than the rest.[29]

Moreover, judgments as to the quality of style are notoriously subjective. S. R. Driver characterizes the style of the Elihu speeches as "prolix, labored, and sometimes tautologous," and Buttenwieser calls the style "pompous and diffuse, with much empty repetition." On the other hand, Marshall pronounces the Elihu speeches to be "on an immeasurably higher plane than the Dialogue," while Cornill declares, "In the entire range of Holy Writ there are few passages which in profundity of thought and loftiness of feeling can compare with the Elihu-speeches: in content they form the summit and crown of the Book of Job."[30] These latter judg-

27. As maintained, e.g., by Rowley, "The Book of Job," p. 173.

28. Cf. my "Quotations as a Literary Usage," pp. 211–218. In Job 12:4—13:3, at the end of the first cycle, the patriarch parodies the position of the friends and dismisses it as irrelevant. In 21:19–34, at the end of the second cycle, he cites and refutes four arguments advanced by the friends. In Job 42:3a, 4, he quotes twice from the words of the Lord (38:2, 3b; 40:7b), with minor variations, as is generally the case.

29. Cf. Psalms 14 and 53 and note the minor variations throughout this dittograph, except for the last two verses (verses 6, 7), which had evidently become largely illegible in some manuscript and had been "restored" in two radically different forms in our Masoretic text. So too, Job, chapter 24, seems to have sustained more textual damage than the surrounding material.

30. The judgments cited in the text are to be found respectively in S. R. Driver, *Introduction*, 9th ed., p. 429, Buttenwieser, *The Book of Job*, p. 85, J. T. Marshall, *Job and His Comforters*, p. 6, and Cornill, *Introduction*, p. 428.

ments are much too flattering, but they serve to counterbalance the all too prevalent view which denigrates the Elihu speeches.

The arguments from structure are also far from decisive. Elihu's absence in the prologue is not at all strange. That the dignified elders have taken no notice of Elihu is entirely understandable in terms of Semitic custom, in view of his being confessedly an interloper and a stripling to boot. The author obviously wishes us to conceive of Elihu as one of the anonymous group of interested bystanders who might conceivably be permitted to listen to the deliberations of their elders, but were certainly not expected to participate in the argument, let alone contradict those wiser than themselves. Elihu's absence from the epilogue, as will be indicated below, is also explicable both in terms of content and the history of the composition of the book.

It is true that if the Elihu speeches are eliminated, the Lord appears immediately after Job's plea for His presence. However, beginning in the very first cycle, Job has repeatedly asked God to enter into fair and open debate with him, and thus offer him an opportunity for self-vindication (9:3, 14ff., 32–35; 13:2, 15–23; 16:18–22; 19:24–27), but to no avail. On the contrary, the debate of the human protagonists continues for two more cycles, with no intervention from God. There is therefore no reason to expect that Job's demand for God's reply in chapter 31 must be answered, and at once. Moreover, it should be noted that the closing portion of Elihu's speech (37:21–24) describes the advent of a storm and its aftermath and thus provides an excellent prelude to the Lord's appearance out of the whirlwind.

V

The heart of the argument against the authenticity of the Elihu speeches lies in the area of content, in the contention that Elihu contributes nothing new or significant to the discussion. But this argument, were it true, would be self-defeating, for it would raise the unanswerable question why an interpolator took the trouble to compose his speeches altogether.

Here again, Budde, in seeking to defend the authenticity of the Elihu section, overstates the case. He argues that Elihu gives the author's main answer to the problem of suffering—that suffering is God's disciplinary measure, designed to prevent men from sinning, an idea expressed by no one else.[31] The fact is, however, that suffering as a Divine chastisement and

31. Cf. his *Das Buch Hiob* (Göttingen, 1896), p. xxxv, "Ausdrücklich gelehrt wird es [sc. das Läuterungsleiden] von Elihu *und von ihm allein.*"

the mark of God's love has already been adumbrated by Eliphaz, though in only one verse (5:17).

What is even more important, if this idea were the principal conclusion of the author, it is incomprehensible that he would have followed it up by another section, the God speeches, which then necessarily take on the character of an anticlimax. As a matter of fact, everything points to the God speeches as being the climax of the author's insight into life and its meaning. Moreover, it is hardly likely that the supremely gifted poet and thinker who wrote Job could seriously regard the disciplinary role of human suffering per se as an adequate explanation of the mystery of pain. He was surely too sensitive to the complexity of life and the depth of human misery to regard this aspect as a sufficient answer. Budde's defense must be regarded as being unconvincing.

Pfeiffer, on the other hand, explains the inclusion of the Elihu interpolations on the view that they are the work of an orthodox reader who "was so shocked, after reading the Book of Job in its original form, that he felt the urge to write a refutation which he placed in the mouth of a character, Elihu, which he invented. It is significant that Elihu's polemic is addressed not only against Job, whose position was decidedly heretical, but also against the friends and even, in a more subtle manner, against the speeches of Jehovah."[32]

It is true that Elihu attacks both the friends and Job bluntly and aggressively. There is, however, no evidence whatever that he challenges the conclusion of the God speeches, either subtly or openly. Their standpoint is summarized by Pfeiffer, albeit too summarily, as maintaining that "God's ways are incomprehensible to man." Nowhere is this idea refuted by Elihu, who, on the contrary, emphasizes that God is too exalted to be affected by human actions (35:4–7) or be understood by man (30:24ff.; 37:14–20). It may also be pointed out that a refutation of the God speeches should have followed, not preceded, them.

Finally, Pfeiffer begins with the critical assumption, frequently made in the past, that heterodox ideas would be subjected to extensive interpolation in order to be made palatable to the orthodox. But this once-popular approach is highly questionable. Thus the present writer has demonstrated that this hypothesis is both unnecessary and erroneous with regard to the Book of Ecclesiastes.[33] In ancient times, a far more effective device was available for countering unorthodox doctrine—since

32. Pfeiffer, *Introduction*, p. 673.
33. See my *Koheleth*, *passim*, for a detailed study of the critical problems of the book.

manuscripts of any given work were few, it was easy to suppress the material by consigning copies of the book in question to the Geniza, and thus condemning it to oblivion.

Virtually all the apocryphal and pseudepigraphical works of the Second Temple period, which were originally written in Hebrew or Aramaic, emnated from groups which differed in greater or lesser degree from the standpoint of normative or Pharisaic Judaism. The leaders of the dominant group in Judaism subjected these books not to critical interpolation but to total neglect. As a result the originals were lost and only translations into Greek, Latin, Syriac, Ethiopic, and other languages survived, safeguarded by the Church, which found these works congenial to its outlook and useful in its work.

It is only as a last resort that one can regard it as methodologically sound to invoke the theory of large-scale interpolation as a technique employed by ancient readers for opposing the main thrust of a literary work. In our case, there is no proof whatever of any such intent in the Elihu speeches.

VI

We are now in position to draw the conclusion to which the evidence points. The style of the Elihu chapters is by no means totally different from the rest of the book, but it does exhibit variations, which are entirely explicable by the assumption that *the Elihu section emanates from the same author writing at a later period in his life.*

A very instructive parallel is fortunately at hand—Goethe's *Faust*. His *Urfaust* goes back to the poet's *Sturm und Drang* period, the third decade of his life; the first part of *Faust* did not appear until more than thirty years later, in 1808, and the second part was completed shortly before his death in 1832. In the sixty-year gestation period of the work, Goethe's conception of his theme and of the characters, as well as his poetic style and vocabulary, underwent a profound transformation. Every reader notices at once the change from the epigrammatic style of Part I to the involved, complicated mode of expression characteristic of Part II. The radical differences in subject matter are summarized by J. G. Robertson in these words: "The Second Part is far removed from the impressive realism of the Urfaust or even the classicism of the First Part. It is a phantasmagory; a drama the actors in which are not creatures of flesh and blood but shadows in an unreal world of allegory. The lover of Gretchen had, as far as poetic continuity is concerned, disappeared with the close of the first part. In the second part, it is virtually a new Faust who, accompanied by a new Mephistopheles, goes out into a world that is not ours. Yet behind the elusive allegories . . . there lies a philosophy of life, a ripe wisdom born of experience, such as no other modern European poet has given us."[34]

Equally worthy of a great poet's entire lifetime would be a masterpiece like the Book of Job, which, though less extensive in compass than *Faust*, is no less profound in theme, moving in spirit, and eloquent in form. In the case of Job, the new insights drawn from the poet's experience found expression in the Elihu chapters which the poet inserted before the great climax of "the Words of the Lord."

The problems of structure are also solved by this theory that the Elihu speeches were added years after the bulk of the book had been written. As the framework for the great debate, the poet utilized and retold the traditional folk-tale of the righteous patriarch, Job, adding only the jointures between the prose and the poetry, both in the prologue (2:11–13) and in the epilogue (42:7–10). Basically, however, the traditional folk-tale remained familiar in every detail to its readers, so that any deviation would at once be recognized and almost surely resented. The prose framework having been written in the poet's earlier period, when the dialogue was composed, he would feel no need in later years, at the time of his maturity or in old age, to recast the text by inserting a reference to Elihu. Moreover, Elihu is not the object of the Lord's condemnation, as are the friends, since his ideas are regarded by the poet as having a substantial measure of validity. Finally, and most important of all, Semitic writers were not concerned with a complete congruence of details when combining various traditions into one consecutive whole.[35]

As for the substance of the Elihu chapters, it is noteworthy that Elihu is at least as antagonistic to the friends as he is to Job. Actually he denies

34. *Encyclopaedia Britannica* (14th ed.), X, 473b.

35. The contradictions between the details in the prologue and the dialogue have long been noted. As one example, we may cite the death of Job's children in the tale and his lament, in the poetry (19:17), about their unfilial behavior. The variant traditions in the Balaam narrative explain why, after he is granted permission to go with the elders of Midian (Num. 22:20), his life is threatened by the angel, and only after the encounter is he permitted to continue (Num. 22:31–35). The same literary practice of retaining variant sources and juxtaposing them unchanged is evident in the Book of Samuel. Thus, according to one account, David became a familiar in Saul's court because of his skill with the harp (I Sam. 16:14–23). According to another source, David is completely unknown to Saul and his court until after the Goliath exploit (I Sam. 17:55–58).

the truth of both positions—but only in part. The friends have maintained that God is just and that therefore suffering is both the penalty and the proof of sin. Job has denied both contentions. He insists that his suffering is not the result of sin and, therefore, he charges God with injustice. Elihu denies the second conclusion of both Job and his friends by declaring that suffering may not be the penalty of sin and yet God's justice remains unassailable.

This position he achieves by injecting a virtually new idea, adumbrated in another form in Deutero-Isaiah, the anonymous prophet of the Exile, who evolved the doctrine of the Suffering Servant of the Lord.[36]

It affirmed for the first time the possibility of national suffering that was not the consequence of national sin. This insight of Deutero-Isaiah was not lost on the author of Job, who applies the doctrine of suffering as a discipline to the life of the individual. This is expressed by Eliphaz in one verse:

> Behold, happy is the man whom God corrects:
> Therefore despise not the chastening of the Almighty.
> (Job 5:17)

But the entire tenor of Eliphaz's address makes it clear that he is referring to suffering as a discipline for sins *already committed.*[37] His position was a familiar one in the conventional Wisdom literature, as for example:

> The corrections of the Lord, my son, do not despise,
> And do not scorn His chastisement.
> For he whom the Lord loves He chastises
> And speaks[38] with him, as a father with his son.
> (Proverbs 3:11, 12)

In any event, the theme is dismissed with this one verse in Eliphaz's discourse—proof positive that at the time the passage was being written, the author, still young, was not particularly impressed with the idea as a key to the problem of evil.

Elihu goes substantially further—he sees suffering as a discipline and warning of the righteous, not only against sins actual and patent, but against offenses potential and latent (33:16–30; 36:9–12). Above all, a frequent tell-tale sign of the imminence of wrong-doing is the sin of the pride of

36. This theme cannot be further discussed in this context.

37. The distinction was acutely noted by Budde, *Das Buch Hiob*, p. xxxvi.

38. On this meaning of *rāṣāh*, see R. Gordis, "Leshon Ha-Miqra᾿ Le-᾿Or Leshon Ḥakhamim" ("Biblical Hebrew in the Light of Rabbinic Hebrew"), in *Sefer Tur-Sinai* (Jerusalem, 5720 = 1960), pp. 163f., where it is applied to several passages in the Psalms (49:14; 50:18; 62:5). The traditional rendering of *rāṣāh* in this passage obviously does not affect the meaning of the first stich.

virtue, the *hubris* or arrogance of those conscious of their own rectitude. One may recall the comment of a modern Hasidic teacher, "Far better a sinner who knows he is a sinner than a saint who knows he is a saint." It was against this insidious threat to spiritual nobility, which Budde calls "the pet sin of the righteous," that Job in his prosperity had tried to guard, by offering up sacrifices of atonement for his children, who might have "cursed God in their hearts" (1:5).

Yet suffering as a discipline is certainly not the whole truth regarding the problem of evil. How could the idea be given its proper weight? Obviously the doctrine could not be placed in the speeches of the friends, with whom the author is manifestly out of sympathy.[39] Nor could it be expressed by Job, who denies that there is any justification for the suffering of the righteous. Finally, were this idea included in the subsequent God speeches, it would weaken the force of the principal answer which is their essential theme. By creating the character of Elihu, who opposes the attitude of the friends as well as that of Job, the author is able to express this secondary idea, giving it due place in his world-view.

Job has contended that God avoids contact with man. On the contrary, Elihu insists, God does communicate with man through dreams and visions, and when these fail, through illness and suffering.

This recognition of the uses of pain is the kind of mature insight that would come to a man through years of experience. For life teaches at every hand how insufferable are those who have never suffered and that frustration and sorrow are men's passport to fellowship and sympathy with their brothers.

A full treatment of the principal insight of the author of Job with regard to the mystery of suffering cannot be attempted here.[40] A brief summary is, however, needed, especially since, in accordance with a far-flung Semitic usage which has not been adequately recognized, it is implied rather than explicated.[41] The God speeches, by their vivid and joyous description of nature, testify that the world is more than a mystery; it is a cosmos, a

39. The full evidence for this conclusion will be presented in our forthcoming book. We may note the greater length and eloquence of Job's speeches and his final vindication by God, who condemns the friends (42:7–8). The passage (42:7–10) which links the dialogue and the prose epilogue, like its earlier counterpart (2:11–13) emanates from the Poet, who needed a jointure to link the prose tale, which served as his framework, and the poetic dialogue which he composed.

40. See "The Temptation of Job," section VII, cited in Note 2 above; and the author's *A Faith for Moderns* (New York, 1960), chapter x, esp. pp. 168ff.

41. A study of "allusiveness" as a basic rhetorical usage in Hebrew and Semitic literature is in progress.

thing of beauty. Just as there is order and harmony in the natural world, so there is order and meaning in the moral sphere. Man cannot fathom the meaning of the natural order, yet he is aware of its beauty and harmony. Similarly, though he cannot expect to comprehend the moral order, he must believe that there is rationality and justice within it. As Kant pointed out, if it is arrogant to defend God, it is even more arrogant to assail Him. After all legitimate explanations of suffering are taken into account, a mystery still remains. Any view of the universe that claims to explain it fully is, on that very account, untrue. The analogy of the natural order gives the believer in God the grounds for facing the mystery with a courage born of faith in the essential rightness of things. What cannot be comprehended through reason must be embraced in love. For the author of Job, as for Judaism always, God is one and indivisible. As nature is instinct with morality, so the moral order is rooted in the natural world.

The author of Job is not merely a great artist and poet. He is too deep a thinker to believe that any neatly articulated system of man can comprehend the beauty and the tragedy of existence. Yet he is too great an intellect to abdicate the use of reason and reflection in pondering on the mystery of evil and comprehending as much of it as we can. He would endorse the unemotional words of the third-century sage, Jannai: "It is not in our power to understand the suffering of the righteous or the well-being of the wicked" (*Aboth* 4:15). There is a residuum of the Unknown in the world, but we have good grounds for holding fast to the faith that harmony and beauty pervade God's world. The mystery is also a miracle.

This is the major theme, and in the superb architecture of the book, it properly comes at the end. But the minor theme, that suffering frequently serves as a source of moral discipline and is thus a spur to ethical perfection, is far from unimportant, and it is placed in the mouth of Elihu.

VII

One more consideration, not hitherto noted, may be advanced in favor of the authenticity of the Elihu speeches. The protagonist of these chapters is given as "Elihu, the son of Barakhel, the Buzite of the family of Ram." The significance attached to names in the ancient world in general and among the Semites in particular is documented on every page of the Bible. Unlike those of the three friends, which have Edomite or South Semitic sources or analogues, most of Elihu's elaborate name is Hebrew in origin. Ram is known as one of the ancestors of David, of Judean or Jerahmeelite stock (Ruth 4:19; I Chronicles 2:9, 25). Buz is the "brother" of Uz, a nephew of Abraham (Genesis 22:21). Barakhel occurs in the business documents of the Murashu family as the name of several Jews in the reign of Artaxerxes I.[42]

But the meaning of the names is more important than their provenance. *Barakhel* means "bless God," or "God has blessed," *rām* means "exalted, high" and *būz* means "scorn, contempt." To one familiar with the deep-seated tendency of Biblical and Rabbinic thought to etymologize names, these names would be an excellent description of the young intruder, scornful of his elders, and conscious of his high role as a defender of God.

But it is the young man's own name which is of the greatest significance. *Elihu*, which is likewise of strictly Hebrew origin, represents a variant orthography of *Elijahu*, the name of the prophet Elijah. The differentiation in punctuation goes back only to the Masoretes, who added the vocalization.[43] The name, meaning "Yah is my God," is highly appropriate for its bearer.

Nor is it accidental that in choosing a name for a protagonist who is to precede God in the book, the author chose a name identical with that of the great prophet Elijah. In history, the prophet plays precisely the role of the "defender of God" (I Kings 17—21). In Malachi, the last of the Prophets, he is "the forerunner of the Day of the Lord" (4:5, 6). In the later literature, the Apocrypha, the Pseudepigrapha, the New Testament, the Talmud, and the Midrash, Elijah becomes the precursor of the "Messiah." In later folklore, he is the reconciler of unsolved contradictions.[44] We may also recall that Elijah is transferred heavenward in a storm, which is described (in II Kings 2:1) by the identical term (*s^{e}ʿarah*) that appears in Job (38:1).

In sum, Elihu's address supplements the major theme of the God speeches with a secondary but important idea. His name suggests to the Hebrew reader, who was thoroughly at home in his Bible and religious tradition, that he is fulfilling the function of his great namesake, the prophet Elijah, as "the forerunner of the Lord" who will appear out of

42. It occurs as *Ba-rik-ili*; see *Babylonian Expedition of the University of Pennsylvania*, series A, IX, 52.

43. Cf. אֱלִיהוּא (I Sam. 1:1; I Chron. 12:20), and אֱלִיהוּ (I Chron. 26:7; 27:18). N. H. Tur-Sinai calls it "an artificial differentiation" (*The Book of Job*, p. 456f.). His elaborate theory on the differences between Barakhel and Elihu is unconvincing.

44. On these roles of Elijah in post-Biblical literature, see L. Ginzberg, *The Legends of the Jews* (Philadelphia, 1909–38), IV, 193–235; VI, 316–342. The belief that Elijah could resolve all difficulties is embodied in the folk-etymology of the Talmudic term, *tēkū* ("let it stand"), popularly interpreted as *tishbi yetarreṣ kushyoth va-ʾabaʿyoth*, "Elijah the Tishbite will answer all difficulties and questions."

the whirlwind. The relative variations in style between the Elihu chapters and the rest of the book suggest the normal changes which an author undergoes with the passing of time, while Elihu's basic idea represents the fruit of years of observing the educative and disciplinary role of suffering. This is not the whole truth with regard to this mystery which lies at the heart of existence. But, as the author of Job has taught us with unequaled clarity and power, the whole truth is not with man, but with God.

The Rise of the Tiberian Bible Text[1]

To N. H. Tur-Sinai—master and friend—on his seventy-fifth birthday

By M. H. GOSHEN-GOTTSTEIN

I. Introduction

1. There can be little doubt that one of the major problems to be tackled afresh in connection with the new critical edition of the Bible, now in progress at the Hebrew University Bible Project, is our understanding of the growth of the Tiberian Bible text. While establishing the authentic character of the renowned Aleppo Codex was the first necessary step,[2] it seems that further study of all the evidence may enable us to get at some broader implications of the discovery of this codex. Much, of course, still remains to be done in furthering our understanding of details of the Masoretic vocalization and accentuation. But the preparation of the new edition also forces us to try to see the forest, not only the manifold trees.

1. The gist of the present paper (finished in July 1961) was read in different stages before various learned audiences during my stay in the United States. While it has been reworked for publication, the original oral manner of presentation is very much in evidence. This will also explain the sometimes unwieldy size of the footnotes. As it stands, the paper contains the backbone of the argumentation of a number of chapters in a forthcoming volume, tentatively termed *Nosaḥ ha-Miqrā ha-Tavrāni*, to be published by the Hebrew University Bible Project. While the present study stands in its own right, many additional issues have been hinted at in the notes to this paper; they will be discussed in detail in that volume.

This paper was written concurrently with my "Biblical Manuscripts in the United States," *Textus* 2:28f. (1962). A number of problems concerning Biblical manuscripts have been dealt with in that paper, and to that extent the two studies will complement each other. Some other points which have been developed here have already been mentioned as "theses" in the introduction to my *Text and Language in Bible and Qumran* (Jerusalem–Tel Aviv, 1960).

While I am fully aware that in my work I have somewhat strayed from the teaching of my masters, I still venture to dedicate this effort to the Nestor of Israeli Hebraists, Professor N. H. Tur-Sinai (Torczyner), whose productivity and brilliance remain an ever-present challenge to his erstwhile students.

2. See Goshen-Gottstein, "The Authenticity of the Aleppo Codex," *Text and Language*, pp. 1f., and also D. S. Löwinger, *Textus* 1:59f. (1960).

2. For the purpose of the present study I should like to use as a starting point the results arrived at earlier. I hope that in the study of the Aleppo Codex I have already shown:

(a) that the manuscript now under investigation at the Hebrew University Bible Project and scheduled to be printed as the basic text is, indeed, the famous Aleppo Codex;

(b) that the text of that manuscript turns out to conform to the accepted characteristics of a Ben Asher text better than any other known early manuscript, so that it must be taken as the superior representative of the tradition of Aaron Ben Asher;

(c) that what was supposed for a century to be a pious legend of the Jewish community of Aleppo and was disbelieved by most scholars—namely, that the Aleppo Codex is the selfsame model codex declared "authoritative" by Maimonides in his great halakhic compendium (the *Code*) with regard to certain fundamental questions of preparing Torah scrolls—is true. The Aleppo Codex *is* the codex of Maimonides, and as such became the halakhically binding model for later generations.

3. In the light of these earlier results with regard to the status and character of the Aleppo Codex we may now try to picture afresh on a broader canvas the history of what has become our *textus receptus*, before the emergence of the Aleppo Codex and after it. However, before turning to our main task on this occasion some general remarks may not be out of place.

The present study is an inquiry into a subject matter, not an analysis of scholarly theories. But trying to gain an understanding of the growth of the Tiberian Bible text means of necessity coming upon the theories of P. Kahle. For almost half a century Kahle's name has been synonymous with the study of the Hebrew Bible text, and what is found today in handbooks on the subject mostly reflects his ideas. Whether directly or indirectly, every student of the Bible text is in Kahle's debt. Only by standing on his shoulders can we try to perceive new vistas.[3]

By the same token, however, it is mainly Kahle's theses that our findings will question. While other scholars have dealt with certain details in most valuable monographs, only Kahle has put forward a general hypothesis of the emergence of the Tiberian Bible text through working into a

3. I should like to use this opportunity to express my gratitude to Professor Paul Kahle for his unfailing courtesy and helpfulness. I am especially in his debt for his permission to use his own transcripts from the fragments of the *ḥillufim* of Mishael. See below, Section V.

whole the results of various studies, carried out since the end of the last century.[4]

4. It was therefore inevitable that our results finally amount almost to an alternative general hypothesis, differing in many respects from the picture painted by Kahle. As such it is to be judged solely by its ability to accommodate the known facts. I would not claim that each particular detail of our thesis has been proved convincingly and that each proof is as sound as, I hope, the proof of the character of the Aleppo Codex itself—our starting point. Certain details will become clearer only after much further work (see below, §50). What I submit at present is that the over-all picture I try to convey allows for the inclusion of a larger number of known details and for a less forced interpretation of many facts than does the picture Kahle has presented. Or, to be less ambitious, the hypothesis to be outlined here is not less probable than his.

By the customary rules of formulating general hypotheses I shall be obliged to accommodate facts only and am not answerable for any theory of Kahle's (or others). At the same time, our hypothesis must allow for later modification of details, and it should not be taken as a final statement of opinions, to be defended stubbornly henceforth.[5]

5. Having grown up, like most of my contemporaries, under the impact of Kahle's teaching, I admit that all this sounds almost sacrilegious. Furthermore, the fate of Kahle's critics in another field of textual studies, the Septuagint text—where practically all the specialists who have investigated the subject on their own stand united against him, while his theories loom largely in the handbooks—does not make my task more enviable. To be sure, I take some comfort from the fact that the teaching of the young Kahle in its time also necessitated a frontal attack on the established authorities on the Hebrew Bible text of those days, such as Baer, Ginsburg, and Strack.[6] Even so I am conscious of embarking on a dangerous undertaking.

4. Kahle has now summed up his views in *Cairo Geniza*, 2nd ed. (Oxford, 1959), and in his German series of lectures, *Der hebräische Bibeltext seit Franz Delitzsch* (Stuttgart, 1961). As far as possible, the most recent statements of his position will be referred to as reflecting his opinions.

5. It is only human that as we advance in our work, we all try to fit new facts into our old patterns rather than to change our theories. Having rechecked Kahle's work as it developed over the decades, I feel—if I may venture such a remark—that his holding fast to the theories submitted in his brilliant pioneer studies (until 1930) has prevented him from much necessary revision.

6. Cf. especially Kahle's introduction to his *Masoreten des Ostens* (Leipzig, 1913), pp. xivf. His attack has not diminished; see *Der hebräische Bibeltext*, pp. 13f.

However, having reached the conclusions on the subject which I have reached, I could not honestly deal with all those questions without getting involved in a major discussion with Kahle and without submitting my findings to all scholars in general and to him in particular. If there is someone alive today who could show the basic fallacy of my position, it surely should be the *Altmeister* of this subject himself. It is in this spirit that I dare to outline my hypothesis. It would be folly to expect that I am completely right; I hope that I am not wholly wrong.

II. Tiberian and Non-Tiberian Traditions

6. Bearing in mind that our point of departure is the new edition of the Bible, no justification is needed for taking the Tiberian Bible text as our central theme. To be sure, the trend of research in Hebrew Bible traditions during the past decades, largely thanks to Kahle's work, has been to concentrate heavily on the study of traditions outside the Tiberian Bible text.

The nineteenth century had witnessed an increasing understanding of Hebrew in the light of Comparative Semitics, and the facts of the Tiberian Bible text, practically the only tradition known then, seemed, so to speak, "exhausted." Nothing was more natural for scholars than to turn to virgin soil. By concentrating their efforts on non-Tiberian traditions—written as well as oral[7]—a new perspective was gained for analyzing the development of Hebrew.

This gain of a new comparative dimension within the realm of Hebrew is one of the fundamental gains of this century in the field of Hebrew and Bible studies. All scholars will accept, therefore, the necessary corollary that every text-form of our Hebrew Bible, including the text of Aaron Ben Asher, represents only a synchronic cut in the flow of diachronic evolution (see my "Authenticity of the Aleppo Codex," §7).

7. But there is another side to the picture, somehow neglected through our preoccupation with non-Tiberian traditions (see also below, §47)—which reminds one of the truism that with all due respect to the side that lost, we should not ignore the fact that there was a winner.[8] It was a particular

7. It would seem that only the few studies undertaken by European scholars on the Samaritan reading tradition have come to Kahle's notice. I should therefore like to stress that the present essay relies in its general outlook on the results of many studies on Masoretic and dialectical questions, especially those by A. Ben David, Z. Ben Ḥayyim, J. Garbell, S. D. Goitein, Y. G. F. Gumpertz, D. S. Löwinger, S. Morag, H. Yalon, and J. Yeivin. See Notes 39, 43, and 54.

8. The question of the neglect of Tiberian Biblical manuscripts has been dealt with in my "Biblical Manuscripts."

Tiberian text-form that became our *textus receptus*, and ninety-nine per cent of the readers of the Hebrew Bible are interested in this form exclusively. In spite of our fullest awareness of the historic circumstances and in spite of the absorbing scholarly interest of other text-forms, our Tiberian Bible text still commands the paramount attention of scholars (see also my "Authenticity of the Aleppo Codex," 1).

Indeed, the great editors of Masoretic Bibles—from the First Masoretic Bible, connected with the name of Jacob Ben Ḥayyim[9] in 1524, to Seligmann Baer, Christian David Ginsburg,[10] and Paul Kahle—saw their task in printing what they believed was the Tiberian Ben Asher text.[11] The recovery of Aaron Ben Asher's model codex is therefore an event which calls for a new attempt to put the Tiberian Bible text into the center of our attention and to trace its emergence and rise to victory.

8. Apart from a new evaluation of the previously known facts, our attempt is based on three lines of inquiry:

(a) the study or perusal of all the Hebrew Bible codices and of most Geniza fragments (outside Russia; see my "Biblical Manuscripts in the United States");

(b) the study of the whole of Mishael Ben ᶜUzziel's treatise on the "differences" (*ḥillufim*) between Ben Asher and Ben Naftali in comparison with the codices mentioned under (c);[12]

(c) a new study of the codices customarily connected today with the

9. I use this formulation in order not to enter the problem of Jacob Ben Ḥayyim's dependence in his *text* (as opposed to the *Masora*) on the work of Felix Pratensis. There seems to be no generally accepted way to make it clear that the First Masoretic Bible is the Second Rabbinic Bible.

10. It has been stressed repeatedly by Kahle (see *Cairo Geniza*, 2nd ed., p. 130) that C. D. Ginsburg was the only one among the editors of the *textus receptus* in recent times who endeavored to reprint exactly the text of Ben Ḥayyim. But Ginsburg did not fully carry out his promise (quite apart from the question of the declared differences between his editions). Any sample collation over a few chapters will reveal this. As far as I can see, only A. Sperber, "Hebrew Phonology," *HUCA* 16:428 (1941), is aware of this fact.

11. This statement needs some qualification. In spite of Kahle's statement (at the moment of writing I find my reference to his chapter in L. Goldschmidt's *Earliest Editions of the Hebrew Bible* [New York, 1950], p. 46; but it probably also appears elsewhere), I cannot find the place where Ben Ḥayyim states that his aim is to print the text of Ben Asher. He intended to print what seemed to him the "correct Masoretic text" (which follows, as he surely believed, the tradition of Ben Asher). This is a slight difference, but still noteworthy. See §44.

12. The results from the analysis of the collations will be given in my *Nosaḥ ha-Miqrā*. I am greatly indebted to Mr. J. Yeivin, assistant at the Hebrew University Bible Project, who took upon himself to copy all the quotations from the various codices and also sent them to the States. In Note 3, above, I expressed my appreciation of Professor Kahle's generosity in making his transcripts available.

Ben Asher family: that is, the Aleppo Codex (A), the codex British Museum Or. 4445 of the Pentateuch (B), the Cairo Codex of the Prophets (C), and the Leningrad Codex B 19a (L).

9. In order to sketch our picture of the rise of the Tiberian Bible text we have to pay attention to the following major problems:[13]

(a) the relationship of Aaron's codex to other "Tiberian" traditions in general and to the Cairo Codex in particular;

(b) the nature of the Ben Naftali tradition—or what is widely accepted as such;

(c) the reason for the victory of Aaron's system.

III. The Position of the Aleppo Codex

10. A study of the Aleppo and Cairo codices[14] and their Masoras, leaf by leaf, gives one the impression, perforce subjective, that these codices are very much personal and individual achievements. The way in which Masoretic notes are put together and corrections introduced is different from that of the twelfth- and thirteenth-century codices. The Aleppo and Cairo codices impress us not as stereotyped copies but as first-hand creations, still bearing marks of occasional changes, not just mistakes,[15] in the light of evidence the author seems to have gathered in the course of his work. Each codex shows its own arrangement and choice of the Masora—substantially different in character from the carefree attitude and "choice" of later copyists. They often offer materials in their margins other than those in the text itself (and sometimes apparently representing an "earlier" stage). Furthermore, the considerable number of Babylonian signs[16] leads us back to a stage when the Tiberian tradition was still under "foreign influence" with regard to the graphic notation, and the extremely rare *ḥaṭaf-ḥiriq* vowels (compare Löwinger, *Textus* 1:83f.) reveal a momentary glimpse of an "experiment" which was immediately discarded.

13. The questions are interconnected and have not influenced the structure of this paper.

14. All Ben Asher manuscripts were studied from photographs, but the Aleppo Codex and British Museum Or. 4445 were also verified from the originals.

15. Completely different from the erasures in the Leningrad Codex (see below, §30). All the codices, of course, have their fair share of "ordinary" mistakes and corrections.

16. Kahle was clearly aware of the significance of this phenomenon in the very early codices (see especially *Theologische Rundschau*, N.S., 5:330f. [1933] reprinted in *Opera Minora* [Leiden, 1956], pp. 70f.). This was stressed again by F. Diez Esteban, *Sefarad* 14:317f. (1954), and with regard to the Aleppo Codex by Löwinger, *Textus* 1:82f.

In short, the codices around 900 C.E. show, so to speak, no stereotype; the last touches of the masters are still fresh. What we see is not the work of copyists, with a tradition of generations of copying the same text, but something which had only just then become fully fledged.[17]

11. In other words: in our submission the early codices which we possess are not only the oldest ones known to us, but they seem to belong to the altogether earliest stratum of codices of the fully developed prototype of the Tiberian Bible text. This impression, gained from working on the codices, tallies exactly with the feeling we get from the unique colophon of the Cairo Codex, written by Moses Ben Asher at the very end of the ninth century.[18] We cannot help noticing the satisfaction of the Masorete that something novel has been achieved, not necessarily by him personally, but through the then-recent common effort of a whole group, something not achieved in the same fashion until that time (see below, § 18f.).

12. Third, and hardly less important: not only are these the earliest known codices,[19] but among all the known Biblical Geniza fragments[20] which have now been perused for the first time, there is not one that can be said to represent basically the Tiberian Bible text and yet be earlier than the ninth- and tenth-century codices.[21]

13. All this is circumstantial evidence and must remain argument from silence. Also, as I stressed elsewhere,[22] the treasures kept in Russia may

17. The chronological implications in the light of the "List of Generations" of the Masoretes (K. Levy, *Zur masoretischen Grammatik* [Stuttgart, 1936], ט) will be dealt with in *Nosaḥ ha-Miqrā*. See below, Notes 65, 112.

18. See *Cairo Geniza*, pp. 80f. See below, Note 57.

19. *Mutatis mutandis* matters apply also to a manuscript like the Sassoon Codex 507 (S).

20. I do not think I exaggerate if I put the number of these fragments, including the very small ones, at ten thousand and above. Selections from these have been photographed by the Hebrew University Bible Project for further study. Only the Russian material and those fragments of the so-called "New Series" in Cambridge which are still in the large wooden crates have not been examined. See my "Biblical Manuscripts," chap. ii.

21. On the basis of my work on Geniza material, both Biblical and non-Biblical, I tend to endorse J. L. Teicher's warning (*JJS* 1:158 [1949]) that in general we should not expect in the Geniza any material antedating that period (see Notes 40, 65, 1.12). But because of the basic character of the Geniza as well as the type of writing materials used, one might have expected that a few Bible manuscripts, a century or two old, should have been ready for the Geniza by the tenth century. In fact, it has been generally held that the Geniza contains much older material (but cf. below, Note 112). Yet no part of an eighth- or ninth-century Tiberian Masoretic manuscript has come to light so far. I include in this statement MS. JTS 226, possibly the earliest Geniza fragment of the Tiberian Bible text, which has not entered the literature so far. See my "Biblical Manuscripts," p. 38. Publication will take place in *Nosaḥ ha-Miqrā* and in forthcoming volumes of *Textus*.

22. See for this matter my *Text and Language*, p. x.

still provide a surprise.[23] Yet from all the indications there emerges, in my opinion, something which we could not suspect until now, something which also throws a completely new light on the astounding action of Maimonides (see my *Text and Language*, pages 43f., especially 46, and below, my Section IX). It sounds, indeed, unbelievable because of its very simplicity.[24] In my submission it has become very probable that the Aleppo Codex was not only one early manuscript out of a few; it was the great event in the history of the Tiberian Bible text. It was preceded, no doubt, by other codices. But this was the *first codex of the complete Bible* with full Masoretic annotation, exhibiting what was to be regarded as the prototype of the Tiberian Bible text. It was the final achievement of the continued work of generations of *the* dynasty of Masoretes,[25] the descendants of "the Old Asher."

14. The stress is on the complete Bible. For our thesis also takes into consideration the fact, often ignored, that for centuries to come codices of the complete Bible remained very rare, and it must have taken a very long time until such a codex was first attempted.[26] Maimonides' description of

23. Although the examination of the Russian collections remains a high-priority desideratum, I am afraid that to some extent our inability to examine them at this moment makes us expect more than there might be. To be more specific: the Günzburg collection does not, to my knowledge, include old Bible codices, and it hardly stands to reason that the Geniza material in the Anṭonin collection is basically different from the material which came to other countries.

In other words, our main hope is undoubtedly the Firkowich collections. But most of that material was examined at the time by H. L. Strack (who was interested in the Ben Asher question; see his pioneer article, "Die biblischen und die massoretischen Handschriften zu Tschufut Kale in der Krim," *Zeitschrift für die Lutherische Theologie und Kirche* 36:585f. [1875]). However, Strack's examination was, according to his own words, rather cursory. Furthermore, we may judge matters differently nowadays. Kahle's own discoveries (*Masoreten des Westens*, vol. I [Stuttgart, 1927], pp. 56ff.), on the other hand, turn out to depend rather heavily on the notes of his predecessors. It is, therefore, not easy to form a picture of what to expect from the manuscripts kept in Russia. See also Note 81.

24. I have wondered for a long time whether any thesis which depends in the last analysis on argument from silence may be suggested. It can never be fully proved and can hardly be disproved. Furthermore, one feels reluctant to assume that the earliest item known is in actual fact the earliest item. Yet the evidence pointing in the direction of our thesis seems so strong that I am personally convinced it is true. Nevertheless, I should like to stress that the other theses of this study—and especially my argument with Kahle—are not dependent on this.

25. This attribute is not based on the ultimate victory of this tradition, but results from the analysis of medieval material (such as that alluded to in Note 17).

26. The only codex of a complete Bible about which we hear the claim that it was earlier than our earliest Tiberian Bible text codices is the legendary Codex Hilleli, long lost. That claim is contained in Zacuto's note which is patently fictitious (dated at the sixth or seventh century!). As a reference I suggest H. L. Strack's *Prolegomena critica in Vetus Testamentum* (Leipzig, 1873), p. 16; all later handbooks seem to have copied their information from him.

the Aleppo Codex as containing the complete Bible[27] thus becomes much more significant than we could imagine. Parts of the Bible were copied much more often, because there was a practical need for them. Such codices with full Tiberian Masoretic annotation may already have been current during the ninth century, and the Cairo Codex may have been spared the fate of other such codices because of its prestige and its superb workmanship. But the idea of a complete model codex,[28] to serve as final arbiter for scribes and scholars, with full Masoretic annotation according to the then most reliable tradition—this idea had yet to be conceived of. Apart from everything else, it must have been extremely expensive,[29] because its author spent many years on it. The Aleppo Codex was the first model codex of this textual type.[30]

15. Although the vicissitudes of Jewish life in the Middle Ages brought about the destruction of many Bible codices, there is no reason on earth why only the codices from before 900 C.E. should have disappeared completely.[31] If there were such codices, some kind of trace should have been left.

It seems therefore much more reasonable to assume that a model codex of the complete Tiberian Bible was attempted only as a crowning undertaking in the mature stage of Masoretic activity. In other words: all the facts known indicate that the practically uniform medieval tradition should be taken at its face value. It was Aaron Ben Asher who was recognized almost universally as the Masorete who had the final word,[32] it was he to

27. *Code*, Book ii, *Ahabha*, *Hilkhoth Sefer Thora*, viii, 4: הספר הידוע במצרים שהוא כולל ארבעה ועשרים ספרים ("The codex known in Egypt which contains the whole Bible"). For a translation of the whole note, see my "Authenticity of the Aleppo Codex," n. 1.

28. For information on differences among the various types of codex, see my "Biblical Manuscripts," pp. 36f. See also below, Notes 136, 138.

29. I understand that information on this subject from Geniza documents will be given by S. D. Goitein in a forthcoming publication.

30. It is useful to remember that there is no such thing as a scroll of the whole Bible. The ancient tradition knows only of parts as the scribal entity.

31. If we may judge at all by the contents of present-day collections and the ratio between the numbers of manuscripts from before and after 1200 C.E., codices of the complete Bible remained very rare, but they are in existence as from the tenth century. It is also illuminating to find that the rarity of complete Bible codices is in evidence elsewhere. Thus from the whole period between the fifth century (the time of the first known codex) until the twelfth century, we possess only four complete codices of the Peshitta. See my "Prolegomena to a critical edition of the Peshitta," *Text and Language*, p. 200. On the other hand, codices of various parts of the Peshitta run into dozens. Furthermore, it took the Syrian punctuators and Masoretes some five hundred years after the invention of diacritic signs before anything faintly resembling a "Masoretic manuscript" was attempted (*Text and Language*, p. 201). For a similar situation with regard to the Vulgate, see S. Berger, *Histoire de la Vulgate* (Paris, 1895), p. 3.

32. היה אחרית השלשלה=כאן אכ׳ר אלסלסלה ("He was the last link in the chain") (Levy, *Zur masoretischen Grammatik*, p. י). For the importance of the facts mentioned here, see below, Note 91. For the development after him, see below, §43f.

whom the collection of Masoretic material, probably partly current in his family for some generations, known as *Dikduke Ha-ṭeamim* was attributed; it was he who was named as the authority in polemic teasings between Rabbanites and Ḳaraites (see below, Note 51); it was his codex that Maimonides relied upon (see below, my Section IX).

As far as our knowledge goes, Aaron Ben Asher did not bring about any revolution in Masoretic notation[33] which would justify his status. Had his father succeeded in preparing a complete Bible codex he would, in all probability, have carried off the palm. In my opinion, then, all the facts point in one direction. *The Aleppo Codex is not only the oldest complete codex of the Tiberian Bible text known to us, but it is altogether the earliest complete codex of that Masoretic subsystem which had been perfected by the Ben Ashers.*

16. This claim does not ignore the possibility that Aaron Ben Asher himself also prepared codices of *parts* of the Bible,[34] probably before the Aleppo Codex was written. But it seems improbable, contrary to what has been believed until now without any positive evidence, that there ever existed another codex of the complete Bible prepared by him. If we bear in mind that even *copying* a codex like the Aleppo Codex, with its ten thousands of annotations, is perforce a matter of years, it seems that the original *preparation* of such a model codex was almost by definition a goal reached once in a lifetime. Being something novel in its execution, even though based on earlier work, it was by necessity the crowning event of many years of endless toil—and we might assume that Aaron began his codex only when his father had laid away his pen forever. Again and again over the years, he introduced slight corrections, just as was hinted by Maimonides (see Note 27) and as was the habit of many authors.[35]

17. To sum up the position so far: in my submission all the facts are

33. For the problem of Aaron versus Moses, see below §33f.

34. The expression הספרים המוגהים והמבוארים אשר עשה המלמד אהרן בן משה בן אשר ("The correct and clear codices prepared by the master Aaron Ben Moses Ben Asher") in the colophon of the Leningrad Codex (fol. 479a) would fit this assumption well, although this is not the only possible explanation. At the same time such an assumption would offer a possible explanation for some differences between the Aleppo and Leningrad codices. See, for the matter, also note 81, below. As far as I can see, no attention has been paid to the wording in the Leningrad Codex as regards its possible relationship with the Aleppo Codex. See also below, §30.

35. Mishael Ben ᶜUzziel testifies when dealing with the *gaᶜyas* of לא יהיה לך (Exod. 20:3; Mishael יב) that such a change of position on the part of Ben Asher took place. The fact of this special mention can, of course, be interpreted in two opposite ways. Unfortunately we do not know the reading of the Aleppo Codex in this instance. (The verse is not mentioned in Jacob Sapir's list; see my "Biblical Manuscripts," chap. v).

interpreted best by assuming that the Aleppo Codex was, indeed, the greatest event in the history of the Tiberian Bible text, the first complete codex of the Bible according to the tradition later to be accepted as *the* Tiberian Masoretic Bible. It is not only the superior manuscript connected with the name of Aaron Ben Asher, but also it is the only complete Bible codex prepared by him (see below, §§31, 43f., 45f.). Its "victory" was due to these circumstances, to its inherent obvious perfection as the acme of achievement of *the* dynasty of Masoretes.

IV. Lower Bible Criticism and Oral Tradition

18. The stress I have put on the unique and novel aspect of Aaron Ben Asher's achievement approaches so dangerously the formulation of Kahle, "dass die tiberische Punktation erst eine Schöpfung der Ben Ascher-Masoreten gewesen ist . . ." (*Der hebräische Bibeltext*, page 51) and similar statements, that our next step must be to try to outline the way which led up to the creation of the Aleppo Codex.[36] This is all the more necessary because the discussions of the last decades have often become reminiscent of the theological feuds of the sixteenth and seventeenth centuries in the wake of Levita's discovery of the late provenience of the vowel points. The analogy is quite striking. Just as Levita's correct critical insights led to the monstrous disregard of facts by later scholars and their cavalier attitude to the Masoretic text,[37] so the modern theories about the development of the Tiberian Bible text, as propounded by Kahle, seem the almost natural outcome of our better acquaintance with non-Tiberian systems, mainly thanks to his work.

19. In order to introduce our point, we may start by looking back at the history of the so-called "Higher Bible Criticism" since Kahle's early days. The theory of evolution was still all-pervading, and it was the aim of

36. With regard especially to the following sections, which develop my main discussion with Kahle, I should like to stress that the arguments are given in greater detail in my *Nosaḥ ha-Miqrā*.

37. The best accounts of these discussions are still those written in the second half of the nineteenth century which deal with the subject in different ways. S. D. Luzzato is still a party to the discussion (*Dialogues sur la Kabbale et le Zohar et sur l'antiquité de la ponctuation et de l'accentuation dans la langue hébraïque* [in Hebrew; Gorice, 1852, pp. 79ff.]). C. D. Ginsburg has written a detailed survey in his introduction to Elia Levita, *Massoreth ha-Massoreth* (London, 1867) while G. Schnedermann has highlighted *Die Controverse des Ludovicus Capellus mit den Buxtorfen* (Leipzig, 1879). I have not found it pointed out that, ironically enough, it was the "discoverer" of the Aleppo Codex himself who again took up the cudgels for the defense of the antiquity of the vowel points (Jacob Sapir, *Even Sapir*, p. ii, end [1874]).

scholars, at least unconsciously, always to detect the line of development. Different phenomena were conceived of as stages in a developmental sequence; the question was only: which preceded which and why.[38]

Whatever our attitude to some extreme contentions of the so-called "oral tradition" school, there is no doubt that during the past quarter of a century it has made scholars aware again of the power of "oral tradition" in Near Eastern cultures. Furthermore, we are much more willing today to acknowledge the existence of traditions side by side, and do not telescope them by force into an evolutional chain.

20. The discussion of all the details of Kahle's theories on the Tiberian Bible text must be left for *Nosaḥ ha-Miqrā*. For the moment, I would suggest that it is precisely by practically negating the role of oral tradition and by forcing the facts into a developmental Procrustean bed, that Kahle was able to build his hypothesis. Since the Tiberian forms are different[39] from those of other traditions they are more recent,[40] and since the Hebrew language had long become extinct, the Tiberian Bible text is really no true tradition at all.[41] It is the invention of the Tiberian Masoretes. They

38. For the general attitude involved see my *Text and Language*, pp. 157ff.

39. See above, Note 7. Kahle, whose revolutionary stressing (since 1902!) of non-Tiberian traditions has made others aware of the problems of dialect traditions in the transmission of Hebrew, apparently never seriously considered the possibility of a plurality of traditions—none of which is necessarily per se inferior to any other—side by side with what may all the time have been the mainstream of tradition. For the present writer this way of explaining facts is an attitude basic both to his viewing the Masoretic consonantal text vis-à-vis the Bible Versions, the Dead Sea Scrolls, variants in Rabbinic literature, and so on, and to his estimation of the Tiberian Bible text vis-à-vis other reading traditions. See my *Text and Language*, pp. ix f., 51f., 156f., 161, and below, Note 43 and §49.

40. Recently Kahle has claimed that A. Murtonen, *Materials for a Non-Masoretic Hebrew Grammar*, I (Helsinki, 1958), has shown that "die Aussprache des Hebräischen in Palästina in der Zeit, ehe die Masoreten von Tiberias mit ihrer Arbeit begannen, im wesentlichen so gewesen ist, wie die Samaritaner heute noch in ihren Gottesdiensten die Tora rezitieren" (*Hebräischer Bibeltext*, p. 29). Furthermore (p. 68), this "palästinische Punktationsmethode . . . die heute noch bei den Samaritanern gebraucht wird [*sic*], von der Dr. Murtonen nachgewiesen hat, dass sie im wesentlichen identisch ist mit der Aussprache des Hebräischen, die . . . in liturgischen Texten [Only ?—*M.G.*] mit palästinischer Punktation . . . einst auch bei rabbanitischen Juden [*sic*] in Palästina bis zum 8/9 Jahrhundert üblich gewesen ist."

I cannot find the slightest basis for this claim in Murtonen's study, nor do I find that Murtonen has claimed this. What Murtonen's investigation of "Palestinian" texts has shown are, in my opinion, certain "Palestinian"–Samaritan isoglosses in addition to those previously known. *Vive la petite différence*! Cf. also below, Notes 65, 112.

41. Having rightly stressed the importance of the non-Tiberian traditions, Kahle went to extremes—in what might have been "discoverer's enthusiasm" at the time. In spite of what purported to be a rejoinder (Marti Festschrift, *BZAW* 41:167f. [1925], collected in *Opera Minora*, pp. 48f.), Kahle never succeeded in answering G. Bergsträsser,

invented, "restituted," and changed arbitrarily (see below, Note 49). Their model was, *horribile dictu*, no one else but the Qoran readers![42]

21. It is not my fault if this sounds like a caricature of critical method (see Note 44). In my submission Kahle's theory does not merely start from outdated ideas.[43] It is contrary to sound historical criticism. It postulates a textual situation unparalleled in the history of philology, and turns into reckless deceivers generations of Masoretic scholars who spent their lives to safeguard the "correct tradition" of the Bible, to the very best of their ability.[44] Even were we to possess what looks like a perfect proof, not just

---

who had protested (*OLZ* 19:582f. [1924]) that Kahle "lässt nur die nicht-'massoretischen' Vokalisationen überhaupt als Überlieferung gelten, so dass schon aus äusserem Grund das von ihnen Gebotene zu bevorzugen, die tiberienische Vokalisation also wie eine nachweislich entstellte Handschrift zu behandeln wäre." Bergsträsser's attitude is, of course, different from that of M. Kober (*Jeschurun* 17:149 [1930]). For Kober, the Tiberian Bible text is obviously the main tradition and the others are "only" dialects. For the problem (cf. also Note 39) see my *Nosaḥ ha-Miqrā*.

In order to prevent any misunderstanding, I should add that becoming aware of the non-Tiberian traditions is of vital importance for understanding the history of Hebrew (see above, §6), but they should not make us turn history upside down. Understanding a problem in historic-comparative linguistics and explaining the history of the Bible text are not necessarily the same thing. Especially with regard to the latter problem Kahle has overplayed his hand and has, besides, ignored any statement to the contrary by specialists. Thus, for example, he continuously adduces Origen's *Secunda* as one of the pillars of his theory. Apart from the fact that, in my opinion, his argument is doubtful, he never refuted in detail the result of what must still be regarded the most thorough monograph on that tradition, E. Brønno's *Studien über hebräische Morphologie und Vokalismus* (Leipzig, 1943), p. 462: "Die grosse Bedeutung der SEC [the Hebrew transcription column in Origen's Hexapla] für die hebr. Sprachwissenschaft liegt u.a. darin, dass diese alte Überlieferung deutlich zeigt, dass das tiberische Formensystem in seinen wesentlichen Hauptzügen eine alte Tradition hinter sich hat." One need not accept Brønno's verdict, but one might at least take the trouble to refute it.

42. Cf. Kahle's summary, *Cairo Geniza*, p. 170: "There need be no doubt that the impetus for revising the reading of the Hebrew text was given to the Masoretes by the Arab readers of the Koran." Not only do I not admit Kahle's claims with regard to the tradition of the Qoran itself, but in all his writings there is not the slightest evidence connecting the activity of the Masoretes with that of the Qoran readers. His whole argument is based on alleged analogy—no doubt a favorite way of proof with Kahle, brought to perfection in his treatment of the Bible versions.

43. Cf. above, Notes 7 and 39, and my *Text and Language*, pp. 157f. It is astonishing that Kahle, who stressed the pluralism of sources with regard to the Bible versions (cf. *Text and Language*, pp. 65f.), did not allow for this possibility with regard to the Hebrew reading traditions. I should like to use this opportunity to stress that while I firmly believe in the pluralism of traditions—and in our inability always to recover the first source *in practice* (*Text and Language*, pp. 156f.)—I do not accept Kahle's thesis that by necessity there was no "*Ur*-Septuagint" (as Strugnell, *JBL* 80:200 [1961], seems to have inferred). My wording in *Text and Language*, p. 160, is deliberate.

For another important aspect of the problem cf. S. Talmon's studies in *Textus* 1:144f., and *Scripta Hierosolymitana* 8:335f. (1961).

44. Cf. Note 50. Statements like those quoted there are painfully reminiscent of what Paul A. de Lagarde in his weak moments had to say about the "Jewish Masoretes."

theories, that the Tiberian Masoretes did what Kahle attributes to them—and what has entered since into most handbooks—we should rather disbelieve our "proofs."

22. One point of detail ought to be made now. Kahle has recently made much of the alleged Ḳaraite beliefs of the Ben Ashers (in both *Cairo Geniza* and *Der hebräische Bibeltext*). He has never paused to ask seriously: Given the relations between Ḳaraites and Rabbanites in the ninth century, is it at all conceivable that anyone could have interfered with the tradition of the Bible text in a way even remotely similar to Kahle's suggestions without causing an immediate outcry by his opponents? Whether the culprits were Rabbanites or Ḳaraites, the other party would have raised a storm.

The polemic literature of that time is not a total blank. Some of it was written very soon after the activity of the younger Ben Ashers, and it contains a good number of teasing remarks on textual and Masoretic matters. There is no doubt that neither side ever suspected the other of any tampering with the text—which according to Kahle was then of very recent occurrence. The very fact that there still exist doubts as to the creed of the Ben Ashers[45] should, indeed, suffice to highlight this point. Ḳaraites and Rabbanites alike must have hushed up their crime—presumably to please the Qoran readers.

23. What Kahle wishes us to assume on this subject is possible only if we completely ignore history.[46] According to him,[47] "from the fact that a Bible text established by Ḳaraite Masoretes [*sic*] was accepted as authorita-

---

It gives some food for thought that the type of Bible criticism prejudiced by evolutionary theory has ended, both in the "Higher" and the "Lower" field, by practically turning our only witnesses into deceivers, even if it was only *pia fraus*. Usurping the attribute "critical" for these theories becomes, of course, a mighty weapon against all "uncritical" dissenters. Cf. below, Notes 89 and 96 and §§ 33 and 47.

45. In "The Authenticity of the Aleppo Codex" I have repeatedly (cf. its § 33 and Notes 16 and 52) spoken of the *alleged* (my italics here) Ḳaraite creed of Ben Asher. This was intended to keep me out of the discussion (a full century old, begun with S. Pinsker's *Lickute Quadmonioth* [Vienna, 1860], pp. 32f.) about the creed of the Ben Ashers, because it was completely immaterial to my subject. On the basis of this expression, however, N. Alloni (*Ha-Aretz*, October 28, 1960) attacked me for my belief that the Ben Ashers were Rabbanites! I ought to state, therefore, that I do not hold such a belief. Although the issue may be included in *Nosaḥ ha-Miqrā* (I have tentatively prepared a chapter on the subject), the interesting fact for me at present is that a good case can be made out for each theory. It is this aspect that is of importance for our discussion.

46. For our argument we do not even have to invoke Bergsträssser's remark (*OLZ* 19:582f.): "Ist in diesen traditionsgebundenen Jahrhunderten eine solch kühne Reform, wie Kahle sie voraussetzt, denkbar?"

47. Cf. *JJS* 7:143 (1956).

tive throughout Jewry, by Rabbanites and Ḳaraites alike, we must conclude that this acceptance must have taken place at a time when the relations between the two parties had not yet come to the critical stage that we know of at a later time."

When, then, did this happen? How did those Rabbanites pronounce "before" and how should we picture the development? I quote from Kahle's latest statement (*Der hebräische Bibeltext*, page 68): "Die Samaritaner haben eine Aussprache des Hebräischen bis auf den heutigen Tag festgehalten, welche die palästinische Punktation in alten Geniza-Fragmenten einst auch für die Aussprache des Hebräischen bei den rabbanitischen Juden bezeugt hat. [Cf. above, Note 40.] Bei diesen rabbanitischen Juden ist diese Aussprache aber abgelöst worden durch eine solche, die von den Masoreten ausgebildet worden ist, die ihren Sitz in Tiberias gehabt haben. Diese haben der im Laufe des 9. Jahrhunderts mächtig aufblühenden Gemeinde der Ḳaräer angehört. Diese Aussprache ist dann [*sic*, necessarily not earlier than 900 C.E.—*M.G.*] aber von den rabbanitischen Juden übernommen und hat sich bei ihnen so vollständig durchgesetzt, dass jede Erinnerung an eine frühere Art der Aussprache des Hebräischen vollständig in Vergessenheit geraten war.[48] Man hat sich sogar mit Erfolg bemüht, alle Spuren zu verwischen, die uns Kunde davon gaben, dass die ḳaräischen Masoreten eine neue Aussprache des Hebräischen ausgebildet und durchgeführt haben [*sic*] und auch den ḳaräischen Ursprung der tiberischen Punktation hat man zu vergessen sich bemüht."

24. According to Kahle's picture, for which we are not offered a scrap of direct evidence,[49] we are requested to believe that there was a unique case of conspiracy between Rabbanites and Ḳaraites in order to falsify

48. To keep chronology straight: according to this hypothesis, all this happened near the lifetime of people like Menaḥem Ben Saruq in Spain and Rabbenu Gershom in Germany—not to mention R. Saᶜadya.

49. In order to give what seems a typical example of Kahle's argumentation, I adduce the following reasoning (*Hebräischer Bibeltext*, p. 67): "Wir müssen also damit rechnen, dass die tiberischen Masoreten eine neue Methode der Andeutung der Betonung der hebräischen Worte durchgeführt haben [Agreed—*M.G.*], die für die hebräische Grammatik, wie wir sie kennen, von grundlegender Bedeutung geworden ist. Das will aber besagen [*sic*], dass die Aussprache des Hebräischen wie wir sie auf Grund der tiberischen Punktation kennen, überhaupt erst eine Schöpfung der tiberischen Masoreten gewesen ist, des prominentesten unter ihnen, insbesonderer erst des grossen Masoreten Mosche ben Ascher, von dem der Kairoer Prophetenkodex eine der ganz grossen Leistungen ist." A perfect example of Kahle's *non sequiturs*. [May 1962: In *Textus* 2:2 (1962) we read that what "became the official language in Tiberias" is a "form of Hebrew created by the Tiberian Massoretes" (*sic*).]

purposely[50] the Bible text, hushed up by all concerned.[51] This took place almost at the height of the anti-Ḳaraite polemic trend (around 900 C.E.), and was accepted by authorities all over the world within a generation or two. Its aim was to enforce (against whom?) a text against live tradition, which had been modeled under the influence of Qoran readers. *Sapienti sat!*

25. I think that for the moment, leaving further details for the forthcoming Hebrew study, I made it clear that I think Kahle's widely accepted theories unfortunate, and that I should not like the stress I put on the novel character of the Aleppo Codex as a *written* document to be interpreted along the lines of Kahle's hypothesis.

In my opinion, the work of the Masoretes, which reached a peak in the Aleppo Codex, is to be understood as the invention and perfection of an ever more refined graphic notation for an age-old oral tradition[52] which endeavored to note down with the greatest possible exactness[53] the smallest details of the customary liturgical way of reading the Bible.[54]

50. Kahle, *Hebräischer Bibeltext*, p. 10: "Schliesslich kann es heute keine Frage mehr sein, dass die Masoreten von Tiberias *absichtlich* [My italics—*M.G.*] Änderungen der Aussprache des Hebräischen vorgenommen haben." (By the way, this is completely different from what some non-specialist *Haskala*-writers who sometimes expressed themselves similarly have meant.)

It is in the same vein that Kahle suggests (*JJS* 7:144 [1956])—again leveling his accusations without any evidence—that in order to hush up their fraudulent conspiracy, the Masoretes committed what by law was a heinous crime (when in fact they would rather have died than have committed it): "The Masoretes eliminated all remnants of earlier pronunciation so radically that no pre-Masoretic texts were allowed to be preserved. The first specimens of earlier punctuation to re-emerge were found in the Cairo Geniza [*sic*] where they had been stored *in order to be destroyed* [My italics—*M.G.*]."

51. In reality, even seemingly insignificant problems formed the subject of "teasing questions" and caused remarks in the polemical literature between Ḳaraites and Rabbanites; each party would surely have seized upon the smallest evidence of doubtful procedure in order to tease the other and to accuse it. These remarks are known in the literature for almost a century. They were republished by Strack in 1879 and 1897 and have appeared on numerous occasions since. Kahle prefers to ignore all this. See my *Nosaḥ ha-Miqrā*.

52. The explanations by medieval grammarians are not to be dismissed without eliciting some information (see Note 55). The need for writing down the tradition was, in my opinion, primarily an *inner* problem (dangers of sectarianism, deviating traditions over the centuries, didactic needs, etc.). Although this assumes that the main reasons were not *exterior* circumstances, which used to be thought responsible, I believe the invention of diacritic notation by the Syriac scribes was of greater importance than, e.g., S. W. Baron, *Social and Religious History of the Jews*, VI (New York, 1958), 241, wishes to allow. Cf. also my remarks on "The Diacritic Points in Syriac," *Tarbiz* 24:105f. (1955).

53. As shown by different opinions on methegs, erasures, and changes. Cf. §§ 10, 27, 30.

54. It should be made quite clear that in this case also, writing down a tradition is not the end of *oral tradition*, a fact not appreciated sufficiently by most European (and American) scholars. Thus the original custom of "indicating the accents" by movement

Critical scholarship should, no doubt, refrain from accepting at their face value the statements of the Masoretes (always including here the early punctuators) about their activity. But it is necessary to find out what those views were. Their testimony is largely identical with our view—with the necessary difference that for them the "tradition from time immemorial" was identified with the Revelation on Sinai,[55] with Ezra, with the Temple, and so on. Our thesis, to be sure, maintains solely that theirs was basically a living tradition (which probably had undergone slight diachronic

---

of the hand continued long after the invention of the signs (which, to be sure, were never introduced into the scrolls). Cf. Rashi's note on the Talmudic dictum (*Berakhoth*, 62a): מפני שמראה בה טעמי תורה ("for one uses it [i.e., one's right hand] for indicating Torah accents"): "One moves one's hand according to the cantillation accent; I have seen readers [doing] this who came from Palestine." Similarly S. Baer and H. L. Strack, *Dikduke*, § 17 (*Die Dikduke Ha-Teamim des Ahron ben Moscheh ben Ascher* [Leipzig, 1879]), speak of an accent יוצאת ביד ברעדה ("going tremblingly forth from the hand"). J. Qāfiḥ mentions (*Sinai* 29:262 [1951]) that this custom is still alive in Yemen.

The relationship between quoting by heart and melodious accentuation was well realized in the Middle Ages; cf. *Tosafoth* on *Megilla* 32a. Cf. J. Yeivin, *Leshonenu* 24:48 (1960), who quotes Saᶜadya's justification for the use of accents in his writings: ליכון אסהל לקראתה ואמכן לחפט׳ה ("so that it is easier to read and to memorize").

It would also seem that the famous fragments from the Cairo Geniza of so-called "Short-hand Bibles" (published first, I think, by A. Neubauer, *JQR* 7:361ff. [1894] and analyzed first by M. Friedländer [*ibid.*, p. 564]) throw an interesting sidelight on the relationship between written text and oral tradition. [May 1962: See also the material published by Yeivin, *Textus* 2:120f.] Another aspect of the problem, merely to be hinted at, is the non-Tiberian reading habits of various Jewish communities in disregard of their Tiberian Bible text (see above, Note 7; see especially—also for non-Biblical texts—S. Morag, *Leshonenu La-ᶜAm* 73:22f. [1957], and the literature there and in *Leshonenu La-ᶜAm* 74:73; also *Tarbiz* 30:121 [1960]). Furthermore, the fate of texts written by scribes of different traditional reading habits—such as "Sefardis" (see below, Notes 65 and 112) and Yemenites who ostensibly tried to reproduce the Tiberian Bible text (see my "Biblical Manuscripts," pp. 39ff.) shows the power of traditions long after the Tiberian Bible text had become "officially" accepted.

55. The varying details as to the origin of the oral tradition and its subsequent graphic fixation are of considerable interest, but they are outside our scope. The usual picture of medieval grammarians—not by necessity identical with that of the Masoretes and punctuators themselves—runs somewhat like this: וכאן אלסייד אלרסול יתלי עליהם אלנץ ויחכמהם קראתה באלרפע ואלצ׳ם ואלנצב ואלכפט׳ ואלמסך ואלפתח ואלקטע ואלוצל וכל אלאעראב. וכאנת כלהא ענדהם חרכאת אללסאן ואליד איצ׳א כמא קאלו "לא יקנח בימין שמראה בה טעמי תורה" (ברכות סב, ע"א). והד׳א הו אלחכם אלחקיקי. וכאן ד׳לך ענדהם תלקין מן צדר אלי צדר. פלמא ראוא אבתדא אלגלות ותשתת אללגה כ׳שוא עלי אנקטאעה ודת׳ורה מן אלמלה פקאמוא ושכלוא וצוורוא . . . ." (A. Neubauer, *Petite Grammaire hébraïque* [Leipzig, 1891], p. 23)—"And Moses used to read the text before them and securely taught them all the different ways of vocalization. All these were movements of the mouth and also of the hand, as the Sages put it: 'One should not wipe oneself with the right hand, because one uses it for indicating the Torah accents.' This is the true custom, and this used to be the way of dictating all of it. But once they saw that the Diaspora had started and that the language had become confused [literally: torn to parts], they were afraid that [the language] might become cut off and forgotten by the Nation. So they started to put signs and marks." To be sure, this is a standard explanation for the change-over from oral tradition. Cf. Rashi *ad Bābā Məṣīᶜā* 33a.

changes).[56] The Masoretes were convinced, rightly in their way, that they were keeping up an ancient tradition, and interfering with it purposely would have been for them the worst crime possible. Yet they were extremely proud, quite justifiedly, of their own achievement:[57] the graphic notation and its perfection, so as to safeguard the ancient tradition for all future generations.[58] It was this double belief in the antiquity of the tradition and

The ideas as to when the fixation in writing occurred are clearly expressed in "Manuel du Lecteur," ed. J. Dérenbourg, *JA* 16:361 [1870]: «ואם יאמר אדם מי חבר אלה המלכים וכן הטעמים והתקין צורתן כמו שהן עתה בידינו, ידע תחלה כי צורתן הוא ממה שחברו עליו האחרונים ואמרו: זו היא צורת הקמצה וזו היא צורת הפתחה וכו׳ . . . וכולן הסכימו על זה ועשו אותן סימנין ללמוד וללמד בהן. יש מי שאומר מימות עזרא הן שכתבו אותן והעלו להן אלו הצורות . . . ויש מי שאומר מקודם עזרא,וזה שאמרנו: בצורתן ושמותן. אבל ענינם ממשה מסיני כמו תורה שבעל פה, והיו על פה כותבין תיבות הפסוק בלא מלכים ולא טעמים וקורין אותו כתקון כמו ששמעו ממשה . . . וכן קבלו איש מפי איש. וכיון שראו שהתחילה הגלות ונתבלבלה הלשון עמדו וסמנום וחקקום ונקדו בהן החומשין כדי שילמדום הכל במהרה ותהיה הלשון הכל צחה בלשון הקדש על פי הדקדוק ששמעו ממשה מסיני.» (My emphasis—*M.G.*) "If someone says: Who invented these vowels and accents and who fixed the forms as we have them now—let him know, to begin with, that their form was decided on by the later generations who said: This is the form of a *qamaṣ* or a *pataḥ* . . . So they all agreed and made the signs for learning and teaching purposes [*sic*]. Some say that the writing down and invention of graphic signs occurred in the days of Ezra . . . and some say before him. But the matter itself comes from Moses on Sinai and was oral tradition like the Oral Law. One wrote without vowels and accents, but read them, just as one heard it from Moses . . . and they handed them from generation to generation. But once they saw that the Diaspora had started and that the language had become confused [Because of נתבלבל in this text I slightly twisted the translation of תשתת above—*M.G.*], they began to mark them and to fix them and they vocalized the codices so that everyone could quickly learn them and use a correct language according to the exact way they had heard from Moses on Sinai."

Allowing for the difference of eleven or twelve centuries, these medieval descriptions are truer to the substance of the facts than the theories of Kahle. For another interesting aspect of medieval attitudes I refer meanwhile to the text in Levy, *Zur Masoretischen Grammatik*, לה.

56. I need not add that the emphasis on the true traditional character of the Tiberian Bible text does not in any way detract from the value of other oral traditions—"dialects," so to speak—whether they were written down or not (see above, §6). That the other traditions finally bowed to the Tiberian Bible text and that the superiority of קראה אלשאמי became universally recognized (cf. Yaᶜqūb al-Qirqisānī, *Kitāb al-ᵓAnwār*, I, 139) is the outcome of historical circumstances, although the feeling that the Babylonian tradition was less accurate (תנבטת קראתהם, *loc. cit.*) is noteworthy. But the fact that it *did* happen seems to me another important indication against Kahle's thesis. See below, Note 118.

57. As is evident from many passages in Baer-Strack, *Die Dikduke*, etc., and from Moses Ben Asher's remarks. See also above, Note 18.

58. This point ought to be stressed because even in the latest discussion of this apparent contradiction (M. Zucker's refutation of B. Klar, *Tarbiz* 27:63f. [1958]) the matter has not been fully explored. As for the views of the Masoretes themselves on the graphic notation, the analysis of the sources adduced by Klar (*Tarbiz* 14:156f. [1943]; 15:36f. [1944], collected in his posthumous *Meḥqārīm wə-ᶜIyyūnīm* [Tel-Aviv, 1954], pp. 276ff.), A. Dothan (*Sinai* 41:280f., 350f. [1957]), Zucker (*Tarbiz* 27:63f.) and Kahle (*JJS* 7:140 [1956]) make me definitely side with all the latter against Klar's contention that the Masoretes themselves believed the graphic signs to be old. (This does not mean that I accept, for example, all the details of Dothan's remarks.) What the Masoretes believed was that the *accents* and so on were old, but not so their *signs*. No quotation adduced

the novelty of the graphic notation[59] which explains, in my opinion, all contemporaneous statements on the subject.[60]

26. In order to avoid unnecessary discussions, let us state that our understanding of the activities of the Masoretes does not deny that the very process of fixing a final graphic notation possibly necessitated certain very minor adjustments which might have been sometimes against the oral custom (of a minority or the majority of Masoretes ?). In certain matters of accentuation—especially with regard to *gaᶜyas*, the vast majority of the *ḥillufim* (see below, Note 109)—the *Systemzwang* might have been strong.[61] But it is precisely the fact ignored until now that such minute differences were noted down with unbelievable exactness and that different Tiberian graphic notations turn out on examination to represent identical phonetic systems (see below, Section VII) that proves the underlying practically uniform[62] oral tradition, common to all, which is the basis of our Tiberian Bible text.

To my knowledge it has never been spelled out that all the much publicized differences in graphic habits[63] among all the Tiberian Masoretes, as far as our knowledge goes, never amounted to more than shades of

necessitates Klar's assumption and, as a personal conviction, I would never assume without clinching arguments that scholars did not know what had happened a few generations before their time. After all, the matter was known in roughly contemporaneous Responsa (cf. Klar, *Tarbiz* 14 : 170, who raises the problem of the authorship of certain Responsa).

59. A good formulation is given by the anonymous author quoted in *Maḥzor Vitry* (cf. Klar, *loc. cit.*, p. 170). While it is continuously quoted in connection with the three vocalization systems its main subject is easily neglected: שטעמי נגינות הם שנאמרו למשה. ... אבל סימני הנגינות סופרים הוא שתקנום, ולפיכך אין נקוד טברני דומה לנקוד שלנו ולא שניהם דומים לנקוד ארץ ישראל. "The cantillation *accents* were, indeed, revealed to Moses . . . but the *signs* [My italics—*M.G.*] were arranged by the Scribes, and for this reason the Tiberian vocalization is not like ours and both are different from the Palestinian one."

60. The Ḳaraite attitude remains to be discussed (see my *Nosaḥ ha-Miqrā*). For the moment suffice it to state (with a reference to Qirqisānī) that the belief in the antiquity of the graphic signs was by no means the accepted Ḳaraite theory around 900 C.E.

61. To give another example: I think it possible that some adjustments were made in questions of the realization of the *zero vowel* after faucals. This is a very far cry from Kahle's theory of "restitution." See Note 64.

62. In certain cases the fixation in writing, accepted by all, surely tended to obscure traditional differences in pronunciation. The *locus classicus* is for me the document republished in Levy, *Zur masoretischen Grammatik* (cf. his pp. 20 and 31 and, earlier, J. Mann, *The Jews in Egypt and in Palestine*, II [London, 1922], 43) that the spelling שתי obscured the tradition of pronouncing *əštē* etc., as pronounced by Ben Asher himself and all other "Tiberians": וגמיע אהל טבריה הד׳א מעהם באלתלקין ואן כאן עלתה לא יערפונהא ולא יעלמון מא הי—"All Tiberians have this by oral teaching even if they do not know its reason."

63. This includes what I think is a Ben Naftali text as well as what Kahle thinks it is. See below, Section VII. Our statement does not deal, of course, with the classical issue of *Inconsequenzen der hebräischen Punktation*.

phonetic realization,[64] one vowel-phoneme (possibly)[65] and the "famous contraction" to *wī*, *lī*, *yē*.[66] To that degree did the Masoretes succeed in disguising the origins of their "artificial invention," until they were unmasked by Kahle.

V. Mishael's *Ḥillufim* and the Ben Asher Codices

27. Having dealt with the origins out of which the work of the Ben Ashers grew, we now have to turn to the codices themselves which are linked

64. The vast literature on the problem of pronouncing *shəva*/*ḥaṭaf*—i.e., the question of free variants of the zero vowel—makes it clear that this was regarded as the gravest problem. In number, of course, the differences on the *gaᶜya* overshadowed everything else. See Note 109.

65. I am paraphrasing mainly the statement about the differences between the Masoretes (Levy, *Zur masoretischen Grammatik*, י): קד אכ׳תלפוא פי אשיא כת׳ירה מן קמץ ופתח ותנתין ולת׳לת׳ה ושוא סאכן ושוא מתחרך. "They differed in many matters with regard to *qamaṣ* and *pataḥ*, *ṣere* and *segol*, quiescent and mobile *shəva*."

While the opposition of the graphemes ‥ versus ∵ cannot be said to be phonemic in the Tiberian Bible text—although there are signs of a beginning phonemization—the opposition - versus ꞊ certainly is. It is conceivable that some of the early Tiberian Masoretes tried, indeed, to represent graphically another tradition which did not have the opposition [å]:[a]—a tradition later on to be labeled "Sefardi"; see Notes 54, 109, and 112. But I doubt that this was felt as a problem within the Tiberian Bible text, or that within that earlier tradition out of which the Tiberian text grew there was a problem as to the phonemic opposition between these vowels. However, although the question does not seem to have been studied until now, I should like to point out that a case can be made out for the Tiberian Bible text type of vocalization being secondary to a "Tiberian grapheme" system which in fact was "proto-Sefardi"; for the way in which all ancient manuscripts write the *qamaṣ* (̄) gives some food for thought. Cf. also Notes 109, 112.

I doubt, however, that this whole problem did exist within the Tiberian Bible text tradition. That is, although I have taken care to indicate the possibility in the text, I believe that within the Tiberian Bible text tradition there were no phonemic oppositions. The text adduced before would hardly have mentioned this matter in such an incidental fashion; moreover, arguments about such a problem would have left their mark in quite a different way. In my opinion, these differences within the Tiberian Bible text refer to exactly the type of *hillufim* quoted for Ben Asher–Ben Naftali, mainly dependent on the degree of stress. See below, Note 109.

To the problem hinted at above, I should like to add that the question of a "proto-Sefardi" vocalization—not merely a reading tradition, which would be obvious—has been on my mind for some time. "Proto-" is to be understood in a similar way to the now already fashionable "Proto-" traditions of the "Latter" Greek versions. (For the Syriac versions see my *Text and Language*, p. 198.) The question is tied up with the "Palestinian" use of graphemes, but our "Tiberian" manuscripts known at present are of too late a date, and arguments are bound to lead to a vicious circle. Were our paleographic knowledge larger, we might at least find out a little more about the vexing question: in what places did reading habits conflict with the intention of scribes to reproduce the "official" Tiberian Bible text? While "geographical paleography" is still a dream, it need not be pointed out—especially after the work of scholars like H. Yalon and Y. G. F. Gumpertz—that "Sefardi" is simply an a posteriori label, both in the historic and in the "prehistoric" (i.e., before 900 C.E.) dimensions. For the whole issue—also with regard to Sperber's claims in *HUCA* 16:450 (1941)—see my *Nosaḥ ha-Miqrā*. See also above, Notes 17 and 21 and my "Biblical Manuscripts," pp. 42f., 47f.

66. The *ḥilluf wəyi* > *wī*, *yəye* > *yē* etc. is, of course, the major phonetic difference between Ben Asher and Ben Naftali. See below, Note 108.

with their name, as well as to Mishael Ben ᶜUzziel's famous treatise on the differences (*ḥillufim*) between Ben Asher and Ben Naftali.

For the last quarter of a century Mishael's treatise had become the proof-stone used by Kahle—especially thanks to the investigations of his student Lipschütz[67]—and others to investigate the possible Ben Asher character of a manuscript. There can be no doubt that Mishael's treatise is largely superior to other lists of differences between the versions of Ben Asher and Ben Naftali[68] and in the first days of our investigation of the Aleppo Codex it was a most welcome help. I feel therefore guilty of ingratitude if I have to stress now that the readings of Mishael prove in no way a rival to the Aleppo Codex. In fact, as regards our knowledge of the Ben Asher text, it has practically become superfluous through the Aleppo Codex.[69] This does not mean that the details of Mishael's list are not instructive or need not be published.[70] But the main importance of the list lies now in its Ben Naftali readings (see Notes 68 and 87). Since the character of the Aleppo Codex has been established, the procedure must be reversed. It is the Aleppo Codex that is now our yardstick for judging the character of other manuscripts—and for judging Mishael.[71]

28. This claim has to be explained. Given the result that the treatise of Mishael has been shown to be generally correct in its quotations of Ben Asher readings, we must ask: "Do these readings practically reflect the text of the Aleppo Codex, or do they differ considerably from it?" If the latter were the case, we would have to explore seriously the possibility that there was in existence *another* text attributed to Aaron Ben Asher,

67. In his introduction and edition of *Ben Ašer–Ben Naftali* (1935). Owing to the persecution in Germany, the dissertation was never published in full. See Note 70.

68. Cf. also H. Yalon, *Kiryat Sefer* 30:258 (1955). To my knowledge, no one has ever seriously troubled to find out whether all the other lists of *ḥillufim*—many of which were published in Ginsburg's *Massorah, s.v.* חלופים—are really as worthless as they were made out to be (cf. Lipschütz, *Ben Ašer–Ben Naftali*, pp. 2f.). The main problem is that we have few means of finding out which of the *ḥillufim* contained in these and not contained in Lipschütz are true ones and whether they have been handed down correctly. However, with the help of the Aleppo Codex some material can probably be salvaged. This would by now be important mainly for the readings of Ben Naftali.

69. The *ḥillufim* remain of practical interest for the Ben Asher text only in the part which is already published—because it is missing in the Aleppo Codex—and in its few readings in the end of the Hagiographa.

70. I understand that the original editor, Lipschütz, who was forced to discontinue his publication (see Note 67), is now ready to publish the whole treatise. [May 1962: Published just recently through the Hebrew University Bible Project, *Textus* 2: אff. (Jerusalem, 1962); see below, Note 109.] In *Hebräischer Bibeltext*, p. 16, Kahle announced that Lacave also is preparing an edition—which seems unnecessary duplication. However, at this stage it is the checking of Mishael's list against the Aleppo Codex on which all the results depend. The data as analyzed by me will be given in *Nosaḥ ha-Miqrā*.

71. I have hinted at this in *Text and Language*, p. x.

apart from the Aleppo Codex, considered equally authoritative, so that a Masoretic scholar like Mishael could use it for his list. That would be a strong indication against the unique position we claim for the Aleppo Codex and might mean that we cannot reach the archetype of the text of Aaron Ben Asher (see my *Text and Language*, pages 156f.)

29. The opposite is the case. A comparison of the whole of Mishael's text to the Aleppo Codex yields about one to two per cent discrepancies. It would be, indeed, against sound practice to make these astonishingly few differences bear the weight of such a far-going hypothesis as suggested above (for argument's sake only). The solution is self-evident: the Aleppo Codex is an original autograph. Mishael's list, as we possess it, is as good a tool as we can hope for. But it is a *copy of a secondary compilation.*[72]

Because of possible future arguments I would like to add that in all publications by Kahle the tenth or eleventh century has been given as the time for Mishael's treatise.[73] It is, however, customary in investigating documents to comment on both the possible date of authorship and of the copy itself. For some reason I do not find that Kahle ever commented on the latter point. A final statement could be made only after examining the original fragments which Kahle used. But a careful analysis of Kahle's transcription makes me suggest that the copy is hardly earlier than the thirteenth century—at least three centuries after the Aleppo Codex.[74] So much for our claim that in spite of its superiority to other lists Mishael's

72. It is difficult to know whether Mishael's original list looked different from the copy we possess. But the astonishing unevenness in adducing readings—sometimes one reading for a large number of chapters leaving serious lacunae, make one wonder what degree of exhaustiveness the author had intended. Or was it just a checklist for scribes? The fact as such as been noted by Lipschütz, *Ben Ašer–Ben Naftali*, pp. 6f.

It certainly strikes one as ironical that the first *ḥilluf* quoted in the "official" technical literature on the Pentateuchal text is not included in Lipschütz. It is quoted by Menaḥem di Lonzano, ᵓ*Or Torah* (Homburg, 1738) on Gen. 1:14 יהי מארת. See below, Note 121.

73. There is no proof for that date but also none against it. Cf. A. Ben David in *Beth Miqrā* 3:17f. (1958). The eleventh century is possible as a *terminus ante quem*, but is not proved. Kahle's suggestion of the tenth century (since *Masoreten des Westens*, II, 60*) is a guess which has not gained force from repetition.

74. My claim is mainly based on the following fact. In Kahle's transcript I find a number of interchanges of *segol-pataḥ*, e.g.:
אֶל באפך (Jer. 10:24), ונבוכדרַצר (Dan. 3:2; Jer. 34:1), ואַתן נזם (Ezek. 16:12) ואַקח לי (Zech. 11:7), אַשתחוה (Ps. 5:8) ואל תַאטר, (Ps. 69:16) etc.

[May 1962: None of these is given in the edition of Lipschütz; see above, Note 70, and below, Note 109.] They are too numerous to be simple mistakes and he must have copied these from the manuscripts (without being aware, at the time, of their importance as evidence). If so, the fragments must be of Yemenite provenance. This leaves the thirteenth century as *terminus post quem* for our copy. This analysis disposes of all exaggerated claims which anyone might care to put forward with regard to our copy of Mishael.

treatise is obviously far from being perfect.[75] In any event we are not entitled to assume because of the few discrepancies that Mishael's list bears witness to another Ben Asher tradition.

30. Our next step is to find out whether our claim for the Aleppo Codex is invalidated by the only other complete codex of the Bible connected with Aaron Ben Asher's name in a colophon: the Leningrad Codex.

If we follow Kahle's pronouncements on the subject carefully, there can be no doubt that he accepted the Leningrad Codex, in the first place, as a basis for the third edition of the Stuttgart Biblia Hebraica only *faute de mieux*. Even though he had never seen more than the photograph of the one page of the Aleppo Codex, he would have preferred to use the Aleppo Codex.[76] However, once the Leningrad Codex had to be chosen, its value rose slowly but steadily in consecutive descriptions, until it became the primary Ben Asher text.[77] But for our recovery of the true Ben Asher text, the Leningrad Codex would have stood unchallenged and all other manuscripts of the Tiberian Bible text would have been judged by it.[78]

Our earlier study[79] left no doubt that the Leningrad Codex is no rival to the Aleppo Codex and that it should not be used as a yardstick to measure other manuscripts. In the best case we might take its colophon at its face value and make the codex a copy harmonized with the Ben Asher text according to some copies which bore Ben Asher's name.[80] But it is clear by now that the Leningrad Codex was basically not a Ben Asher codex. It was secondarily brought into harmony with a Ben Asher *Vorlage* by

75. From a different angle Ben David (*Beth Miqrā* 3:17f.) has come to a similar result, without any connection with the problem of the Aleppo Codex.

76. See the introduction to the Biblia Hebraica, p. vi.

77. In Kahle's *Hebräischer Bibeltext*, p. 9, we finally come upon the unbelievable statement that the Leningrad Codex is the "älteste vollständige Ben Ascher–Handschrift." Or does Kahle wish to elevate the Leningrad Codex to that position because the Aleppo Codex has recently been mutilated by vandals? (See President Ben-Zvi's description, *Textus* 1:1f. [1960].)

78. This is not quite correct. Without having the Aleppo Codex at his disposal, Yalon had become suspicious of the many erasures in the Leningrad Codex (*Kiryat Sefer* 30:259 [1955]; cf. *ibid.* 32:100 [1957]). See also F. Perez-Castro, *Sefarad* 15:27f. (1955). Kahle says now (*Hebräischer Bibeltext*, p. 77) that the corrections and erasures were known to the editors of the Biblia Hebraica. It might have been useful to state all the facts thirty years ago. From R. Kittel's introduction to the Biblia Hebraica (p. iv) these could hardly be inferred.

79. See my "Authenticity of the Aleppo Codex," §13f. See also Löwinger, *Textus* 1:64f. (1960).

80. See above, Note 34. For the moment I do not wish to press the point that the Leningrad Codex has a colophon in the first person singular which does not put forward the claim of connection with Ben Asher (fol. 474a). It is the colophon in the third person (fol. 479a) that does this. At the time of writing I have no means of checking on the question of handwriting.

endless erasures and changes. This procedure is, in my opinion, of great importance as proof for the status which Aaron's text must have had in the generation after he passed away and should be taken as strengthening our claims as to his position (see below, Note 91). The Leningrad Codex was turned very successfully into a Ben Asher codex and was not too bad a substitute. But it stands to reason that if no direct copy can be a rival to the archetype, a harmonized manuscript can do this even less well. We have no way of knowing whether the deviations of the Leningrad Codex from the Aleppo Codex can even be taken to represent the readings of Ben Asher codices (assumed for argument's sake) of *parts* of the Bible.[81] But surely they challenge the unique position of the Aleppo Codex.

As matters stand today we have no right to assume that the Leningrad Codex represents in any way a genuine Ben Asher tradition where it differs from the Aleppo Codex.[82] Needless to add, that this makes its reproduction as the basic text of a new scholarly edition of the Bible an anachronism.[83]

31. None of our sources, then, disproves the unique position we have claimed for the Aleppo Codex—although I should like to stress that there is naturally no possibility of obtaining clinching positive proof. While the codices of *parts* of the Bible are still of interest, we can study at the moment only British Museum Or. 4445[84] and have to wait until the Leningrad

81. It should be stressed that for my general hypothesis I do not have to assume that there was no other authentic Ben Asher tradition apart from the Aleppo Codex. It happens to be a fact that there remains no basis for such an assumption and, as far as we can see now, there is no text which clearly represents such a tradition. Were we to find such a manuscript, it could be taken as representing other codices by Ben Asher of parts of the Bible. Note that the colophons speak of ספרים מוגהים in the plural, and the copyist surely did not intend to present an eclectic text-edition of Ben Asher codices! I speak of colophons in the plural because of the codex from Tschufutkale (allegedly written in 989 C.E.; referred to in Baer-Strack, *Dikduke*, p. xxvii). For the time being the matter of the genuineness of that codex from Firkowich's collections must naturally be left in abeyance. (This question should not be confused with the completely different issue of fifteenth-century Yemenite manuscripts; see below, Note 133, and my "Biblical Manuscripts," pp. 47f.)

At the moment it is anybody's guess whether any other manuscript in the Firkowich collections puts forward similar claims and whether the suspiciously similar wording is a sign of early widespread esteem for Aaron Ben Asher—or whether it indicates Firkowich's tampering with the colophon. See above, Note 23, and my "Biblical Manuscripts," p. 50.

82. I need hardly add that this is different from the negative judgment passed on the Leningrad Codex by A. Harkavy and later by J. L. Teicher. Cf. A. E. Harkavy and H. L. Strack, *Catalog der hebräischen Bibelhandschriften der Kaiserlichen Öffentlichen Bibliothek in St. Petersburg* (St. Petersburg, 1875), pp. 263f.; Teicher, *JJS* 2:20f. (1950). See also below, Note 89.

83. Just as an eclectic edition of the text of the "Ben Asher family" would be. See my "Authenticity," n. 55, and below, Note 90.

84. The most exhaustive study of sample passages of that codex is the somewhat unknown article of A. Ramirez, *Biblica* 10:200ff. (1929), 11:108ff. (1930), 14:303ff. (1933). On this occasion I should like to query the statement, copied by one author from

material mentioned by Kahle in *Masoreten des Westens* (I, 56f.) becomes available again.

After examining the British Museum codex in the original I have no doubt that this is not a harmonized manuscript—there are, of course, the normal few erasures. But I am afraid I cannot agree that it could be a substitute for the missing part of the Aleppo Codex. To be sure, it is very close to the subsystem of Ben Asher, and if we put the (wrong) alternatives: Ben Asher or Ben Naftali—according to Lipschütz's *Mischael*—it definitely looks like Ben Asher.[85] But one of the valuable aspects of Mishael's list is that it also lists cases where Ben Asher and Ben Naftali agree against some other Masorete who, generally speaking, belonged to the same tradition. In a certain number of cases British Museum Or. 4445 agrees with such a reading which is neither Ben Asher nor Ben Naftali.[86]

In this case our investigation leads, indeed, to a clear result which is no less astonishing: as far as our present knowledge of manuscripts goes, the Aleppo Codex is not just the superior known representative of Aaron Ben Asher's text; *it is the only known true representative.*

VI. Moses Ben Asher and Moses Ben Naftali

32. The next step must be to examine anew the relationship of the Aleppo Codex—and the codices which are similar to it—with the Cairo Codex of the Prophets written by Aaron's father, Moses Ben Asher. This question is inextricably bound up with the age-old problem of the so-called Masoretic rival systems of Ben Asher and Ben Naftali.

Even though we objected (above, §29) to any possible claims for absolute correctness on the part of Mishael's list, we nevertheless found it to be an excellent working tool. If its quotations from Ben Asher are, in

the other (Ramirez, 10:203), that the Masoretic annotator of that manuscript must have lived during the lifetime of Aaron Ben Asher. The alleged reason is the lack of the eulogistic formula when Ben Asher is mentioned in the margin. In my opinion this is an unsatisfactory criterion to prove the age of a document. No one has ever shown that a note, supposedly written in the tenth century, mentioning somebody's name in the margin (not in a colophon!) should have added the formula if the person mentioned was no longer alive.

85. I hinted at this in *Text and Language*, p. x, by calling both the Leningrad Codex and British Museum Or. 4445 *codices mixti* from the point of view of the Aleppo Codex. See also below, §42f.

86. Perez-Castro (*Sefarad* 15:27f.) seems to have neglected this necessary part of the examination. For this reason the British Museum Codex seemed to him more of a Ben Asher text than it actually is. I understand from J. Yeivin that he has meanwhile come to similar conclusions with regard to the character of the British Museum manuscript, whereas Löwinger (*Textus* 1:93) takes the latter as the best possible Ben Asher text to serve as a complement to the Aleppo Codex.

the main, correct, it stands to reason that a similar degree of correctness should be assumed for its quotations from Ben Naftali. The latter we must, for the moment, accept solely on the authority of Mishael,[87] since we possess no manuscript which claims, or is proved to represent, the text of Ben Naftali.[88] Mishael's list is then by necessity our sole proven criterion.

33. It is precisely this decisive document that seems to cast suspicion on the oldest dated Biblical manuscript in our possession: the Cairo Codex of the Prophets. For, judging by Mishael's list, the Cairo Codex is much more a Ben Naftali manuscript than a Ben Asher manuscript. In fact, but for the colophon, the Cairo Codex would have surely been acclaimed as the outstanding distinguished representative of the Ben Naftali tradition. Hence we are led, so it seems, to the logical conclusion that the colophon of this earliest dated Hebrew Bible manuscript is a forgery.[89]

87. Hence our statement above (§ 27) that the main importance of Mishael's list now lies in its quotations from Ben Naftali.

88. See my statement in *Text and Language*, pp. ix f. No one seems to have considered the possibility that there was never such a thing as a "pure" Ben Naftali manuscript and that Ben Naftali's main contribution was to compile his dissenting annotations on the Ben Asher tradition, to which he adhered in general (see below, Note 117). There is nothing to prove such an assumption, but for that matter nothing to disprove it either, and we should at least be aware of the possibility. In fact, I doubt very much whether Ben Naftali ever produced a model codex of the complete Bible comparable in its scope to the Aleppo Codex. See below, Note 100.

On the other hand, the fragment (Strack, *Zeitschrift für die Lutherische Theologie*, 36:617; in Baer-Strack, *Dikduke*, p. xii) of which Kahle (*Masoreten des Westens*, II, 50*) tried to dispose in order to develop his own theory (see below, Section VII), and on which Ben Naftali's name apparently occurs, is still a possibility as a Ben Naftali text. However, the matter cannot be proved. The whole issue hinges on exactly one accent, and this is hardly enough to go by. Yeivin has recently discussed the problem (*Tarbiz* 29:346 [1960]), and his conjecture as to that one accent is borne out by Mishael's list.

Incidentally, I would think that after Mishael we must finally accept Moses Ben David Ben Naftali as the correct name (not Jacob Ben Naftali, as accepted especially on the authority of Levita, who, in any case, did not know too much about Ben Naftali; see below, Notes 109, 133). The above fragment is obviously defective, and to call Ben Naftali David Ben Naftali, as Yeivin does, may cause additional confusion.

All the other manuscripts recently suggested as possibly from Ben Naftali's hand are by necessity at best *codices mixti*. Cf. Yalon, *Kiryat Sefer* 30:258f.; Perez-Castro, *Homenaje a Millas-Vallicrosa*, II (Barcelona, 1950), 141f., and Yeivin, *Tarbiz* 29:346. See also Ben David, *Beth Miqrā* 3:15 (1958). Sassoon Codex 507 may come nearest to the subsystem connected with Ben Naftali's name. See below, §42f.

89. For the most recent accusations along these lines and my position, see my "Authenticity," nn. 55, 15. Löwinger (*Textus* 1:93) tries to solve the problem by assuming that the Cairo Codex is "a secondary copy made on the basis of a manuscript written at the time by Moses ben Asher, but that during the process of copying, fundamental changes in punctuation and accents were made on the basis of considerations unknown to us." This is nothing else but denying the colophon of the Cairo Codex. It should be stated that during the last decade only Kahle has stood up against this trend.

For our purpose it is immaterial whether we assume a forgery or the transfer of the colophon from another manuscript. These doubts with regard to the Cairo Codex are, of course, again materially different from those of nineteenth-century scholars who denied

In my opinion, this type of solution to our difficulties should never be suggested except as a very last resort, the more so since scholars are apparently prone by nature to prove their critical acumen by casting suspicions on our most distinguished and ancient sources (see above, Note 44). My own thesis is, I submit, a bit less drastic. To my mind it is our own habit of talking of a "Ben Asher text"—without qualifying *which* Ben Asher, and tacitly assuming the identity of the texts of father and son[90]—that has created this problem which has led, in the last instance, to accusations of forgery or willful tampering.

34. Medieval scholars talking of Ben Asher were exclusively referring to the one whose text had become the final authority. Once history had been changed through the great achievement of a complete Bible codex, all earlier attempts became prehistory, and no one bothered much about Aaron's father.[91]

---

the Ben Asher relationship because the early codices did not fit the Baer–Wickes rules on the *metheg*. See above, Note 82, and my "Authenticity," §3f. For that view see A. Neubauer, *Studia Biblica et Ecclesiastica*, 3:25 (1891). In this case, too, Strack did not accept the judgment, but again gave no reasons; see my "Authenticity," n. 14.

I cannot help directing the reader's attention to the commonsense remark of Richard Gottheil (*JQR* 18:566 [1906]), who never claimed to be an authority on the Masora, against the absurd results of critics (see above, Note 44). According to the authorities of the day, he muses, the same strange fate has overcome our two most ancient Hebrew Bible manuscripts. Both the codex of the father (Cairo Codex) and the codex of the son (Aleppo Codex) have turned out to have forged colophons!

90. This tacit assumption has, in my opinion, misled Cassuto and made him attempt a reconstruction of a text which never existed (see my "Authenticity," n. 55, and Note 83, above). Kahle, on the other hand, wishes to minimize the differences between the Aleppo and Cairo codices so as to make Aaron into almost the copyist of his father's work. Although he allows for slight changes of mind—Or. 4445 is for him a "Text aus Ahron ben Ascher's früherer Zeit" (*Hebräischer Bibeltext*, p. 77)—the Ben Asher text is basically one entity, and the Cairo Codex is just a "Ben Ascher Kodex aus noch früherer Zeit." See also next note.

91. This does not mean that all authors knew who was who and that some nonspecialist did not sometimes confuse the two. Such mistakes can also happen to modern scholars (see my "Authenticity," nn. 2, 24). For the general problem of the Cairo Codex, see "Authenticity," §20f.

I should, however, like to voice strongest dissent from a remarkable position recently adopted by Kahle. While everyone will agree that Moses Ben Asher was "one of the prominent Masoretes," as Kahle used to call him (my reference at the moment is to his chapter in Goldschmidt, *Earliest Editions of the Hebrew Bible* [1950], p. 49), it seems an extraordinary coincidence that since the Aleppo Codex was made available to serve as the basis for the new edition of the Bible, Kahle insists on repeatedly referring to Moses as "*the prominent* Masorete" and practically turns his son into his amanuensis. In *VT* 10:35 (1960), Moses has become the "Hauptmasoret von Tiberias" and in *Hebräischer Bibeltext*, p. 76, the "Prominenteste der Masoreten."

This flies in the face of all the evidence (cf. above, §15). Kahle cannot get rid of the judgment of generations by a mere stroke of his pen. Similarly he might have learned from the volume of *Textus* (which he quotes, *Hebräischer Bibeltext*, p. 83) that the opposite is true of what he claims: "Eine genaue Gegenüberstellung der beiden Texte hat ergeben,

We have stated before (above, §10f.) that the ninth century was (at least until 900 C.E. and slightly after that) a time of *individual* creations, each Masorete refining the notation and sifting the material assembled before him. These were not yet stereotyped works of copyists who worked from accepted models, but the very personal creations of "Masters of the Masora" on the basis of their lifelong studies. The graphic notation was in a constant process of refinement.[92] Even though the founder of the Ben Asher dynasty and his contemporaries—a century and more before Aaron Ben Asher—had taken decisive steps toward refining the notation and had taught their system to their sons and disciples, yet the "young" Ben Ashers, Moses and Aaron, were still busy perfecting it. Both were masters in their own right, and nothing on earth could stop them from holding certain different opinions as regards some minutiae—and minutiae they were.[93] It was Moses' bad luck that only his son, standing no doubt on his father's shoulders, made the final step and produced the complete model codex.

We have no reason to doubt the tradition that the scribe[94] of the Cairo Codex was the father of the scribe of the Aleppo Codex. But there is no reason whatsoever why the son should merely have copied his father,[95] nor why the father should have written his codex according to the subsystem finally perfected and adopted by his son.

35. In our view there is no need to expect the Cairo Codex to conform in

---

dass der Aleppo Kodex in allen Einzelheiten [*sic*] von Text und Vokalisation genau mit dem Kairoer Prophetenkodex übereinstimmt. Das ergab aber mit Sicherheit, dass der Aleppo Kodex im wesentlichen auf die Fassung des Kairoer Prophetenkodex zurückgeht und auf ihm beruht und dass als der *massgebende Mann für den tiberischen* Bibeltext durchaus der Vater Mosche ben Ascher anzusehen ist" [My italics].

In order to avoid any misunderstanding of my position, I should stress that I regard the Cairo Codex as a most valuable source, the importance of which for our understanding of the history of the Tiberian Bible text is perhaps, in its way, equal to that of the Aleppo Codex. But the Cairo Codex *was not the model for our textus receptus*. (Cf. below, §42f.) It was the bad luck of Moses Ben Asher that he did not succeed where his son was to succeed—which would have made him into The Masorete. But this was not what happened, and in the judgment of later generations it was Aaron who was regarded as "the most prominent Masorete." Kahle will have to explain away all the facts before his claim will be acceptable.

92. The developments which we can trace in Babylonian punctuation may give an idea of the developments which led up to the Cairo and Aleppo codices. But this is no more than a possible illustration.

93. See for this issue, Note 64f. above and Note 109 below.

94. For our purpose it is immaterial whether we speak of scribe, author, etc., and whether the Masorete also wrote the consonantal text.

95. See above, §15. The formulation in the text Levy, *Zur masoretischen Grammatik*, p. ט, אברהם ריקאט וריקאט אבוה מן קבלה ("Abraham Riqaṭ and his father Riqaṭ before him") might provide an interesting parallel.

all its details to the system of the Aleppo Codex. Consequently, all the suspicions raised against the Cairo Codex are baseless.[96]

Yet one question remains. If the Cairo Codex need not conform to the Ben Asher column of Mishael's list, it seems extraordinary that it conforms so much better to the Ben Naftali column. How, then, can we account for what seems the Ben Naftali character of the Cairo Codex?

36. This alleged character of the Cairo Codex is, in my opinion, history turned topsy-turvy. The tiny differences between Aaron Ben Asher and Moses Ben Asher were not their inventions. They handed on, each in his own slightly different way, some earlier tradition. What finally became crystallized and connected to the name of Ben Naftali was essentially the tradition of his predecessors, among them Moses Ben Asher, even though Ben Naftali probably deviated in some minutiae. But for the fact that history made that subsystem finally stick to the name of Ben Naftali—just as it happened with Aaron Ben Asher—it would not be too far from the truth to speak of the two subsystems inside the Ben Asher family and to term the contrast of readings: *Ben Asher versus Ben Asher.*[97]

Both Aaron Ben Asher and Ben Naftali mark, so to speak, final steps,[98] slightly apart, in the development of that subsystem of Masora, in which the last stage but one has left us only one known representative: the codex of Moses Ben Asher. For illustration's sake one may picture both Aaron and Ben Naftali being educated in the old tradition of the Ben Ashers,[99] both ripening and developing and refining their work, but Ben Naftali in the last instance remaining more faithful to that subsystem to which Aaron's father adhered.[100] Only once the contrast had become finally

96. I am not concerned for the present with the kind of criticism which allows itself any kind of liberty because the author of the document concerned cannot rise from his grave to testify. See also above, Note 44.

97. I have hinted at this in *Text and Language*, p. ix. The formulation here is meant to be provocative, but I think I made it clear that there was, in my opinion, a development from the Cairo Codex to Ben Naftali. My position is therefore different from that of Yeivin (*Tarbiz* 29:345 [1960]) who formulates: "The Ben Naftali text is represented, to a smaller or larger extent, by manuscripts like the Cairo Codex."

98. But we should not forget for a minute that this final development among the master Masoretes does not mark the final development of the text itself, as is shown by the immediate rise of what from their point of view were *codices mixti*—the direct ancestors of our *textus receptus*. See below, §43.

99. And those Masoretes whose system was similar. Cf. Levy, *Zur masoretischen Grammatik*, ט.

100. For argument's sake we could work out a theory which would make Ben Naftali a "master Masorete" in the generation before Moses Ben Asher. Certain details would then have to be changed, but the general thesis would not be affected. The possibility is remote. Because of the picture of later sources and the absence of Ben Naftali's name

crystallized into the Ben Asher–Ben Naftali "controversy," could we be misled in retrospective to mistake the Cairo Codex for a manuscript which could not have been written by "a" Ben Asher.

VII. Receptus and Non-Receptus Traditions

37. Our theory assumes that the two traditions, crystallized into the pigeon-hole opposition Ben Asher–Ben Naftali, which seemed two major rival systems of the Tiberian Masora, are basically alike. This is exactly what is borne out by the facts, and it is only on this basis that many readings attributed to Ben Naftali slipped into our "Ben Asher" ***textus receptus*** (see Note 98 and below, §43).

Without going here into all the details[101] I therefore have to add that the type of manuscript accepted on Kahle's authority[102] by practically all scholars to this day as Ben Naftali manuscripts has been wrongly labeled so.[103] These manuscripts—the best known of which is, of course,

---

in the list of Masoretes (cf. Levy, *Zur masoretischen Grammatik*), the only reasonable theory is to make Ben Naftali roughly contemporaneous with Aaron Ben Asher.

We may speculate, of course, on why it was not the subsystem of the Cairo Codex and Ben Naftali that carried off the palm—supposing, for the sake of argument, that Ben Naftali did produce a model codex similar in its way to the Aleppo Codex (see Notes 88, 128) and that our assumption about the novel character of the Aleppo Codex is wrong. It may be, then, that Aaron benefited from his descent from Ben Asher forefathers, while Ben Naftali was an outsider. For all we know, Aaron may have taken after his grandfather and returned to the "original" family tradition. All this is idle speculation. One point, however, already seems quite clear to me (although I should not like to say much before completing the analysis for *Nosaḥ ha-Miqrā*): Ben Naftali's "defeat" is not due to any inherent difference between his system and that of Aaron Ben Asher. (For such a theory, see Ben David, *Tarbiz* 26:384f. [1958].)

101. This subject will be dealt with in a special chapter.

102. Kahle, *Masoreten des Westens*, II, 45*. Much of the work seems to have been carried out by Edelmann.

103. Lipschütz must have realized that Kahle's identification was wrong, but in the published part of his book which I use I cannot find any protest on his part. (However, he was Kahle's student, and this was his dissertation!) A. Sperber obviously did not accept Kahle's idea and finally called those manuscripts "pre-Masoretic." See his "A Grammar of Masoretic Hebrew," *Corpus Codicum Hebraicorum Medii Aevi*, II (I use the 8[vo] edition of his treatise, Copenhagen, 1958; see below, Note 112). S. Morag, *JSS* 4:234 (1959), is clearly against calling the Codex Reuchlinianus a Ben Naftali manuscript, while he regards the problem of Ben Naftali manuscripts in general as outside the scope of his paper (see below, Note 108). Ben David, *Beth Miqrā* 3:415 and *Tarbiz* 26:384f. and Yeivin, *Tarbiz* 29:345 (1960) are the only ones clearly to criticize Kahle. A. Diez-Macho (since *Estudios Biblicos* 15:187f. [1956]) has tried to build his understanding of the issue around the problems of certain "Palestinian" fragments. (To be sure, the possible existence of such a "proto-Ben Naftali" need not have prevented anyone from continuing to talk about Ben Naftali manuscripts. See Note 65, above.)

On the other hand, the latest and most competent summary of our subject (H. Rabin's article on Ben Naftali in *Encyclopedia ʿIvrith*, IX [Jerusalem, 1958], *s.v.* "Ben Naftali") accepts Kahle's view, and Yalon (*Kiryat Sefer* 1957:108) leaves the question open for

the Codex Reuchlinianus 3 (CR = Kennicott 154)[104]—were declared by Kahle to be Ben Naftali manuscripts in the face of the only existing criterion, the very same manuscript which Kahle had used correctly for proving the genuineness of the Ben Asher manuscripts. This refers, it goes without saying, to Mishael's list.

38. For the present suffice it to say that at the very moment when Kahle fully realized the fallacy of medieval compilers of Masoretic lists who reduced variants indiscriminately to the stereotyped contrast Ben Asher–Ben Naftali (see also below, Note 121), and when he recognized the value of Mishael's treatise, he committed a similar error with regard to what he termed Ben Naftali manuscripts. Taking up hints dropped by earlier scholars[105] and closing his eyes to the most conspicuous[106] marks of those manuscripts,[107] he identified them as Ben Naftali manuscripts on the basis of little more than one phonetic isogloss.[108]

---

discussion but neither discusses it nor opposes Kahle. For this reason it seems that Yeivin (*Tarbiz* 29:345) is rather optimistic when he claims that "today the accepted view is that these manuscripts are not by Ben Naftali and not by his school." Agreed—but just by three or four scholars, and it will take some time until Kahle's mistaken identifications will be dropped from the handbooks.

104. To the manuscripts listed by Kahle we have not only to add Prijs, *ZAW* 69:171 (1957), as noted by Yeivin, but also J. Hempel's "Codex Wolters" (*Nachrichten der Göttingen Gesellschaft der Wissenschaften*, 1937, *Phil.-Hist. Klasse, Fachgruppe III*:227f.), which seems to have disappeared from the recent literature. By the way, Hempel naturally accepts Kahle's authority, but with a cautionary note: "Darf man diese Gruppe mit Kahle für Ben Naftali in Anspruch nehmen, so hätten wir im Codex Wolters eine BN-Handschrift zu sehen. . ." For fragments see also my "Biblical Manuscripts."

105. Ginsburg in particular had dealt with the subject (not just "auch bereits"; cf. Kahle, *Masoreten des Westens*, II, 51*f.) The idea of that identification was apparently "in the air" after the Delitzsch-Baer edition of Jeremiah in 1890 (cf. Kahle, *loc. cit.*). Graetz wrote about this type of vocalization in 1887 (*MGWJ* 36:489) and did not know of such a theory.

106. In *Masoreten des Ostens* (1913), p. xvi, he was much more aware of these marks and spoke correctly of "eine besondere Gruppe . . . die, wie es erscheint, weder mit Ben Ascher noch mit Ben Naftali zu tun hat."

107. Because of the importance of the practical unity of all Tiberian systems from the phonetic (and certainly phonemic) point of view (see above, Notes 64f.), it should be stressed again that these are only graphic differences, but most conspicuous ones indeed. See next Note and Note 112.

108. In spite of his wording—which indicates the difference between him and me—Morag was aware of the linguistic question involved when he wrote (*JSS* 4:234): "This comparison shows that only a small number of CR [Codex Reuchlinianus] features in this table can be defined as belonging to the school of Ben Naphtali." In my opinion, there is a clear structural difference between the case of the *dagesh* in בן־נון—a completely isolated instance in the system of Ben Naftali which may or may not link up with the system of some other manuscripts (see Note 116)—and the perpetual syllable indicator in the Codex Reuchlinianus and kindred manuscripts. This leaves us, then, with the haplological contraction *yəye* > *yē*, etc. (see above, Note 66), which must have been quite widespread as a phonetical phenomenon and was certainly not restricted to one particular type of tradition. In other words: the one isogloss is far from being significant.

39. If we, however, leave these alleged Ben Naftali manuscripts aside and turn to the only admissible evidence of Ben Naftali's readings—Mishael's list—there remains no doubt that the two systems are practically one. The judgment of scholars before Kahle, that the lists of *ḥillufim* are, on the main, lists of minutiae, is correct.[109] Although there are a few items

---

The question may, of course, be asked whether this type of contraction was a general phenomenon in Ben Naftali texts (as I believe it was) or whether its notation is meant to indicate that the phenomenon was sporadic and could be found only in the places indicated. If I see correctly, there are fewer than ten places where the *ḥilluf* is attested; cf. Jud. 19:6, 9—Ben Asher, וְיִיטַב; Ben Naftali, "וִיטַב "לא יכ׳רג אליוד" (the *yodh* is not pronounced). There is only one case of haplology with identical consonants, and this is the only case in which the phenomenon does not occur at the juncture after a syntactical prefix; this is (ו)יְיֵלִיל/יֵילִיל in Isa. 16:7 and Hos 7:14. (All other cases after copulative *waw* except Ps. 119:38: לְיִרְאָתֶךָ.) See next Notes.

109. Cf. above, §26, and below, Note 120. The judgment of Ginsburg (*Introduction* [1897], p. 278) is not far from the truth: "It is the presence or absence of the *metheg* or *gaya* which constitutes fully nine-tenths of the differences between these two redactors of the text." (Ben David has echoed this sixty years later in *Beth Miqrā* 3:1f.). Against this basically correct judgment Kahle's identification had assumed much larger differences, which, in their way, although substantially different, were as large as those presupposed some hundreds of years ago. For the idea that Ben Naftali was actually the representative of the readings of the "Orientals"—still echoed by Ginsburg, mainly introduced into scholarly literature on the authority of Levita, *Massoreth ha-Massoreth*, p. 114, but in existence at least as early as Ibn Balʿam (cf. Baer-Strack, *Die Dikduke*, p. 83)—assumed considerable differences by necessity.

For this reason Ginsburg, although he had already become aware of the character of the *ḥillufim* (while still allowing the evidence of certain marginal notes which claimed real textual variants; *Introduction*, p. 246), could still speak of Ben Asher and Ben Naftali as "two rival textual critics, engaged in the redaction of two rival recensions of the Hebrew Bible" (*Introduction*, p. 241).

Nevertheless, there may be a few real textual differences not recorded in Lipschütz, *Ben Ašer–Ben Naftali*, but noted in the margins of ancient codices. The problem is to find out and to prove how trustworthy these are. A good example is the note recurring in the margins of ancient codices (adduced by Strack, *Zeitschrift für die Lutherische Theologie* 36:611 on Jer. 29:22: בן נפתלי: כצדקיהו וכאחב כתיב וכאחיו קרי; בן אשר: וכאחב כתיב וכן קרי. But it is this expression which is recorded elsewhere as part of the *ḥillufim* between "Orientals" and "Occidentals"; cf., e.g., the discussion, in this connection, of S. Pinsker, *Einleitung in das babylonisch-hebräische Punktationsystem* (1863), p. 126. See also C. D. Ginsburg, *The Massorah*, I (London, 1880), p. 595. While such a case illustrates the old (erroneous) identification of the Ben Naftali readings as "Orientals," it also illustrates the difficulties in reclaiming *ḥillufim* not recorded in Mishael.

In general, however, the analysis of all the material in Mishael's list shows that Levita, *Massoreth ha-Massoreth*, p. 114, was actually not wrong in his description of the differences, but his lack of quantitative differentiation between the phenomena (which is indicative of the whole issue) was misleading. He describes: והפלוגתות שביניהן בטעמים אינן אלא בטעמים הקטנים, כגון מתג ומקף ומונח ובפשטא אחד וב׳ פשטין . . . גם הפלוגתות שביניהן בנקודות אינן אלא בחולם ובקמץ חטוף ובקמץ גדול ופתח ובשוא ובחטף פתח וכן בדגשין ורפין ומלעיל ומלרע ("The differences of opinion between them in matters of accent only appear in minor accents, such as *metheg* . . . Also the differences in matters of vocalization are only questions of *ḥolam* and *qamaṣ ḥaṭuf*, etc.")

where the two Masoretes differ in text or vocalization, I am afraid—without being very facetious, I hope—that the vast majority of present-day Bible scholars would not notice without special study any difference in a Ben Naftali manuscript (if there were one in existence).

To give a first idea of the material I summarize the following notes from the list of Mishael.

(a) Addition and omission of *waw* (of course there are always other sources which show the same change): Jer. 7:25: Ben Asher עד היום, Ben Naftali ועד היום; Jer. 11:7 Ben Asher—ועד היום, Ben Naftali—עד היום; Dan. 9:8: Ben Asher למלכינו לשרינו, Ben Naftali למלכינו ולשרינו.

(b) Change of Tetragrammaton: Lam. 5:21: Ben Asher—יהוה, Ben Naftali—אדני.

(c) Change identical with *qere/ketibh* in other sources: Job 6:21: Ben Asher—הייתם לא Ben Naftali—לו.

(d) Orthography in one or two words: Isa. 54:9: Ben Asher—כימי, Ben Naftali—כי־מי; Ps. 48:15: Ben Asher—על־מות, Ben Naftali—עלמות; Cant. 8:6: Ben Asher—שלהבתיה, Ben Naftali—שלהבת־יה.

(The question of the Aleppo Codex versus the Leningrad Codex in these cases needs special discussion.)

(e) Odd differences in matters of *dagesh* which cannot be reduced to a common denominator: Jer. 9:3: Ben Asher—יַ֫עְקֹב Ben Naftali—יַ֫עְקֹּב, (like the Cairo Codex!) reminds us of the tendency to insert a *dagesh* after syllable-final faucals (see Note 116). But it should be stressed that one example in Ben Naftali—supposing that he accepted all the other readings indicative of this tendency which are in Ben Asher—is not really of a sign. I Sam. 16:7: Ben Asher—כי לא, Ben Naftali—כי לּא with *dagesh* (like the Cairo Codex!) is interesting because of the accentuation pattern *in loco*. Job 20:26: Ben Asher—לצפּוניו (thus the Aleppo and Leningrad codices, not as in Biblia Hebraica), Ben Naftali—לצפֿוניו (no *dagesh*) may illustrate a grammatical point. Why Ben Naftali in II Chron. 31:7 has החלֿו without *dagesh* in the *lamedh* I cannot figure out at the moment.

(f) In connection with the *ḥilluf* discussed in the preceding note, Neh. 11:25: Ben Asher—וּבִיַֽקְּבְצְאֵל (with *dagesh* against Ben Naftali) seems important. This kind of indication surely cannot be divorced from Ps. 45:10: Ben Naftali—בְּיִקְּרוֹתֶיךָ (I cannot make out from the transcript whether the Ben Asher form is written with a *dagesh*; cf. Biblia Hebraica). The problem whether there is a Ben Naftali system in this case and whether also in Mishael the two Masoretes could "exchange places" remains to be discussed.

(g) The largest group among the non-accentual *ḥillufim* are changes of vowels, practically all in connection with stress conditions. Well known already are Gen. 41:50; Ben Asher—וליוסף ילַד, Ben Naftali—ילָד and the strange Deut. 31:21: Ben Asher—אשר נשבַעתי (in pause), Ben Naftali—נשבָעתי. Cf. also my "Biblical Manuscripts," pp. 56ff. Ezek 15:15: Ben Asher—ושכלָתה, Ben Naftali—ושכלַתה. Ez. 27:13: Ben Asher—תֻּבַל, Ben Naftali—תובָל, seems a problem of a proper name.

There seems to be only one case with *e*-vowels: Job 9:33: Ben Asher—יֵשׁ בינינו, Ben Naftali—יֶשׁ בינינו (with *segol*). All the other cases deal with the *ḥolam-qamaṣ* series and are to be found, curiously enough, in the three poetic books (Psalms, Proverbs, Job). In this case there is a discernible pattern: an "imperfect"-imperative *qal*-form connected to a complement with *maqqef* is read by Ben Asher with *qamaṣ* and by Ben Naftali with *ḥolam*. Thus: Ps. 49:25: Ben Asher—שְׁפָךְ־עליהם, Ben Naftali—שפֹךְ עליהם;

The very fact that these minutiae were recorded in Mishael's treatise—together with a listing of cases where Ben Asher and Ben Naftali agree (against some other Masorete [see above, §31 and below, Note 117]) proves to me that what had seemed, after Kahle's identifications, a major difference between basically different graphic systems, are nothing but the very last minute differentiations between the exponents of the same school.[110]

40. In the light of what we found I would therefore suggest the following picture of the rise of the Tiberian Bible text.

The earliest stages of the "Tiberian" attempt—as opposed to the "Palestinian"—to note down the oral tradition are unknown to us. We can only assume that the Masoretes, about most of whom we know nothing but their names (see Note 117), gradually refined their system of notation. By the end of the ninth century (?) two main Tiberian systems had emerged, each of which presented the same reading tradition in a graphically different way, by using the same "Tiberian" signs: the one I propose to term *proto-receptus*, the other *non-receptus*.

41. The *non-receptus* tradition is the one used by the Reuchlinianus and kindred manuscripts.[111] While there are obvious differences among these

---

Ps. 121:8: Ben Asher—יִשְׁמָר־צֵאתְךָ, Ben Naftali—יִשְׁמֹר־צֵאתְךָ, and so on. Similarly, Job 3:5: תִּשְׁכָּן־עָלָיו, 24:14: יִקְטָל־עָנִי, Prov. 4:4: יִתְמָךְ־דְּבָרַי. Only in Ps. 10:15, do we find that it is Ben Naftali who has a *qamaṣ* without *maqqef*! The remaining case is also apparently one of *matres*-orthography: Ben Asher spells in both Job 13:27 and 3:11 אָרְחוֹתַי with *qamaṣ*, whereas Ben Naftali spells it with a *waw*.

These are almost all the differences in Mishael with regard to text and vocalization, as far as they can be made out from Kahle's transcript. [May 1962 (see above, Note 70): Between Kahle's transcript and the text now published by Lipschütz there are certain slight differences. The most important one is the lack of the telling vocalization, mentioned above, Note 74. The differences will be discussed, together with the full evaluation of the material, in *Nosaḥ ha-Miqrā*. For the moment I should like to point out that the suspicious *plene* אורחותי of Ben Naftali in Job 13:27, 33:11, is not borne out by the text of Lipschütz. On the other hand, the alleged ציצית of Ben Naftali, in Isa. 28:4 in Lipschütz' text, seems a simple misprint.]

110. That is to say: Ben Naftali is basically an exponent of the tradition of the Ben Ashers (in the plural), and developed in particular the subsystem of which Moses Ben Asher was the outstanding exponent in the generation before him. See also above, Note 100.

111. Just as the ancient codices of the Tiberian Bible text type show clear connections with the Babylonian system (see above, Note 16), it stands to reason that we should search for parallel connections of the *non-receptus* tradition. At present I merely want to hint at the fact that certain features of "Babylonian" manuscripts—including the Codex Petropolitanus of the Prophets (ed. Strack, 1876) and noticed in part already in their own right by Pinsker, *Einleitung*, esp. p. 111—show certain affinities with the *non-receptus* tradition (and kindred types). I suppose that the hint dropped by Ben David (*Leshonenu* 22:21 [1958]) is meant to refer to such features. However, as they stand, the manuscripts of the *non-receptus* tradition have to be regarded as a *Tiberian* system, and not just as a

manuscripts which remain to be analyzed in order to establish possible subsystems, their common features are conspicuous enough to justify our term as a unity—at least for the time being.

These are neither Ben Naftali manuscripts nor are they *pre-Masoretic* or *post-Masoretic*[112] or *non-Masoretic*.[113] They were, in their way, as

---

"Tiberian" counterpart to the opposite phenomenon symbolized by the existence of the Codex Petropolitanus. See below, Note 118.

112. This is to say I agree with Kahle (*Cairo Geniza*, p. 123) and Morag (*JSS* 4:216f.), who do not admit Sperber's claims. On the other hand, I do not agree with Morag when he—perhaps somewhat in a polemical vein—regards these manuscripts as *post-Masoretic* (*JSS* 4:229, 237). While the thesis that a more developed phonetic notation is not only a typological but also a chronological criterion is valid in general (this is not Morag's phrasing, but I think that is what he means), I cannot see why "the *CR* [Codex Reuchlinianus] *vocalization system is far more phonetic in its principles than the usual Tiberian system*" (p. 229, his italics). To be sure, it uses certain graphic devices much more than does the Tiberian Bible text, but this does not make it necessarily "more phonetic." The relationship as regards the graphemic complexity between the two Tiberian systems is *not* similar to the ostensibly parallel problem of the Babylonian systems. I have not found in the tradition of the Codex Reuchlinianus any graphic notation indicative of a phonetic phenomenon not known from the Tiberian Bible text. (If anything, the only partial notation of the *pataḥ furtivum* might have been taken to point to the opposite.)

While I take the *non-receptus* tradition as a whole as chronologically neither earlier nor later than the emergence of the Tiberian Bible text (for this whole issue see also Notes 17, 21, 40, 65), I agree that the particular subsystem as shown by the Codex Reuchlinianus exemplifies a comparatively later stage inside that tradition. My main reason is (but cf. above, Note 65) that the Codex Reuchlinianus does not differentiate between certain vowel graphemes (ַ : ֳ , etc.) which stand in opposition within other manuscripts of that tradition. In my opinion (cf. also Prijs, *ZAW* 69:180 [1957], against Yeivin, *Tarbiz* 29:347), the Codex Reuchlinianus is an example of a particular, comparatively later, subsystem, which is to be judged in accordance with what we have remarked on the "Sefardi" codices (see above, Notes 54, 65). But the *non-receptus* tradition in general is typologically (and probably chronologically) neither pre- nor post-Tiberian Bible text.

This whole problem is bound up not only with the question of early reading traditions in general, but also especially with that of the "Palestinian" vocalization. I might therefore add (see my *Nosaḥ ha-Miqrā*) that because Kahle's claims were widely accepted, the problem of typological versus chronological evaluation, with regard to the Palestinian vocalization, has never been tackled seriously. Kahle's "High chronology" for the Palestinian fragments—which are a decisive part of his theory on the Tiberian text (see above, Note 41)—is exclusively based on a priori evolutional reasoning. Paradoxically, he has always claimed dates but never dealt convincingly with the question of dates of Geniza fragments (see above, Note 21)—presumably because he did not bother much about the Geniza material apart from the fragments with non-Tiberian vocalization (as can be seen from his book entitled "Cairo Geniza"). I am not aware of any paleographical study ever having been carried out by him (or by his followers). Even though the fragments may not be as late as suggested by Ben David (*Kiryat Sefer* 33:484), who has sharply criticized Kahle, also this part of Kahle's theories is without the slightest factual basis. Perhaps the Geniza may yield some further "Palestinian"–Tiberian fragments to help us to solve this problem and to base claims on a sounder paleographical basis. See also "Biblical Manuscripts," pp. 35ff.

113. As Yeivin terms them (*Tarbiz* 29:345f.). Since Mr. Yeivin has been kind enough to arrange for me various collations within the framework of the Hebrew University Bible Project and since we have had the opportunity to discuss many questions of

Masoretic as "our" Tiberian Bible text and were in use, it seems, especially in the Franco-German area, until the thirteenth or fourteenth century.[114] Although they must always have been very rare,[115] it is not impossible that they were finally doomed only by the advent of printing. All this will explain that the least misleading term at the moment seems to be "Tiberian *non-receptus* tradition."

VIII. Prehistory and History of the Tiberian Bible Text

42. No typology can get rid of borderline phenomena. There were, no doubt, mutual influences between the traditions,[116] and yet we can clearly

---

common interest, I might stress, that as regards this subject, each of us has come to his conclusions on his own, both where we differ and where we agree.

114. This is already obvious from the descriptions by Ginsburg, *Introduction*, pp. 556f., 605f., 632f.

115. Since I suspect that there is a local preference, one cannot really judge from the scarcity of fragments of this tradition in the Cairo Geniza. I would estimate that the fragments of *non-receptus* material in the Geniza are less than half of one per cent. For this reason the few ones in existence deserve careful study. See also my "Biblical Manuscripts," pp. 43f.

116. Those manuscripts which consistently put a *dagesh* after a syllable-final faucal and/or in the second of two similar letters need special investigation; see above, Note 108. (The question whether this dot is a *dagesh* should be left open for the moment.) Ben Naftali does not have this system, and the one or two cases in which the Ben Naftali reading has such a "*dagesh*" which is not in the Ben Asher text should not really be taken as suggesting any definite connection. Since Ginsburg's *Introduction* (see also below), this type of manuscript becomes somewhat mixed up with the "pure" *non-receptus* and as far as I can make out at the moment, Yeivin's fragment (*Tarbiz* 29:345f.) also does not belong to the "pure" type. Whatever term we use, in my opinion, these manuscripts which put a *mappiq* in consonantal *alefs* and mark the beginnings of syllables as a constant rule—not just in a very special case—have to be taken as a group by themselves. The importance of the *mappiq* as the essential sign of a certain group was first stressed by L. Prijs, *ZAW* 69:171f. (1957). But Prijs never questions Kahle's identification as such. Whether we can establish any connection between the *non-receptus* manuscripts and those which have a special "*dagesh*" (as mentioned in the beginning of this note) remains to be seen. Certainly, talking of the two systems as "primitive" and "elaborate"—if I interpret some recent suggestions rightly—might again lead us into creating a new evolutional chain without any real basis.

Furthermore, the connection—if there is any—with certain "*dageshes*" of Tiberian Bible text manuscripts has to be examined. What I refer to is the kind of dot which since the time of Michaelis (and later through W. Gesenius' *Lehrgebäude* [Leipzig, 1817] §§3, 19) has been sporadically introduced into grammars under such promising names as *dagesh neutrum, orthophonicum, orthosyllabicum*, etc., sometimes with some censoring remarks of the author that this is an "Übertreibung" (F. Böttcher, *Lehrbuch* [Leipzig, 1866], §227) or "purism" (Ginsburg, *Introduction*, pp. 556f., 605f., 632f.).

The "academic" Hebraists do not seem to be aware of the fact that the Jewish grammarians have had remarks to make on manuscripts of the *non-receptus* type and have been alert to some of its characteristics—at least since the eighteenth century. It is fascinating to follow up this lead which—this much I shall say here—seems to go back to the famous punctuator, Yequtiel Hakohen, who is supposed to have flourished in Prague in the thirteenth century. (To be sure, our term is not meant to indicate that the *non-receptus*

distinguish between the *non-receptus* and the (*proto*)-*receptus* traditions. The *proto-receptus* tradition may for the moment be identified with that of the dynasty of the Ben Ashers (and their adherents), including the *Vorlagen* of what seem to us Ben Naftali manuscripts as well as codices which contain readings which are neither those of Aaron Ben Asher nor of Ben Naftali (like the Cairo, Sassoon, and British Museum codices, et cetera).[117] The differences between all those must have been rather small. All these belonged to *one* tradition, even though a particular subsystem, represented by the Aleppo Codex, was finally to gain fame.

43. By the end of the ninth century this tradition was fully developed,[118] and the Aleppo Codex emerged out of it as a perfect specimen, crystallizing the tradition in a model codex of the complete Bible. But it was part and parcel of that tradition. In spite of its unique prestige it remained near the other subsystems. It could serve as a model. But scribes, while ostensibly reproducing it, could easily keep deviating readings to which they had been accustomed. In contradistinction to the *non-receptus* codices these minute deviations amounted to very little.

---

vocalization is found in Biblical manuscripts only. This fact should have been clear at least since M. Zulay's *Meḥqəre Yannai* [Berlin, 1936], p. 326.) For the whole problem see my *Nosaḥ ha-Miqrā*.

117. There are only a very few cases where tradition has elaborated on the question of *three* different readings within the *proto-receptus* tradition. The classical example remains, of course, the proper name ישׂשכר (since Pinsker's *Lickute Qadmonioth*, pp. 98f.; cf. Ginsburg, *Introduction*, p. 252, and Ben David, *Beth Miqrā* 3:415). The Masoretes who apart from the Ben Ashers come alive somewhat through our sources, are Pineḥas, head of the Academy, and especially Moshe Moḥa (Moḥe). See my *Nosaḥ ha-Miqrā*.

But only very seldom can we find out against whom Mishael stressed the agreement between Ben Asher and Ben Naftali. One example must suffice here: for Exod. 3:8 Mishael stressed their agreement very strongly: ... והד׳א מא לם יכ׳תלף פיה בתה . . . . וארד להצילו ("There was absolutely no *ḥilluf* on these"). To my mind this means that some earlier listing of differences—there must have been such a listing against which Mishael stressed his better tradition!—mistakenly quoted some difference of opinion on this subject and attributed it to Ben Asher and Ben Naftali (as happened throughout the Middle Ages). There was no such difference between them, says Mishael. But if we happen to look up Pinsker's *Lickute Qadmonioth*, p. 30, we find who *did* differ: R. Pineḥas' reading is like our Ben Asher version: להְצילו, while R. Ḥabib read להְֽצילו, with *gaᶜya*. See also Pinsker, *Lickute Qadmonioth*, p. 30, for another case.

Such instances account, in my opinion, for the existence in the *proto-receptus* period of what in our eyes are *codices mixti*, containing also readings which are neither Ben Asher nor Ben Naftali. Of course we should not expect at that stage that there were *three* codices, each exhibiting a "pure" subsystem of *proto-receptus*. It will be clear that my position agrees to some extent with that of Yalon, *Kiryat Sefer* 32:101 (1957). See also above, Note 88.

118. Geiger has already suggested (*Urschrift* [Breslau, 1857], p. 169) that around 900 C.E. the Tiberian system conquered areas which had previously used the "Babylonian"

It is this basic similarity between the "model" Aleppo Codex and other codices of the *proto-receptus* tradition—some of which may have been esteemed codices of certain parts of the Bible—which explains in my submission that in spite of the immense prestige which was accorded to Aaron Ben Asher very soon after his death (see above, §15), ostensible copies of his text were, in fact, *codices mixti* from the point of view of the Aleppo Codex.[119]

The Aleppo Codex was not the absolutely final step. It was the peak which marks the transition from the *proto-receptus* to the *receptus* period. This was a completely smooth transition, hardly noticeable at the time, and yet there was a distinct later development, as can be seen especially by the use of methegs.[120] Those *codices mixti* were, indeed, the direct continuation

---

system. This idea has now been taken up in detail by Morag, *Sefer Tur-Sinai* (Jerusalem, 1960), pp. 234f. I admit that I hesitate somewhat to believe that one system yields to another because of some relative decline in the life of the community. The decline in Babylonia in the ninth century was not so sharp and the upward trend in Palestine not that decisive. Furthermore, I suspect that the very term "Babylonian system" has been too much identified in this case with the system of Babylonian Jewry—contrary to our sources.

But the whole history of the victory of the "Tiberian" system becomes more comprehensible to me if we assume that it was precisely in the ninth century that the Tiberian system had been finally perfected. Its system of accentuation (not of vocalization!) must have been recognized as vastly superior to the "Babylonian" system, and was taken by the users of the "Babylonian" system as the true and "original" Palestinian tradition for liturgical recitation. As a further suggestion, just as the "Tiberians" had tried, as an "experiment," to enhance the utility of their graphic vowel-notation by such an invention as the *ḥataf-ḥiriq*, obviously drawing on Babylonian custom (see above, §10), so the other side tried to combine the achievements of both Tiberian and Babylonian systems; both experiments failed. But it seems to me extremely significant that we possess a specimen like the Codex Petropolitanus of the Prophets from exactly that time. See above, Note 111.

In my submission, it was this recently achieved perfection which was a decisive factor in the victory of the Tiberian system—allowing, of course, for the possible "prestige appeal" of the Palestinian tradition. See Benjamin Klar, *Meḥqārīm wə-ᶜIyyūnīm* (1954), pp. 45f. See also above, Note 56.

119. This consideration may force us again to discuss the problem whether in the Masora apparatus of a critical edition (see *Text and Language*, p. x) we should not really also include those manuscripts written prior to the thirteenth century which are actually *codices mixti*—but lean heavily toward the *non*-Ben Asher subsystems of the *receptus* tradition. If we include the Cairo Codex in the apparatus, there is little sense in leaving the Sassoon Codex out!

120. Having repeatedly called questions of *gaᶜya* "minutiae" (see, e.g., Note 93 above, and especially Note 109), I should add that this is only a relative evaluation within the system. In point of fact, the *gaᶜya* fulfilled a considerable task in exact phonetic notation. Its neglect by many modern students of Hebrew can be explained only by the fact that the attempts inside the *receptus* tradition after Ben Asher to remedy what seemed like deficiencies in the Tiberian system finally led to the worst confusion in our *receptus* prints, with editors trying to bring order into the system—according to what they thought that order was. Yeivin's forthcoming study of the subject (cf. *Textus* 1:211) should help to remedy the situation.

of the *proto-receptus* tradition, with the one difference that the vast majority were now leaning heavily toward that subsystem which had been the basis of the Aleppo Codex (not toward the Cairo Codex, and so on).[121]

44. This is, in my opinion, the story of the rise of the Tiberian Bible text, and these manuscripts are the ultimate basis of our *textus receptus* prints, basically similar to the Aleppo Codex, and yet slightly removed from it.[122]

According to our picture it becomes obvious, for the first time, why generations took those *codices mixti*, which were finally used by Jacob Ben Ḥayyim, to represent the Ben Asher tradition. Looking back in our secure possession of the Aleppo Codex, we might even allow for a broadness of terminology and say that calling these *receptus* manuscripts "Ben Asher codices" was not really as wrong as scholars were led for the past generation to believe.[123]

IX. Maimonides and the Ben Asher Text

45. A final word may be permitted now on the role of Maimonides in

121. See my "Authenticity," §§1, 8. To put it differently: in the self-estimation of scribes and writers, the text of the "in-group" was declared to be a Ben Asher text, and the readings of the "out-group" were often termed Ben Naftali! Thus, e.g., the first example of a *ḥilluf* given by Lonzano (see above, Note 72) is very illuminating because he terms one reading, the one of *this area* (הגלילות האלו), the "correct" one, the reading of Ben Asher; whereas the other reading is that of the Ashkenazi codices (ספרי אשכנזים) which are unreliable (אין לסמוך עליהם)—and that is the reading of Ben Naftali! See also above, Note 11.

122. It appears from the picture I have tried to present that there is a kernel of truth in Sperber's grossly nihilistic and misleading dictum (*Grammar of Masoretic Hebrew*, p. 51): "*There never existed The Masoretic Text, and consequently never will be*" (his italics). To be sure, there never was a "canonization" (see below, Note 130). But when all is said and done, it is misleading to create the impression that the "Masoretic text" is practically the invention of Jacob Ben Ḥayyim (see above, Note 11). Sperber is one of the few scholars who were privileged to study Bible codices by the hundreds, and it must have occurred to him that—allowing for the differences often mentioned in this study—the *receptus* tradition emerges clearly from the vast majority of the codices. It would seem that only by disregarding the position of each phenomenon in its structural context and by treating the overwhelming majority and the hardly noticeable minority alike in his system, could Sperber reach his results which have—in his words (*Grammar of Masoretic Hebrew*, p. 17)—"reduced to shambles" all the work of other Hebrew grammarians.

123. See for this problem my "Authenticity," n. 17. [May 1962: In the light of these facts we need not wonder that N. H. Snaith could recently have published an edition of the Hebrew Bible (London, 1958) on the basis of fourteenth- and fifteenth-century manuscripts, being convinced that he had discovered a "way of obtaining the Ben Asher text independently of Leningrad Codex B 19 a." His understanding of the facts is highlighted by his judgment that the Aleppo and the Leningrad codices on the one hand and the "first hand of the best Sephardi MSS" (!) on the other hand are all equally "sound representatives of the true Ben Asher tradition." See *Textus* 2:11ff. (1962) and *Vetus Testamentum* 7:207f. (1957). Kahle has rightly hinted (*Cairo Geniza*, 2nd ed., p. 140, and *Hebräischer Bibeltext*, p. 17) that if Snaith had at least reproduced the thirteenth-century manuscript used by Norzi, his edition would have had value.]

connection with the "victory" of the Ben Asher text. In spite of the importance of Maimonides' authoritative acceptance of the Aleppo Codex for certain halakhic questions, I have already expressed doubts[124] as to the assumption, constantly repeated by Kahle[125] and others,[126] that it was the authority of Maimonides to which the victory of Ben Asher was due. I now submit that that view is untenable in every respect.

46. In view of the apparently ineradicable mistake reiterated by scholars,[127] it should be stressed first that Maimonides never dealt in as much as one word with the text of Ben Asher—and certainly not with Ben Naftali.[128] None of the textual problems which were of interest to medieval grammarians—let alone to modern students of the Bible—was of interest to him.[129]

Furthermore the assumption of the victory of Ben Asher in the wake of Maimonides' "decree" comes dangerously near to what can only be called a canonization. It looks as if on the authority of Maimonides and by some apparently arbitrary act, a text hitherto not accepted by the whole of Jewry became all of a sudden authoritative for all Jewish communities—two and a half centuries after Aaron Ben Asher (and a century and a half, according to Kahle's theory, after the "Tiberian pronunciation" had been "substituted" for the "original" one).

This is completely off the mark. There was never any "decree" which

124. For "Authenticity," §1, I did not have to investigate this point. But I felt uneasy even then about this accepted theory.

125. While in most of Kahle's statements on the subject Maimonides is simply made responsible for the victory of Ben Asher, he admits in *Hebräischer Bibeltext*, p. 69, that Aaron Ben Asher was in Maimonides' eyes the long-established Masoretic authority.

126. In lieu of many examples I choose the formulation in one of the most widely used handbooks on the Bible text (B. Roberts, *The Old Testament and Versions* [Cardiff, 1951], p. 64): "During the first half of the tenth century A.D.[!] there flourished in Palestine two main families of Massoretes, that of ben Asher and that of ben Naphtali [!], and it was not until the twelfth century that it was decided, by the decree of Maimonides [!], that the text and vocalization of the former family was to be regarded as standard."

127. See my "Authenticity," §8. I cannot rid myself of the suspicion that most scholars copying this myth from somebody else never troubled to look up the statement of Maimonides in its context in the *Code*. The "Urtext" is nowadays possibly Kahle, *Masoreten des Westens*, I, 12: "Freilich möchte ich darauf hinweisen, dass Maimonides in dieser viel zitierten Stelle in erster Linie [*sic*] auf die in diesem Kodex vorliegende massgebend korrekte Schreibung des Konsonantentextes der Tora hinweist [*sic*] und auf die Minutiae der Punktation [*sic*] nur nebenher Bezug nimmt." The Maimonides text bears no relation to what is imputed to it in this statement.

128. As far as I can see, only Prijs, *ZAW* 69:180 (1957) and Rabin, *Encyclopedia ʿIvrith*, IX (1958), *s.v.* "Ben Naftali," correctly stress that the decline of Ben Naftali cannot be attributed to the decision of Maimonides.

129. For the issue see my "Authenticity," §8.

had the character of a "canonization"[130] and it is impossible that in the halakhic literature of the twelfth and thirteenth centuries there should be no trace of it—had it existed. But it is completely out of the question that anything like that could have happened around 1200 C.E. Great as Maimonides' authority was, he would never have dared to do such a thing nor would he have dreamed of doing it. Had he done so, all other halakhists would have put him under ban.[131] But it was not in the power of any one person at that stage of history to make all communities accept a text contrary to their age-old traditions.

To be sure, Maimonides did not succeed too well in settling those (comparatively minor) halakhic questions of certain details in writing Torah scrolls, for which he had invoked the authority of the Aleppo Codex[132]—he would have been less successful in questions which he never tackled. The most that can be said is that through his reliance on the Aleppo Code as a model codex for those halakhic purposes, he indirectly strengthened the prestige of the *receptus* codices—which were the vast majority anyhow—that were held to represent the Ben Asher tradition.[133]

130. For the crime allegedly committed already earlier by the Masoretes see above, Note 50. It might still be useful to point out that it is not a Jewish way to "canonize" a text by declaring that as from now, such and such a text is "holy."

131. While Maimonides is the one all-round genius known to the gentile world, too, he was not at all regarded as the undisputable halakhic authority—neither in his time nor later on. This position was accorded to him only by the Yemenite Jews. See below, Note 133.

132. See the discussion in my "Authenticity," esp. §33.

133. Later scholars never credited Maimonides with having brought about the general acceptance of a textual tradition (see next Note). Although I cannot check the text at present, I remember having been struck while working on ha-Meiri's *Kiryat Sefer* (cf. "Authenticity," §31f.) by the fact that he deals at great length with Maimonides' views without mentioning Ben Asher in that context; on the other hand, when discussing the widespread acceptance of the *receptus* ha-Meiri does not allude to Maimonides. I would suspect that modern scholars were perhaps misled by their usual source for Masoretic information. We have seen that Levita, *Massoreth ha-Massoreth*, p. 114, is not too well informed about the Ben Asher–Ben Naftali problem (see above, Note 88). He is the first one to mention the decision of Maimonides and the acceptance of Ben Asher's readings in one breath, implying some faint causal connection: ״וכתב הרמב״ם . . . ועליו סמכתי בספר תורה שכתבתי כהלכתו״. וכן אנחנו סומכין על קריאתו בכל הארצות האלה ואנשי מזרח סומכין על קריאת בן נפתלי ("Maimonides wrote . . . And similarly we rely on his [Ben Asher's] reading in all these countries, whereas the 'Orientals' rely on Ben Naftali.") Only for one community did Maimonides' decision mean a real change of their habits, precisely because they had still a completely different type of codex (according to the "Babylonian" system; these were the Yemenites). Cf. on this issue and the importance of Maimonides in this respect Qafiḥ, *Sinai* 29:262f. (1951). The only way for the Yemenite Jews to implement their full acceptance of Maimonides' authority was to change their type of codex altogether, and the analysis of Yemenite codices in the libraries leaves no doubt that the changeover to Tiberian tradition started with the Hebrew text of the Pentateuch. As late as the sixteenth century a certain school of Yemenite scribes used to stress

Scribes, grammarians, and Masoretic scholars became more conscious of the facts and started stressing the point that their tradition was the tradition of Ben Asher—whether that claim was justified or not (see above, Note 121). This trend may also have hastened the final decline of other traditions, especially that of *non-receptus*. But it was a gradual and natural process,[134] not an active and conscious suppression.

47. But on the whole—and this is the main point—the excellence of Aaron Ben Asher's textual achievement was acknowledged[135] for two centuries before Maimonides. The *receptus* tradition, which the Aleppo Codex had helped to bring about and into which it had merged again, had already become by 1200 C.E. the accepted form of the Hebrew Bible for the vast majority of Jewry.[136] Only by speculating on the Bible text *in vacuo* and by neglecting what we know from the pulsating Jewish literature of those days, only by concentrating exclusively on the few fragments of non-Masoretic texts kept in libraries—important as they are in their own right (see above §6f. and Note 112)—and by ignoring the evidence, up to the thirteenth century, accumulated in collections all over the world, only thus could history be turned upside down.

In my opinion, Maimonides' act—rather drastic from the halakhic point of view, even though of minor consequence—can be understood only on the assumption that he did exactly as he said. Also in this case Maimonides

---

that their codices were according to the halakhic tradition declared authoritative by Maimonides. But this had absolutely nothing to do with the details of the Ben Asher vocalization and accentuation, and the comparison of those codices shows clearly that they had no access to the Aleppo Codex or to any direct copy from it. No special claims in this respect—as put forward by Morag (May 26, 1961, and June 16, 1961)—seem plausible, and it will take some skill to convince us that the Aleppo Codex should be judged by the yardstick of these late Yemenite manuscripts. See above, Note 81, and my "Biblical Manuscripts," pp. 47f.

134. The formulation I find given by Lonzano, ᵓ*Or Thora*, on Gen 1:3 mirrors precisely the correct feeling people had about the issue and can be taken as classsic: ונהגו כל ישראל בגלילות האלו לסמוך על קריאת בן אשר כאלו יצאה בת קול ואמרה: בן אשר ובן נפתלי הלכה כבן אשר. ("And the whole of Israel in these countries got accustomed to rely on the reading of Ben Asher, as if a Divine voice [not Maimonides!—*M.G.*] had declared: The decision is always according to Ben Asher.")

135. The colophon of the Leningrad Codex (and other codices? See above, Note 81) and the fact that the scribe of the Leningrad Codex took upon himself the trouble to harmonize the manuscript are good indications (see above, §30). To be sure, while the literature shows that Aaron's tradition carried most prestige, it was not yet towering high above everyone else's as happened later on. A fair example of the prestige, yet not absolutely binding, of Ben Asher can be found in Levy, *Zur masoretischen Grammatik*, p. 39. Cf. also Ben David, *Beth Miqrā* 3:12f.

136. What is decisive in this respect is the nature of the "Masoretic model codices," not the "teaching" or "private" codices. Cf. my "Biblical Manuscripts," chapter iii.

had his usual excellent information about valuable ancient manuscripts.[137] The Ben Asher text and the Aleppo Codex did not become authoritative because Maimonides chose them, but Maimonides chose the codex, because he considered it authoritative! This is what he says,[138] and again it might be useful to listen to our source before engaging in speculative criticism (see above, Note 44).

48. The Aleppo Codex was accepted as a model codex—as is quite obvious from the note which was appended to it[139]—long before Maimonides. By referring to it he tried to remedy a halakhically disturbing situation by going back to what he took to be—most justifiedly, as it has turned out—the best ancient codex available. Indirectly his act raised the prestige of Ben Asher and of the Aleppo Codex as a whole, not only in those matters with which he had dealt. But, generally speaking, the act of Maimonides is additional and extremely important evidence for our thesis as to the status of the Aleppo Codex.

49. As I said at the outset, scrutiny of all the facts known today has led me, against the teachings I used to take for true, to formulate a general hypothesis which differs in its decisive aspects from the picture accepted on Kahle's authority by many students of the Bible. Where he sees abrupt changes, artificiality, invention, and what amounts to fraudulent tampering, I see a live tradition, endless toil for safeguarding a sacred text, and gradual development. Where he speculates about the Bible text without properly taking into consideration the data of Jewish history and non-Biblical documents, I have tried to paint the picture of the rise of the Tiberian Bible text within living communities, listening to what history tells us about Ḳaraites and Rabbanites, about Masoretes and grammarians, about Maimonides and his contemporaries. Where he sees life in every tradition except the "official" Tiberian one, I see plurality around the ancient mainstream which finally led to our Masoretic *textus receptus*.

137. His use and acceptance of certain ancient manuscripts is well known in halakhic literature. While the discussion of the assumed Ḳaraite creed of Ben Asher will be dealt with in *Nosaḥ ha-Miqrā* (see above, Note 45), I should like to say meanwhile that the argument of the acceptance of the Aleppo Codex by Maimonides against the assumption of Ben Asher's Ḳaraite leanings has been grossly overplayed. Cf. Dothan, *Sinai* 41:307.

138. The full quotation has been given in my "Authenticity," n. 1.

139. Most recently published by President Ben-Zvi (*Textus* 1:13f.) and in Kahle, *Hebräischer Bibeltext*, pp. 84f.

What I claim is that my general hypothesis accommodates all the facts no worse—and I venture to hope better—than does his.

50. Many details, however, are still in need of further examination,[140] and I pray that my colleagues and I may be allowed to continue our work, filling in what is missing and correcting what is wrong. Meanwhile it will be left to fellow scholars to decide which picture they wish to accept.

140. I need not repeat that only certain details known already have been given in the footnotes to this paper. See *Nosaḥ ha-Miqrā*.

How Much Greek in Jewish Palestine?

By SAUL LIEBERMAN

Before approaching our subject, let us first determine its exact area and scope. From the conquest of the East by Alexander the Great until the end of the Talmudic period the Jews of Palestine lived amidst nations with a more or less developed Hellenistic culture (at least among the upper classes of society). At the same time, the Palestinian Rabbis shaped Rabbinic Judaism, which has influenced the life of the Jewish people up to modern times. Rabbinic literature has been studied by the Jews for two thousand years, and has left deep imprints on their minds and hearts throughout the generations. Ancient Rabbinic works reflect certain attitudes toward the behavior, thinking, and teaching of the non-Jewish Hellenistic world. It is therefore pertinent to ask: "Were the views of the ancient Palestinian Rabbis based upon knowledge of the surrounding Hellenistic culture, or were they the product of ignorance, or, at least, the result of misunderstanding?" Hence, "How much Greek in Jewish Palestine?" is to be understood mainly as the question: "How much knowledge of the world which surrounded them did the builders of Rabbinic Judaism possess?"

It is, therefore, obvious that we shall have to eliminate from our discussion pre-Maccabean Hellenistic Judaism, the Hellenism of the Jewish aristocracy, the high priests and their families, apocryphal and pseudepigraphic writings, the many Greek inscriptions found in Jerusalem and in the rest of Palestine, and even the long hexametrical Greek epigram discovered in Beth-Sheᶜarim, the central burial place in the very heart of Rabbinic Palestine of the third and fourth centuries. Relevant though that material may be, we must limit ourselves to the main stratum which influenced Judaism: namely, Rabbinic literature.

It is natural that modern Jewish scholars have been particularly interested in the influence of Greek philosophy on the Rabbinic mind. We are greatly indebted to the works of Joel,[1] Bacher,[2] Neumark,[3] Kaminka,[4] and many others who pointed out numerous parallels between some Rabbinic passages and the sayings of Greek philosophers. These include cosmological topics, questions about the soul and its immortality, about ethics and practical wisdom. It is highly probable that some purely Greek ideas penetrated into Rabbinic circles. Some were accepted and many were rejected, cognizance of the latter being taken in the form of arguments trying to prove the fallacy of the ideas concerned. It would require a series of lectures to treat in elaborate fashion all the passages in the Rabbinic books which may be associated with the views and sayings of the Greek philosophers. For our purpose it will suffice to state that the researches of Jewish scholars have shown the center of contact between Rabbinic and Greek philosophy, particularly the philosophy of the Stoics, to lie in the ethical principles with which both philosophers and Rabbis were deeply concerned.

Kaminka[5] collected many quotations from the Stoics which, in his opinion, are identical with Rabbinic statements. And since the early and middle Stoa preceded the Rabbis in question, it was reasonable to assume that the latter borrowed from the former. However, most of the cited examples are ethical aphorisms and apothegms which could be formulated by any intelligent person raised on the teachings of the Hebrew Bible. Some of them were the apanage of the entire civilized ancient world. The Jews and the Greeks may have drawn them from a common source. And, finally, some topics seem to have only a superficial similarity to those raised by the Stoics, and one may doubt whether the points argued by the Stoics and the Rabbis are identical.

Nevertheless, upon closer examination we may sometimes discover that some seemingly questionable conjectures of Jewish scholars are much sounder than they appear prima facie. We shall illustrate this point by reference to a well-known text.[6] "Supposing two people are walking in a waterless desert. One of them has in his possession a canteen of water.

1. *Blicke in die Religionsgeschichte . . .*, vols. I–II (Breslau, 1880–1883).
2. In his notes on the pertinent passages of the *Aggada* throughout his monumental work, *Die Agada der Tannaiten* (Strassburg, 1890), and *Die Agada der palästinensischen Amoräer* (Strassburg, 1892).
3. תולדות הפילוסופיה בישראל, pp. 39–95.
4. מחקרים בתלמוד, תל־אביב תשי״א, pp. 42ff.
5. *Ibid.* and in his article in *REJ* 82:233ff. (1926). Cf. also J. Bergmann, "Die Stoische Philosophie und die jüdische Frömmigkeit" in *Festschrift zu Herman Cohen's siebzigsten Geburtstage* (Berlin, 1912), pp. 145ff.
6. *Sifra Behar*, VI, 3 (ed. Weiss), 109c; BT *Baba Meṣiʿa* 62b.

Were he alone to drink from it, he would survive and reach an inhabited place; but were he to share this water with his companion, both would perish. 'Let them both drink and die,' said Ben Peturi. Rabbi ᶜAkiba objected: 'Your life comes before the life of your brother.'"

Bacher,[7] Juda Bergmann[8] and Kaminka[9] associated this passage with the question raised by Hecaton (a Stoic of the second century B.C.E.) as quoted by Cicero:[10] Supposing a ship was wrecked in the sea and two people took hold of a plank; if one man clings to it, he has a chance to be saved, but if both cling to it, both will perish. The answer of the Stoic is that the plank should be left to the man whose life is more valuable, either for his own sake or for that of his country. Since Hecaton flourished about one hundred and fifty years before Rabbi ᶜAkiba, it was plausible to assume that the Rabbis borrowed the problem from the Stoics.

Upon second thought, however, it appears that the said two questions are far from being identical. The case of two men who try to save themselves on the plank of a sinking ship represents no problem to a Rabbi; if one of them pushed the other way, or wrested a plank from another person in the middle of the sea, he would be considered a sheer murderer. He who kills an innocent person in order to save his own life is guilty of murder. The problem posed by the Rabbis was: should a man give away his property upon which his very life depends (in our case, some of the water in his canteen) in order to prolong somebody else's life? Normally a man is master of his property, but he is never master of his life. Nobody has the right to decide that his own life is less important than the life of another single individual. In case his life depends on his property, he actually gives his life away when he surrenders his property. It is for this reason that Rabbi ᶜAkiba ruled: your life comes before the life of your brother; you are not supposed to give your life away with your own hands in order to save the life of another person. It is the factor of ownership which determines the ruling in the Rabbinic case.

The above-mentioned scholars did not, however, quote Cicero *in toto*. He reports in the same context another question in the name of Hecaton: "What about the owner of the ship? May he take away the plank? The answer is: until they reach the place for which the ship is chartered, she belongs to the passengers, not to the owner." This answer solves our problem too. It is evident that the Stoic raised here the question of ownership: has the owner of the property any special rights in a case like ours?

7. *Die Agada der Tanaiten*, I, 62, n. 1.
8. "Die Stoische Philosophie," p. 160.
9. מחקרים, p. 155.
10. *De officiis* III, 23.

He dismissed the question by deciding that in this case the ship does not belong to her master only, but also to the passengers; the master has therefore no advantage of ownership. Now it is almost unthinkable that the sophist stopped with that problem. Since he had already raised the problem of ownership, he could not be content with the answer that in this particular case ownership did not apply. It must have occurred to him that a similar question might arise under circumstances of indisputable ownership, like the case cited by the Rabbis, or one similar to it. A famous sophist can hardly be suspected of such a flagrant omission. Cicero begins his chapter as follows: "The sixth book of Hecaton, *Moral Duties* [*De officiis*] is full of questions like the following," and he then proceeds to quote the problems we have just mentioned. In the light of what we said it is more than probable that Hecaton did deal with the question whether unchallenged ownership of a life-saving object could decide the proper moral behavior of two men fighting for their lives. Cicero himself explicitly admits that he did not report all the cases cited by Hecaton.

Fortunately, our conjecture can be fully corroborated. Solomon Pines discovered[11] in a work by the physician and philosopher al-Rāzī[12] the following passage: "Or like two people in a waterless desert. One of them has in his possession an amount of water sufficient to sustain himself, but not enough for both of them. Under such conditions it is proper that the water be assigned to the one more useful to mankind." Pines rightly pointed out that the instance quoted by al-Rāzī is exactly identical with the example cited by the Rabbis; moreover, that it was unlikely that al-Rāzī drew his information from a Rabbinic source. For the answer was the one offered by the Stoics in the case of a plank from a sinking ship, and not the answer given by the Rabbis. Hence he concludes that al-Rāzī drew on the book of the Stoic Hecaton. We demonstrated above that Hecaton could not have failed to ask the same question as the one raised by the Rabbis. Pines' conclusion can hardly be refuted. We thus have before us a problem of the Stoics discussed by the Rabbis, and answered by the latter not on the basis of expediency (*utilitas*), but according to the principles of Jewish law.

What was a mere conjecture on the part of Bacher, Bergmann, and Kaminka can now be considered substantiated. The problem posed by the Stoics assumes a legal character with the Rabbis. None of the Rabbis suggested that the owner of the water should deliver it to the other person;

11. See *Tarbiṣ* 16:241ff. (1945).

12. Flourished in the first half of the tenth century.

for as soon as the water is surrendered, the other, on his part, must act in the same manner as the first. The fact that he was not the original owner of the water does not give him any precedence over the former. The only question is whether they should both share the water, and subsequently perish together, or whether the owner should retain his property entirely for himself. The Stoic principle of *utilitas*—that is, that of preferring the person "whose life is more valuable, either for his own sake or for that of his country"—is applied by the Rabbis only in case a third person has to make his choice between two other human beings.[13] Thus the Babylonian Talmud (*Nazir* 47b) states explicitly that the "Anointed for Battle" is to be saved first (that is, before his superior, the *Sagan*, the adjutant to the High Priest), because the welfare of the community depends upon him; in other words, because his life is more valuable to his country.

It is, indeed, fairly reasonable to assume that some elements of Greek philosophy penetrated into Palestinian Rabbinic circles; the question, however, is: "How much?" In recent years Professor I. F. Baer, the prominent Israeli historian, advanced the thesis that the Rabbis were strongly influenced by Platonic ideas, and that Rabbinic methods of interpretation were directly affected by the dialectic of the Greek philosophical schools.[14] He modestly disclaims competence in the Rabbinic field but feels called upon to undertake his task, being not too happy, it appears, with the historical perspective of the scholars in the field.[15] He admits, however, that his thesis is to be regarded as no more than a primary outline for future orientation.[16]

The present writer regrets to say that the simple meaning of the texts and common scholarly methods do not justify the conclusions arrived at by Professor Baer. None of the sources cited indicates direct Greek philosophic influence. Most of the texts, though correctly interpreted by him, are either irrelevant or do not bear out the conclusions. In the few cases in which the sources, according to Baer, betray evident influence of Greek philosophy, they were totally misunderstood. We shall illustrate our contention by two examples.

Professor Baer cites[17] the famous saying of Beth Shamai[18] about the three

13. See Mishnah *Horayoth* III, 7–8; Mishnah *Baba Meṣiᶜa* II, end, and parallels. Cf. Tosafoth *Nazir* 47b, s.v. והתניא, and *Shaᶜar Joseph* by Azulai on *Horayoth* 113b.

14. ישראל בעמים (Jerusalem, 1955) and in his articles in *Ṣiyon* 23–24:3ff., 141ff. (Jerusalem, 1958–59). Cf. also *Ṣiyon* 21:1ff. (1956).

15. ישראל בעמים, p. 130, n. 1.

16. *Ibid.*

17. *Ṣiyon* 23–24:6.

18. Tosefta *Sanhedrin* XIII, 3; BT *Rosh Hashanah* 16b.

groups on the day of judgment: one perfectly righteous, the other utterly wicked, and the third intermediate. The intermediate will go down to Hell (*Gehinom*) and squeak and rise again. He argues that the expression מצפצפין in this Rabbinic text can be understood only on the basis of the Greek text of Plato (*Phaedo* 114a):[19] *ἐνταῦθα βοῶσί τε καὶ καλοῦσιν* . . . ("Therein they shout and call," et cetera). If this were true, there might be good reason to believe that the Rabbis were aware of the Greek text of Plato. However, צפצף corresponds neither to the Greek *βοᾶν* nor to *καλεῖν*. The Hebrew word usually means to chirp, to whistle. One may wonder at the chirping and the whistling of the intermediate group in Hell, but it is certainly not explained by the Greek text of Plato. The correct meaning of the word צפצף in this context was first established by C. Yallon,[20] who proved it to coincide with that of ספסף ("singe"): the intermediate group will not be consumed by the fire of Hell but will be only *singed* by the flames, to give them, as it were, some taste of Hell. It has therefore nothing to do with the Greek text of Plato.

Baer further states[21] to have found "clear proof" to the effect that the Greek term *νόμος ἄγραφος* ("unwritten law") used by the Greek philosophers and Philo to mean the Divine natural law, occurs in the Talmud. If this were true, we would be compelled to admit clear evidence in this case of a Greek philosophic term. For although the Rabbis were aware of natural law,[22] the designation of this law by the Greek term *νόμος ἄγραφος* is very strange in the mouth of a Rabbi. Let us therefore quote the text:[23] "Rabbi Ele^cazar said *παρὰ βασιλέως ὁ νόμος ἄγραφος*.[24] Ordinarily, when a human king issues a decree, if he chooses, he obeys it, otherwise [only] others obey it; but when the Holy One, blessed be He, issues a decree, He is the first to obey it." This is the verbatim translation from the Hebrew, and its sense is quite clear: a human king obeys his own laws only when he chooses to do so, while God always obeys His own laws. Hence the Greek phrase can only mean: The law is not written for the king; that is, on the king the law is not binding.[25] This is how the passage has been uniformly understood by medieval authorities and modern scholars. A Greek contemporary of our Rabbi quoted the proverb: *μωρῷ καὶ*

19. .הבטוי מצפצפין אינו מובן אלא על יסוד הנוסח היוני
20. See S. Lieberman, *Tosefeth Rishonim* (Jerusalem, 1937–39), II, 161.
21. *Ṣiyon* 21:28.
22. See, for example, BT *^cErubin* 100b.
23. PT *Rosh Hashanah* I, 3, 57b. The correct reading is available in *The Yerushalmi Fragments from the Genizah*, ed. L. Ginzberg (New York, 1909), p. 145.
24. The Greek words are in Hebrew characters in the original text.
25. See S. Lieberman, *Greek in Jewish Palestine* (New York, 1942), p. 144, n. 2.

βασιλεῖ νόμος ἄγραφος[26] ("On the fool and the king the law is not binding.") The existence of such a Greek proverb justifies the use of Greek by the Rabbi. Baer, however, renders the statement in the Palestinian Talmud as follows: παρὰ βασιλέως ὁ νόμος ἄγραφος—("From the King, the King of the world, emanates the unwritten law.") He explains the Hebrew text in these words: "The laws of the emperor are transitory, and their fulfillment depends on the arbitrary will of a human being, whereas the laws of the true King, the King of the universe, are first fulfilled by God himself, who sustains and preserves everything, and the true worshiper has but to follow His ways." There is nothing in the Rabbinic text to suggest this noble sentiment in sermonizing or to justify this kind of translation and interpretation. Professor Baer mentions in a note that the usual explanation of the Greek sentence is not in accordance with the rules of Greek grammar, for παρά with the genitive case means "from" and not "on." Obviously, he follows the routine method of modern research in ancient Hebrew or Aramaic texts. Granted, however, that παρά was never used in this sense in Greek, we have no right to distort the simple meaning of the sentence on the basis of Greek grammar. In our case we have before us a Babylonian Rabbi who immigrated to Palestine at a mature age, and it does not irk us at all if we suppose that he did not make proper use of the grammatical cases of nouns, and said παρὰ βασιλέως instead of παρὰ βασιλεῖ.[27] Whoever is familiar with Greek inscriptions in the East knows that such grammatical mistakes are found by the dozens, and nobody alters the meaning of the inscriptions in order to squeeze them into the frame of Greek grammar. There is absolutely no evidence for the use of the philosophic term νόμος ἄγραφος in Rabbinic literature, and there is certainly no "clear proof" to that effect.

From among the famous Greek philosophers only two names are mentioned, namely: Epicurus and Oenomaus of Gadara.[28] The Rabbis maintained:[29] "No philosophers like Balaam the son of Beᶜor and Oenomaus of Gadara ever existed among the nations of the world." In the minds of the Rabbis, Oenomaus of Gadara was the greatest Gentile philosopher of all

26. *Ibid.*, p. 38, n. 51.

27. Incidentally, our Rabbi is not alone in this mistake in Greek grammar. Sophocles (a learned Greek) in his Lexicon, p. 839, quotes from the *historia* by Nicephorus of Constantinople παρὰ Ῥωμαίων as "apud Romanos" (=παρὰ Ῥωμαίοις). I checked the reference and found that Sophocles was not exact in his translation, but our Rabbi is at least in good Greek company.

28. An orator and Cynic philosopher of the second century.

29. *Bereshith Rabba* LXVIII, 20 (ed. J. Theodor and C. Albeck, Berlin, 1912–36), p. 734.

ages! Of course, this may only mean that in their eyes he was the only true monotheist and sympathizer with the laws of Moses, and therein lay his true greatness. Nevertheless, the fact remains that the ancient Rabbis never mention Plato, or Aristotle, or some of the famous Stoics. The only Greek philosopher of the pre-Christian era mentioned by name is Epicurus.[30] He served as the symbol of heresy.

We read in *Midrash Tehilim* (ed. Buber, I, 22): "Those are the heretics who say that the universe is an *automaton*."[31] The word *automaton* is not found anywhere else in Rabbinic literature, and the Rabbis probably heard that the Epicureans said: *τὸν κόσμον αὐτόματον εἶναι*. Or, as Josephus puts it:[32] *ἀφρόνιστον τὸν κόσμον αὐτομάτως φέρεσθαι λέγουσιν*.[33] ("They say that the world moves automatically and uncared for.") Epicurus was chosen as a symbol of heresy not only because of his immense popularity but also because of the particular danger inherent in his philosophy. Complete atheism was not fashionable in the first centuries of the Christian Era, and polytheism was not too difficult to combat. The Epicurean doctrine that the gods care about nothing and nobody, thereby denying reward and punishment for men's actions, was regarded by the Rabbis as worse than atheism. We have noted above that Josephus too chose Epicurus as the target for his attack on the heretics. There is, however, no evidence that the Rabbis knew about the teaching of Epicurus more than the current general phrases.

In the Palestinian Talmud[34] we read: "And he who destroys whatever is given to him is [perhaps] a קינוקוס (*κυνικός*)." A general impression of the cynic philosophy was probably conveyed to the Rabbis through personal contact with these eccentric teachers who so much aroused the curiosity of the populace.

Professor Harry A. Wolfson declared (*Philo*, I, 92) that he was not able to discover any Greek philosophic term in Rabbinic literature. I want to state more positively: Greek philosophic terms are absent from the entire ancient Rabbinic literature. Such phrases as "the world is an *αὐτόματον*"

30. See S. Krauss, *Griechische und lateinische Lehnwörter in Talmud Midrasch und Targum* (Berlin, 1898–99), p. 107, *s.v.* אפיקורוס.

31. טומטום read: [א]טומום, or, as Rabbi Benjamin Mussafia had it in his manuscript: אטומטוס.

32. *Ant.* X, end, 278. Dr. Gershon Cohen drew my attention to Dr. Menachem Stein's דת ודעת (Krakow, 1938), p. 46. Dr. Stein anticipated me with regard to the association of the passages in Midrash and Josephus.

33. Cf. the quotation from Hippolytus in H. Usener's *Epicurea* (Leipzig, 1887), 359, p. 240.

34. *Gittin* VII, 1, 48c. The parallel passage in PT *Terumoth* I, 1, 40b is corrupted in our editions, but Cod. Rome reads correctly: קיניקוס, *κυνικός*.

have, of course, nothing to do with Greek literary philosophic terminology. A sentence like this was picked up by mere hearsay. The Rabbinic use of the Greek word κυνικός has no more significance than the word φιλόσοφος used by the Rabbis.

The Rabbis drew their information from personal conversations with philosophers and other intelligent people. The Talmuds and the Midrashim frequently mention such intercourse between the Rabbis and men whom they styled "philosophers." It is reasonable to assume that there were many learned Jews among the upper classes of Jewish Palestine who communicated some of the Greek doctrines to the Rabbis. We should bear in mind that in the third century C.E. there was at least one synagogue in Palestine (in Caesarea) where the *Shemaᶜ* was recited in Greek,[35] which indicates that Greek was the spoken language of the Jews resident in that locality. We likewise know that some Rabbis often visited Greek-speaking communities outside of Palestine, and engaged in learned discussions there. It appears that Alexandria in Egypt supplied to the Rabbis a constant source of information about Greek wisdom, as has been observed by various scholars. I have written elsewhere[36] about the influence of the Alexandrians on the Palestinian Rabbis. We have explicit evidence and direct testimony concerning halakhic dialectics coming from Alexandria in the form of puzzle problems posed to Rabbi Joshua.[37] These problems were subsequently embodied in the Tannaitic literature.[38]

It is noteworthy that the main body of the entire tractate of the Mishnah of קינים ("Nests") consists of difficult puzzle problems, and the author of this tractate is none other than the same Rabbi Joshua.[39] Again, we have puzzle problems in a *baraita* quoted in the Babylonian Talmud *Niddah* (54a), and once more its author is the same Rabbi Joshua, as is evident from the Mishnah (*ibid.*, VI, end). The Rabbis were aware of the peculiarity of these two sources, קינים and פתחי נדה and they remarked to this effect:[40] "[The problems of] קינים and פתחי נדה are the essentials of the *halakhoth*, but astronomic calculations and גימטריות [that is,

35. See Lieberman, *Greek in Jewish Palestine*, p. 30.

36. *Proceedings of the Rabbinical Assembly in America* 12:273ff. (1949).

37. Tosefta *Negaᶜim*, end, BT *Niddah* 69b.

38. Mishnah *Negaᶜim*, end; *Sifre Zuta*, ed. Horowitz, p. 305.

39. See BT *Zebaḥim* 67b. Cf. also the puzzle problem in the Mishnah *Nazir* VIII, 1 (a problem similar to that raised in Alexandria); again the author is Rabbi Joshua, as is clearly stated in the Mishnah.

40. Mishnah *Aboth* III, end.

γεωμετρία, manipulation with numbers][41] are aftercourses of wisdom." This is to my mind the only simple meaning of that statement. The Rabbis felt that puzzle problems were not the regular genre of Tannaitic literature, and that they appeared at first glance similar to the calculations and manipulations with numbers. Nevertheless, these particular problems, קינים ופתחי נדה dealt with law and were therefore "essentials," as Rabbi Joshua himself expresses it in his comment on a halakhic puzzle posed by the Alexandrians: This is a דבר חכמה[42] which may be formulated: This is halakhah.[43] In contradistinction to it, תקופות וגימטריות are only פרפראות לחכמה, aftercourses of wisdom.

In our opinion it is legitimate to draw parallels between Rabbinic dialectics and the dialectics of the non-Jewish law schools. Whereas we have no Greek philosophic terminology in Rabbinic literature, the situation is quite different with regard to Greek and Latin legal terms, as we shall presently try to demonstrate. Rabbinic books are full of Greek words. Many of them became part and parcel of the Aramaic language as a result of the practical contact in life between Jew and Gentile. From the newly discovered Bar Kozba Aramaic letters and the recently published copper scrolls we learn that Greek words which occur only once or do not appear at all in Rabbinic literature were common in the Aramaic and Hebrew of Jewish Palestine. In other words, we have good reason to suppose that the Aramaic spoken by the Jews included more Greek words than those preserved in Rabbinic writings. Certain elements of most of the Greek sciences of that time were known to the Rabbis in Palestine, and the formulations and the definitions in natural sciences are very similar to those of the Greek scholars.[44] But here again there is no evidence for Rabbinic quotations from first-hand sources; all their information may have been derived from secondary sources.

The situation is quite different when we turn to the Oriental-Hellenistic law which was prevalent in the Mediterranean basin in the time of the Mishnah and the Palestinian Talmud. The Rabbis had a special interest in first-hand knowledge of that law. They themselves sometimes had to resort to this law in cases when two Gentiles,[45] or a Jew and a Gentile,

41. See S. Lieberman, *Hellenism in Jewish Palestine* (New York, 1950), p. 69, n. 173.

42. Tosefta *Negaʿim*, end.

43. On the identity of *ḥokhmah* and *halakhah* (in many cases) see Professor L. Ginzburg's comment in פירושים וחידושים לירושלמי, IV, 19–31.

44. See Lieberman, *Hellenism in Jewish Palestine*, pp. 180ff.

45. PT *Baba Ḳamma* IV, 1, 4b.

agreed to be judged by a Rabbinic court.[46] Actually, the Rabbis taught that the Gentiles were under a Divine Commandment to follow a system of laws of their own.[47] The Rabbis would recognize only those Gentile laws as valid among non-Jews even under Rabbinic jurisdiction in a sovereign Jewish state. They recognized their law of *divortium* when given by the husband and the *repudium* given by the woman when she sued for divorce.[48] It is almost impossible to assume that the Rabbis would not be anxious to claim first-hand information about the ethics and the justice of the law applied by the Gentile courts of the time. In their interpretation of the Bible they sometimes made good use of their acquaintance with the Gentile law. Thus, for example, according to Rabbinic tradition Pharaoh did not inflict any harm on the matriarch Sarah. Why, then, did the Lord plague Pharaoh with great plagues (Genesis 12:7)? A Rabbi of the third century answered (PT *Kethuboth* VII, end, 31d): על דטולמיסן למגע בסמת דמטרונה. Except for the word למגע the whole sentence is in Greek: "Because he ἐτόλμησε ματρώνης σώματος ἅψασθαι" ("Because he dared to seize the body of a matron.") I have shown elsewhere[49] that the Greek sentence is a verbatim quotation from a law book which forbids seizing a matron for unpaid debts. The penalty for such seizure is corporal punishment. Consequently, Pharaoh was justly punished in full accordance with the Gentile law prevalent in Egypt in Rabbinic times. As pointed out above, the Rabbis maintain that the Gentiles must obey their own laws, and if they transgress them, they are subject to the penalties imposed by their law. The Talmud did not even bother to translate the Greek sentence, or to elaborate on it; its meaning and its implication were evidently well known.

Again Plutarch in his *Quaestiones Romanae* (30) states: "The Jurists employ the names of Gaius Seius and Lucius Titius [as fictitious names], and the philosophers speak of Dion and Theon." Similarly, whenever the Palestinian Rabbis want to use fictitious Gentile names, they cite the names of Gaius and Lucius.[50] They never mention the names of Dion and Theon.

46. *Sifre*, Deut., sect. 16; BT *Baba Ḳamma* 113a.

47. Tosefta ᶜ*Abodah Zarah* VIII (IX), 4 (ed. Zuckermandel), p. 473, line 13; BT *Sanhedrin* 56a, 56b, and parallels. Cf. PT *Ḳiddushin* I, 1, 58c.

48. *Bereshith Rabba* XVIII, 5 (ed. Theodor), p. 166; PT *Ḳiddushin* I, 1, 58c (according to Cod. Leiden). The text as well as the whole problem was finally illuminated by Professor Boaz Cohen in the *Proceedings of the American Academy for Jewish Research* 21: 10ff. (1952).

49. *Greek in Jewish Palestine*, p. 42ff.

50. PT *Terumoth* X, 7, 47b; *Gittin* I, 1, 43b; *Pesikta Rabbathi* XXI (ed. Friedmann), 107b. Cf. S. Lieberman in *Mélange Grégoire* (Brussels, 1949), p. 412.

The concern of the Jews with Gentile law predominant in Palestine is self-understood. The people had a vested interest in it. The procedure in the courts was a daily occurrence. The inhabitants listened to the speeches of the rhetors, and the art of rhetorics had a practical value. It is no wonder that certain methods of the legal *progymnasmata* (exercises) in the Gentile law schools were also adopted by the Rabbis. At the very back door of Palestine, in Beirut, a famous law school was established in the beginning of the third century C.E.[51] True, the language of instruction in that school was Latin,[52] a language with which Palestinian Jews were not familiar; but the very existence of such a famous school near Palestine undoubtedly stimulated legal science among the intellectuals of that country. The interest of the Rabbis in the ethical doctrines of the middle and later Stoa was an additional factor in exciting their curiosity about the application of those principles to practical law.

The result was that the Rabbis did not criticize the justice of the Hellenistic or the Roman laws per se but condemned the cruelties in capital punishment, the legal procedure in practice, the catch questions, the forced confessions, briberies, and so on.[53] The Rabbis did not belittle the wisdom of the Gentiles; they said:[54] "If you are told that there is wisdom among the Gentiles, believe it." But they censured the behavior and practices of the pagans. Two special chapters in *Tosefta Shabbath* (VI–VII) are devoted to the description of heathen superstitions. We find there a long catalogue of Oriental, Greek, and Roman superstitions which were forbidden to the Jews. The Rabbis did not exaggerate. Greek and Latin literature corroborates the evidence offered by the Rabbis in this respect.

Mutual criticism was current among all nations. Only the nations of the extreme North, the people at the end of the inhabited world (ἔσχατοι ἀνδρῶν), were idealized by the ancient writers. These nations were no competitors in any way. The mutual abuse among the several nations should not be taken too seriously. However, it was the special misfortune of the Jews that many learned Greek and Roman writers condemned their laws and invented fantastic stories about their ritual, practices, and customs.[55] These calumnies and the false charges brought against the Jews were not

51. See Paul Collinet, *Historie de l'école de droit de Beyrouth* (Paris, 1925), pp. 17ff.

52. *Ibid.*, pp. 26ff.

53. See S. Lieberman, "Roman Legal Institutions in Early Rabbinics and in the Acta Martyrum," *JQR* 35:13ff. (1944).

54. Midrash *Ekha Rabba* II, 9 (ed. Buber), p. 114.

55. A situation which the Christians of antiquity shared with them.

only a product of ill will but partly the result of gross ignorance of Judaism. The Jews knew much more about the Greeks and Romans than the latter knew about them.

To summarize: We do not know exactly how much Greek the Rabbis knew. They probably did not read Plato and certainly not the pre-Socratic philosophers. Their main interest was centered in Gentile legal studies and their methods of rhetoric. But the Rabbis knew enough Greek to prevent them from telling stories about Greek principles and their civil laws. Jewish opinion on the non-Jewish world was the product of knowledge and not of ignorance, and this knowledge was undoubtedly a great asset.

Appendix

In the preceding study we have avoided mentioning Gnostic "philosophy" and the relation of the Rabbis to it. There is no doubt that the Gnostics made good use of the Greek classics and their interpretation of Greek mythology.[1] But can we seriously consider their teaching as something similar to Greek philosophy? With his usual lucidity Professor H. A. Wolfson has demonstrated[2] the character of the "philosophy" of the Gnostics.[3] The newly discovered Gnostic writings at Chenoboskion do not alter the main conclusions arrived at by Wolfson. However, our previous discussion may seem incomplete if we entirely ignore this branch of "philosophy" and the Rabbinic reaction to it. Nonsense is nonsense, but the history of nonsense is a very important science. In certain respects it is more revealing than the history of sciences based on reason.

It is now evident that the Rabbis were aware of the Gnostic teachings.[4] There can also be no doubt that in many cases the *Minim* mentioned in Rabbinic literature designate Gnostics.[5] However, no direct allusions to the maxims of the Gnostics (except generalities of their theology) were ever identified in Rabbinic literature. But I believe that such allusions do exist.

1. See J. Doresse, *The Secret Books of the Egyptian Gnostics* (New York, 1960), pp. 190ff.

2. *The Philosophy of the Church Fathers* (Cambridge, Mass., 1956), I, 559ff.

3. Esp. *ibid.*, p. 574.

4. See G. Scholem, *Major Trends in Jewish Mysticism* (New York, 1946), pp. 40ff. and Index, *s.v.* Jewish Gnosticism, and, especially, his recent excellent book *Jewish Gnosticism, Merkabah Mysticism and Talmudic Tradition*, (New York, 1960), pp. 9ff.

5. See *Major Trends* . . ., p. 359, n. 24.

Let us start with the classic formula of the Gnostics. We read in the so-called *Evangelium Veritatis*:[6] "He who thus possesses the Gnose knows whence he is come, and where he is going," et cetera.[7] He also knows "who he is."[8] In the Gospel according to Thomas,[9] 55, we read: Jesus says "If people ask you: Where do you come from? Tell them: We have come from the Light, from the place where the Light is produced," et cetera. The meaning is clear:[10] the Gnostic should remember that his essence is derived from the Propator (or the *ἐξουσία*, *αὐθεντία*, et cetera), and not from the inferior "demiurge." He is descended from light and returns to light.

On the other hand, we read in the Mishnah *Aboth* III, 1:" ᶜAqabiah ben Mahalaleel[11] said: "Consider three things and thou wilt not come into the hands of transgression. Know whence thou comest; and whither thou art going; and before whom thou art about to give account and reckoning. Know whence thou comest: from a fetid drop, and whither thou art going: to worm and maggot," et cetera. It is clear that the Rabbi reminds man of the lowly nature of his body, of the virtue of humility and the fear of the Lord. There is no inner contradiction between the formula of the Gnostics per se and that of the Rabbis. And indeed the medieval Rabbinic commentaries remarked[12] that one may ask also about the soul: "Whence comest thou?" and answer: "Hewn from the Throne of Glory"; and ask: "Whither art thou going?" and answer: "Returning to God whence the soul was taken," et cetera. They, of course, need not have been aware of the teaching of the Gnostics.[13]

6. 22, 13ff. (ed. Malinine, Puech and Quispel, 1956).

7. *Ibid.*, p. 54, see the editors' note, and the excellent discussion by A. D. Nock in *The Journal of Theological Studies*, N.S., vol. 9, 2 (1958), pp. 322ff. Cf. also the quotation from *Sophia of Jesus* by Doresse, *The Secret Books of Egyptian Gnostics*, p. 200.

8. See Irenaeus, *Adv. haer.*, I, 21, 5, and cf. *Eranos-Jahrbuch* 20:100 (1951), referred to by Nock, *Journal of Theological Studies*, N.S., 9, 2:322ff.

9. Doresse, *The Secret Books of Egyptian Gnostics*, p. 363.

10. See Irenaeus, *Adv. haer.*, I, 21, 5.

11. Flouished around the beginning of the first century.

12. According to מנחה חדשה, a, 1, 28a.

13. The several groups took this maxim in the different senses which conformed to their own teachings. Kaminka (מחקרים, p. 50) called attention to Seneca, *Epist.*, 82 (6), who said: *sciat quo iturus sit, unde ortus*, etc. "Let (a man) know whither he is going and whence he came," etc. It is indeed verbally the Rabbinic saying, but I doubt that it had the same meaning. From the context of the letter it appears that Seneca had in mind the nature of things in the philosophic sense, whereas the Rabbis' stress was on "Before Whom thou art about to give account and reckoning." The formula was a classical Stoic phrase, and again, the several groups applied it in their own ways. Cf. also Epictetus, *Dissert.* III. 12.15.

But the minor tract *Derekh Ereṣ Rabba*[14] III records in the name of Ben ʿAzai[15] a long discourse on the above-mentioned saying of ʿAqabiah ben Mahalaleel. He declares: "Whence did he come? From a place of darkness; and whither is he going? To a place of darkness and gloom. Whence did he come? From an impure place; and whither is he going? To defile other people,"[16] et cetera. In other words: man does not come from light and does not return to light, but comes from darkness and returns to darkness and gloom. Man does not come from a holy source and does not return to a holy source, but comes from an impure source and goes to defile other people. This obvious elaboration on the Mishnaic source breathes protest and anger. It is a refutation of the Gnostic's fundamental answer to this question.

However, we find in *Aboth de-R. Nathan* II, 32 (ed. Schechter, 35a): Rabbi Simeon ben Eleʿazar[17] said: "Whence did he come? From a place of fire, and he returns to a place of fire. And whence did he come? From a place of compression [ממקום לחוץ], and he returns to a place of compression [that is, the grave]. And whence did he come? From a place that nobody can see, and he returns to a place that nobody can see. Whence did he come? From a place of impurity, and when he returns, he defiles other people." It appears that there is an inner contradiction between the first answer of Rabbi Simeon ben Eleʿazar and his following answers. Perhaps the text is defective, and the other answers do not belong to that Rabbi. But the first answer is verbatim the answer of the Gnostics, as recorded in the Gospel of Thomas 55, quoted above. It is possible that the Rabbi recorded an old orthodox saying referring to the soul, which the Gnostics appropriated and applied, in their own way, to their own doctrines. But from the subsequent answers in *Aboth de-R. Nathan* as well as from the explicit statements of Ben ʿAzai cited above, it is evident that the fundamental question of the Gnostics was well known to the Rabbis of the second century, and they accordingly expressed their reaction to it.

In the light of the preceding we shall be able to understand an obscure passage in the Midrash. We read there:[18] "Simeon ben Zoma[19] was sitting

14. (Ed. Higger), p. 155, and parallels.

15. Flourished in the first half of the second century. He was a close associate of Ben Zoma, and both of them belonged to the school of Rabbinic mystics.

16. Who carry or touch his dead body, or who bend over his grave.

17. Flourished in the second half of the second century.

18. *Bereshith Rabba* II, 4.

19. See above, Note 15.

and meditating when Rabbi Joshua[20] passed by and greeted him once and twice but received no reply. The third time he answered hurriedly. Then he asked him: Where do the legs come from? He said: I was contemplating [מעיין הייתי]. He [Rabbi Joshua] insisted: I call upon heaven and earth as my witnesses that I will not budge from here until you tell me where the legs are from. He answered: I was contemplating the Story of Creation [מעשה בראשית], and there was only a space of two or three fingers between the upper and lower waters, for it is not written 'And the Spirit of God blew,' but 'hovered' [Genesis 1:2], like a bird flying and flapping with its wings, its wings barely touching [the nest]. Thereupon Rabbi Joshua turned to his disciples and remarked to them: Ben Zoma has gone." This is the literal translation from the *editio princeps*. All the parallel passages[21] record as the first question of Rabbi Joshua: מאין ולאין (לאין) בן זומא ("Whence and whither, Ben Zoma?") And thereupon follows the answer: "I was contemplating the Story of Creation," et cetera. The first answer of Ben Zoma and the second question of Rabbi Joshua are missing in all the parallel sources, and it is exactly in the omitted part that the secret of the passage is hidden.

Before explaining the text, let us first establish its correct reading. All the codices in the critical edition by Theodor, page 17, read in Ben Zoma's first answer: לא מאיין (מאין) ר׳. We may add that an ancient manuscript from the Geniza (overlooked by Theodor), written on a palimpsest, and reproduced by Lewis and Gibson in *Palestinian Syriac Texts*[22] (London, 1900), Plate II, also reads לא מאין רבי. In the Soncino translation of this midrash (of the text edited by Theodor) Ben Zoma's answer is rendered: "From nowhere, Rabbi." It is needless to say that לא מאין cannot have this meaning in good Hebrew; its only possible meaning is "nothing from nothing": that is (a human being who is) nothing (coming) from nothing.[23] The significance of the story is fully understood in the light of the classic answer of the Gnostics cited above. When Ben Zoma failed to reply to the greetings of Rabbi Joshua, the latter asked him in complete innocence

20. We have pointed out above, Page 131, that this Rabbi visited Alexandria, where he held learned discussion. We should bear in mind that Christian Gnostics abounded in Egypt, and the Alexandrian Jews were most probably well acquainted with their doctrines.

21. Tosefta *Ḥagigah* II, 6 (ed. S. Lieberman), pp. 381ff.; PT *Ḥagigah* II, 1, 77a bot.; BT *Ḥagigah* 15a.

22. According to the editors, the manuscript is probably of the tenth or eleventh century, see *Palestinian Syriac Texts*, Introduction, p. xii.

23. This application of לא and אין to human beings is found in other Rabbinic sources; see *Debarim Rabba* (ed. Lieberman), p. 119, and n. 2.

whence he was coming seeing that he was so engrossed in his thoughts as not to have noticed the greetings of his teacher. Ben Zoma answered evasively and rhetorically: "Nothing from nothing":[24] that is, I am nothing who comes from nothing. Rabbi Joshua did not like this evasive answer; it indicated to him only that Ben Zoma's mind was occupied with questions raised by the Gnostics, pretending as he did that he had not understood the simple question of his teacher. The answer given by Ben Zoma was orthodox, exactly in the spirit of his associate and colleague Ben ᶜAzai (see above, Note 15), but it betrayed his thoughts. Yet there was no sufficient basis to draw any definite conclusion from Ben Zoma's answer. Rabbi Joshua therefore repeated his question and said: "I will not budge from here until you tell me where the legs are from": that is, I want a direct answer to my question. After Ben Zoma answered what he answered, Rabbi Joshua turned to his pupils and said: "Ben Zoma has gone." It is not quite clear what was wrong with Ben Zoma's answer.[25] It appears from the context that Ben Zoma was talking about the Spirit hovering between the upper and lower waters,[26] and that there was a very small interval between the waters. The Sethian Gnostics taught:[27] "The Light is on high and the Darkness below, and the Breath between the two. This Breath which is between the Darkness which is below the Light which is on high is not a Breath like a gust of wind nor a gentle breeze . . . but it is like a perfume exhaled from an ointment, or a wisely compounded incense," et cetera. We learn from here that the Gnostics engaged in speculations about the nature of the Spirit hovering between the upper and lower waters. We now understand why Rabbi Joshua did not like Ben Zoma's second answer. The former's suspicions were strengthened by the latter's first answer which betrayed his preoccupation with the question: "Who am I, and whence do I come?"

24. A good Epicurean phrase: οὐδὲν γίνεται ἐκ τοῦ μὴ ὄντος (*Epist. ad Herodotum*, 38; Usener, p. 5); "gigni de nihilo nihilum, in nihilum nil posse reverti," see the commentary of C. Bailey on Lucretius (*De rer. nat.* I, 150), II (Oxford, 1947), 624ff., 636. Cf. also Marcus Aurelius, *Medit.*, IV, 4. On the medieval Jewish formulation of the corresponding formula, see H. A. Wolfson, "The Kalam Problem . . .," *JQR*, 36:388ff. (1946). The Epicurean phrase was quite current among the writers and intellectuals of antiquity. The twisting of the phrase in a quite different meaning is natural and understandable. This was the usual practice of that time with regard to classical texts, and verses from the Bible shared the same fate.

25. See M. Joel, *Blicke in die Religionsgeschichte . . .*, I, 163ff., and Theodor's note *ad loc.*, p. 18, n. 2.

26. See יפה תאר *ad loc.* Cf. Gen. 1:6–7, Rashi *ad loc.*, and Midrash *Bereshith Rabba* (ed. Theodor), p. 26, line 10, and p. 29.

27. Doresse, *The Secret Books . . .*, p. 150.

Again, we read in the Babylonian Talmud[28] in the name of Rabbi Simeon ben Ele^cazar:[29] "A man should always be careful in the formulation of his answers, for it is from Aaron's answer to Moses that the heretics[30] derived their heresy, as it is said: [Exodus 32:24] *And I cast it into the fire, and there came out this calf.*" The statement is very vague, and it is not clear to which heretics the Rabbi refers, nor how they could have derived their heresy from that verse. Rabbi Todros Abulafia[31] in his אוצר הכבוד on *Megilla ad loc.* already associated this passage with a tradition in the Aggada that the Golden Calf was fashioned after the pattern of the calf in the *Merkabah*, which the people saw during their passage through the Red Sea, or on Mount Sinai. This is an old tradition alluded to by Rabbi ᶜAkiba and his colleagues.[32] It appears from the Midrashim that the Golden Calf drew life from the original model, and therefore leaped alive out of the fire. The Gnostics, on the other hand, assert:[33] "The body of this man is fashioned from earth in the image of the high God, a reflection of Whom has just been seen by the Archons in the waters below." And again we read in the Gospel of the Egyptians:[34] "The image of the celestial Man is at once reflected in the waters. Sacla [that is, Sacla the demiurge] and his colleagues, in imitation of this, fashion the first human creature."

Now, the saying of Rabbi Simeon ben Eleᶜazar makes good sense. He claims that the wording of Aaron's reply, "This calf came out," suggests that the calf came out by itself: that is, came out alive.[35] Aaron revealed that it came out alive, and this is impossible unless we suppose that Aaron fashioned it in the likeness of the ox in the *Merkabah*; which is indeed the Rabbinic tradition, as mentioned above. This implied meaning of Aaron's reply, the Rabbi contends, gave support to the doctrine of the heretics—that is, the Gnostics—that the first man was created by the demiurge who shaped him after the model in the likeness of the superior

28. *Megilla* 25b. Cf. Tosefta *Megilla* III, 37 (ed. Lieberman), p. 363.

29. See above, Note 17.

30. המינין. This is the reading in all uncensored editions, manuscripts, and Tosefta *locis citatis*.

31. Flourished in the second half of the thirteenth century.

32. See the sources referred to in my Appendix to G. Scholem's *Jewish Gnosticism, Merkabah Mysticism* . . ., p. 122, n. 24.

33. *Hypostasis of the Archons*, according to Doresse, *The Secret Books* . . ., p. 160.

34. Doresse, *The Secret Books* . . ., pp. 178–179.

35. As correctly explained by Rashi 25a, *s.v.* ומעשה עגל, and corroborated by the Midrashim, see above, Note 32.

God, and consequently he was endowed with life. This belief in the power of the likeness—that the knowledge of the likeness of heavenly beings enables man to penetrate the secrets of creation—is not unorthodox. We read in *Aboth de-R. Nathan* (chap. XXXIX, ed. Schechter, page 116):[36] "Because of his sin it is not granted to man to know *what likeness is on high*; and but for that, the keys would have been handed over to him and he might have known *what heaven and earth were created with.*"[37] Here again the general belief is Rabbinic, but the Gnostics used it for their doctrines.

All the above sources indicate[38] that certain basic teachings of the Gnostics were not entirely foreign to the Rabbis, and that the latter had much more information about Gnosticism than was hitherto supposed. However, even in this domain the early Rabbinic literature never mentions a single Greek "philosophic" term used by the Gnostics.

36. Translation by Judah Goldin, p. 161.

37. This differs in purpose and in function from sympathetic magic, although there may be a possible relation between them.

38. Though not of each of them with the same degree of certainty.

Observations on Hekhalot Rabbati

By MORTON SMITH

Hekhalot Rabbati is not a very common work in any form, and the particular text which I have used is that of an as yet unpublished edition prepared by Professors Scholem and Wirszubski; therefore I shall begin by outlining the content of this text.

It is a collection of teachings almost all attributed to R. Ishmael—in only one or two at the end does R. ᶜAkiba appear as the speaker. R. Ishmael sometimes speaks for himself, sometimes reports the teachings of others, usually of R. Neḥunya ben Hakkanah, but occasionally of R. ᶜAkiba, R. Eliezer, or Rabban Simon ben Gamaliel, to say nothing of his celestial interlocutors, like Surya, the Prince of the Presence. In the majority of the sections, however, the speaker does not figure in what he is reported to have said. If the names of the speakers were obliterated the essential content of most of the text would not be affected. Therefore we may simply lay these attributions aside.

The text begins with the question, "What are the virtues of the spells to be recited by a man who wishes to behold the vision of the *Merkabah* [the chariot throne of God, seen by Ezekiel] and to survive the experience unharmed?" The spells are "songs," of course, like the Latin *carmina* and the Greek *epoidai*, and their virtues are all we should expect: they enable their possessor not only to ascend to the highest heaven and see the Throne, but also to know the future and the secrets of men's minds and of the past; they secure for him Divine protection and assure that his enemies will be blasted. Then comes a brief warning against interrupting the recitation, and then the spells themselves. They are mostly descriptions of the region and happenings around the Throne.

After about 125 lines of these we have an interruption to demonstrate their efficacy: R. Ishmael reports how, in the face of Rome's mistreatment of Israel, R. Neḥunya ben Hakkanah sent him down to the *Merkabah* and he secured an explanation of Rome's temporary rule and an assurance that accounts would be squared in the end. Moreover, Surya, the Prince of the Presence, was commanded to transpose "Lupinus Caesar" and R.

Ḥananya ben Teradyon, who was about to be executed. He also exchanged their appearances, so that "Lupinus Caesar" was executed and R. Ḥananya reigned over Rome for six months, during which he killed six thousand high Roman officials. At the end of that time the Roman populace caught him and burned him alive. But it was not he they burned alive, it was "Lupinus Caesar," who had been opportunely resuscitated for the purpose.

After this come three apocalypses: in the first, Seganzagel, the Prince of the Presence, shows R. Ishmael how the daily recitation of the *Ḳedushah* prevents the execution of the Divine decrees against Israel. Then Hadariel the Prince takes him to a service in the *Bet Hammidrash* of the firmament, where David and the Kings of Judah and Israel are in attendance. David is a supernatural personage who sits on a throne of fire forty miles high. In the second apocalypse Akhtariel Yah, Lord God of Hosts, declares his purpose to punish Israel but preserve it, and a Divine voice gives Ishmael certain figures on the basis of which he tries to calculate the time till the end. In the third apocalypse Meṭaṭron, the Prince of the Presence, tells Ishmael how in the end the Messiah will come out of prison, with the scrip and staff of a wandering philosopher, and challenge the great powers to a contest which he will win by raising the dead, who will then assemble the living of Israel. This section concludes with two brief stories, one of the efficacy of penitence—Meṭaṭron used it to plead before the Throne for the pardon of Israel—the other of how R. Ishmael saw Akhtariel Yah, Lord of Hosts, sitting on a lofty throne in the Temple. Akhtariel asked him for a blessing and Ishmael blessed him with the prayer that, among his attributes, mercy might prevail.

With this we return to the hymns for another 180 lines. After that comes a brief prose section of what is called *Shiᶜur Ḳomah* material, that is, lists of dimensions of the deity. (His right eye is 33,000 parasangs wide, and so is his left eye, and he is 770,000 parasangs from shoulder to shoulder. And so on.) Then comes another brief section of hymns; then a statistical account of the crowning of the creatures around the Throne, evidently cognate to the *Shiᶜur Ḳomah* material; another brief section of hymns, and a long prose account of the ritual of heaven: it cannot begin until the prayers of Israel have begun on earth. As soon as these are heard in heaven, the angels who have been charged with the pacification of the world (and consequently have been exposed to pollution) go down into rivers of fire and immerse themselves to burn off the odor of men. Then they go up a ladder of fire to stand before the Throne when all creatures cover their faces and God reveals his face and they sing (and any who sings too loud or soft or fast or slow immediately falls into the river of fire and is burned up). This leads into another forty lines of verse, which in turn are concluded with a prose confession of the greatness of God, containing a long list of His magical names (Ṭoṭrosiʾi, Ṭoṭrosiyah, and so on, evidently formed on the Greek *tetras*).[1]

This brings us to chapter 13, a little past the middle of the book, in terms of length, and here we come to what is clearly a new and distinct section: a full, coherent account of the ascent through the *Hekhalot*—that is, the palaces or temples of heaven—to the Throne. This account has two pseudohistorical introductions, or, perhaps, a single incoherent one, which begins with the statement,

> R. Ishmael said, When R. Neḥunya ben Hakkanah saw Rome was planning to destroy the mighty of Israel, he at once revealed the secret of the world as it appears to one who is worthy to gaze on the King and his Throne and the host of heaven. What is it like to know the secret of the *Merkabah*? It is like having a ladder in one's house and being able to go up and down at will. This is possible for anyone who is pure of idolatry, sexual offenses, bloodshed, slander, vain oaths, profanation of the Name, impertinence, and unjustified enmity, and who keeps every positive and negative commandment. R. Ishmael said, When I heard this I said to R. Neḥunya ben Hakkanah, If so, there is no end to the matter, for there is no living man so pure. Accordingly R. Neḥunya ordered an assembly of all the leading scholars, that he might declare to them the secrets of the ascent [*sic*]. R. Ishmael assembled every Sanhedrin, great or small, at the third gate of the Temple and R. Neḥunya sat and instructed the chosen few who sat before him, while the rest of the scholars stood at a distance, separated from them by globes of fire and torches of light.

When a man wanted to go down to the *Merkabah* he would call on Surya, the Prince of the Presence, and conjure him 112 times (no more, no fewer—that might be fatal) by Ṭoṭrosiʾi Yahweh, who was called—a long string of magical names.

R. Ishmael said, R. Neḥunya ben Hakkanah said, Ṭoṭrosiʾi Yahweh dwells in seven palaces, one inside the other, and at the gate of each palace there are eight doorkeepers, four on either side. Here follow the names of the doorkeepers for the first six palaces, and a terrifying description of the gigantic doorkeepers of the seventh palace and their fiery horses. Fortunately, the description is followed immediately by the assurance that

1. Cf. *Ṭeṭrasi = to enteles* in the *Etymologicum Magnum*, ed. T. Gaisford (Oxford, 1848). The influence of the Neo-Pythagoreans, for whom the tetrad was the source of the eternal *physis*, is presumably behind this usage as it is behind that of Philo; see the material under *tetrakys* in H. Stephanus, *Thesaurus Graecae Linguae* (London, 1824), vol. VI.

they are harmless to those who go down to the *Merkabah* and that Ṭoṭrosiʾi Yahweh welcomes visitors from Israel to see his glory, to see the destined end, and to go up and tell what has been seen.

After a burst of song and recitation of the Divine attributes, the text goes on, in the name of Rabbi Ishmael, to describe in detail how the traveler is to show, at each gate, specified seals to the specified angels in charge. In each case, on seeing the seals, these angels will take him on to the next gate. So, eventually, he arrives at the sixth. Now, the gatekeepers of the sixth palace made a practice of destroying those who went down to the *Merkabah* and did not go down to the *Merkabah*. . .

At this point some of the listeners wanted to ask a question: What is meant by "those who go down to the *Merkabah* and do not go down to the *Merkabah*"? They did not dare interrupt R. Neḥunya directly, since he was not only describing the descent, but himself making it as he spoke. Accordingly, they approached R. Ishmael and asked him to call R. Neḥunya back to earth. This he did by securing an object with the least possible contact with a woman whose condition might, by a rigorist minority, have been considered impure. As soon as this object was brought into contact with R. Neḥunya he was dismissed from before the Throne and was able to answer the question. It turned out that "those who go down to the *Merkabah* and do not go down to the *Merkabah*" are persons asked by those who really go down to the *Merkabah* to sit before them and write down whatever they say. If such amanuenses are not worthy, the doorkeepers of the sixth gateway attack them. Therefore be careful to choose pure men and tested scholars.

The question thus answered, the text jumps back to the gate of the sixth palace and describes at some length the chief doorkeepers, Dumiel (Divine silence) and Kaṣpiel (Divine wrath)—such names composed of abstract nouns plus the divine name, *el*, are the most common of the various sorts of angelic names found in these texts. When shown the proper seals, Dumiel and Kaṣpiel will bring the visitor, in a carriage of light drawn by a storm, to the gatekeepers of the seventh palace, but the text interrupts the procession to remark that Dumiel makes the visitor declare his legal knowledge and observance (for ideally no one who is not a student of all forms of Rabbinic tradition and who does not observe all the commandments can go down to the *Merkabah*). But if the visitor can lay claim to *either* knowledge *or* observance, Dumiel is satisfied, and Gabriel the scribe records both knowledge and actions and attaches the record to the carriage. When the gatekeepers of the seventh palace see the cortège approaching, "they cover their angry faces and thereupon unstring their drawn bows and put back their polished swords into their sheaths. None the less one must show them the great seal and fearful crown, *Chaos*,[2] *Urano*(*s*), *Ges*, and *Despotes* [that is, chaos, heaven, earth, and Lord] Yahweh God of Israel. Then they will bring [the visitor] in before the Throne of God's glory and will bring out before him all kinds of music and song, and will go before him making music until they bring him up and seat him with the Cherubim, with the Ophanim, with the Holy Beasts, and he sees wonders and powers, loftiness and greatness, holiness and purity, fear, humility, and rectitude." Thereupon R. Ishmael said, All the scholars compared this method to a man's having a ladder in his house and being able to go up and down at will. "Blessed art thou Yahweh, wise in secrets and lord of hidden things. Amen. Amen."

After this conclusion comes a pseudohistorical appendix. R. Ishmael reports that Rabban Simon ben Gamaliel was angry with him because the names of the gatekeepers of the seventh palace had not been declared. He complained of this to R. Neḥunya who explained that they had been omitted because they were compounded with *Yahweh*. However, he consented to declare them, went on to a description of their chief, Anaphiel Yahweh (the Divine ramification), then gave a different list, for the descent from the Throne. In this second list Anaphiel figures again, which leads to a further account of his functions. Above all he opens the gates of the seventh palace, before the Throne of Glory, which is opposite these gates. Now the Holy Beasts which bear the Throne have 256 faces, and 512 eyes, and their eyes are like lightnings, and around them are the Ophanim and Cherubim innumerable, and their eyes are like flames of fire. When a man wants to go down to the *Merkabah* Anaphiel opens the gates for him, and he enters and stands on the threshold, and all these creatures look at him with all their eyes and he is terrified, but Anaphiel and the gatekeepers of all the palaces encourage him, and recite the attributes of God, and a trumpet sounds above the firmament which is above the heads of the Beasts, and the Beasts cover their faces, and the Cherubim and Ophanim turn away their gaze, and he enters and stands before the Throne of God's glory and recites the song.

After sixty lines of song we come to a prose fragment: "And I saw one like to the lightning who . . . stood and distinguished the worthy among those who go down to the *Merkabah*, from the unworthy"—this by means of the way they behave when invited to enter the palaces. Fools rush in

2. My emendation; the text reads *Taos*.

where wise men wait to be asked twice. At the sixth palace, moreover, there is a special test: there the unworthy are deceived by an appearance of water (which is really the marble facing of the palace). When the visitor reveals his unworthiness by asking about the water, he is crushed beneath thousands of iron bars. Thereupon we have another 125 lines of song, including the great acrostic, *Ha-aderet we ha-emunah le-ḥey ha-ᶜolamim*, and concluding with the prose statement that as the wonders of God are unsearchable, so is Meṭaṭron, the decad, inconceivable, and listing Meṭaṭron's magical names.

This is practically the end of the book, but a number of short pieces are now tagged on. First R. Ishmael tells how, for three years, he was unable to remember what he learned. Therefore he went into deep mourning and refused food. Thereupon R. Neḥunya took him into the Temple, adjured him by various magical names of God, and revealed to him the secret of the Torah, after which he forgot nothing. Next R. Ishmael reports in the name of R. ᶜAkiba in the name of R. Eliezer, some eighty-five lines in verse of a type quite different from that of the hymns. This is an account of how, when the second Temple was built and the *Shekhinah* did not dwell in it, God decided to console Israel by revealing to them the glory of the Torah, which had never been revealed before. The ministering angels opposed the decision, but God carried it out none the less. In prose again, R. ᶜAkiba said he heard a voice from beneath the Throne of Glory telling how Enoch had been exalted above the angels and transformed into the Little Adonai whose name is Meṭaṭron. ᶜAkiba also reported the order of morning prayer in the heavens. R. Ishmael said R. ᶜAkiba said in the name of R. Eliezer, Our fathers did not consent to put one stone on another in the Temple until they forced the King of the World to reveal to them the secret of the Law and how to use it. Therefore the Throne came down in front of the place where the Temple was to be built and the King of the World, through Zerubbabel, instructed his people in the names and seals of the Princes of the Torah. There follow detailed instructions for the use of the secret of the Torah: rigorous immersion, twelve days' confinement in a single room, fasting from evening to evening, a diet of bread and water, and continual repetition—interrupted only by prayers—of the midrash on the secret of the Torah, finally, the names with which the Princes of the Torah are to be conjured. R. Ishmael said this method has been tried and makes even fools masters of the Torah. Moreover, R. ᶜAkiba has shown, by experiment, that it works outside the land of Israel. And what should a man say before praying this secret of the Torah?

Twenty lines of the hymns, concluding, "Holy, Holy, Holy is the Lord God of Hosts, all the earth is full of his glory."

Such is the text. As suggested in the course of the outline it breaks quite distinctly into two parts, chapters 1 to 12, the spells which are to be said by one who desires to see the *Merkabah*, and chapters 13 to 30 (the end), an account of the ascent through the palaces of heaven, culminating in a session with the Cherubim, the Ophanim, and the Holy Beasts, "being throned together," as Clement of Alexandria said, "with the other gods, who were first established in their orders by the Saviour."[3]

Both of these parts now contain a number of obviously separable sections. Let us avoid the question of authorship, since that would involve detailed stylistic analysis and attempts to distinguish between authorship and editing, which might not be fruitful. Regardless of who wrote them, the anti-Roman and apocalyptic prose sections in the first part obviously interrupt what is otherwise a collection of poems. So does the *Shiᶜur Ḳomah* material and the prose account of the ritual of heaven, though these are clearly more germane to the subject than are the apocalypses, of which the principal interest for us lies in the basis for dating afforded by the calculations in the second one. There Rabbi Ishmael hears a heavenly voice declare, "At the end of the completion of seven hundred years [reckoned according] to the building of the temple of the Kings of Persia, all things will end, and they will end from the face of all the earth, and this will be the finishing of iniquities. As [the children of Israel] abandoned me seven hundred years and served the Baᶜalim, so I too shall abandon them and cast them off into the hand of cruel [men] seven hundred years." In this same apocalypse Ishmael has reckoned for Babylon seventy years, for Media fifty-two, for Greece one hundred eighty; these are the standard Rabbinic figures, so we may attribute to the author the rest of the Rabbinic reckoning as we find it in *Seder ᶜOlam* 30 and *Abodah Zarah* 8b–9a. This allows four hundred twenty years from the building of the Temple to its destruction. Since the Rabbinic date for the destruction of the Temple works out as 69/70 of the common era,[4] the author's date for the end is 700—(420 − 69) = 349 C.E., the time of the Christianization of the Roman Empire and the accompanying anti-Jewish legislation, to which the text in fact refers. The third apocalypse may be somewhat later, since it contains

3. This is the goal of Clement's gnosis; *Opera*, ed. Stählin, III, 41, lines 24f.

4. This information and the preceding references I owe to Professor Gerson Cohen. The figures are, Persia 34 years, Greece 180, Hasmoneans 103, Herodians 103. (The end of the Herodians coincides with the destruction of the Temple.)

what is perhaps a reflection of the rebuilding of the Temple proposed by Julian after 361.

The passage preceding the apocalypses, on the transformations and transpositions of R. Ḥananya ben Teradyon and Lupinus Caesar, probably served as the occasion for adding the apocalypses at this point. Its use of the title "Caesar" for the Emperor suggests a date prior to Diocletian, the *-inus* termination and the slaughter of the Roman administrators reflect the troubled years of the mid-third century when relations between the emperors and the Senate were particularly bad. Maximinus, for instance, is said to have killed more men in Rome itself than he did in his bloody defeats of the barbarians.[5] The folk-tale motif of transformation and substitution of persons was popular at that time; we find it, for instance, in the third-century strata of the Pseudo-Clementine Homilies.[6]

The second main part of *Hekhalot Rabbati* also contains a number of passages easily separable from its chief element, the account of the ascent through the palaces of heaven. The second list of the gatekeepers of the seventh heaven, for instance, could be dispensed with, and the second account of the traveler's entrance, to which it leads, stands in clear contradiction to the first. In the first, the entrance is a triumphal procession, in the second, it is the final trial. The little fragment on tests for the worthy and unworthy comes from a somewhat different tradition from the main account, which conceives the dealings with the doorkeepers in more formal terms. The character of the songs changes markedly as we approach the end of the book, becoming obviously closer to the liturgical tradition of the synagogue. The concluding fragments on the secret of the Torah—that is, a magical method of learning it without labor and retaining it without forgetfulness—show the adaptation of the *Merkabah* tradition as a magical technique for a particular practical purpose. The same spirit is apparent in the prose introduction to the first part of the book, and the above references to the songs as *spells* (which is justified by this framework) rather than as *hymns* (which is the term their content would suggest) may have already called attention to this contrast.

Thus what we have in *Hekhalot Rabbati* is not so much a single composition as a collection of pieces illustrating different aspects of a single tradition of speculation concerning the Throne of God and the heavens beneath it. Its two main elements are a collection of songs, which are magni-

5. Herodian 7.3.1.

6. At 20.12 following: for the date, O. Cullmann, *Le Problème littéraire . . .* (Paris, 1930), p. 115.

loquent descriptions of the Throne, and a detailed account of the ascent, but beside these there are other songs which show the adaptation of this tradition for liturgical purposes, and there are prose passages which show its use in folk-tales and in apocalyptic speculations. The pseudohistorical framework of the ascent section, and the imposition of midrashic form on the whole, shows how this speculative tradition was attached to the authoritative figures of Rabbinic Judaism. Finally we can see clearly how it has appropriated magical elements for its own purposes, and has in turn been exploited by orthodox Jewish magicians for purposes of their own.

Now, this speculative tradition is represented by other works beside *Hekhalot Rabbati*. Professor Scholem in his recent book *Jewish Gnosticism, Merkabah Mysticism and Talmudic Tradition*[7] has listed eight examples of *hekhalot* literature, and has discussed a number of the literature's characteristic themes, with especial reference to their appearances in Gnostic, Talmudic, Christian, and magical material. His principal findings are as follows.

First, the notion of the ascent of the soul through a series of heavens is frequent in the pseudepigrapha, some of which are pre-Christian, and appears at the very beginning of Christianity (Paul was caught up into the third heaven) and in the *baraita* on the four who entered paradise, to say nothing of its frequent occurrence in Gnosticism.[8] The use of seals is prominent in later Coptic Gnostic works, and Marcosian gnosis uses Aramaic magical formulae in Greek material to control the hostile heavenly powers just as the *hekhalot* use Greek formulae in Aramaic or Hebrew contexts.[9] The peculiar use of "descent" instead of "ascent" to the *Merkabah* probably represents a transference to *Merkabah* speculation of the liturgical expression "going down before the ark" in prayer; this transference presumably resulted from comparison to the *Merkabah* of the synagogal ark containing the scrolls of the Pentateuch.[10] The transference was a late development, and numerous traces of the earlier usage (which spoke of an "ascent" to the *Merkabah*) have survived.

Second, much of the celestial personnel of the *hekhalot* is found also in the magical papyri and in Gnosticism.[11] Not only have the papyri and the

7. New York, 1960.

8. Scholem, *Jewish Gnosticism*, pp. 14–19.

9. *Ibid.*, p. 33.

10. *Ibid.*, p. 20, n. 1.

11. *Ibid.*, pp. 41ff., 67ff.

Gnostics taken over Hebrew names, but the *hekhalot* have taken over Greek names and sometimes have even taken back Greek corruptions of names which were originally Hebrew.[12] There was evidently a period of interchange between these traditions, and since the material exchanged shows no sign of Christian influence, Scholem argues that the period was probably pre-Christian.[13] Meṭaṭron is peculiar to the *hekhalot* and Rabbinic traditions, but he is a late development; his name has been imposed on two figures, one the angel Yahoel or the Lesser Lord (*Adonai*—or Yahweh—*hakkaṭan*) who appears in the pseudepigrapha, the magical papyri and Coptic Gnostic literature, and is presupposed in several Talmudic passages, the other the transformed Enoch, who appears in the pseudepigrapha.[14]

Third, the *hekhalot's* magical names of the deity have the same affiliations as those of the angels, while their metaphrastic expressions, "the power" (*geburah-dynamis*) and "the glory" (*kabod-doxa*), are common in the pseudepigrapha, the Christian and the Rabbinic material as well.[15] The expression "the place" (*makom-topos*), also used in the *hekhalot*, is common in Rabbinic material and appears in the Gnostic and Christian traditions in Clement's *Excerpts from Theodotus*, where is found also the *hekhalot's* identification of "the place" with the Demiurge (*yoṣer bereshit*) as the highest god.[16] Not only the names of God but also the description of His body—that is, the *Shiʿur Ḳomah* material, and (what is another form of the same thing) the description of his garment of light—have second- and third-century parallels in Rabbinic exegesis, especially that of the Song of Songs, in Gnosticism, in the magical papyri, and in pagan Greek and Iranian material.[17] Indeed, the *Shiʿur Ḳomah* material has a parallel which is probably from the first century, for it is found in the book of Elchasai, which promised a new forgiveness of sins in the third year of Trajan (*ca.* 101) and was presumably written some time prior to that date (Hippolytus, *Philosophumena*, 9, 13–15).

Finally, the *hekhalot* hymns are certainly prior to the synagogal *piyyutim*

12. *Ibid.*, pp. 76ff.

13. *Ibid.*, p. 34.

14. *Ibid.*, pp. 41–51. The transformation had already appeared in II Enoch 22:10, Charles = IX, end, Vaillant, and in the Ethiopic *Ascension of Isaiah* 9:9 (Charles = Tisserant).

15. Scholem, *Jewish Gnosticism*, pp. 67f.

16. *Ibid.*, pp. 34f.

17. *Ibid.*, pp. 36–41 and 58–64. Scholem's observations on the midrash on *Song* have been supplemented by a conclusive study by Saul Lieberman, printed as Appendix D of Scholem's book.

(therefore they cannot be later than the fourth or fifth century), and they are closely paralleled by a hymn reported by the Palestinian Rabbi, Isaac Napḥa, of the third century, a hymn he says was sung by the kine who pulled the ark of the Lord in I Samuel 6:12.[18] Therefore the literary form of these hymns is at least as old as the third century, and the concept of hymns being sung by the angels, the beasts, and the Throne itself is found in yet earlier pseudepigraphic and Christian material.[19]

Such are Scholem's findings: the notion of the ascent of the soul, the names of the angels and of God, the description of the body and garment of God, and the literary form of the hymns sung around the Throne, are all traceable at least to the third century. The fact that there are no traces of the literary form prior to this time, and the fullness with which the occult world is described (by contrast to the Tannaïtic practice of giving the student merely the main headings) incline Scholem to think that this literary tradition took form only in the third century.[20] But he himself points out that these are merely arguments from silence, and he evidently supposes that prior to the present literary formulation there was a tradition of mystical speculation concerning the ascent, the names, and the deity, which went back to some pre-Christian synthesis, since the magical and Gnostic borrowings of Jewish material, and the Jewish borrowings of magical and Gnostic material, are alike without any important trace of Christian contamination.[21] Christian, magical, Gnostic, and Jewish material of this sort, therefore, must all derive from some common stock which existed, at the latest, in the first century C.E.

This conclusion is of immense importance for the history of early Christianity and of the beginnings of Rabbinic Judaism. It adds a new dimension—that of the mystery, the *sod*, the secret doctrine—to our conventional conceptions of these movements. There is now a background in the picture, and we suddenly become aware that much of what we have hitherto been seeing was foreground. We recall with a shock of recognition stories like that of Rabbi Yoḥanan ben Zakkai. A Gentile once said to him, "The rituals you perform look like some sort of witchcraft. You bring a cow and burn it and reduce it to powder and take its ashes and when one of you is polluted by a dead body you sprinkle on him two or three drops and say to him, 'You are pure.'" R. Yoḥanan replied . . . "Have you seen

18. Scholem, *Jewish Gnosticism*, pp. 24ff.

19. *Ibid.*, p. 23.

20. *Ibid.*, pp. 28, 31.

21. *Ibid.*, p. 34.

a man into whom the demon of shaking has entered?" "Yes." "And what do you do to him?" "You bring roots and fumigate him with their smoke and you sprinkle water on him and the demon flees." Rabbi Yohanan asked him, "Can your ears hear what your mouth says? The same is the case with this spirit, which is the spirit of uncleanness... We sprinkle the water of purification on him and it flees." After the Gentile left, Rabbi Yoḥanan's students said to him, "Master, you pushed this fellow off with a reed. What do you say to us?" He said to them, "By your life, neither does the dead body render impure, nor do the waters purify, but the Holy One, Blessed be He, said, 'I have engraved a statute, I have decreed a decree. You are not free to transgress my decree.'"[22]

"Neither does the dead body render impure, nor do the waters purify!" It is easy to understand why such a teaching should be kept in the background, taught only to the inner circle of the master's pupils. But not all teachers were so discreet. When Jesus was asked a question on purity law, "Why do your disciples eat with unwashed hands?" he is said to have taught openly: "There is nothing outside a man which, going into him, can profane him." Nevertheless, "when he went into a house away from the crowd, his disciples asked him about this parable," and he explained it at length.[23] And the evangelist Mark, who tells us this story, is elsewhere at pains to insist that Jesus spoke to the people only in parables, "but privately, to his own disciples, he explained everything."[24] His disciples were those to whom he had given "the mystery of the Kingdom of God."[25]

Of course, scholars have long since explained away such traditions, and will doubtless continue to do so. But it is amazing how the evidence from quite diverse bodies of material, studied independently by scholars of quite different backgrounds and temperaments, yields uniform conclusions which agree with the plain sense of these discredited passages. Scholem's study of the materials in the *hekhalot* tradition, for instance, has just led us to conclusions amazingly close to those reached by Goodenough from his study of the archeological remains:[26] to wit, the Hellenistic period saw the development of a Judaism profoundly shaped by Greco-Oriental thought, in which mystical and magical (Goodenough would probably

22. *Numbers Rabbah* 19, 4; *Tanḥuma* (ed. Buber), *Ḥukat* 26.
23. Mark 7:5–23.
24. Mark 4:34.
25. Mark 4:11. Note the tense of the verb. It cannot refer to the following explanation. Consequently, there is no contradiction in verse 13. Contrast E. Klostermann's commentary (4th ed., Berlin, 1950).
26. E. Goodenough, *Jewish Symbols in the Greco-Roman Period*, 8 vols. to date (Bollingen Series 37: New York, 1953ff.)

say, "sacramental") elements were very important. From this common background such elements were derived independently by the magical papyri, Gnosticism, Christianity, and Hellenistic and Rabbinic Judaism. I may add that in all of these traditions such material was passed on as secret doctrine.

Having thus recognized the general relationship of *Hekhalot Rabbati* to these cognate esoteric traditions, let us now turn to the particular content of its teachings. Scholem has undoubtedly picked out the main elements: the accent, the magical names and formulae, the material on the Body and Garment of God, and the hymns. To these we should add, I think, the framework material on the preparation necessary for the ascent and the advantages which accrue to the master of the secret. As I said in the outline, these have their closest parallels in magical material. "The Sacred Secret Book of Moses called Eighth or Holy,"[27] for instance, for "the praxis of the name which includes all things" prescribes forty-one days' preliminary purification and a room on the ground floor of a house in which no one has died during the preceding year. The door must be on the west side, proper incense must be used, and one must sleep on the ground the night before the praxis is attempted. This sort of thing is so common in the magical papyri that the principal interest of the parallel is to show that the *hekhalot* books are not merely theoretical or imaginative works, but reflections of an actual practice. This is shown also by their differences from the magical papyri, for instance, in the matter of amanuenses. The magical papyri occasionally prescribe the use of a medium, usually an uncorrupted boy, who, under the magician's direction, sees the gods and describes what he sees.[28] In the *hekhalot*, on the other hand, it is the master who sees and describes, the assistant who writes what is revealed. This cannot be referred to literary imitation, and the further warning that the amanuenses are apt to be attacked by the hostile spirits is true to the phenomena of psychic contagion as reported, for instance, in the witchcraft trials, and is undoubtedly derived from actual experience.

This fact deserves emphasis not only for its own sake, but because magical practice and secrecy are very closely connected. Theoretically, no doubt, a philosophical or religious doctrine without any practical consequences might be kept secret; perhaps, even, some instances can be

27. Pap. Leyden J 395, folio I, lines 1ff., and VIII, lines 32ff., as given by A. Dieterich, *Abraxas* (Leipzig, 1891), pp. 169ff.

28. Such mediums appear in *The Demotic Magical Papyrus of London and Leiden*, ed. F. Griffith and H. Thompson (Oxford, 1921), I. 8, 18f., II. 1ff. and in *Papyri Graecae Magicae*, ed. K. Preisendanz, vol. I (Leipzig, 1928), pap. IV, lines 89ff.

found. But there is no doubt that secrecy is much more apt to be taken seriously if there is some practice involved. As in politics one was free to preach of liberty, but conspiracy to procure it was punishable by death, so in philosophy one might teach at will about supernatural beings, but particular practices calculated to establish communication with them were magic and magic was a capital crime, about which, therefore, injunctions of secrecy were apt to be taken seriously. A corollary of this practical attitude is the formation of small, secret groups. These groups, because of their nature, were in danger not only from the civil authorities, but also from their own practices, which exposed them to what would be called, in our terms, serious psychological strains. In their terms, anyone who attempted the ascent while unworthy, or who did not know the names of the doorkeepers or the proper forms of behavior, would be burned with supernatural fire or crushed beneath a myriad of iron bars. Therefore the unworthy and the unprepared must not be given information which would permit them to venture into this dangerous territory. The consequent secrecy which surrounded these teachings was completely serious. To dismiss it as conventional theosophical rhetoric would be to misunderstand completely the sort of material with which we have to do.

From all this it follows that the practical side of the *Merkabah* tradition had considerable influence on its intellectual development. Therefore, let us do what we can to date the beginning of the praxis. A *terminus post quem* is furnished by the tradition itself. The conclusion of *Hekhalot Rabbati* dates the revelation of the secret method at the building of the Second Temple, and says quite specifically that it had not been revealed before. The negative side of this statement, the refusal to claim Mosaic origin, is surprising and may reflect some special historical tradition. A *terminus ante quem* is given by the general Rabbinic tradition in its reports of the four who entered paradise in the early years of the second century. The same report[29] tells us that the men of the preceding generation were also familiar with speculation about the *Merkabah*, but it says nothing of their ascending to heaven; on the contrary, when they discussed the subject the holy spirit came down to them, as it did a generation earlier on the followers of Jesus.[30] Paul's report of being caught up to the third heaven[31] clearly refers to an involuntary experience and as such is an example of the ancient apocalyptic tradition in which the initiative is taken by the

29. *Ḥagigah* 14b, *T. Ḥagigah* 2.2 (Zuckermandel, p. 234), etc.
30. Acts 2:2ff.
31. II Cor. 12:1ff.; cf. Rev. 4:1ff.

deity, or is, at least, a special response to a prayer which might not have been answered. There is no notion of a technique in which the man takes the initiative and which enables him to ascend whenever he wants, as if—in the *Hekhalot's* words—he had a ladder in his house.

On the other hand, the technique seems to have existed in Paul's day. In his letter to the Colossians (2:8ff.) Paul is concerned among other things to warn the new converts against those who would capture them and carry them off by philosophy and empty deceit according to the tradition of men concerning the elements of the world. Against these deceivers he emphasizes that in the Messiah is embodied the whole pleroma of the divine, that the Messiah is the head of every power (*arche*) and authority, and that in him the Colossians have been disembodied and raised from the dead to immortality. The Messiah has overcome the obstacles before them, has stripped himself of the powers and authorities, has led the powers and authorities as captives in his triumph. Therefore, Paul argues, let no one judge you in food or drink or in matter of festival or new moon or Sabbath, which are mere shadows of the things to come and only the body of the Messiah. Do not let yourself be kept from the goal by anyone concerned with what is less important, even with service of the angels, the things he saw when going in, a man vainly puffed up by fleshly thoughts and not holding to the Head, from which all the cosmic body derives its order and direction. If you died with the Messiah from the elements of the world, why do you still teach, as if you still lived in the world, Do not touch, and Do not taste, and so on?

"The things he saw when going in" are admittedly obscure and their identity has long been disputed in the commentaries on the passage, but I think in the context they are best understood as the elements of the world; that is, the celestial bodies, who are also conceived as angels, spiritual powers and authorities. The variety of terminology is confusing because Paul, like other writers of his time, borrows indiscriminately from the different intellectual traditions of the world around him.[32] But behind the various terminologies the thought is simple. The world is the body of God, specifically it is the body of the Messiah, by whom and through whom and in whom God made it.[33] Miraculously, however, the Messiah has now come into this world, in order to save his chosen out of it, he has died to his cosmic body, stripped it off him, and risen free of it from the dead, in order that those who are magically united with

32. Cf. H. A. Wolfson, *Philo* (Cambridge, Mass., 1947), I, 102f.
33. Col. 1:15–17.

him may sacramentally share his death to the world and, consequently, his freedom.[34] Being free of the world, they should no longer reverence the cosmic powers, the angels, whom the false teacher, opposed by Paul, saw when going in. To what? Presumably, to the palaces of heaven.

It has recently been shown[35] that Colossians and Ephesians had some literary relationship to the hymns of the Dead Sea sect—the same peculiar rhetoric appears in them all, and this rhetoric, by the way, with its turgid piling up of abstract notions and its concern for supernatural dominations and powers, is not without similarities to that of the *hekhalot* hymns. Therefore it is tempting to look for traces of this technique of ascent in the literature of the Dead Sea sect, but the vague verbosity of its style affords no certain evidence. The *War* makes it probable that the sectarians thought God and His angels were in their camps,[36] or at least expected they would be with them in the final struggle against the powers of evil. The conclusion to the *Manual of Discipline* and, yet more clearly, certain passages of the *Hymns*, declare that the chosen of God is or is to be a companion of the angels, to share their lot and their secret knowledge and be joined with them in their praise of God.[37] But whether this is already realized or merely is to be in the end, is obscure, and in any event I have found no clear trace of a special technique beyond the general discipline of the sect by which this companionship might be secured. Similarly Philo's account of the *Therapeutae* does not quite state what is necessary. He concludes[38] with an account of their great festival, prepared for by the usual long period of abstinence. We hear of their assembling, robed in white, for prayer, of their forming two companies—one of women, the other of men—of their liberal potations of cold or (as a luxury) lukewarm water, of an allegorical exposition of the Scriptures, like one of Philo's, which they nonetheless follow with keenest interest, of hymns sung solo by each member of the company, of a meal so meager that one thinks it was probably sacramental, and of their spending the whole night singing and dancing in two choirs which finally merge into one. That their singing and circling choirs represented the planets and the angels is altogether likely. That the songs and dancing raised some of them to the heights of visionary ecstasy, so that the celebration was actually a technique

34. Col. 2:20—3:4.
35. By Professor K. Kuhn, in his paper at the meeting of SNTS, 1960.
36. XII, 6ff., so they were with R. Yoḥanan ben Zakkai when the doctrine of the *Merkabah* was taught; *Ḥagigah* 14b.
37. III, 21ff.; VI, 14, etc.
38. *On the Contemplative Life*, end.

enabling the soul to ascend into the cosmic and angelic heavens, is not unlikely, but it is not demonstrable, either. Both Philo and the Dead Sea sectarians speak often about "mysteries" of which they do not explain the nature, so it is not impossible that both may have known of such techniques as we have described and deliberately have said nothing about them.

Now it would be very surprising to find in the Judaism of this period any development wholly unparalleled in the surrounding Greco-Roman world. Therefore we naturally look thither for parallels to the *hekhalot* material and we find striking ones. The "Great Magical Papyrus of Paris" contains a ritual to enable the magician to ascend to heaven and see all the things which are there and so obtain immortality. It reads as follows (the magical names and cries being omitted):[39]

Draw breath from the rays [of sunlight] three times, breathing as deeply as you can, and you will see yourself becoming light and ascending on high, so that you seem to be in mid air. You will hear no sound of any creature, neither of man nor of any other animal, nor will you see at that time anything of the mortal things on earth, but you will see all immortal things. For you will see the divine constellation of that day and that hour, the presiding gods rising into heaven and others declining. The routs of the visible gods through the disc of the god, my father, will be seen, and likewise, too, the so-called tube, the source of the serviceable wind... And you will see the gods staring at you and rushing at you. You, then, immediately put your right index finger on your mouth and say, "Silence, Silence, Silence, symbol of the incorruptible living God, guard me, Silence!" Then give a long hiss, then smack your lips, saying [magical words], and then you will see the gods looking at you kindly and no longer rushing at you, but going to the proper order of their ranks. Accordingly, when you see the world above clear and revolving and none of the gods or angels rushing at you, expect to hear the crash of a thunderbolt so great as to terrify you. But again say, "Silence, Silence, [the spell], I am a star moving with you and rising radiant from the deep." At once, when you say these words, the disc [of the sun] will expand. And after you say the second spell in which is "Silence, Silence," and so on, hiss twice and smack your lips twice and forthwith you will see many five-rayed stars coming forth from the disc and filling all the air. But you again say, "Silence, Silence." And when the disc is opened you will see a circle free of fire and fiery doors, closed. And you immediately go on with the following spell, closing your eyes. Spell 3: "Hearken to me, hear me, N.N., Lord who hast bound together by spirit the fiery bars of the four-fold band[?], Thou who walkest in fire, creator of light, eternal sun, who breathest fire, fire-spirited Iao, spirit of light, oaI, rejoicing in fire, beautiful in light, aeon, ruler of light, whose body is fire, giver of light, sower of fire, shaker of fire,

39. Preisendanz, *Papyri Graecae Magicae*, IV, 537ff. I omit the beginning of the text.

strong of light, whirling fire, mover of light, thunderer, fame of light, increaser of light, who holdest light in fire, master of stars, open to me, for I call, because of the pressing and bitter and inexorable necessity, the immortal and living and honoured names which have never yet come into mortal nature nor been uttered in articulation by human tongue or mortal speech or mortal voice: [magical combinations of the vowels]." Say all this with fire and spirit, finishing the first recitation then similarly beginning the second until you finish the seven immortal gods of the world. When you have finished you will hear thunder and reverberation of the surrounding [heaven] and, in the same way, you will feel yourself shaken. And you say again, "Silence, [the spell]." Then open your eyes and you will see the doors opened and the world of the gods, which is inside the doors, so that from the pleasure and joy of the sight your spirit runs towards them and ascends. Then, standing still, gazing fixedly, at once draw your spirit from the divine into yourself. When, therefore, your soul has returned, say, "Come, Lord, [magical words]." When you say this the rays will turn toward you. Gaze into the midst of them. Then, when you do this, you will see a youthful god, well-favored, fiery-haired, in a white chiton and scarlet cloak, wearing a fiery crown. Forthwith greet him with the fiery greeting, "Hail, Lord, great in power, great ruler, king, greatest of the gods, Helios, the Lord of the heaven and the earth, god of gods, mighty is thy breath, mighty is thy power, O Lord. If thou seest fit, announce me to the greatest god, thy begetter and maker."

Following Helios the initiate sees yet further doors opened, meets the seven fates of the heaven and the seven rulers of the pole (each of whom must be greeted by his proper name), and eventually meets the supreme deity, the mover of the heaven, from whose eyes lightnings flame and from whose body stars leap forth. The account concludes with directions to be followed, "If you wish to use a fellow initiate so that he alone may hear with you what is said,"[40] perhaps the closest approach in the magical papyri to the amanuenses of the *hekhalot*.

It is impossible to deny the relationship of this material to the *hekhalot* tradition. The contrast between mortal and immortal beings, the ascent from the realm of mortality to that of the immortals, the jealous guards to be mastered by the use of magic names, the entrance of the heavenly realm, when the hostile gods all stare at the intruder, the thunder from the heaven above these inferior deities and the opening of the fiery doors and the vision of the world of the gods within and, finally, the fiery god from whose body the stars stream forth—all these characteristics are common to the Jewish and the magical material. The role of Helios in the magical text may well be the explanation of his frequent appearance (in his chariot, or *Merkabah*) on the center of Palestinian synagogue floors roughly

40. Lines 752ff.

contemporary with this fourth-century document. As the sun was the image of the invisible god, the psychopomp which led the beholder to the contemplation of the transcendent being, so perhaps the chariot of the transcendent god was imaged by the chariot of the sun, the chariot of fire in which the soul might ascend to the heavens. We have seen that behind the *hekhalot* material lies an actual technique traceable to the first century C.E. Similarly, Professor Hans Lewy has traced a pagan technique like that of the Paris papyrus to the end of the first century.[41] Behind this, unquestionably, lies a long liturgical and speculative development of which Bousset[42] and Dieterich[43] have begun the exploration, but which here lies beyond our immediate concern.

41. H. Lewy, *Chaldean Oracles and Theurgy* (Publications de l'Institut Français d'Archéologie Orientale, Recherches d'archéologie, XIII; Cairo, 1956), chaps. iii and iv.
42. W. Bousset, "Die Himmelsreise der Seele," *ARW* 4: 160ff. (1901).
43. A. Dieterich, *Eine Mithrasliturgie*, 3rd ed. (Berlin, 1923).

The Beginnings of Mishneh Torah Criticism

By ISADORE TWERSKY

Maimonides, sharing the philosopher's innate propensity for universals and concomitant disdain for particulars, may not have thought highly of historiography; some of his parenthetic observations on the subject are quite nihilistic.[1] It may also be that he had no penchant for history and never developed a critical historical sense; occasional historical illustrations or chronological statements in his writings are not always precise.[2] One thing, however, is certain: he evaluated his own historic position accurately and sensitively. Displaying great powers of discernment—and omitting the stereotyped overtures to modesty—Maimonides emphatically called attention to the innovating aspects of all his major works.[3] With regard to the *Mishneh Torah* in particular, he candidly declared that a work of such scope and arrangement was absolutely unprecedented. Some of his Geonic predecessors produced fragmentary codifications of Jewish law, but not since R. Judah the Patriarch has any individual undertaken to rework and reformulate the entire Halakhah. This, he implies, is his intellectual act of daring.[4]

Together with this confident realization of primacy went the undaunted

1. See *Mishnah Commentary*, *Sanhedrin*, X, 1; *Moreh Nebukim*, I, 2; S. Baron, "The Historical Outlook of Maimonides," *PAAJR* 6:8 (1934–35), n. 4. Cf. Abraham ibn Ezra, *Yesod Mora*ʾ (Prague, 1833), I, p. 11b; Abraham Maimonides, *Responsa*, ed. A. Freimann and S. Goitein (Jerusalem, 1937), 82 (p. 108).

2. E.g., *Moreh Nebukim*, I, 71; *Mishneh Torah*, introduction.

3. See his introductions to the *Mishnah Commentary* and *Sefer ha-Miẓwot*; in the introduction to *Moreh Nebukim* he claims to write about topics "which have not been treated by any of our scholars . . . since the time of our captivity."

4. *Ḳobeẓ Teshubot ha-Rambam* (Leipzig, 1859), I, 140 (p. 25): לפסוק הלכות בכל התלמוד ובכל דיני התורה לא קדמני אדם אחר רבנו הקדוש וסיעתו הקדושה. also, introductions to *Sefer ha-Miẓwot* and *Mishneh Torah*. This is the emphasis of Aaron ben Meshullam in his letter to R. Meïr Abulafia, *Ḳobeẓ*, III, 11d, ha-Meʾīrī, *Bet ha-Beḥirah* on *Nedarim*, *Nazir*, *Soṭah* (Halberstadt, 1860), p. 5b (והוסיף אומץ לכתוב . . . כל עניני התלמוד.) and P. Duran, *Maʿaseh Efod* (Vienna, 1865), p. 19. The parenthetic remarks in the letter to Joseph ben Judah (*Iggerot ha-Rambam*, ed. D. H. Baneth [Jerusalem, 1946]), I, 50, strike one as a deliberate understatement.

anticipation of criticism and opposition. Maimonides not only feared that inbred conservatism which instinctually leads people to oppose innovation and change,[5] but also he foresaw specific reasons for *Mishneh Torah* criticism. The occasion for the anticipatory classification of the various kinds of critics that would undoubtedly arise to find fault with his *Mishneh Torah* was the plaintive letter of his trusted disciple Joseph ibn Aknin, who was grievously irritated by the vehement anti-Maimonidean criticism generated in the school of Baghdad and was eager to retaliate in kind in defense of his master. In his very revelatory reply, counseling Joseph to accept the restraint, tolerance, and detachment which age, experience, and wisdom have imparted to himself, Maimonides enumerates the following types of critics:

> I knew and it was perfectly clear to me at the time that I composed it that it would undoubtedly fall into the hands of a wicked and jealous person who would defame its praiseworthy features and pretend that he does not need it or is in a position to ignore it; and [that it would fall] into the hands of a foolish ignoramus who will not recognize the value of this project and will consider it worthless; and [that it would fall] into the hands of a deluded and confused tyro to whom many places in the book would be incomprehensible, inasmuch as he does not know their source or is unable to comprehend in full the inferences which I inferred with great precision; and [that it would fall] into the hands of a reactionary and obtuse man of piety who will assail the explanations of the fundamentals of faith included in it.[6]

This acutely sensitive prediction, with its emphasis on jealousy, confusion engendered by the lack of sources, and unenlightened rejection of his explanation of theological principles as three potential reasons for criticism, is certainly noteworthy. However, these categories of criticism, while relevant—in greater or lesser degrees, depending on the particular critic[7]—are by no means exhaustive. There are many features of the *Mishneh Torah* which would invite legitimate criticism of a less personal nature. For all the overtures to anonymity and self-effacement notwithstanding, the *Mishneh Torah* bears an unmistakable Maimonidean imprint. Its

5. *Moreh Nebukim*, I, 31; cf. Judah ibn Tibbon, introduction to *Ḥobot ha-Lebabot*.

6. *Iggerot ha-Rambam*, ed. Baneth, I, 50–51; see *Iggeret Teḥiyat ha-Metim*, ed. M. D. Rabinovitz (Tel Aviv, 1951), pp. 347–348.

7. An interesting misapplication is the case of Rabad of Posquières, to whom scholars, collectively, attributed all these motives, thus making him the bugbear of Maimonidean criticism. See, e.g., H. Graetz, *Toledot ʿAm Yisraʾel*, IV (Warsaw, 1894), 403, n. 2, and A. Harkavy, *Ḥadashim gam Yeshanim*, p. 56; H. Gross, *Gallia Judaica* (Paris, 1897), p. 450; A. Geiger, *Wissenschaftliche Zeitschrift für jüdische Theologie* 5:558 (1839); I. H. Weiss, *Dor Dor we-Doreshaw*, IV, 300; S. Eppenstein, in *Moses ben Maimon*, ed. J. Guttmann (Leipzig, 1914), II, 72; H. Tchernowitz, *Toledot ha-Poskim* (New York, 1946–47), I, 285. I have discussed these in my study *Rabad of Posquières* (Cambridge, Mass., 1962).

rearrangement and systematization of Rabbinic law, although drawn from ancient sources, was known to be original; the choice of a term and the turn of a phrase were invested with significance and taken to reflect peculiar Maimonidean opinions. The personality and intellectual temper of the author emerge quite distinctly. This is the case not only with regard to the *Sefer ha-Madda*ᶜ and the other pockets of Maimonidean intellectualism so skillfully, often inconspicuously, woven into the warp and woof of the *Mishneh Torah*,[8] or the selective use of haggadic motifs (especially in concluding chapters of the various books),[9] but in purely halakhic contexts as well. Although Maimonides defined with great exactitude the structural and stylistic differences between an independent treatise (*ḥibbur*) and a commentary (*perush*) and relentlessly insisted that the *Mishneh Torah* was a *ḥibbur*,[10] it was inevitable that Maimonides the codifier should emerge also as a commentator. For example, in his restatement of a law, he frequently substituted a lengthy expository paraphrase for the key word or *terminus technicus* of the underlying Talmudic passage. This commentatorial strain is most pronounced in those sections whose subject matter abounds in lexicographical and terminological difficulties—*Sefer Tohorot*, for instance, particularly *Hilkot Kelim*.[11] These instances of Maimonidean paraphrase, while revealing that Maimonides realized the essential interrelationship of codification and commentary, drive in a wedge for the potential critic. Students of the *Mishneh Torah*, confronted with these explanations, may prefer what they believe to be superior explanations, which they will surely bring to the fore.[12]

When Maimonides, choosing the path of least resistance, evades the latent interpretive function incumbent upon the codifier by incorporating

8. See, e.g., the novel emphases in *Talmud Torah*, III, 12; *Issure Bi*ᵓ*ah*, XIV, 2; *Gezelah*, VI, 11 (for which cf. J. Anatoli, *Malmad ha-Talmidim* [Lyck, 1866], 173). Also, *Roẓe*ᵓ*aḥ*, VII, 1.

9. E.g., *Kesef Mishneh*, ᶜ*Abadim*, IX, 8 (הם דברי רבנו ראויים אליו.); see M. Berlin, *Sefer ha-Rambam*, ed. J. L. Fishman (Jerusalem, n.d.), II, 247ff.; J. Leiner, "Halakah wa-Aggadah besofē ha-Sefarim shebe-Mishneh Torah," *Talpiyot* 7:214–222 (1957). Cf. A. Cronbach, "The Maimonidean Code of Benevolence," *HUCA* 20:473 (1947). Appending an edifying haggadah to halakhic discussion has Mishnaic and Talmudic precedent; see J. N. Epstein, *Mabo le-Nusaḥ ha-Mishnah* (Jerusalem, 1948), pp. 974ff.

10. *Ḳobeẓ Teshubot ha-Rambam*, I, 25b

11. E.g., *Kelim*, XI, 20; *Ṭume*ᵓ*at Met*, X, 4; XI, 10; XIII, 3; *Shabbat*, XVIII, 10 (cf. S. Lieberman, *Hilkot Jerushalmi la-Rambam* [New York, 1947], p. 9). *Bet ha-Beḥirah*, VII, 5; *Nizḳe Mamon*, XIII, 12. The need to "extract the lexical material from Maimonides' halakhic writings" was noted parenthetically by B. Cohen, *Rashi Anniversary Volume* (New York, 1941), p. 246. This material is often inconspicuous, e.g., *Ḳeri*ᵓ*at Shema*, II, 1.

12. See *Hassagot*, *Ṭume*ᵓ*at Met*, XIV, 7; XVII, 3; *Malweh we-Loweh*, V, 5.

essentially equivocal words or problematic phrases into his restatement of the law, his readers will often have to provide explanations which vivify or actualize the given law. This is particularly so when there is no scholarly consensus upon which Maimonides can implicitly rely in his verbatim reproduction of an initially obscure or perplexing passage.[13] The standard line followed by Maimonidean protagonists—that Maimonides is only a codifier or compiler and does not purport to be a commentator[14]— is weakened by the fact that Maimonides frequently does interpolate commentary into his code.

Furthermore, notwithstanding all of Maimonides' announced intentions of eliminating indeterminate debate by selecting the most cogent view and then presenting unilateral, unsubstantiated decisions, he occasionally felt compelled to cite two or more opinions or to elaborate the reasons for his preferential treatment of a specific position.[15] In such cases, the reader may align himself with one of the views or question Maimonides' argumentation.

Perhaps the freest invitation to divergence of opinion was in the extensive area of actual Talmudic study and analysis, where curt normative formulations reflect Maimonides' latent explanation of Talmudic texts or halakhic concepts, and incorporate his inferences, deductions, and interpretive tours de force. Again, although Maimonides claims to have reproduced only those Talmudic statements whose meaning is indisputable,[16] the *Mishneh Torah* abounds with instances of originality of interpretation, harmonistic summation of disparate passages, calculated selection of variant readings, deliberate choice of one of many possible interpretations, independent determination of the normative decision when the Talmudic context is inconclusive, and the like. These instances far outnumber the approximately one hundred original statements and novel insights, unmistakably heralded by the formula, "It seems to me."[17] As a matter of fact, Maimonides admits elsewhere that much invisible paper work and

13. E.g., *Ṭumeʾat Met*, XVI, 5; *Ṭumeʾat Ẓaraʿat*, IV, 5; *Maʾakalot Asurot*, XII, 1; *Maʿaser Sheni*, III, 20; *Kelim*, V, 1; *Ṭumeʾat Oklin*, XIII, 11. See *Or Zaruʿa*, I, 760 (כי כן דרכו שכותב פסקיו דרך קריאה.)

14. E.g., *Kesef Mishneh*, *Ṭumeʾat Met*, XVI, 5; אין זה תפיסה על רבנו מפני שרבנו בספר הזה מחבר לא מפרש. *Migdal ʿOz*, *Genebah*, II, 1.

15. *Shabbat*, XXIX, 14; *Maʾakalot Asurot*, VII, 9; *Yom Ṭob*, II, 12; *Sheḳalim*, III, 9; *Nedarim*, II, 4; *Malweh we-Loweh*, XXI, 1. See Z. H. Chajes, *Tiferet le-Mosheh* (Zolkiew, 1840), 8a.

16. *Responsa*, 152: לא נניח תלמוד ערוך ונפסוק הלכה ממשא ומתן של גמרא. See H. J. Michael, *Or ha-Ḥayyim* (Frankfort, 1891), p. 540. Also, *Migdal ʿOz*, *Gerushin*, V, 14, *Maʾakalot Asurot*, III, 18.

17. See the list compiled by Maimon, in the introduction to the photostat of the 1480 Rome edition of the *Mishneh Torah* (Jerusalem, 1955), p. 6, n. 19.

incalculable mental effort went into the implied explanation of texts and derivations of laws in the *Mishneh Torah*.[18] Sometimes the style alludes to this originality or unconventional emphasis; the relative verbosity in such remarks as "these are reasonable statements and it is proper to adjudicate accordingly" is understandable only as underscoring a special point or innovation.[19] It was, therefore, all too natural for students of the *Mishneh Torah* to attempt a meticulous reconstruction of these submerged explanations, to analyze them, correlate them with others, and—if and when they appeared to be erroneous, inconsistent, or unconvincing—to take issue with them. Sometimes, even the cumulative resourcefulness of successive generations of scholars has failed to unravel a perplexing Maimonidean statement.

It should especially be noted that there was a large area of learning and interpretation in which complete unanimity could not be and was not expected. The admissibility of two or more equally tenable interpretations of a uniform text was a widespread principle—almost a rule of thumb—in medieval halakhic study and accounts for a good measure of its polemicism. This concept of relativism—or lack of objective determinacy characteristic of the mathematical sciences—was most strikingly formulated by Naḥmanides in his defense of Alfasi against the strictures of R. Zeraḥyah ha-Levi,[20] but it is implicit in Maimonides as well. In the introduction to the Mishnah Commentary, Maimonides pays homage to the excellence of Alfasi's *Halakhot* and declares that one would be hard put to find as many as ten errors in this monumental work.[21] Yet, in a responsum to an inquiry concerning a discrepancy between his view and Alfasi's, Maimonides reveals that he had prepared the first draft of a number of tracts and

18. *Responsa*, 69, 106, 143; *Iggerot ha-Rambam*, I, 51. Maimonides repeatedly called attention to the painstaking preparation, meticulous research, and architectonic construction that characterize all his writings. See introduction to *Pereḳ Ḥeleḳ* (*Sanhedrin*, chap. 10), end: אני לא חברתי . . . אלא לאחר עיון גדול והתבוננות *Moreh Nebukim*, introduction: לא נפלו בו הדברים כאשר נזדמנו אלא בדקדוק גדול ובשקידה רבה. *Sefer ha-Miẓwot*, introduction: ואקדים מה שיחייב העיון. See also introduction to *Tohorot Commentary*, end and other passages strewn throughout his writings.

19. *Malweh we-Loweh*, XXI, 1 (against Alfasi); *Sekirut*, II, 3 (against R. Joseph ibn Migas). Sometimes he specifies that he is rejecting his masters' opinions; e.g., *Ishut*, V, 15; *Zekiyah u-Matanah*, III, 8.

20. *Milḥamot ha-Shem*, *Berakot*, introduction: ואתה המסתכל בספרי אל תאמר בלבבך כי כל
תשובותי על הרב רבי זרחיה ז״ל כולו בעיני תשובות נצחות ומכריחות אותך להודות בהם על פני עקשותך,
ותתפאר בהיותך מספק אחת מהן על לומדיה או תטריח על דעתך להכנס בנקב המחט לדחות מעליך הכרח ראיותי.
אין הדבר כן. כי יודע כל לומד תלמודנו שאין במחלוקת מפרשיו ראיות גמורות ולא ברוב קושיות חלוטות
שאין בחכמה הזאת מופת ברור כגון חשבוני התשבורות ונסיוני התכונה.

21. *Mishnah Commentary*, introduction: ואין תפישה עליו בהם אלא בהלכות מועטות לא יגיעו עד
עשר בשום פנים.

treatises enumerating all those places where Alfasi may be criticized.[22] There are, in fact, scores and scores of places in the *Mishneh Torah* where the normative formulation differs from that in Alfasi.[23] In other words, the *Halakhot* contained not more than ten glaring mistakes which were indefensible and which one was bound to excoriate, but one could register one's reservations and queries, or submit alternate hypotheses with regard to many others. There were standing controversies which had never been definitively resolved and scholars could align themselves with one side or the other.[24] There were degrees of plausibility which had to be considered in the appraisal of divergent views and these could not be decided on the basis of purely scientific criteria.

Students of the *Mishneh Torah* would undoubtedly be aware of this element of relativism and be guided by comparable standards. On one hand, they would not mechanically reproduce all of their own stock views and pit them against those of the *Mishneh Torah*—which means, of course, that the argument *ex silentio* is not always valid.[25] A critic's silence does not invariably signify concurrence. On the other hand, though, students of the *Mishneh Torah* would not hesitate to introduce tentative alternatives to rigid Maimonidean formulations—which means, of course, that they did not have to be unreservedly committed to these views. Just as Naḥmanides could weaken a view of Razah and thereby rehabilitate a view of Alfasi merely by suggesting *possible* interpretations and conjectural constructions, students of the *Mishneh Torah* could at least reservedly question—if not peremptorily dismiss—a Maimonidean statement by submitting an alternative. Their purpose may be to deflate Maimonides' sense of certitude and authoritativeness, when this is very pronounced or, more generally, to

22. *Responsa*, 353: וזה שאנחנו חלקנו עליו בקצת מקומות כמו ל׳ מקום או יותר, מה שתפס עליו תלמידו רבי׳ יוסף הלוי ז״ל . . . וקצתם אנחנו הערנו עליהם . . . וכבר עשינו קונדרסין באותם המקומות אמנם עדיין לא יצאו לתכלית הפעולה. See also his letter to Joseph ben Judah, *Iggerot ha-Rambam*, I, 69: ותעסוק בתלמוד תורה על דרך האמת ולא תלמוד אלא הלכות הרב ז״ל בהעריכו אל החבור וכאשר תמצא חלוף ביניהם תדע כי העיון בתלמוד יורך הדבר ויתגלו לכם המקומות הסתומים.

23. The critics sometimes note this divergence; see *Yom Ṭob*, I, 14; *Ishut*, XVIII, 28; *Zekiyah u-Matanah*, X, 2; *Yibbum wa-Ḥalizah*, VI, 27, and others.

24. See, e.g., *Shabbat*, I, 7 (מלאכה שאינה צריכה לגופה) and commentaries *ad loc.*; cf. the important article of A. Freimann, "Teshubat ha-Rambam le-R. Joseph ha-Maᶜarabi," *Sefer Yobel le-B. M. Lewin* (Jerusalem, 1940), p. 30. The commentators repeatedly observe: זו מחלוקת ישנה היא· see *Yom Ṭob*, III, 8; *Shofar*, III, 4; *Ishut*, XVIII, 19; *Ḥameẓ u-Maẓah*, VIII, 8; *Nizḳe Mamon*, XII, 8, and others.

25. Many Rabbinic scholars maintained that silence is tantamount to support. See, e.g., *Kenesset ha-Gedolah*, *Kelale ha-Rabad*, printed at the beginning of most *Mishneh Torah* editions; ᶜAzariah dei Rossi, *Meᵓor ᶜEnayim* (Vilna, 1863), *Imre Binah*, 242; *Maẓref ha-Kesef*, 13. R. Solomon Luria apparently also maintained that silence equaled agreement: see *Yam Shel Shelomoh*, *Ḥullin*, I, 42: ואף שהרמב״ם גדול בתורה היה . . . והראב״ד ג״כ לא השיג עליו, מכל מקום לא אשא פנים בתורה.

stimulate further research and analysis by underscoring the existence of cogent, conflicting views. Sometimes, they merely reflect one's own uncertainty about the correct theory or proper practice.[26]

II

Now, indeed, this criticism, much of which Maimonides fully anticipated, was quickly forthcoming. By the middle of the thirteenth century there must already have been a considerable volume of criticism, for by approximately that time Naḥmanides could observe in passing that Maimonides' "great treatise" had been subject to sustained questioning.[27] Earlier, Alḥarizi had commented rather amorphously on the widespread critique of Maimonides' work—tendentiously suggesting that it was *all* biased and inconsequential.[28] Such an accumulation of critical literature —and one must subsume under this category not only the animadversionary writings of avowed critics but the explanatory works of neutral students as well—is comprehensible only in light of the speed and intensity with which the *Mishneh Torah* spread.

Completed in 1180, or probably 1178,[29] it became known with amazing rapidity,[30] first in Oriental countries (Palestine, Syria, Babylon, Yemen)[31] then in the Mediterranean area (including Spain and Provence), and finally in the Franco-German orbit as well. In 1191, Maimonides already spoke

26. Those annotations which are introduced by noncommittal phrases—"There is one who says," "Some explain," "It is possible to say"—are not necessarily binding; see *Kenesset ha-Gedolah*; *Bet Joseph* on *Ṭur Oraḥ Ḥayyim*, 582. There are over forty of these in Rabad's *Hassagot*.

27. Naḥmanides' *Hassagot* on the *Sefer ha-Miẓwot* הקדמה לפרטי המצוות: דברים הכתובים לו בחבורו הגדול, בין שכבר הקשו עליו חכמי הדורות או שמחלו עליהן. The last phrase indicates that there was more disagreement and criticism than was articulated. It implies that they refrained from calling attention to flaws which could easily be exposed. Compare the following exchange: R. Zeraḥyah ha-Levi, *Sefer ha-Ẓaba*, *middah* 12: הרב אלפסי כתב ... ואנן לא ס״ל הכי ... וגם אלו מן המחילות שמחלנו לו ולא השגנום בספר המאור. To which Naḥmanides retorts: ועדיין בעל הספר הזה מערער על דבריו. כי אחר שמחל לו בספר המאור. ומה זו מחילה שהלה חוזר וגובה ממנו.

28. *Taḥkemoni*, chap. 46: ויהי אחרי מות משה, נועדו כל איש עז וקשה, וכל כסיל פיהו פער, בספרד וצרפת וארץ הצבי ושנער, ויועצו להשיב על חבורו דברים רקים וענינים צנומים דקים.

29. See S. Gandz, "Date of the Composition of Maimonides' Code," *PAAJR* 17:1–9 (1948); E. Weisenberg, Appendix to *Code of Maimonides*: *Book III* (Yale Judaica Series, XIV, New Haven, 1961), p. 561.

30. Cf., e.g., the spread of Rashi's commentary, which is not yet mentioned in the *Sefer ha-Ḳabbalah* of Abraham ibn Daud; see L. Ginzberg, *Ginze Schechter*, II (New York, 1929), 382; S. Assaf, *Tarbiz* 8:162 (1937), n. 2; *idem*, *Be-Oholē Yaᶜakob* (Jerusalem, 1943), pp. 16–18.

31. E.g., the *Hassagot* of R. Daniel in *Birkat Abraham*, ed. Goldberg (Lyck, 1859); see the references cited by A. Freimann, "Teshubat ha-Rambam," *Sefer Yobel Lewin*, pp. 27–28.

of its renown in all corners of the earth,[32] even though in 1193 it had apparently not yet reached southern France.[33] By the turn of the century, it was firmly rooted in the Provençal-Castille region and was the subject of intense study.[34] In northern France also it quickly established itself and circulated widely.[35] One can discern the transition, in a matter of decades, from casual, irregular use and selective study of the *Mishneh Torah* to habitual, almost routine reference to it on all occasions. The earliest quotations, those by R. Judah ben Isaac of Paris, R. Isaac ben Abraham (Riẓba) and R. Samson of Sens, appear as sporadic references to "the book of R. Moses."[36] By 1236, R. Moses of Coucy refers to that praiseworthy composition of Maimonides which "enlightened the eyes of Israel" and strengthened Talmudic study as it spread "in the lands of Christendom and Islam."[37] Still later, by the time of R. Meïr of Rothenburg, it had achieved special prominence as an indispensable reference work, comparable metaphorically to the *Urim we-Tumim*.[38] Extensive quotations from it—sometimes anonymous—turn up in the *ᶜArugat ha-Bosem* of Abraham ben ᶜAzriel, *Sefer Ḥasidim*, *Sefer ha-Roḳeaḥ* of R. Eleazar of Worms, responsa collections of R. Meïr of Rothenburg,

32. *Iggeret Teḥiyat ha-Metim*, 357: וכאשר התפרסם חבורנו זה בארצות והתפשט בקצוות

33. Maimonides' Epistle on Astrology, ed. A. Marx, *HUCA*, vol. III (1926). והדבר ידוע כי לא הגיע עדיין לידכם החבור אשר חברנו במשפטי התורה שקראתיו משנה תורה. See A. Geiger, "Moses ben Maimon," *Nachgelassene Schriften* (Berlin, 1876), III, 90–91. From his very important letter to Joseph ben Judah (*ca.* 1192), it would appear that the *Mishneh Torah* (as was later to be the case with the *Moreh Nebukim*) was circulated in installments; cf. *Iggerot ha-Rambam*, ed. Baneth, I, 52: כל שכן שהגיעו אלי אגרות מחכמי צרפת ואחרים בשמותם שהם מתפעלים מהמפעל ומבקשים לקבל את ההמשך, וכבר נפוץ החיבור עד לקצות הארץ הנושבת. If the references to הרב הבבלי in the *Sefer ha-ᶜIṭṭur* of R. Isaac ben Abba Mari (d. 1193) designate Maimonides, this would significantly support the view that the *Mishneh Torah* reached France in piecemeal fashion, book by book. See J. Dienstag, "Yaḥasam shel Baᶜale ha-Tosafot la-Rambam," *Mirsky Jubilee Volume* (New York, 1959), pp. 353–354. On the date of the composition of the *ᶜIṭṭur*, see A. Neubauer, "Der Itur," *MGWJ* 20:173–176 (1870). Also, L. Blau, "Das Gesetzbuch des Maimonides historisch betrachtet," Moses ben Maimon, ed., J. Guttmann (Leipzig, 1914), II, 339, n. 4.

34. In 1232, R. Meïr ha-Levi Abulafia wrote to Naḥmanides: אף כי זה ימים רבים הרבה משלשים שנה, בהגיע תור משנה ספר התורה בארץ הזאת see *Ḳobeẓ Teshubot ha-Rambam*, III, 7a. Also, Abulafia's elegy on Maimonides, ed. H. Brody, *Tarbiz* 6:7 (1935).

35. See, in general, Abraham Maimonides, *Milḥamot ha-Shem*, ed. R. Margaliyot (Jerusalem, 1953), pp. 52–54.

36. See E. Urbach, *Baᶜale ha-Tosafot* (Jerusalem, 1955), 272–273; M. Abulafia, *Kitāb Al-Rasāʾil*, 132: (נמצא ביד החברים שעמנו מקצת ספרי הרמב״ם ז״ל) Naḥmanides' letter, *Ḳobeẓ*, III, 9: וראיתי לרבנו הצרפתי ז״ל בתשובותיו (הריצב״א) במצוות הנוהגות עתה בארץ ישראל, שהגיעו ספרי הרב הגדול לידו והיה מתברך בהם בשפה ברורה ובלשון מהודרת . . .

37. *Sefer Miẓwot Gadol* (Venice, 1522), introduction.

38. *Responsa* (Lemberg, 1860), 426: אמנם משבא לידי ספר רבינו משה בן מיימון זצ״ל נשאלתי מאת כבודך שאלה זו, אמרתי בלבי אשאל באורים ותומים ודבר מה יראני וכיבדתי לך.

not to mention the *Midrash ha-Gadol*, *Tanḥuma*, and other works.[39] In short, less than a century after its composition, the *Mishneh Torah* was well on its way to becoming "the most celebrated codification of Jewish law."[40]

Much has been written about the nature of this criticism and the motives which spurred scholars on to review the *Mishneh Torah* in its encyclopedic totality. The Maimonidean allegation of jealousy—begrudging Maimonides the honor which was almost universally bestowed upon him—is often repeated; it was echoed immediately by Aaron ha-Kohen of Lunel and Sheshet of Saragossa.[41] Instinctive polemicism—critique for critique's sake—is sometimes suggested.[42] Responsibility is also placed upon ideological convictions: suspicion of heresy and antipathy to unbridled popular philosophic inquiries.[43] Arbitrary opposition to codification, to any definitive, systematic formulation of halakhah, is also submitted in explanation of the anti-Maimonidean critique.[44] All these motivational analyses, to my mind, merely skirt the periphery, without coming to grips with the crux of the problem: how much of the opposition was personal and petty, psychological and ideological, and how much was scholarly and methodological? What was objectionable even to scholars who themselves excelled in codification and were not averse to philosophizing? What made a student move from obviously great admiration to reservation and even rejection?

Deeper study would indicate that the nature and motives of this criticism can be determined only in the broad perspective of the total reception

39. See ᶜ*Arugat ha-Bosem*, ed. E. Urbach (Jerusalem, 1941) and Urbach's article in *Tarbiz* 10:30 (1939); *Sefer Ḥasidim*, ed. Freimann, p. 17; E. Urbach, " Ḥelkam shel Ḥakmē Ashkenaz we-Ẓarefat ba-Pulemos ᶜal ha-Rambam," *Zion* 12:150–151 (1947); *Tanḥuma*, ed. S. Buber, introduction, chap. 9; *Midrash ha-Gadol, Genesis*, ed. M. Margaliyot, p. 8.

40 R. Joseph Karo, introduction to *Bet Joseph*.

41. Aaron's letter to Abulafia, *Kitāb al-Rasāᵓil*, 34: ומבין ריסי אגרתך נכר כי לא חפצת צדקו במחשבתך כי אם בהתגלות לבך ואתה לא החילות כי אם להראות חכמתך. Sheshet's letter to Lunel, ed. A. Marx, *JQR* 25:414 (1935). See also the anonymous letter published in *Kerem Ḥemed*, 5:10 (1841). This is implicit in Alharizi's characterization of Abulafia; *Taḥkemoni*, 46. See Note 7. Joseph Sambary (A. Neubauer, *Mediaeval Jewish Chronicles* [London–New York, 1887–95], I, 124) suggested that Rabad envied the success of Maimonides' code: הרמב״ם ז״ל שמיה גרים ־ הר״מ במז״ל; שזכה מזלו ונתפשט חבורו. והראב״ד ז״ל שמיה גרים ־ הר׳ אבד ז״ל; שלא זכה ואבד חבורו.

42. E.g., *Kesef Mishneh*, *Bet ha-Beḥirah*, IV, 5; *Ḥameẓ u-Maẓah*, VI, 6; R. David ben Zimra, *Maᶜaser Sheni*, I, 14. *Sefer ha-Menuḥah* on *Shofar* I, 1; II, 8.

43. E.g., Menaḥem ᶜAzariah Fano, *Sefer Teshubot*, 108 (p. 111). See *Jewish Encyclopedia*, I, 104; S. Winniger, *Grosse jüdische National-Biographie* (1925), I, 22; I. Zinberg, *Toledot Sifrut Yisraᵓel* (Tel Aviv, 1955), I, 306.

44. Tchernowitz, *Toledot ha-Posḳim*, I, 11; S. Atlas, introduction to *Rabad's Commentary on Baba Ḳamma* (London 1940), 42.

of the *Mishneh Torah*, where stricture and supplement, criticism and commentary, dissent and elaboration are inseparable.[45] Scholars everywhere turned to its exhaustive study rather than its exclusive criticism, as had previously been the case with Alfasi's *Halakhot*. Bias and personal temperament, to be sure, may play a part; scholars were "involved" persons with likes and dislikes, deep-seated sentiments and decided propensities, and did not write with emotional detachment. However, reaction to the *Mishneh Torah* was motivated primarily by a sense of intellectual freedom and independence which expressed itself in pointed criticism and/or reasoned corroboration—animadversions or scholia. The common purpose of all Maimonidean literature was to scrutinize Maimonidean statements—criticize them, interpret them, modify them, relate them to the sources. Most of the twelfth- and thirteenth-century writers—R. Daniel ha-Babli, R. Abraham ben David of Posquières, R. Moses ha-Kohen, R. Jonathan of Lunel, R. Meshulam ben Moses of Béziers, R. Samson of Sens, R. Meïr ha-Kohen—are as much commentators as they are critics while, to a measurable extent, the writings of the Maimonidean "armbearers" of the fourteenth century and later, starting with R. Manoaḥ (*Sefer ha-Menuḥah*), R. Vidal of Tolosa (*Maggid Mishneh*), Shem Tob ibn Gaon (*Migdal ᶜOz*) and R. David ben Zimra (*Leshonot ha-Rambam*; *Yeḳar Tiferet*), contain much substantive critique. The same is true for the Maimonidean statements quoted and discussed in the general halakhic literature of the period—such as the *Sefer ha-ᶜIṭṭur* of R. Isaac ben Abba Mari, responsa of R. Meïr ha-Levi Abulafia, collective studies of the sages of Lunel, early *Tosafot* of R. Judah ben Isaac of Paris, Isaac ben Abraham and Solomon ben Judah of Dreux, *Or Zaruᶜa* of R. Isaac ben Moses of Vienna, commentaries of R. Jonah Gerondi and his disciples, novellae and codificatory writings of Naḥmanides and Rashbah, compendium of R. Asher ben Yeḥiel. The common characteristic of this heterogeneous literature vis-à-vis Maimonides is neither unquestioning subservience nor uninformed rejection but searching analysis of the subject under consideration. The results—blanket endorsement, qualified approval, partial dissent, or relentless criticism—vary.

Allowing for varying emphasis, two major trends are discernible in all subsequent Maimonidean studies: (1) criticism of Maimonides for omitting

45. Cf. M. Hagiz, *Mishnat Ḥakamim* (Tchernovitz, 1864), 176, Z. H. Chajes, *Tiferet le-Mosheh* (Zolkiew, 1840), p. 3; J. Reifmann, "Rabad Baᶜal ha-Hassagot," *Bet Talmud* 4:380 (1885); S. Assaf, "Yaḥaso shel ha-Rabad el-ha-Rambam," *Ḳobeẓ Rabbenu Moses b. Maimon*, ed. J. L. Fishman (Jerusalem, 1935), p. 276.

what we may loosely call the apparatus criticus from his *Mishneh Torah* and, concomitantly partial disqualification of this work as an ultimate guide in codification; (2) conversely, concerted efforts to supply the necessary sources and explanations for his statements and thus rehabilitate the *Mishneh Torah* as an authoritative code. These two approaches, apparently antithetical yet in many respects mutually complementary, are the axes around which all commentaries, supercommentaries, and critical supplements revolve. Both—and this is the main point—are articulated and to some degree implemented in the early decades of *Mishneh Torah* investigation by those very writers usually described as hypercritical and anti-Maimonidean.

A good example of the early critic-commentator foreshadowing both these aspects in theory as well as in practice is Rabad of Posquières. The argument concerning the lack of sources, which led to a systematic exposé of other weaknesses and errors—alleged flaws, apparent discrepancies, strained interpretations—was fully articulated by Rabad in one of the early *hassagot*, where he castigates Maimonides for "forsaking the way of all authors who preceded him."[46] Precisely because Maimonides mentions no names and adduces no proofs, because the derivation of normative judgments from hylic Talmudic debates is not traced, Rabad illustrated that the *Mishneh Torah* was not the last word in codification, that some statements were erroneous, others were based on faulty inferences and still others were merely one possible alternative, arbitrarily selected. Errors, real or apparent, serious or trivial, of various sorts—textual, stylistic, theoretical, methodological, codificatory, consuetudinary, classificatory, but mostly interpretive—evoked various critical reactions from Rabad.

This critical note, once struck, reverberates throughout later literature and helps establish a major category of interpretive and critical annota-

46. *Hassagot, Mishneh Torah*, introduction:

"He intended to improve but did not improve, for he forsook the way of all authors who preceded him. They always adduced proof for their statements and cited the proper authority for each statement; this was very useful, for sometimes the judge would be inclined to forbid or permit something and his proof was based on some other authority. Had he known that there was a greater authority who interpreted the law differently, he might have retracted. Now, therefore, I do not know why I should reverse my tradition or my corroborative views because of the compendium of this author. If the one who differs with me is greater than I—fine; and if I am greater than he, why should I annul my opinion in deference to his? Moreover, there are matters concerning which the Geonim disagree and this author has selected the opinion of one and incorporated it in his compendium. Why should I rely upon his choice when it is not acceptable to me and I do not know whether the contending authority is competent to differ or not. It can only be that 'an overbearing spirit is in him.'"

tions. Rabad's immediate successors in Maimonidean critique, such as R. Moses ha-Kohen, shared this concern. It is expressed or implied in a host of other contemporary statements from the pen of both antagonists and protagonists, such as R. Samson of Sens, Joseph ben Todros Abulafia, Sheshet ha-Nasi of Saragossa, and an anonymous partisan of the *Mishneh Torah*.[47] R. Moses of Coucy, author of the *Sefer Miẓwot Gadol* which is actually based on the *Mishneh Torah* and organized in accord with Maimonidean principles of classification, mentions the lack of sources as a serious deficiency impairing the value and restricting the usefulness of the *Mishneh Torah*.[48] His own book cites sources and includes summary presentations of explanations and inferences. R. Asher ben Yeḥiel correlated the ability—even the possibility—to use the *Mishneh Torah* with one's knowledge of the sources: "One should not rely upon his reading in this book to judge and issue decisions unless he finds proof in the Talmud."[49] Ha-Meʾiri also stresses this deficiency, even though he does not explicitly condemn it.[50] Joseph ibn Kaspi chides the scholars of his day for seeking proofs and explanations of the commandments rather than being content with the codified traditions of the *Mishneh Torah*.[51] Ḥasdai Crescas, who had contemplated a comprehensive work on law as well as dogma, practically reproduces Rabad's objections.[52] R. Isaac ben Sheshet Perfet endorses R. Asher ben Yeḥiel's view concerning the need to trace all decisions back to original sources; people who rely exclusively on the code are denigrated

47. Letter of R. Samson, *Kitāb al-Rasāʾil*, 131–132: ואיש אל ישים יגיעו בספרים הסתומים . . . וכל האומר דבר בשם אומרו מביא גאולה לעולם· Joseph Abulafia, *Jeshurun* 8:39–40 (ed. J. S. Kobak, 1872): היחשבו כל הספר הסתום למשה מסיני הלכה . . . Letter of R. Sheshet, published by A. Marx, *JQR* 25:414 (1935): ואחרי אשר איננו מביא ראיות מדברי חכמי התלמוד לדבריו, מי ישמע אליו. A. S. Halkin, "Sanegoriyah ʿal Sefer Mishneh Torah," *Tarbiz* 25:413–428 (1956). See also D. Kaufmann, "The Etz Chayim of Jacob b. Jehudah of London," *JQR*, O.S., 5:368 (1893): ועל כי הגאון לא הביא בספרו ראיה לדבריו, גם לקצת דבריו חלוקין גאוני עולם האחרונים . . . ועמד הרב ר׳ משה מקוצי וחבר חבור מכל התורה על פי ספר הגאון . . . והביא ראיות לרוב דבריו.

48. *Sefer Miẓwot Gadol*, introduction: לא הביא הגאון שום ראיה בספריו וכל אדם שיורה מתוך ספריו ויבקשו ממנו כתב ראיה מנין· אם לא למד הראיה או אפי׳ למדה ואינו זוכר יהא לו הדבר ההוא כחלום בלא פתרון.

49. *Responsa*, *Kelal*, XXXI, 9.

50. *Bet ha-Beḥirah* on *Nedarim*, *Nazir*, *Soṭah*, p. 5b. See also Jeruham ben Meshullam, *Sefer Mesharim* (Kapust, 1908), p. 2.

51. Will of Joseph ibn Kaspi, in *Hebrew Ethical Wills*, ed. I. Abrahams (Philadelphia, 1926), I, 153: כי לא יספיק לכם הקבלה מספר משנה תורה שחבר רבנו משה ואעפ״י שאמר הוא ז״ל ואינו צריך לספר אחר ביניהם. Earlier, Jacob Anatoli had written in the introduction to *Malmad ha-Talmidim*: אבל הדבר הגדול היום בעיני חכמינו בעלי הגמרא הוא העסק בסוגיות התלמוד ולא העסק בפסק הנברר ממנו.

52. *Or Adonai* (Vienna, 1860), p. 32.

as "rendering decisions in haughtiness."[53] Faint echoes of this refrain may be heard even from R. Joseph Karo, who admits that he would have liked to pattern his book on that of Maimonides but was compelled to alter his plans "because he brings only one opinion while I had to elaborate and write the opinions of other codifiers and their reasons."[54] This attitude—and its critical consequences—is uniformly reflected in the sustained refusal of halakhists to use the name *Mishneh Torah*, which struck them as somewhat audacious in its presumption to serve as the sole companion to Scripture.[55] Indeed, what more need be said than to call attention to the fact that Maimonides himself was conscious of this shortcoming, discussed it a number of times in his correspondence, and anticipated the criticism it would provoke.[56]

The second trend in Maimonidean study—corroborating and elucidating the *Mishneh Torah* by unearthing its Talmudic sources and revealing its latent processes of reasoning—also had its origin in Rabad's *Hassagot*. He was the first to emphasize the need of such work and, in part, to undertake its implementation. His *Hassagot* contains many positive, appreciatory elements, starting with a sustained quest for sources and continuing to

53. See A. Hershman, *Rabbi Isaac ben Sheshet Perfet* (New York, 1943), p. 69.

54. *Bet Joseph*, *Ṭur Oraḥ Ḥayyim*.

55. See defensive statement of Solomon Duran, *Milḥemet Miẓwah*, end. Usual references are: כתב הרב רמב״ם (*Temim Deᶜim*, 120); חבור חדש (*ᶜIṭṭur*, p. 152); וכן בספר הרב ר׳ משה (*Or Zaruᶜa*, I, 332); לשון הר׳ משה (*ᶜArugat ha-Bosem*, II, 269); מקצת ספרי הרמב״ם (*Kitāb al-Rasāʾil*, 132); ספר הרמב״ם (Responsa of R. Asher ben Yeḥiel, XXXII, 11); חבור הרמב״מ ז״ל (Responsa of Rashbah, 253). See also *Sefer ha-Makriᶜa* (Munkacz, 1900), pp. 28, 89, 91. Chroniclers and poets, however—whose concern is not halakhic—do not hesitate to use the title *Mishneh Torah*; see, e.g., Judah ben Samuel ibn ᶜAbbas, *Yaʾir Netib*, quoted by Assaf, *Meḳorot le-Toledot ha-Ḥinnuk*, II, 30; Shem Tob Falaqera, *Sefer ha-Mebaḳesh*, Assaf, II, 47; poem printed by Steinschneider, *Moreh meḳom ha-Moreh* (Berlin, 1885), 65 (p. 19); Abraham ben Solomon, Supplement to *Sefer ha-Ḳabbalah*, ed. A. Neubauer, *Mediaeval Jewish Chronicles*, I, 102; Profiat Duran, *Maᶜaseh Efod*, 19. In his polemical exchange with Abulafia, Aaron ben Meshullam still refers in passing to *Mishneh Torah*; *Ḳobeẓ*, III, 11d. See also Notes 34, 51. Apparently the first person to substitute *yad ha-ḥazaḳah* for *Mishneh Torah* was Jesse ben Ḥezeḳiah, the exilarch of Damascus; *Ḳobeẓ Teshubot ha-Rambam*, III, 21c (היד החזקה אשר קראו משנה תורה). See B. Cohen, "The Classification of the Law in the Mishneh Torah," *JQR* 25:529 (1935), n. 41. This is noteworthy: a confirmed Maimonidean protagonist—in a letter threatening to excommunicate those who keep writings antagonistic to Maimonides—already shows his reluctance to use the term *Mishneh Torah*.

Finally, it should be remembered that Maimonides frequently used the term *ḥibbur* to designate his code; cf. L. Blau, "Das Gesetzbuch des Maimonides historisch betrachtet," *Moses ben Maimon*, ed. J. Guttmann (Leipzig, 1914), II, 338–339. Blau's statement, however, that the term *Mishneh Torah* is never repeated by Maimonides is untenable; cf. *Responsa*, 334; *Iggeret Teḥiyat ha-Metim*, 347.

56. *Ḳobeẓ Teshubot ha-Rambam*, I, 140 (p. 26). See the well-documented study by I. Kahana, "Ha-Pulemos mi-Sabib le-Ḳebiᶜat ha-Halakah keha-Rambam," *Sinai* 26:391–411, 530–537 (1955).

pointed lexical annotation as well as lengthy halakhic clarification. All the standard commentators, starting with R. Shem Tob ibn Gaon and Vidal of Tolosa through R. David ben Zimra and R. Joseph Karo and continuing until this very day, were preoccupied with this task; the center around which their commentaries revolve is the enumeration of sources and their explication in a Maimonidean vein. Karo provides an excellent description of the inherent difficulties of the *Mishneh Torah* and the attempts to resolve them: "The generations that followed him could not understand his works well . . . for the source of every decision is concealed from them . . . One wrote a commentary *Maggid Mishneh* in which he revealed the source of every law . . . But he illuminated only six [of the fourteen] parts . . . So I the youngster arose . . . to write on the source of every decision and explain his statements."[57] To this day, the quest for *Mishneh Torah* sources in unknown midrashim, Geonic responsa, variant readings, et cetera, continues unabated as one of the main forms of rabbinic scholarship. What more need be said than to call attention to the fact that Maimonides himself, fully cognizant that his method would invite criticism, contemplated the composition of a *Sefer ha-Beʾur*, some kind of sourcebook which would serve as a supplement to the *Mishneh Torah.*[58]

Another interesting example is provided by the writings of R. Meïr of Rothenburg—to take a later scholar whose attitude to the *Mishneh Torah* already had time to be conditioned by the steadily increasing venerability and authoritativeness of Maimonides. On one occasion, he subordinates himself completely to Maimonides for "who am I and what is my reasoning, my heart is like the fullness of the eye of a very fine needle and [I cannot] dissent from the reasoning of our Master which is as wide as the Temple door." The *Mishneh Torah* is like the *Urim we-Tumim.*[59] Yet he himself initiated the systematic glossing of the *Mishneh Torah* (completed by his disciple R. Meïr ha-Kohen in the *Hagahot Maimuniyot*) which aimed to bring it into harmony with current Franco-German practice and opinion, and did not hesitate unreservedly to reject certain Maimonidean views. Just the listing of alternate views and different customs, although merging formally with the text, most often repudiated it. The initial assertion of dependence is tempered by actual independence

57. *Kesef Mishneh,* introduction. See a similar statement by R. David ben Zimra, *Yeḳar Tifʾeret,* ed. S. B. Werner (Jerusalem, 1945), p. 11.

58. Abraham Maimonides, *Birkat Abraham,* ed. Goldberg, p. 8; *Ḳobeẓ Teshubot ha-Rambam,* I, 140; *Iggerot ha-Rambam,* ed. Baneth, I, 51.

59. See Note 38; *ʿErubin,* 53a.

to such an extent that the cumulative result is the familiar combination of stricture and supplement.[60]

The axiological orientation and literary achievements of R. Jonathan ha-Kohen of Lunel, younger contemporary and erstwhile student of Rabad, illustrate the same dialectical position from a slightly different vantage point. On one hand, he is the spokesman for the Lunel Scholars and communicates the famous twenty-four questions, respectful but trenchant, to Maimonides. These questions, many of which are repeated in the *Hassagot* of Rabad and Ramak, reflect the cooperative-critical endeavor of the Lunel school (and indicate parenthetically the immediacy with which they turned to the study of the *Mishneh Torah*).[61] On the other hand, Jonathan ha-Kohen is described by contemporaries and successors as a zealous, erudite champion of the *Mishneh Torah* who "explained and corroborated the words of Maimonides."[62] David Messer Leon puts his writings in the same category as the *Maggid Mishneh* and *Migdal ᶜOz*, which usually "refute the criticisms."[63] Actually, his attitude to the *Mishneh Torah* should be correlated with his treatment of Alfasi's *Halakhot*. His commentaries on Alfasi's compendium of law initiate that process whereby the *Halakhot* are transformed into a "miniature Talmud,"[64] embellished with commentaries just like the Talmud itself. Nonetheless, although operating within a theoretical framework which was overtly favorable to Alfasi, he periodically modified or dissented from certain views.

The ramified activity of R. Jonathan suggests an extension of the dialectical principle we have just formulated with regard to the *Mishneh Torah*: all writing on major works (Rashi's Commentary and Alfasi's *Halakhot* take their place alongside of Maimonides' *Mishneh Torah*) was of this character—partly approbatory, partly negative. First of all, the terminology itself is significant. The literature stimulated by the aforementioned epochal works consists of *Tosafot*, *Sifre Tashlum*, *Hashlamah*, *hagahot*, and *hassagot*. Even the latter term, which, in the course of time and contrary to its original connotation, acquired the sense of negative

60. See Urbach, *Baᶜale ha-Tosafot*, 434–435; G. Wellesz, "Hagahot Maimuniyot," *Ha-Goren* 7:36ff. (1908).

61. Maimonides' *Responsa*, ed. Freimann, introduction.

62. David of Estella, *Ḳiryat Sefer*, in Neubauer, *Mediaeval Jewish Chronicles*, II, 232; N. Wieder, "Sifro ha-Nisraf shel Judah ibn Shabbetai," *Meẓudah* 2:124 (1944).

63. *Kebod Ḥakamim*, ed. S. Bernfeld (Berlin, 1899), p. 120; גם אין כאן לא מגיד משנה ולא מגדל עוז. ולא רבינו יהונתן הרגילים להשיג על ההשגות.

64. R. Menaḥem ben Zeraḥ, *Ẓedah la-Derek* (Warsaw, 1880), 6; Isaac Israeli, *Yesod ᶜOlam* (Berlin, 1848), II, 34b. The phrase is first used apparently by Abraham ibn Daud, *Sefer ha-Ḳabbalah*, in A. Neubauer, *Mediaeval Jewish Chronicles*, I, 76.

critique—demolition tactics exclusively—originally denoted supplement of all kinds, fairly objective and frequently favorable.[65] It is noteworthy that many scholars—R. Samuel ha-Sardi, R. David ben Levi of Narbonne, Naḥmanides, R. Aaron ha-Kohen of Lunel, R. Manoaḥ, Rashbah, Ha-Meʾiri, the author of *Kol Bo*, R. David ben Zimra, R. Jacob Landau (*Agur*)—use the words *hassagot* and *hagahot* interchangeably. Rabad himself uses both terms to designate his scholia.[66] Secondly, a number of authors publicly declare their intention of devoting their works to exhaustive review rather than exclusive criticism of a given text. The avowed goal of the *Sefer ha-Hashlamah* (פעם לחזק דבריו ופעם לתמוה עליהם) is not, in theory, very different from the alleged purpose of the *Sefer ha-Maʾor*: דורש ושואל וחוקר ומאיר ומעורר. פעם סומך ועוזר ופעם כמשיב ושובר.

Rabad also introduces his criticism of Alfasi in similar terms: לא נמנעתי לחפש אחריו כאשר תשיג ידי. פעם לסתור ופעם לחזק.[67] What is more, even if such an a priori declaration of intent is not forthcoming, the actual literary practice is the same. For example, in his defense of Alfasi against the *Sefer ha-Maʾor*, Rabad frequently supports Razah, expands his statements or elaborates his theories. He points out correlations and coincidences between their views, refers to his own criticisms of Alfasi, and even has an occasional word of praise for Razah. A striking indication of the complexity or dialectical involvement of this defense–criticism is the statement of Naḥmanides, most vigilant guardian and comprehensive expounder of Alfasi, that Rabad's attempted defense of Alfasi is futile, for Alfasi's position is really indefensible.[68] The critical attitude of Rashi's descendants and disciples toward his commentaries is, of course, another case in point.

III

In a detailed study of Rabad, I hope to have demonstrated that his *Hassagot*—glosses, scholia, and animadversions—can be understood only as a comprehensive review of the *Mishneh Torah*, as the natural outcome of the concentrated critical study by the greatest Provençal Talmudist of the greatest work of halakhic codification, produced by the most outstanding Spanish-Egyptian Talmudist. They contain every conceivable

65. See Jonah ibn Janaḥ, *Sefer ha-Riḳma*, ed. M. Wilensky (Berlin, 1929), p. 19, n. 7.

66. E.g., *Terumot*, III, 7; *Meḥusrē Kapparah*, IV, 2; *Ṭumeʾat Met*, VI, 9; *Sanhedrin*, I, 5. I discuss this at length in my book.

67. *Hassagot* on Alfasi, *Ketubot*, 14b.

68. *Milḥamot*, *Shabbat*, 7b.

form of annotation, and the only common denominator forthcoming to give them a semblance of unity is this concept of a scholar's professional, microscopic review. All narrow characterizations of the contents and objectives of the *Hassagot* are emphatically defied by their heterogeneity and complexity, their breadth and diversity. They are truly protean. One finds, in the first place, many shades of criticism: authoritative, decisively triumphant, and frequently scornful; firm and steadfast but minus all traces of personal invective; courteously dissenting; diffident, incomplete, and occasionally conjectural. They refer to a range of interpretive matters, textual problems, local customs, and the like. There are, in addition, many forms of interpretive and commentatorial notes: listing the source—often obscure or unknown—of a statement and explaining it; reconstructing Maimonides' explanation of a difficult text; showing the derivative process followed by Maimonides in the formulation of a law; approving a Maimonidean view and elaborating it; warding off possible criticism; agreeing with but modifying a view. Sometimes an annotation is nothing more than a mental note in writing, a candid, fluid discussion, indicating the pro and con arguments for various possible interpretations and conclusions, including the Maimonidean ones. There are scores of cases where, for the sake of academic completeness or stimulus, Rabad cites an alternative view, without necessarily committing himself to this view or automatically discountenancing the view of Maimonides. A note may on occasion provide supplementary details which Maimonides himself mentions elsewhere but which are necessary for a complete on-the-spot picture, thereby obviating the need of collating the other scattered references. The *Hassagot* also serve as a mere vehicle of expression for Rabad; he incorporated into them extraneous material which was not directly relevant to a specific statement of Maimonides but was suggested by it. In sum, most of the matters a sensitive scholar systematically studying the *Mishneh Torah* or discursively browsing through any of its sections might discover is to be found in Rabad's *Hassagot*.

By singling out recurrent types of annotations which constitute distinct categories, I attempted to identify certain hypothetical principles of selectivity in Rabad's critical approach to the *Mishneh Torah*. Rabad nowhere formulates any a priori principles which led him to seek out specific kinds of Maimonidean statements, but most of his animadversions conveniently subsume themselves under a number of characteristic rubrics, constructive and negative. In reviewing a representative amount of the total output of the critical-commentatorial literature of this early period of

Mishneh Torah study, I found that this classification of recurrent types of annotations, approbatory and dissenting, applies more or less to the literature as a whole. Consequently, while Maimonides' anticipatory explanation and motivation of criticism is penetrating and realistic, the hard core of *Mishneh Torah* literature, all its accoutrements and diversionary motifs notwithstanding, remains substantially halakhic.

IV

Some scholars have suggested that one of the reasons for the eruption of the prolonged controversy in the thirteenth century concerning philosophic studies in general and Maimonides' *Sefer ha-Madda*ᶜ and *Moreh Nebukim* in particular was the anxiety of the Maimonidean antagonists lest the admittedly great halakhic authority of Maimonides lend weight to his philosophic views and make rationalist speculation as a whole more fashionable. This unprecedented conjunction of Talmudic scholarship and philosophic acumen helps explain why the antiphilosophic forces, hitherto dormant, were so violently aroused precisely at that period, even though philosophy had already for some time before taken root in Judaism.[69] Actually this is the view of the sixteenth-century Talmudist and mystic, Menaḥem Azariah Fano, who asserted that Rabad threw down the gauntlet at Maimonides the Talmudist only in order to discredit Maimonides the philosopher. Rabad criticized the *Mishneh Torah* as thoroughly as he did "in order that everybody should not be drawn after him to study and teach religious beliefs from the *Guide*."[70]

It would appear rather that a proper understanding of both phases of the Maimonidean controversy demands that the halakhic strictures be treated apart from the philosophical refutations. The two are basically independent. Sometimes, to be sure, the two appear as concentric circles on the same target. Samuel ben Eli, the learned Gaon of Baghdad,[71] or Meïr ha-Levi Abulafia, the buoyant young Talmudist of Toledo, may perhaps assail Maimonides' authority in the more central, influential realm of halakhah, in order that his philosophic stature should automatically be cut down to size as well. But their major concern is theological. Abulafia was convinced

69. E.g., Aḥad Haᶜam, "Shilṭon ha-Sekel," *Kol Kitbe Aḥad Haᶜam* (Tel Aviv, 1950), p. 366; J. Guttmann, *Ha-Pilosofiah shel ha-Yahadut* (Jerusalem, 1953), p. 169; J. Sarachek, *Faith and Reason* (Williamsport, 1935), p. 10.

70. M. A. Fano, *Sefer Teshubot*, 108 (p. 111).

71. See S. Assaf, "Ḳobeẓ shel Iggerot R. Samuel b. Eli," *Tarbiz* 1:102–130, 43–84, 15-80 (1929).

that Maimonides had unambiguously denied corporeal resurrection and he would not be silent in the face of such a dangerous breach.[72] Indeed, he was quite truculent. Thirty years later, in his letter to Naḥmanides, who was seeking his support in a newly intensified phase of the struggle, he reiterates his early—practically exclusive—interest in the theologically objectionable passages of the *Mishneh Torah*.[73] In the *Yad Ramah* on *Sanhedrin*, he reviews the problem and articulates his original misgivings about the Maimonidean position. The halakhic critique in his writing is incidental, and once it is forthcoming, should be viewed independently. Almost as a postscript to his first letter to Lunel, he interjects a note of apprehensiveness about the presumptuous finality of the *Mishneh Torah* as a whole and in order to substantiate his anxieties, he presents some halakhic queries.[74] These, however, are not artificially contrived. Many of them are well taken and can only be answered by "wishful hoping" on the part of the Maimonidean partisans; "perhaps some concealed source will appear in corroboration of Maimonides."[75] This is the consistent pattern of all his writings. His correspondence with R. Samson of Sens and other French rabbis—which helped spread knowledge of the *Mishneh Torah* in northern France—is also theologically oriented. His relentless agitation is nourished by concern for the literal truth of the doctrine of resurrection. It is only after R. Samson refuses to be drawn into this quibbling that Abulafia turns to halakhic disputation—as if to show that he can hold his own in that domain as well.[76]

The opposite is also true. Those Maimonidean protagonists involved in the philosophic controversy—Alḥarizi, David Ḳimḥi, Sheshet of Saragossa, Aaron of Lunel—will utilize every possible occasion to underscore Maimonides' undisputed centrality in Talmudic studies in order to build up his general authority. This explains the fact that when Naḥmanides assumed the role of mediator between the apparently irreconcilable factions, he parenthetically praises Maimonides as a Talmudist in order to

72. *Kitāb*, 7: אף כי השולח יד ביסוד היסודות ועמוד התעודות·

73. *Ḳobeẓ*, III, 6b.

74. *Kitāb*, 16: אף לזאת יחרד לבי . . . באמרכם איש אל רעהו כי יפלא ממנו דבר לאמר הגישה האפוד· ואולם כי התבוננתי בדברי הספר והנו נותן אמרי שפר· אך זאת שמעה אזני ותבן· כי אין בר בלא תבן . . . והנה מעט מן הקש אשר קששתי בעמריו.

In his responsa (*Or Ẓaddiḳim* [Salonica, 1799]), he uses the *Mishneh Torah* frequently; see nn. 210, 211, 259, 262, 266.

75. *Kitāb*, 46: דבריך נכונים · · · ומי יודע אולי אתו משען ועזר מהירושלמי או ממקום אחר או מן הברייתות הנסתרות אלינו והנגלות לו· Some of Ramah's questions troubled later students as well; e.g., *Kitāb*, 18, and *Teshubot R. Joshua ha-Nagid*, ed. A. Freimann, *Ḳobeẓ al Yad*, III (1939), 84 (question 2).

76. *Kitāb*, 4.

make his philosophic views more easily defensible and to prevail upon the French rabbis to discountenance a proposed anti-Maimonidean ban. It is clear, however, that his major concern here—in this letter to the rabbinic authorities of northern France—is not halakhic but theological: to prove that there is nothing heretical or damnable in Maimonides' writings.[77]

For the most part, however, halakhic criticism and philosophic controversy are rather neatly compartmentalized. The Talmudists concentrate only on halakhically objectionable passages, while those who imagined an ideological threat to Judaism exposed the weaknesses, dangers, and pernicious potential of his philosophic system. For the latter, the debate revolved around the merits and liabilities, benefits and disadvantages, of a rationalized Judaism. Judah al-Fakar, the celebrated physician of Toledo who was an eloquent and respected spokesman for the anti-Maimunists, clearly defines his sphere of interest: Maimonidean Aristotelianism and the indiscriminate spread of philosophizing which it engendered. He genuinely admired the *Mishneh Torah* and excluded it from the arena of controversy.[78] His quarrel was with the *Moreh*. The same is true for R. Solomon of Montpellier, usually depicted as the arch-villain and nemesis of the Maimunist liberals; the words of the *Mishneh Torah* are "dear and sweet" to him and his colleagues, who labor assiduously in order to fathom their meaning.[79] Also, Joseph ben Todros Abulafia, who—as Professor Baer has emphasized—focused very precisely upon the sociological implications and repercussions of the controversy, merely says in passing that occasional criticism of the *Mishneh Torah* is neither arrogant nor condescending. His aim, however, is to expose the insincerity of the alleged followers of the *Moreh*: they are either secret nonbelievers, or assimilated aristocrats.[80]

The validity of this approach is strengthened by the fact that it is applicable also to the kabbalistic opposition to Maimonides. The boundaries are rarely crossed. Early kabbalists, such as Sheshet ben Jacob, devote themselves to a discussion of metaphysical and theosophical views. Their objective is to discredit the philosophic system and enthrone the kabbalistic one, but no attention is given to the *Mishneh Torah* problem. There

77. *Ḳobeẓ*, III, 9a. See also A. Marx, "Texts by and about Maimonides," *JQR* 25:426 (1935).

78. *Iggerot Ha-Moreh* (Fürth, 1846), p. 15.

79. *Ginze Nistarot*, ed. J. J. Kobak, 4:13 (1878). כי חביבים וערבים עלינו דבריו מאד, ובכל שמועה ושמועה אנחנו רואים פסקיו, ונושאים ונותנים בדבריו וטורחים בכל כחנו להעמידם.

80. *Jeschurun* 8:44 (1872). See F. Baer, *Toledot ha-Yehudim Bi-Sefarad ha-Noẓrit*, p. 71; *Devir* 2:316–317 (1924). For a later phase, see M. Rosenmann, "Das Lehrhaus des R. Nissim Gerundi," *Festschrift Adolf Schwarz* (Berlin, 1917), pp. 489–499.

are no efforts to belittle Maimonides' halakhic achievements. This holds even for R. Moses Taku, usually described as the obscurantist par excellence. His quarrel is with philosophy as such and therefore he simply dismisses Maimonides as a shameless heretic: "His allegiance was with the philosophers who do not believe in the Torah."[81]

The halakhic critics display the same consistency. Although they occasionally treat nonhalakhic themes—and this is because the *Mishneh Torah* by its nature invited nonhalakhic criticism as well[82]—their focus is clearly set. R. Samson of Sens insists that Maimonides be treated as a Talmudist and that the debate be conducted according to the canons of halakhic scholarship.[83] He refuses to intervene in the speculative problems, much to the distress of Abulafia, who does not conceal his disappointment and tells R. Samson that his answer was essentially irrelevant. This is all the more striking because R. Samson happens to share Abulafia's views on resurrection and tacitly endorses the condemnation of Maimonides, but when he finally takes up the issue he treats it as a concrete problem in Talmudic exegesis, involving the interpretation and reconciliation of texts.

Rabad's *Hassagot* convey the same impression. His primary concern was halakhic and therefore, as a rule, he maintained a discreet silence concerning secular sciences. When, however, such extraneous learning impinged upon halakhah and even affected normative decisions, he was as articulate as ever. This is the import of the following animadversion:

> Because the author raises himself up and boasts about this science and in his opinion he reached the very ultimate [in knowledge of it], while I, on the other hand, am not among those proficient in it, for also my teachers did not attain to it—consequently I have not intruded upon his statements to check up on him, but when I encountered this statement which he wrote it was remarkably strange in my eyes.

Only because Maimonides appears "as one who is straying," because

81. See G. Scholem, "Mi-Ḥoḳer li-Meḳubbal," *Tarbiz* 6:91–93 (1935); Moses Taku, "Ketab Tamim," *Oẓar Neḥmad* 3:65 (1860). Also Scholem, *Reshit ha-Ḳabbalah*, pp. 133–134. An extreme case of compartmentalization of interest would be the (Muhammadan?) commentary which deals with the "general philosophico-theological" section of the *Sefer ha-Madda*ᶜ; see G. Margoliouth, "A Muhammadan Commentary on Maimonides' Mishneh Torah," *JQR*, O.S., 13:488–507 (1901).

82. E.g., knowledge of God, free will, eschatology.

83. *Kitāb*, 131–132, 138: הרב משה אשכול הכופר· ממנו פנה ממנו יתד· שמענו שמער כי נגלו לו שערי בינה· ותורה היא וללמוד אני צריך· לא תקעתי עצמי לדבר הלכה אך השומע ישמע וכל הרוצה להשיב יבא וישיב· see Urbach, *Ba*ᶜ*ale ha-Tosafot*, pp. 226–227. For the last phrase (תוקע עצמו לדבר הלכה), cf. *Yebamot*, 109b, and Rabad, *Katub Sham* on *Rosh ha-Shanah*, ed. B. Bergmann (Jerusalem, 1957), p. 74. This stresses the attention paid to the practical implications of the disputed teachings.

knowledge derived from secular sources in the solution of calendrical problems was erroneous for practical religious purposes, does Rabad expose his errors. It was not the use of secular astronomical learning as such which was objectionable.[84]

The attitude of R. Asher ben Yeḥiel provides another illustration. He certainly gave little thought to problems of philosophy and secular sciences. In the third phase of the controversy, he somewhat flippantly disclaims all interest in the subject.[85] It is therefore interesting that this avowed antagonist of secularism commissioned his pupil Isaac Israeli to arbitrate a controversy between Maimonides and Rabad covering a complex statement in *Kilayim* VI, 2, which involved advanced geometrical computations. The geometrical accuracy per se was neither here nor there in his opinion, but the practical halakhic implications were crucial. This approach apparently carried over into his pupil's extensive treatise on astronomical and calendrical problems, the *Yesod ᶜOlam*, whose practical purposes are repeatedly emphasized. As a matter of fact, the work is presented as an informative handbook, systematically listing premises and conclusions, rather than as a scholarly text meticulously demonstrating and verifying all its hypotheses.[86]

His objectivity emerges from the fact that in this case he throws his weight behind Maimonides' formulation, explains all his scientific premises and endorses his halakhic implications. But when he takes up the astronomical problem, he praises Rabad's concise refutation and proves that the Maimonidean position is absolutely indefensible.

84. *Ḳiddush ha-Ḥodesh*, VII, 7. See my discussion of this in *PAAJR* 26:169ff. (1957). The same is true of the problem of free will; *Teshubah*, V, 5.

85. *Minḥat Ḳenaᵓot* (Pressburg, 1838), p. 138.

86. *Yesod ᶜOlam*, introduction; II, 17.

Spinoza's Dogmas of Universal Faith in the Light of their Medieval Jewish Background

By ARTHUR HYMAN

When Spinoza in his *Theologico-Political Treatise*[1] sets out to dissolve the medieval synthesis between religion and philosophy,[2] he formulates a new understanding of Scriptural religion in the process. This new understanding of Scriptural religion takes its place within the threefold meaning that religion has for him. Religion in its primary sense is the religion of the philosopher. Described as "universal religion" (*religio catholica*) or as "divine law" (*lex divina*), the religion of the philosopher is common to all men. Not depending for its truth on any historic narrative—as do revealed religions—not demanding the performance of ceremonies, it is its own reward. The religion of the philosopher is the product of man's reason.[3]

Opposed to the religion of the philosopher is the "religion of the masses" (*vulgi religio*). Also described as "superstition" (*superstitio*), the religion of the masses is the religion of particular groups of men. Depending on historic narratives, demanding the performance of ceremonies, it is practiced because of fear and doubt. The religion of the masses is the product of man's imagination.[4] Between the universal religion of the philosopher and the superstitious religion of the masses lies what might be

1. All Spinoza references are to *Spinoza Opera* in *Auftrag der Heidelberger Akademie der Wissenschaften herausgegeben von Carl Gebhardt* (Heidelberg, 1924–26). The *Theologico-Political Treatise* is found in the third volume of this edition. It will be cited as *Tractatus* and the page and line references in parentheses are to the third volume of the Gebhardt edition. I also used the portions of the text of the *Tractatus* which appears in Benedict de Spinoza, *The Political Works*, ed. and trans. by A. G. Wernham (Oxford, 1958). For the English quotations I used the Elwes translation and, for the *Tractatus*, also that of Wernham. I felt free to change these translations whenever they did not appear to do justice to the Latin text.

2. See *Tractatus*, chap. 14 (p. 174): "... quod quidem in hoc capit facere constitui, simulque fidem a Philosophia separare, quod totius operis praecipuum intentum fuit." Cf. *Tractatus*, Introduction (p. 10, lines 16–18).

3. *Tractatus*, chap. 4 (pp. 61–62).

4. For a characterization of the religion of the masses, see *Tractatus*, Introduction, beginning. Also chap. 7 beginning.

called Scriptural religion, in the good sense of that term.[5] Spinoza has no special term for this kind of religion, but its content is formulated in seven "dogmas of universal faith" (*fidei universalis dogmata*) or "fundamental principles which Scripture as a whole aims to convey" (*universae Scripturae intenti fundamentalia*).[6] These dogmas, according to Spinoza, are: God's existence, unity, omnipresence, power, and will, and man's worship of Him, salvation, and repentance.[7]

In formulating his dogmas of universal faith, Spinoza makes use of the medieval—particularly medieval Jewish—discussion concerning fundamental principles of religion, transforming, as was his custom, the opinions of his predecessors to bring them into accord with his own philosophic views. It is the purpose of this paper to summarize the medieval backgrounds of the content and purpose of Spinoza's dogmas, to analyze the transformation he effected, and to examine how the understanding of Scriptural religion contained in the dogmas is related to his other philosophic views.

In explaining the backgrounds of Spinoza's dogmas, some historians of philosophy have examined them in the light of their purpose, while others have investigated their content and arrangement. Manuel Joel, the pioneer of the former group, was the first to note the strong affinity existing between Spinoza's dogmas and Maimonides' fundamental principles of religion as discussed in chapters twenty-seven and twenty-eight of the third part of his *Guide for the Perplexed*.[8] Harry A. Wolfson[9] and Leo Strauss,[10] in their discussions of Spinoza's dogmas, elaborated on Joel's suggestion.

Among those who investigated the content and arrangement of the dogmas, J. Freudenthal found a similarity between them and those of Herbert of Cherbury,[11] while Julius Guttmann viewed them as an extension of Joseph Albo's three fundamental principles.[12] However, my own

5. Spinoza was of the opinion that Scriptural religion, as practiced by most of his contemporaries, had descended to the level of superstition. Cf. *Tractatus*, Introduction.

6. *Tractatus*, chap. 14 (p. 177, lines 14–15).

7. *Tractatus*, chap. 14 (pp. 177–178).

8. Manuel Joel, *Spinoza's Theologisch-Politischer Traktat auf seine Quellen geprüft* (Breslau, 1870), pp. 66–69.

9. Harry A. Wolfson, *The Philosophy of Spinoza*, II (New York, 1958), 325–330. This work will be cited as *Spinoza*.

10. Leo Strauss, *Die Religionskritik Spinozas als Grundlage seiner Bibelwissenschaft* (Berlin, 1930), pp. 129–181.

11. J. Freudenthal, *Spinoza: Leben und Lehre*, I (Heidelberg, 1927), 322.

12. Julius Guttmann, "Mendelssohns Jerusalem und Spinozas Theologisch-Politischer Traktat," *Achtundvierzigster Bericht der Hochschule für die Wissenschaft des Judentums* (Berlin, 1931), p. 66, n. 45.

studies lead me to suspect that Spinoza's debt to Maimonides extends not only to the discussion of the purpose of the dogmas but also to the order and arrangement of part of them.

The seven dogmas may be grouped into two sections: the first four containing propositions about God and His attributes, the other three dealing with man's religious acts. The formulation and conclusion of the last three dogmas make it seem likely that Spinoza derived them from a Christian rather than a Jewish context. For, in commenting on the last dogma, he writes: "He who firmly believes that God . . . forgives the sins of men . . . he, I say, does really know Christ according to the spirit, and Christ is in him."[13] The first four, according to my analysis, show, however, a striking similarity to Maimonides' discussion of fundamental principles of religion in the already-mentioned passage of the *Guide*.

Maimonides, in chapter twenty-eight of the third part of the *Guide*, divides the fundamental principles of religion, which every believer must affirm, into two categories: "true opinions," which convey certain truths about God and His attributes, and "necessary beliefs," which are required for regulating man's social relations.[14] As examples of "true opinions" Maimonides lists the existence of God, His unity, omniscience, omnipotence, will, and eternity. This list of fundamental principles differs from Maimonides' other enumerations, primarily in the *Commentary on the Mishnah*,[15] in that the attribute of omniscience follows immediately after God's existence and His unity.

With the exception of the attribute of God's eternity, which he omits, Spinoza derives the content and arrangement of his first four dogmas from Maimonides' "true opinions." Spinoza, like Maimonides, begins with God's existence and His unity. Next follows omnipresence. However, in defining omnipresence in the sense that "all things are open to [God],"[16] Spinoza, though changing the term, retains the meaning Maimonides gives to omniscience. Finally, Spinoza's fourth principle, that God has "supreme right and dominion" and that "He does nothing under com-

13. *Tractatus*, chap. 14 (p. 178, lines 7–10): ". . . qui autem hoc firmiter credit, videlicet Deum ex misericordia, et gratia . . . hominum peccata condonare . . . is revera Christum secundum Spiritum novit, et Christus in eo est."

14. This distinction is discussed in greater detail below, Pages 188–190.

15. Maimonides, *Commentary on the Mishnah, Sanhedrin*, chap. 10, Introduction (for text, see J. Holzer, *Zur Geschichte der Dogmenlehre . . .: Mose Maimuni's Einleitung zu Chelek* [Berlin, 1901]).

16. *Tractatus*, chap. 14 (p. 177, lines 27–28): ". . . vel omnia ipsi patere . . ."

pulsion,"[17] is an amalgam of Maimonides' principles of omnipotence and will. Thus it appears that Spinoza derives the content and arrangement of his first four dogmas from Maimonides' "true opinions." But, whereas Maimonides' "true opinions" derive their significance from the truth they contain, Spinoza's dogmas will be seen to be important for the obedience they instill. This transformation will be examined further on.

Just as Spinoza is indebted to Maimonides for the content and arrangement of his first four dogmas, so is he obligated to him for his discussion of the function and the purpose of all seven. Using as our starting point some similarities in Maimonides' and Spinoza's philosophy of man and in their philosophy of the state, we shall next analyze how Spinoza used Maimonides' opinions concerning the function of Scriptural principles and how he adapted these opinions to his own philosophic views.

Maimonides, agreeing with the Aristotelian tradition, bases his analysis of human nature on the various functions or faculties possessed by men. Among these faculties reason is the highest. Through its exercise which results in the acquisition of the intellectual virtues, man attains his highest perfection and immortality comes to him.[18]

Sharing Maimonides' conclusion concerning man's highest perfection, Spinoza writes: ". . . a man's true happiness consists only in wisdom and the knowledge of the truth."[19] And in another passage he states: "Inasmuch as the intellect is the best part of our being, it is evident that we should make every effort to perfect it as far as possible. . . For in intellectual perfection the highest good should consist."[20]

Though intellectual perfection is the highest goal of man, through man's natural powers it is attained by but a few. Most men, Maimonides and Spinoza agree, do not possess the natural ability for independent philosophic speculation, and, even those who do, develop their intellect only

17. *Tractatus*, chap. 14 (p. 177, lines 30–32): "ipsum in omnia supremum habere jus, et dominium, nec aliquid jure coactum, sed ex absoluto beneplacito, et singulari gratia facere."

18. See Maimonides, *Guide for the Perplexed*, III, 54: "The fourth kind of perfection is the true human perfection, and it occurs when the intellectual virtues are attained by man, I mean to say, the conception of intellectual principles from which one might learn true opinions concerning divine [metaphysical] matters. This perfection is man's final goal, and it gives him true perfection. It remains to him alone, and because of it he is worthy of immortality and on its account he is called man."

19. *Tractatus*, chap. 3 (p. 44, lines 21–22).

20. *Tractatus*, chap. 4 (p. 59, lines 29–32).

with great difficulty and after much labor.[21] Most men function on the basis of their imagination or, at best, by means of their imagination and reason combined.

Finally, as political philosophers, Maimonides and Spinoza agree that the life of the philosopher as well as that of the common man is best lived in the state. To function well, the state must lay down rules for correct conduct. Were men guided only by their reason, they would obey these rules because they are good. But, since the majority of men is guided by imagination—following their desires rather than what is right—states must formulate laws to which sanctions are attached.[22] A state for ordinary men requires a set of beliefs or fundamental principles designed to instill obedience to its laws. Addressed to large masses of men, these principles are directed primarily to the human imagination.[23]

Agreeing on this point, Spinoza writes: "People prefer to be taught by experience, rather than deduce their conclusions from a few axioms and set them out in logical order. Whence it follows," he continues, "that if anyone wishes to teach some doctrine to a whole nation (not to speak of the whole human race) . . . he will support his teachings with experience and will suit his reasoning and the definitions of his doctrines as far as possible to the understanding of ordinary people [*ad captum plebis*]."[24]

Though in agreement on these basic points concerning human nature and on the need for political beliefs, Maimonides and Spinoza differ in their application of these philosophic views. Maimonides, affirming that Scripture is the product of Divine communication, must attempt to harmonize these philosophic conclusions with the Scriptural view of man. Spinoza, holding that Scripture is produced by men, may use Scriptural teachings if they should turn out to be of use. But for Spinoza no need exists to bring his philosophic views into agreement with Scriptural religion.

21. For Maimonides' discussion of this issue, see *Guide*, I, 34–35.

Discussing the same point Spinoza writes in *Tractatus*, chap. 5 (p. 77, lines 5–9): "But since to deduce conclusions from intellectual principles alone usually requires a long chain of arguments, and, moreover, very great caution, acuteness, and self-restraint—all qualities which are rarely met with in human beings . . ." ("Verum quia ad res ex solis notionibus intellectualibus deducendum, longa perceptionum concatenatio saepissime requiritur, et praeterea etiam summa praecautio, ingenii perspicitatis, et summa continentia, quae omnia raro in hominibus reperiuntur . . .")

22. This aspect of Maimonides' philosophy was developed by Leo Strauss in his *Philosophie und Gesetz* (Berlin, 1935), pp. 87–122.

23. For Spinoza's discussion of this point, see *Tractatus*, chap. 5 (p. 73, line 27–p. 74, line 3).

24. *Tractatus*, chap. 5 (p. 77, lines 10–15).

Maimonides, holding that intellectual perfection and, with it, immortality comes naturally to but few men, finds this opinion in contrast with Jewish religious belief. For Jewish tradition affirms that all Israelites as well as all the righteous of the nations have a part in "the World-to-Come," that is, immortality is possible for all.[25] Furthermore, experience shows that states based on human principles alone are imperfect. Such states are incapable of providing the right environment for the attainment of the highest human happiness. Only a perfect state can produce such perfection, yet the perfect state appears to lie beyond the grasp of natural human powers.

For Maimonides, Scripture provides the answer to these two dilemmas. Being the product of direct Divine communication, Scripture contains the means for making immortality possible for all men[26] as well as the beliefs required for setting up the perfect state. To attain these ends, Scripture sets down fundamental principles of religion, which, according to Maimonides, as we have seen, may be divided into two kinds: "true opinions" and "necessary beliefs." "True opinions" are those fundamental principles a literal belief in which is required by Scripture. It is their purpose to teach some truth about God. As examples of "true opinions" Maimonides cites, as we have seen, the existence of God, His unity, omniscience, omnipotence, will, and eternity.[27] "Necessary beliefs" are those which are communicated by Scripture in figurative form. They may be accepted in that form by those who cannot understand their deeper truth. Their purpose is to regulate men's social relations by instilling obedience to God's law. As examples of "necessary beliefs" Maimonides cites God's anger toward those who disobey Him[28] and His mercy toward those who do His will.[29]

The "true opinions" of Scriptural religion permit Maimonides to resolve the conflict between his philosophic and religious views concerning

25. *Mishnah*, *Sanhedrin*, X, 1. Cf. Maimonides' *Commentary*, *ad loc.*, and *Mishneh Torah*, *Teshubah*, III, 5. Also, *Mishneh Torah*, *Melakim*, VIII, 11.

26. In my discussion of this point I follow the suggestion of Julius Guttmann in his *Die Philosophie des Judentums* (Berlin, 1933), pp. 201–202 (Hebrew: *Ha-Pilosophia shel ha-Yahadut* [Jerusalem, 1953], p. 165).

27. Maimonides in *Guide*, III, 28, writes: "It is necessary to bear in mind that Scripture only teaches the final conclusions of those *true opinions* which lead to the ultimate perfection of man. . . Thus Scripture teaches the existence, unity, omniscience, omnipotence, will, and eternity of God. All of these are given in the form of final results . . ."

28. Maimonides, *Guide*, III, 28: "Scripture further demands to affirm certain beliefs, the *belief* in which is *necessary* for regulating our social relations, such as our belief that God is angry with those who disobey Him, for it leads us to the fear and dread of disobedience [to the will of God]."

29. Maimonides, *Guide*, III, end of chapter.

immortality. For in listing "true opinions," Scripture provides those truths concerning God necessary for that development of the human intellect which leads to immortality. In demanding that every believer must affirm these propositions in a literal way, Scripture guarantees a part in the "World-to-Come" (that is, immortality) to all believers.

The "necessary opinions," on the other hand, make it possible for Maimonides to resolve the difficulty in his political views, for, though human reason cannot provide the fundamental beliefs for the perfect state, a law based on Divine authority can. Scripture in enumerating "necessary beliefs" designed to instill obedience provides the fundamental principles on which the perfect state can rest. Since these beliefs are of considerable complexity and since they are addressed to large masses of men, they are communicated in a manner intelligible to all. They are communicated in figurative rather than in literal form.

In discussing "necessary beliefs" Maimonides stresses their role in instilling obedience, leaving it open in this context whether they are merely convenient political "lies," or whether they contain some cognitive truth. To use the terminology of medieval logic, he leaves it open whether they are sophistic propositions—that is, propositions which are without any truth—or whether they are dialectical: that is, propositions which are true in some respect though not in another.[30] If the "necessary beliefs" are sophistic, they are simply convenient for instilling obedience and others might do just as well. Are they, however, dialectical, their advantage over other propositions useful for instilling obedience lies in the truth they possess.

That the "necessary beliefs" are dialectical rather than sophistic becomes clear once they are considered in the light of other aspects of Maimonides' philosophy. In discussing anthropopathic terms applied to God—God's anger being one of his examples—Maimonides shows that propositions containing such terms are not completely false. "The Torah uses the language of ordinary men." Though it is false to ascribe passions to God, it is correct to state that God produces actions similar to those resulting from man's anger.[31] This correct interpretation of the proposition

30. The distinction between dialectical and sophistic propositions and arguments was a commonplace in medieval logic. Maimonides formulates the distinction as follows: "When, however, one or both premises of the syllogism belong to convention [or, as we have said, are dialectical], we call it a dialectical syllogism . . . There is also a kind of syllogism used for deception and falsehood, where one or both premises are such wherewith . . . a man falsifies. Such syllogisms are called sophistic . . ." (*Millot ha-Higgayon*, ed. Israel Efros [New York, 1938], p. 41, Hebrew section).

31. Maimonides, *Guide*, I, 54.

yields its truth. Thus, Maimonides' "necessary beliefs" are seen to be dialectical propositions which attain their "correctness" from the cognitive content they possess. It is their cognitive content which makes them superior to other propositions which may be useful for instilling obedience.

Turning to Spinoza we find that, since he denies the Divine origin of Scripture, he is not compelled to harmonize his philosophic views with any Scriptural teachings. Holding that most men are incapable of philosophic speculation he can stand by his conclusion that intellectual perfection, the highest goal of human life, is attained only by few men. For Spinoza there exists no Scriptural religion which through authoritative pronouncements will remedy the lack of intellectual accomplishments of most men. However limited human reason may be and however few are able to follow its call, human reason is all man possesses. This is the view which underlies Spinoza's *Ethics*, the book addressed to the philosophically gifted few. Had Spinoza been the author only of the *Ethics* and had he lived at another time, "he could have," as Professor Wolfson puts it so perceptively, "demanded the overthrow of the old order with its effete institutions so as to build upon its ruins a new society for a new generation raised on his new philosophy. He would thus, perhaps, have become the first apostle of the rebellion."[32] Spinoza could simply have ignored Scripture.

But the world in which Spinoza lived was one in which Scripture still commanded the respect of many men. For these the Bible conveyed true knowledge concerning God and for them Scriptural truth was the source of man's happiness and immortality. Thus, though Spinoza the speculative philosopher writing for a few kindred spirits might have ignored Scripture, Spinoza the student of history and society could not. To establish his claim that truth belongs to philosophy alone, he had to disprove the views of those opponents who found speculative truths in Scripture. To the task of separating philosophy from Scripture the *Theologico-Political Treatise* is primarily devoted.

The separation of philosophy from religion is accomplished by Spinoza by means of a new method of Scriptural exegesis.[33] Assuming that the Bible

32. Harry A. Wolfson, *Spinoza*, II, 330.

33. See the statement in the Introduction to the *Tractatus* (p. 9, lines 22–25): "... I was determined to examine the Bible afresh in a careful, impartial, and unfettered spirit, making no assumption concerning it, and attributing to it no doctrines, which I do not find clearly therein set down." ("... sedulo statui, Scripturam de novo integro et libero animo examinare, et nihil de eadem affirmare, nihilque tanquam ejus doctrinam admittere, quod ab eadem clarissime non edocere.") Cf. also chap. 7 (p. 98, lines 16–30).

is a book like any other book, he proceeds to argue that it must be interpreted in accordance with the ordinary canons of historical and literary exegesis.[34] The new method of exegesis leads him to the conclusion that the Bible is intellectually rather naive, so that one should not expect to find philosophic profundities in it. The Bible in no way intends to teach philosophic truths, for these fall within the province of human reason. As Spinoza puts it: "Thus to suppose that knowledge of natural and spiritual phenomena can be gained from prophetic books is an utter mistake which I shall endeavor to expose."[35]

In denying that Scripture contains speculative truths, Spinoza denies that Scripture has any direct function in the production of the highest kind of human happiness, intellectual perfection. Consequently he denies Maimonides' first category of Scriptural principles, that of "true opinions," which on the basis of Divine authority provide speculative truths which lead to immortality. Having discredited the speculative claims of Scriptural religion, Spinoza could have once again denied that Scripture makes any contribution toward human happiness.

But instead of rejecting the Bible altogether, Spinoza recognizes in it a certain usefulness for the moral and political life of the majority of men.[36] Scripture, according to his view, contains much that is irrelevant for the good life,[37] and many Scriptural beliefs are considered superstitious by him.[38] But Scripture in its noblest core teaches "obedience to God in the singleness of heart and the practice of justice and charity."[39] The principles on which these teachings rest are the seven dogmas of Scriptual religion.

Designed to instill obedience and formulated "according to the opinions and understanding of those among whom the apostles and prophets preached,"[40] the seven dogmas in their purpose and in the manner of their formulation possess the same characteristics as Maimonides' "necessary beliefs." Thus it is clear that Spinoza's dogmas have their origin in Maimonides' "necessary beliefs," though these are now stripped of their divine origin. Spinoza can no longer accept Maimonides' category of "true

34. For these canons, see *Tractatus*, chap. 7 (p. 99, bottom ff.)

35. *Tractatus*, chap. 2 (p. 29, lines 29–32).

36. That the philosopher for himself has no need for Scripture is evident from the passage cited in Note 3, above. Cf. *Tractatus*, chap. 5 (p. 78, lines 8–10).

37. Such as ceremonial precepts.

38. See Introduction to the *Tractatus*.

39. *Tractatus*, Introduction (p. 10, lines 27–28): ". . . Deo integro animo obedire, justitiam et charitatem colendo."

40. Cf. *Tractatus*, chap. 3 (p. 44, line 33): ". . . Scriptura . . . ad eorum [Hebraeorum] captum tantum loquitur." This is virtually a parody of Maimonides' exegetical principle, "The Torah speaks in the language of ordinary men."

opinions" to describe one of the purposes of Scripture, but the category of "necessary beliefs" provides him with the means for finding some room for the Bible within his over-all views. The Scriptural dogmas are useful as foundations of popular morality and as fundamental beliefs for the state.

That Spinoza shares Maimonides' view that Scriptural dogmas are useful for instilling obedience is evident enough, but how he views their cognitive content is less clearly set down by him. Are the dogmas for Spinoza, in the language of medieval logic, sophistic propositions, or are they dialectical? Interpreters of Spinoza have differed in their answer to this question.

Some interpreters of Spinoza argue that, for him, the dogmas contain no shadow of truth.[41] Pointing to his sharp distinction between philosophy and religion and recalling that he demands that dogmas be pious rather than true, they conclude that the dogmas are politically useful "lies." In the language of medieval logicians, they are sophistic propositions. The Scriptural dogmas were still effective in the seventeenth century at a time when the Bible was still revered by many. But according to this interpretation, Spinoza holds that at some future time other dogmas might conceivably provide a better foundation for popular morality.

Against this interpretation of the dogmas it may be urged that, though Spinoza emphasizes that religious dogmas should be pious, he nowhere states that all of them are false. On the contrary, in stating that there *may be* many religious dogmas which "contain not a shadow of truth,"[42] he implies that there are some which may. More than that, assuming that the dogmas are merely useful, there is no way of distinguishing the beliefs of superstitious religion from the dogmas of Scriptural religion—a differentiation which Spinoza clearly implies.[43] This difficulty in Spinoza's view had

41. Cf. Julius Guttmann, *Die Philosophie des Judentums*, pp. 299–300 and p. 400, n. 705 (Hebrew: pp. 257–258 and p. 407, n. 705). It is my impression that Leo Strauss in his "How to Study Spinoza's *Theologico-Political Treatise*" (in *Persecution and the Art of Writing* [Glencoe, 1952], pp. 195–197, esp. bottom, p. 196–top, p. 197) interprets the dogmas along these lines. This interpretation appears to me to differ from the one he offers in his *Die Religionskritik Spinozas* (see page 193, below).

42. *Tractatus*, chap. 14 (p. 162, lines 18–20): "Wherefore it follows, that faith does not so much require true or pious dogmas, that is, such, which will move the heart to obedience; even though there be many among them, which do not contain a shadow of truth." ("Sequitur denique fidem non tam requirere vera quam pia dogmata, hoc est, talia quae animum ad obedientiam movent: Tametsi inter ea plurima sint, quae nec umbram veritatis habent . . .")

43. This interpretation finds further support from Spinoza's statement that ". . . we do not wish to affirm absolutely that Scripture contains no doctrine in the sphere of speculative knowledge [*speculationis*] . . ." (*Tractatus*, chap. xiii [p. 168, lines 5–7]).

already been noted by Manuel Joel when he stated that Spinoza's opinion that dogmas of belief are completely independent of a man's philosophic convictions "is untenable."[44]

Leo Strauss in his *Die Religionskritik Spinozas*[45] sets out to solve this difficulty inhering in the purely utilitarian interpretations of the dogmas on the basis of Spinoza's own views. Admitting that, for Spinoza, the dogmas are primarily useful for instilling obedience, Professor Strauss argues that they are not merely so. Since Spinoza holds that "*all* men can obey the dogmas,"[46] he implies that the possibility for obedience lies within the nature of all men. The basis of this possibility lies in the fact that "God's eternal word is inscribed in the hearts of men."[47] Even ordinary men possess sufficient knowledge of God to understand that the dogmas are truer than the tenets of superstitious religion. In maintaining that the dogmas contain some truth, Professor Strauss has provided, on the basis of Spinoza's own philosophy, a criterion for distinguishing them from other dogmas useful for instilling obedience.

Comparing these two explanations of Spinoza's dogmas, I find my own intepretation closer to the second. However, I would differ from it in assigning the dogmas a different place within Spinoza's theory of knowledge.

In the *Ethics*, Spinoza divides human knowledge into three kinds: (1) opinion or imagination, (2) reason, and (3) intuition. Clear and adequate knowledge is found only in the last two categories, those of reason and intuition, while inadequate and confused knowledge is found in the first.[48]

Professor Strauss, in holding that the dogmas derive their superiority from the fact that "the word of God is inscribed in the heart of men," appears to imply that even ordinary men possess an intuitive knowledge of God; that is, they possess knowledge of the third kind. Against this view it may be argued that intuition, in spite of its name, is the result of a speculative process.[49] Thus it seems unlikely that ordinary men possess an

44. Joel, *Spinoza's Theologisch-Politischer Traktat auf seine Quellen geprüft*, p. 69 top.
45. Pp. 240–246.
46. Strauss, *Religionskritik*, p. 243.
47. *Ibid.*, p. 245.
48. *Ethics*, II, prop. 40, schol. 2 (*Opera*, II, 122).
49. Though Spinoza's statement, "Hence we see that the infinite essence of God is known to all" (*Ethics*, II, prop. 47, schol. [*Opera*, II, p. 128, II. 13–14]) appears to support Professor Strauss' interpretation, it seems to me on the basis of other consideration—such as the extensive discussion of God and His attributes in the first book of the *Ethics*—that the knowledge of God comes at the end of a speculative process rather than at its beginning. Cf. Wolfson, *Spinoza*, II, 140–145, 155–158. Cf. also *Tractatus*, pp. 252–253, n. 6. For a discussion of "intuitive knowledge," see also G. H. R. Parkinson, *Spinoza's Theory of Knowledge* (Oxford, 1954), chap. ix, esp. pp. 182–185.

intuitive knowledge of God which would be knowledge of the third kind. The dogmas must thus be placed into a different category.

My analysis of the dogmas leads me to suspect that they should be placed within the first category of knowledge, that of opinion and imagination, rather than in that of intuition. For in discussing beliefs—the dogmas being one example of belief—Spinoza states that they belong to the category of opinion.[50] And though opinions are primarily characterized as doubtful, they can be true. The criterion for distinguishing true beliefs from false ones is provided by knowledge of the second and third categories. Thus, true beliefs, according to Spinoza, would be composed of adequate ideas—derived from the second and third categories—and inadequate ideas of the imagination. False beliefs would be composed of inadequate ideas alone. While the philosophically gifted few can make use of reason and intuition alone, the masses, functioning primarily through their imagination, must make use of opinion, and thus belief. Yet for the masses, actions based on true beliefs are superior to those based on false beliefs.

This analysis of true beliefs permits us to describe the superiority of Spinoza's dogmas over the tenets of superstitious religions. Whereas superstitious dogmas are composed of false beliefs alone, Spinoza's dogmas are composed of true beliefs—such as God's existence and His unity—as well as false beliefs—such as the anthropomorphic expressions applied to God. The latter component has been added as an accommodation to the understanding of ordinary men who function primarily through their imagination. But even ordinary men can appreciate some philosophic truths if these truths are transmitted to them on the authority of those who know these truths in a truly philosophic way. It is this cognitive content which provides the pre-eminence of the Scriptural dogmas over the tenets of superstitious religion.[51] Thus, at least some of the Scriptural writers must

50. For a discussion of "belief" in Spinoza, see Wolfson, *Spinoza*, II, 145ff. In this passage Professor Wolfson shows that, for Spinoza, "true beliefs" belong to the second category of knowledge, that of reason. But it seems to me that a place can be found for them also within the first category, that of opinion. Cf. Wolfson, *Spinoza*, II, 152.

51. In this context it is striking to note that in formulating the content of his dogmas, Spinoza used primarily Maimonides' "true opinions," which contain speculative propositions about God and His attributes. It is also to be noted that all the Divine attributes mentioned in the dogmas are discussed in a "philosophic" context in the *Ethics*. Furthermore, I find support for my argument in the example of the "tradesman" used by Spinoza (in *Ethics*, II, prop. 40, schol. 2) to illustrate the first kind of knowledge. For in finding the required number, the "tradesman" is envisaged as making use of a rule received from a master (". . . quia scilicet ea, quae a magistro absque ulla demonstratione audiverunt, nondum tradiderunt oblivioni . . ." [*Opera*, II, 122, lines 22–24]). This suggests that he accepts the validity of the rule on the basis of the master's authority. The master, apparently, knows the reasons why the rule is true.

have been philosophical enough to understand the truths contained in the dogmas.

In describing the dogmas of Scriptural religion in the sense of true belief described above, Spinoza once again shows his indebtedness to Maimonides. For Spinoza's dogmas, considered from the point of view of their function, are nothing but Maimonides' "necessary beliefs." Since for Spinoza they contain cognitive truths, they are for him—as for Maimonides—dialectic propositions, not sophistic ones. Thus Scripture in its innermost core, for Spinoza, is not simply a convenient political "lie," but the foundation for popular morality in harmony with the dictates of human reason.

To conclude, it is of interest to note that, though human reason, according to Spinoza, may discover the best beliefs on which to base popular morality, it is a fact that Scripture happens to contain them too. Scripture, for Spinoza, no longer contains the means for ultimate human happiness and immortality—as it did for the medievals—but it can still provide the foundations of popular morality addressed to all "decent men."[52]

52. *Tractatus*, chap. 14 (p. 177, lines 4–6): ". . . there can be no doctrines in the universal religion, which can give rise to controversy among decent men [*inter honestos*]."

The Delphic Maxim in Medieval Islam and Judaism

By ALEXANDER ALTMANN

The Islamic Ḥadīth attributes to Muhammad (or ᶜAlī) a saying which is obviously based on the famous Delphic exhortation, "Know thyself." It appears, as Ibn al-ᶜArabī testifies,[1] in two formulae: "He who knows himself knows his Lord" and "He among you who knows himself best knows his Lord best."[2] The Ikhwān al-Ṣafāᵓ quote both in the name of the Prophet.[3] The author who first introduced this sentence as a *ḥadīth* is the early mystic Yaḥya b. Muᶜādh (d. 871).[4] Ibn Sīnā,[5] who quotes the first of the two formulae, describes it as a saying (*kalima*) on which the philosophers (*al-ḥukamāᵓ*) and the Saints (*al-awliyāᵓ*) are in agreement. As for the philosophers, he recalls a statement by the "Head" (*raᵓīs*) of the philosophers: "He who is incapable of the knowledge of himself, will naturally be incapable of the knowledge of his Creator. How will he consider what is reliable in the science of any of the things, being ignorant of himself?" The "Head" of the philosophers to whom this saying is attributed is, no doubt, Aristotle. The quotation must be assumed to derive from some apocryphal text similar to the one from which ᶜAlī ibn Rabban Sahl al-Ṭabarī (d. after 855) cited Aristotle's alleged statement: "Whosoever possesses the knowledge about the intelligent soul recognizes his essence, and whosoever recognizes his essence is able to recognize

1. *Kitāb ᶜuqlat al-mustawfiz*, ed. H. S. Nyberg (*Kleinere Schriften des Ibn Al-ᶜArabī*) (Leiden, 1919), p. 52.

2. (1) *Man ᶜarafa nafsahu faqad ᶜarafa rabbahu*; (2) *ᵓaᶜrafukum bi-nafsihi ᵓaᶜrafukum bi-rabbihi.*

3. *Rasāᵓil Ikhwān al-Ṣafāᵓ* (Cairo, 1928), III, 351.

4. Cf. L. Massignon, *Essai sur les origines du lexique technique de la mystique musulmane* (Paris, 1929), p. 107 (quoted by S. van den Bergh, *Die Epitome der Metaphysik des Averroes*, Leiden, 1924, p. 250). For the literary history of this *ḥadīth*, see Muḥammad Thābit al-Fandī, *Mashriq* (1934), p. 325, n. 7 (quoted by G. Vajda, *Archives d'histoire doctrinale et littéraire du moyen age*, XV (Paris, 1946), 193, n. 3). On Yaḥya b. Muᶜādh, see L. Massignon, *Recueil des textes inédits . . .* (Paris, 1929), p. 27.

5. In his early *opusculum* on the soul published by S. Landauer, "Die Psychologie des Ibn Sina," *Zeitschrift der deutschen Morgenländischen Gesellschaft* 29:340, 374 (1875).

God."[6] As for the Saints, Ibn Sīnā does not cite any religious authority but links the *ḥadīth* with the Qur᾿ān verse (59,19): "Be not as those who forget God, and so He caused them to forget their souls." He points out that according to this verse the knowledge of God and the knowledge of the soul are interdependent.[7] Al-Ghazālī likewise quotes this verse and interprets it in the same way.[8] He may have borrowed this piece of exegesis from Ibn Sīnā or from a source common to both. It should be noted that "knowing oneself" is understood here as "knowing one's soul," the Arabic *nafsahu* having both meanings.[9]

A third formula expressing the same idea is still closer to the original Delphic inscription. It reads, "Know thyself [thy soul], O man, and thou wilt know thy Lord."[10] Ibn Sīnā introduces it in the same context as the first one in the following words: "I have read in the writings of the Ancients that they invited profundity in the knowledge of the soul on account of a revelation [*waḥy*] that came down to them in one of their sacred temples, saying . . ." He adds that according to his source this saying was found on the altar (*miḥrāb*) of the temple of Aesculapius, who was known to them as a prophet.[11] This third formula is thus not considered a *ḥadīth* but is recognized as of Greek origin. Ibn Sīnā's source confused the temple of the Pythian Apollo at Delphi with the temple of Aesculapius and shows other inaccuracies, but he at least preserves some semblance of historical record.[12] It should be noted that in his quotation the Delphic maxim appears with the addition, "and thou wilt know thy Lord." There existed then an Arabic version of some "ancient," most probably late-Hellenistic, text which stated the Delphic inscription in the full-fledged form "Know thyself and thou wilt know thy Lord" or simply: "God." Ibn Rushd quotes the same formula from "the Divine laws"[13] which seems to be a vague reference to the Ḥadīth and the Qur᾿ān exegesis mentioned above,

6. Quoted by F. Rosenthal, "On the Knowledge of Plato's Philosophy in the Islamic World," *Islamic Culture* 14:410 (1940).

7. *Ibid.*

8. See *Kitāb Mīzān al-ᶜamal* (Cairo, 1946), p. 23.

9. Cf. Landauer's remark, "Die Psychologie des Ibn Sina," p. 375, n. 5, and M. Steinschneider, *Hebräische Bibliographie*, XV (1875), 43.

10. *Iᶜrif nafsaka, yā insān, taᶜrif rabbaka.*

11. Landauer, "Die Psychologie des Ibn Sina," 341, 374–375.

12. Alexander of Aphrodisias' *De anima* contains at the beginning a reference to the Delphic maxim by stating the necessity of obeying the injunction given and proclaimed by the Pythian (Apollo). See *De anima*, ed. I. Bruns, p. 1, lines 4–6. But the Arabic version—as we may infer from the Hebrew one which was based on it—substituted "the Prophet" for "the Pythian" (*Ibid.*, ed. Bruns, p. 1, lines 3–5).

13. In his *Epitome* of Aristotle's *Metaphysics*. Cf. S. van den Bergh, *Die Epitome*, p. 117.

but there is no reason to doubt the clear and detailed statement of Ibn Sīnā concerning his "ancient" source. It is possible to assume that the *ḥadīth* actually originated in some such source. If the Delphic maxim already existed in the two-stage form (self-God) in some Hellenistic text translated into Arabic, it was a simple matter to recast it from the imperative into the indicative form, "He who . . ." That the two-stage formula is found earlier in the Hellenistic tradition is attested also by Ḥunain ibn Ishāq, whose Florilegium of Sayings of the Philosophers (*Kitāb al-ādāb al-falāsifa*) contains a paraphrase of it in the name of one of "Seven Greek Philosophers": "It is fitting that we should first know ourselves before attempting to know God."[14]

From Islam the concept of self-knowledge leading to the knowledge of God passed also into medieval Judaism. The earliest references to this notion appear in some Karaite authors of the ninth and tenth centuries (Daniel al-Qumīsī, Qirqisānī, Joseph al-Baṣīr)[15] but use neither the *ḥadīth* formulae nor the enlarged Delphic maxim. They quote as *locus probans* a verse from Job (19:26), "From my flesh I behold God," which is understood to mean that God's existence can be inferred from His creation. This Scriptural proof continues to be employed throughout medieval Jewish literature. It occurs—still unconnected with the *ḥadīth* formulae or the Delphic maxim—in such twelfth- and thirteenth-century writers as Abraham bar Ḥiyya, Joseph ibn Ṣaddīq, Samuel ben Nissīm Masnūt, Baḥya ben Asher, and others.[16] Isaac Albalag, on the other hand, connects the Job verse with the saying, "Know thy soul and thou wilt know thy Lord," which he introduces as "the word of the Sage."[17] He points out that the Arabic word *nafs* is homonymous, meaning both "soul" and "essence," and that in this particular instance it denotes the latter. Likewise, the Hebrew word *basar*, he says, means either "flesh" or (as in Genesis 2:24) "essence." In the Job verse it stands for the latter.[18]

14. See A. Loewenthal's edition of Jehuda ben Solomon al-Ḥarīzī's Hebrew version, *Sēfer Musērē ha-Pilōsōfīm* (1896), p. 11.

15. Cf. G. Vajda, *Archives*, XV, 193, n. 3, and *Revue de l'Histoire des Religions* (January–March 1959), p. 89, where he points out that the interpretation of Job 19:26 in the sense of self-knowledge leading to the knowledge of God is attested for the ninth century, if the Karaite text edited by J. Mann (*JQR*, N.S. 12:274 [1921–22]) has indeed Daniel al-Qumīsī for its author.

16. See Abraham bar Ḥiyya, *Sefer Hegyon ha-Nefesh* (Leipzig, 1860), p. 1b; Joseph ibn Ṣaddīq, *Sefer ᶜOlam ha-Qatan*, ed. A. Jellinek (Leipzig, 1854), p. 20 and XIX; *idem*, ed. S. Horovitz (Breslau, 1903), p. 21; Samuel ben Nissīm Masnūt, *Maᶜyan Ganīm*, ed. S. Buber (Berlin, 1889), p. 61; Baḥya ben Asher, *Beʾūr ᶜal ha-Torah* (Amsterdam, 1726), fol. 9*r*, col. a; Joseph ben Jehuda, *Sefer Musar*, ed. W. Bacher (Berlin, 1910), p. 75.

17. Cf. G. Vajda, *Isaac Albalag* (Paris, 1960), p. 117.

18. *Ibid.* and Steinschneider, *Hebräische Bibliographie*, XV, 43.

In Hebrew texts the Arabic *rabbaka* ("thy Lord") is usually rendered *elohekha* ("thy God") or *bōrʾekha*, also *yōṣerkha* ("thy Creator").[19] Thus, Shemtob ibn Falaqēra and Simon ben Ṣemaḥ Durān quote the formula, *daᶜ nafshekha wa-tedaᶜ bōrʾekha.*[20] Jehuda Hallevi's poem, *im nafshĕkha yeqarah be-ᶜēnēkha* contains a paraphrase of it: "If thy soul be precious in thine eyes, know thou her essence [*mā hīʾ*] and seek her Creator."[21] Abraham ibn Ḥasday's Hebrew version of al-Ghazālī's *Mīzān al-ᶜamal* translates it: *Ben adam, daᶜ nafshĕkha, tēdaᶜ elohēkha.*[22]

What was the meaning associated in the medieval Islamic and Jewish mind with this exhortation to know oneself in order to know God? The formula as such is rather vague and lends itself to a variety of interpretations.[23] Porphyry's treatise, "On *Know thyself*,"[24] lists several distinct ways of understanding the Delphic sentence. We shall endeavor to answer our question by sifting the various strands of interpretation in the sources at our disposal.

1. *The motif of the Soul's "Likeness" to God.* The inscription on Apollo's temple at Delphi originally meant: "Know that you are but man, not divine." It was a warning against *hubris* and taught the Apollinic virtue of temperance (σωφροσύνη). Thus it expressed the essence of Greek piety.[25] In Socrates, the Delphic oracle assumes a new significance. Turning away from the cosmological speculations of his predecessors, he poses the problem as to the nature of man. He wants to examine himself. Hence, he chooses the maxim: "Know thyself." Plato goes beyond Socrates' use of the Delphic saying. In his *First Alcibiades*[26] he introduces Socrates as offering a fresh

19. Vajda, *Isaac Albalag*, p. 117.

20. Shemtob ibn Falaqēra, *Iggeret ha-Wikuaḥ*, ed. A. Jellinek (Vienna, 1875), p. 13 (quoted by Steinschneider, *Hebräische Bibliographie*); Simon ben Ṣemaḥ Durān, *Magen Abōt* (Leghorn, 1785), fol. 49a (quoted by L. Dukes, *Philosophisches aus dem zehnten Jahrhundert*, Nakel, 1868, p. 59).

21. Quoted by L. Dukes, *Shīrē Shĕlomoh* (Hannover, 1858), p. 82 from an Oxford MS.; see *Dīwān des Abū-l-Ḥassan Jehuda ha-Levi*, ed. H. Brody (Berlin, 1903), p. 242.

22. *Sefer Moʾzĕnē Ṣēdeq*, ed. J. Goldenthal (Leipzig–Paris, 1839), p. 28.

23. In the Confucianist School (*The Mencius*, VIIa, I) it was similarly stated: "He who knows his nature knows Heaven" (see *History of Philosophy Eastern and Western*, ed. S. Radhakrishnan, London, 1952, I, 564).

24. In Stobaeus' *Florilegium*, ed. A. Meineke, I (Leipzig, 1855), 332ff. For the history of the Delphic maxim in the Classical and Hellenistic periods, see also Ulrich von Wilamowitz-Moellendorff, *Reden und Vorträge*, II (Berlin, 1926), 171–189.

25. Cf. W. Jaeger, *Aristotle* (Oxford, 1934), p. 164; Karl Kerényi, *Apollon*, 2nd ed. (Amsterdam—Leipzig, 1941), p. 268; Martin P. Nilsson, *Greek Piety* (Oxford, 1948), pp. 47–52. Philo, *Spec. Leg.*, I, 10, 44, reflects this interpretation of the Delphic maxim.

interpretation. "I will tell you what I suspect to be the real advice which the inscription gives us." Just as an eye viewing another eye will see itself as in a mirror, the soul too, if she is to see herself, must look at the Divine. For the best part of the soul resembles God, and it is only by looking at the Divine that she will gain the best knowledge of herself. The Divine, to be sure, is true prudence or temperance, and here the original meaning of the Delphic oracle again emerges. But the new thing is the idea of God being akin to the soul, and the implicit use of the Empedoclean motif of "like being known only by like." "Know thyself" now means: "Know thyself by knowing God"; in other words, "He who knows God knows himself." As W. Jaeger has shown, this theological trend is evident also in other literary documents of the later Academy. It appears in Plato's *Epinomis* and in Aristoxenus' *Life of Socrates*, in which an Indian (representing the later Plato) explains that man cannot know himself until he knows God.[27] The connection of self-knowledge and knowledge of God is reasserted in the Platonizing Stoa. Posidonius' *Commentary* on Plato's *Timaeus* says that "Just as light is apprehended by the luciform sense of sight, and sound by the aeriform sense of hearing, so also the nature of all things ought to be apprehended by its kindred reason."[28] This elaborates the Empedoclean principle of "like knowing like" which Plato had used in the *Timaeus* (45 C),[29] and Sextus Empiricus reports that "Empedocles called himself a god because he alone had kept his mind free from evil and unmuddied and by means of the god within him apprehended the god without."[30] Cicero's interpretation of the Delphic maxim, "*ut ipsa se*

26. At 127e, 132b; see also *Philebus*, 48c; *Charmides*, 164d. On the influence of Proclus' *Commentary* on the *First Alcibiades* see my account in A. Altmann and S. M. Stern, *Isaac Israeli* (Oxford, 1958), pp. 184ff., 204ff.

27. Cf. W. Jaeger, *Aristotle*, pp. 164–166. The Aristoxenus fragment referred to by Jaeger (from Eusebius, *Prep. Ev.*, XI, 3) reads: "*Nisi divina . . . prius perspecta et cognita habeam praevideri a nobis humana non possunt.*" Cf. *Fragmenta Historicorum Graecorum*, II, ed. C. Müller (Paris, 1878), 281.

28. See Sextus Empiricus, *Adversus Dogmaticos*, I, 93 (ed. R. G. Bury, *Loeb Classical Library*, II, 49).

29. See Sextus Empiricus, *Adversus Mathematicos*, I, 303 (ed. R. G. Bury, *Loeb Classical Library*, IV, 174–177).

30. *Ibid.* From Sextus Empiricus' testimony we gather that Posidonius said of "the nature of all things" that it ought to be apprehended by its kindred reason; and that Empedocles said of himself to be able to apprehend the god without because of the god within. Karl Gronau (*Poseidonius und die Jüdisch-Christliche Genesisexegese*, Leipzig, 1914, p. 170) confounds these two distinct testimonies when declaring that, according to Sextus Empiricus, Posidonius used Plato's image of the luciform eye in order to prove the soul's ability to know God by virtue of its kinship with God. This statement goes beyond the evidence furnished by the above texts. Its veracity can, however, be confirmed by reference to the Cicero passages adduced by I. Heinemann, *Poseidonios' metaphysische Schriften*, I (Breslau, 1921), 69–70.

mens agnoscat conjunctamque cum divina mente se sentiat" (*Tusc.* V, 70) and similar statements have been traced to Posidonius.[31] The kinship between God and the ruling part (ἡγεμονικόν) of the soul is frequently stressed in Stoic doctrine.[32] Even as God sees and hears everything, so the soul perceives everything.[33] In the purity of the *pneuma* the soul is divine.[34]

Chalcidius (fourth century) in his *Commentary* on the *Timaeus*[35] combines the Empedoclean motif with the Biblical notion of the Divine "spirit" in man. Re-echoing Philo's statement that "in many passages the Law of Moses pronounces the blood to be the essence of the soul,"[36] he explains, like Philo,[37] that this view applies only to the irrational part of the soul. The likeness between God and the soul is due to the fact that God breathed the Divine Spirit into man. "Knowledge [*cognatio*] is common to us with Divinity, and we are said to be children of God."[38] It is strange, however, that Chalcidius failed to connect the Empedoclean motif with the Biblical notion of man being created in the "image" of God.[39]

Similarly, Gregory of Nyssa (end of the fourth century) uses the Empedoclean motif when saying that by the Divine Spirit within him man knows God, and by the senses which are part of his earthly nature he knows things earthly.[40] The Biblical notion of the "Spirit" is woven into the discussion but, again, the *homo imago Dei* concept is not taken into account. There is, on the other hand, an earlier attempt to combine the Delphic maxim with the *homo imago Dei* motif, though without any reference to the Empedoclean principle. It occurs in Origen's homily on the verse, Canticles 1:8[41] (translated by him: "Unless thou know thyself,

31. See end of preceding note.

32. Cf. Emile Bréhier, *Chrysippe et l'Ancien Stoicism* (Paris, 1951), p. 166.

33. "Quem in hoc mundo locum deus obtinet, hunc in homine animus" (Seneca, *Ep.* 65, quoted by Gronau, *Poseidonius*, p. 165, where also further references are given). The Talmudic fivefold comparison of God and the soul in BT *Berakhot* 10a reflects this Stoic theme.

34. Cf. Gronau, *Poseidonius*, p. 165.

35. *Chalcidii Commentarius in Timaeum Platonis* in *Fragmenta Philosophorum Graecorum*, II, 226–227.

36. See H. A. Wolfson, *Philo* (Cambridge, Mass., 1947), I, 387.

37. *Ibid.*

38. Chalcidius, chap. 207.

39. He quotes the Empedoclean principle, "*similia non nisi a similibus suis comprehendi*," but connects it only with the Biblical concept of the inbreathing of the Spirit into man.

40. Cf. Gronau, *Poseidonius*, p. 170, where the relevant passages are quoted.

41. See Origen, *The Song of Songs, Commentary and Homilies*, trans. and annotated by R. P. Lawson (London, 1957), pp. 128–139 (in *Ancient Christian Writers*, no. 26). See also Walter Völker, *Das Vollkommenheitsideal des Origenes*, in *Beiträge zur Historischen Theologie* (Tübingen, 1931), p. 23; H. Crouzel, "L'image de Dieu dans la théologie d'Origène," *Studia Patristica*, ed. K. Aland-F. L. Cross (Berlin, 1957), II, 194ff.

o fair one among women . . ."). The Greek maxim "Know thyself," Origen declares, had been anticipated by King Solomon, who addresses the soul: "Unless thou hast known thyself and hast recognized whence the ground of thy beauty proceeds—namely, that thou wast created in God's image, so that there is an abundance of natural beauty. . ."[42] The soul is exhorted to know "both what she is in herself, and how she is actuated."[43] The first of the two tasks is not immediately explained. All interest seems to concentrate on the second aspect: the soul should examine her dispositions, inclinations, and actions. "Know thyself" is an invitation to reflect on one's moral and spiritual condition. But the soul should also know the Trinity and God's creation. Knowing the creation implies "a certain self-perception"; that is, "how she [*scilicet*, the soul] is constituted in herself" —reverting to the first of the two tasks—"whether her being is corporeal or incorporeal, and whether it is simple, or consists of two or three or several elements," et cetera.[44] There follows a listing of practically the whole gamut of problems of the nature of the soul posed in Patristic and medieval psychology. Origen's exegesis of Canticles 1:8 in the sense of "Know thyself" has a solitary later parallel, obviously without any literary connection, in a passage in the *Zohar Ḥadash* on Canticles which will be discussed below.[45]

In Islam the Biblical *homo imago Dei* motif had found expression in the *ḥadīth*, "Allāh created Adam in his image," which seems to have given rise to some perplexity and conflict among the theologians.[46] Al-Ghazālī accepted it as authentic, and devoted a great deal of effort to its interpretation.[47] What interests us here is the way he combined this particular *ḥadīth* with the theme of self-knowledge. This he did in his esoteric works, especially in the *Mishkāt al-Anwār* ("The Niche of Lights"), which he wrote toward the end of his life. It is in this fusion of the two *ḥadīths*, the one stemming from the Biblical, the other from the Hellenic tradition, that his deepest thought on the subject is provoked. In his early *Mīzān al-ᶜAmal* ("The Balance of Action") he interprets the *ḥadīth* on self-knowledge without any reference to the image motif.[48] In the *Iḥyāʾ*

42. Origen, *The Song of Songs*, p. 128.
43. *Ibid.*, p. 130.
44. *Ibid.*, p. 134.
45. See page 212.
46. Cf. Farid Jabre, *La Notion de la Maᶜrifa chez Ghazali* (Beirut, 1958), p. 86.
47. Cf. Jabre, *La Notion de la Maᶜrifa*, pp. 86–108; W. H. T. Gairdner, *Al-Ghazzālī's Mishkāt Al-Anwār*, A Translation with Introduction (London, 1924), pp. 31ff.; A. J. Wensinck, *La Pensée de Ghazzālī* (Paris, 1940), pp. 39ff.
48. Cf. *Mīzān al-ᶜAmal*, ed. Kurdi (Cairo, 1342[1923]), p. 18; Hebrew version, *Mozĕnē Ṣedeq*, ed. J. Goldenthal (Leipzig–Paris, 1839), p. 28.

ᶜUlūm al-Dīn, his great compendium on theology, and in his *Kitāb al-Imlāʾ*, which answers some doubts concerning a certain section in the *Iḥyāʾ*, he elaborates two ways of interpreting the *ḥadīth* on Adam's creation in God's image without linking them with the theme of self-knowledge.[49] But once he is on esoteric ground, he connects the two. This happens in the *Al-Maḍnūn al-ṣaghīr*,[50] one of the books "to be guarded stingily against those unworthy of them," where the two *ḥadīths* are placed alongside each other, and Ghazālī records an actual question asked of him: What is the meaning of the sentence, "He who knows himself knows his Lord"? He answers that things are known by virtue of kinship, and that man could not know his Creator by knowing himself unless a certain kinship existed between man and his Creator. This, clearly, is an echo of the Empedoclean theory, and it is by no means an isolated utterance of al-Ghazālī's. In the *Iḥyāʾ* (IV, 263) he speaks of the necessity of loving God as founded on a "hidden correspondence" between God and man,[51] and in his *Al-Maqṣad al-asna fī asmāʾ Allāh al-ḥusna* ("Exhortation to the Imitation of the Divine Qualities") he develops the notion of a "common term" existing between God and man.[52] But in the *Maḍnūn ṣaghīr* he adds that the kinship spoken of consists in man being a microcosm and, more specifically, in possessing a soul which resembles God.[53]

The microcosm motif is one which seems to have been very dear to al-Ghazālī. We find it in the *Mīzān al-ᶜAmal*: "It is an effect of the mercy of God that man is a copy *en miniature* of the form of the universe; by contemplating it he comes to know God."[54] The *Imlāʾ* offers a detailed list of correspondences between man as a microcosm and the world at large.[55] But it is hard to see how the knowledge of the macrocosm achieved by introspection can yield a knowledge of God. Al-Ghazālī therefore adds that it is the soul which by virtue of her kinship with God leads us to the knowledge of the Creator. The soul, he says distinctly, and hereby reflects Plato's view, is the essence of man, and thus the *ḥadīth* describing man as created in the image of God must be understood to refer to the

49. Cf. *Iḥyāʾ ᶜUlūm al-Dīn*, ed. Ḥalabi, IV (Cairo, 1352/1933), pp. 215–216; *Kitāb al-Imlāʾ*, printed in the margin of *Iḥyaʾ*, I (Cairo, 1346/1927), pp. 138–141, 165–171. These passages are reproduced as Appendices 11 and 12 in Jabre, *La Notion de la Maᶜrifa*, pp. 186–193.

50. Cf. Wensinck, *La Pensée de Ghazzālī*, pp. 40–42.

51. *Iḥyāʾ*, IV, 263; cf. Jabre, *La Notion de la Maᶜrifa*, p. 88.

52. Cf. *Al-Maqṣad*, ed. Sharaf (Cairo, 1324/1905), pp. 17–27; cf. Jabre, *La Notion de la Maᶜrifa*, p. 93.

53. Cf. Wensinck, *La Pensée de Ghazzālī*, p. 40.

54. See Note 48.

55. Cf. Jabre, *La Notion de la Maᶜrifa*, pp. 96–97.

soul of man.[56] Hence, we conclude, only he who knows his soul knows his Lord.

The two *ḥadiths* are even more fully discussed in the *Mishkāt al-Anwār*[57] where the theme crops up again and again. In one of the major passages on this topic[58] al-Ghazālī starts out by explaining that Adam was created in the image not of Allāh himself but of "the Merciful One." A distinction is thus drawn between God in his transcendence and what al-Ghazālī also calls the "Divine Presence" (*ḥaḍara*). "For it was the Divine mercy that caused the image of the Divine Presence to be in that 'image.' And then Allāh, out of his grace and mercy, gave Adam a summary 'image' embracing every genus and species in the whole world, insomuch that it was as if Adam were all that was in the world, or were a summarized copy of the world." Adam created in the image of the Merciful One, therefore, means simply that his being a microcosm is due to God's mercy. We assume that the exegesis implied in this view is identical with the one offered in the *Imlāʾ*: "in *his* image" signifies the macrocosm which is "his," that is, belongs to God; as distinct from the other (second) exegesis which interprets "his" image as God's attributes.[59] Our passage in the *Mishkāt* would seem to adopt the (first) interpretation and to elaborate it in the sense that as Adam's creation in the image of the macrocosm was due to the Divine mercy, the *ḥadīth* may also be understood as saying that Adam was created in the image of the Merciful One. He actually quotes a version (according to Bukhari) which reads: "Allāh created Adam in the image of the Merciful One."[60] We may note that this exegesis or, for that matter, this text is already presupposed in the passage in the *Mīzān al-ᶜAmal* (quoted above) which attributes man's being a miniature copy of the world to the "effect of the mercy of God." "But for this mercy," al-Ghazālī says in the *Mishkāt* passage, "no son of Adam would be capable of knowing his Lord; for 'only he who knows himself knows his Lord.'"[61] Thus the two *ḥadīths* are once more connected with each

56. Cf. Wensinck, *La Pensée de Ghazzālī*, p. 42.

57. Gairdner's translation is based on the text of the Cairo edition of 1322/1903; see *Al-Ghazzālī's Mishkāt*, p. 1, note 1; Jabre's analysis on the text in *Al-Jawāhir ʾl-ghawāli*, pp. 110–146; cf. his *La Notion de la Maᶜrifa*, p. 142. The work was rendered twice in Hebrew. The third section of Isaac ben Joseph al-Fazi's version has been published by L. Dukes, *Shīrē Shelōmō*, pp. ix–xiii, 90. M. Steinschneider quotes Joḥanan Alemano's comparison of al-Ghazālī's grading of lights with the kabbalistic doctrine (*Hebr. Übersetzungen*,# 196, p. 346).

58. Cf. Gairdner, *Al-Ghazzālī's Mishkāt*, pp. 75–76.

59. Cf. Jabre, *La Notion de la Maᶜrifa*, pp. 89–90.

60. Cf. Gairdner, *Al-Ghazzālī's Mishkāt*, p. 76.

61. *Ibid.*

other. The microcosm motif, it would appear, holds the key to the understanding of the *ḥadīth* on self-knowledge.

But this is not the whole story in this highly esoteric treatise. In an earlier passage of the same work[62] al-Ghazālī discusses the "light" of the intellect (*al-ᶜaql*). "In the twinkling of an eye it [*scilicet*, intellect] ascends to the highest heavens above, in another instant to the confines of the earth beneath . . . For it is a pattern or sample of the attributes of Allāh. Now the sample must be commensurate with the original, even though it does not rise to the degree of equality with it. And this may move you to set your mind to work upon the true meaning of the tradition: 'Allah created Adam after his own likeness.'" It is to be noted that here the *ḥadīth* is quoted differently from the usual text. Obviously, a new exegesis is worked into the quotation. Allāh created Adam after *his own* likeness. We may recognize in this exegesis the one offered as a second possibility in the *Imlāʾ*: "his" image meaning the image of God's own attributes. Moreover, it is the intellect which is here described as being in the image of God. This links up with the passage in the *Maḍnūn ṣaghīr* which speaks of the soul as the true essence of man. Man in the image of God here, therefore, means the intellect as "a pattern of the attributes of Allāh." And our mind that is to be set working on this new interpretation is directed toward the mystery of the intellect as a spiritual "light." Al-Ghazālī refuses, at this stage, to be drawn more deeply into the matter.[63]

There is, however, a third passage in the *Mishkāt*[64] which brings us to the acme of al-Ghazālī's mystical interpretation of the *ḥadīth* on self-knowledge. It relates to the experience of mystical union. In that experience man may, like the Prophet, become so fully immersed in the Divine Unity as to utter in rapture: "I have become His hearing whereby He heareth, His vision whereby He seeth, His tongue wherewith He speaketh"; or as to exclaim, like al-Ḥallāj, "I am the ONE REAL!"; or, like another, "Glory be to ME!" Al-Ghazālī sees in this assertion of identity with Allāh a self-delusion comparable to mistaking the form seen in a mirror for the mirror itself.[65] Yet, as W. H. T. Gairdner remarked,[66] the *Mishkāt* could have been written only after al-Ghazālī had been deep in the study of al-Ḥallāj, and "his inmost thought may have been, 'Perhaps al-Ḥallāj has penetrated here to something of what the Koran itself left obscure. I neither

62. Gairdner, *Al-Ghazzālī's Mishkāt*, p. 48.
63. *Ibid.*
64. Gairdner, *Al-Ghazzālī's Mishkāt*, pp. 64–65; see also pp. 60–61.
65. *Ibid.*, p. 61.
66. *Ibid.*, pp. 33–34.

assert nor deny.'" We have to bear this thought in mind when contemplating al-Ghazālī's final hint at what the *ḥadīth* on *homo imago Dei* may mean: "From that heaven of intellect he [*scilicet*, the mystic] fares upward to the limit of the ascension of created things . . . thereafter 'settleth he himself on the throne' of the Divine Unity, and therefrom 'taketh command' throughout his storied heavens. Well might one, in looking upon such an one, apply to him the saying, 'Allāh created Adam after the image of the Merciful One.'" There is the sobering afterthought that such an interpretation stands condemned just like the self-delusory "I am the ONE REAL" or "Glory be to ME."[67] But it is noteworthy that al-Ghazālī considered, albeit for a fleeting moment and with great hesitation, the possibility of understanding the *ḥadīth* about man being in the image of God and, obviously, also the *ḥadīth* about self-knowledge, in terms of an ultimate identity.

Although al-Ghazālī rejects the claim of the mystic to union with Allāh, he seems to suggest that in the experience described the human intellect merges with the supernal Intellect. In the third section of the *Mishkāt*, which deals with the degrees of ascent, the third grade is said to be reached when God ("the Lord") is conceived in terms of the Vicegerent, the first Mover of the Heavens, who is, however, but one of His creatures, an Angel who issues the command (*amr*), and is "the Obeyed One" (*al-Muṭāʾ*).[68] Gairdner has argued that this Vicegerent is the Spirit of Allāh, the Divine Word of Command or *Logos* but does not include, as R. Nicholson had suggested, the archetypal spirit of Muḥammad, the Heavenly Man, nor, as L. Massignon had proposed, the figure of the *quṭb* ("axis") as embodied in an earthly mystic who, unknown to the world, administers the affairs of the heaven and the earth.[69]

We suggest that this figure of "the Obeyed One" is identical with Philo's *Logos* as "ruler" and "second God" in whose image man is created (man thus being an image of the image of God),[70] and that he is, therefore, the archetypal man. Moreover, he is identical also with the Plotinian Intellect, as has already been pointed out by Jabre.[71] In his *Kitāb al-Maʿārif al-ʿaqliyya*[72] al-Ghazālī quotes a *ḥadīth* of Neoplatonic origin in which the

67. *Ibid.*, p. 65.
68. *Ibid.*, p. 96.
69. Cf. Gairdner, *Al-Ghazzālī's Mishkāt*, pp. 10–25.
70. Cf. H. A. Wolfson, *Philo*, I, 339, 234.
71. Cf. Jabre, *La Notion de la Maʿrifa*, p. 107.
72. Cf. M. Asín Palacios, *La Espiritualidad de Algazel*, III (Madrid, 1936), 254–255; Dario Cabanelas, "Un Opusculo inedito de Algazel," *Al-Andalus*, 21:28 (1956).

Intellect is described as the first of God's creations. He says of this Intellect (which obviously represents the Plotinian *Νοῦς*) that *it knows its Lord*, humbly *obeying* His command, and *exercising dominion* over the decrees of Providence and the mystery of predestination contained in the Word (*kalima*) of the Creator. The supernal Intellect, thus, possess the features of the Vicegerent ("exercising dominion") and of the *Muṭāʾ* who is obeyed because he obeys the Divine Command. What is of particular interest to us here is the characterization of this figure as "knowing its Lord." This phrase is clearly taken from the *ḥadīth*, "He who knows himself knows his Lord." Intellect, knowing itself, knows its Lord.

If we put all the threads together, the final interpretation of the two *ḥadīths* as implied in al-Ghazālī's doctrine is as follows. Man is essentially intellect. He is created in the image of the Merciful One, which we take to signify the supernal intellect or Vicegerent. In the act of union the mystic becomes identical with this supernal intellect and, like it, by virtue of the intellect's self-knowledge knows his Lord. But as experience shows, the mystic rather tends to mistake this identity with the Intellect for one with Allāh Himself. Here the danger lurks which al-Ghazālī tries to warn against.

Ibn al-ᶜArabī follows in the footsteps of al-Ḥallāj and al-Ghazālī. The soul or self referred to in the *ḥadīth* formulae is the Intellect (*ᶜaql*); it is the "Pen," a symbol of the "handwriting of Allāh," by which, in a passage in the *Mishkāt*, al-Ghazālī had described Adam's form; it is the Spirit of Allāh, again as in al-Ghazālī. There is also the reference to the mystic's "settling oneself on the throne" as expressed by al-Ḥallāj.[73] But Ibn al-ᶜArabī goes beyond al-Ghazālī in identifying the perfect soul or self with the Vicegerent of God on earth. Here he resumes entirely al-Ḥallāj's tradition which saw in the perfect saint a semi-divine power put in charge of the governance of the world, and who taught that the saint becomes *al-Muṭāʾ* (the Obeyed One) and *Quṭb* (Axis) of his time.[74] In a more specific sense Muḥammad is the "perfect man," the *Logos proforikos* of Christian theology.[75] But potentially every man is a claimant, as it were, to the throne. For man is created in the image of God.[76] "God formed a knowledge of Himself; thereby He knew the world, and for this reason,

73. See *Kitāb ᶜuqlat al-mustawfiz* (ed. Nyberg), p. 52.

74. Cf. Gairdner, *Al-Ghazzālī's Mishkāt*, pp. 14ff.; R. A. Nicholson, *The Idea of Personality in Sūfism* (Cambridge, 1923), pp. 44ff.

75. Cf. H. S. Nyberg's account in his Introduction to *Kleinere Schriften des Ibn Al-ᶜArabi*, pp. 100ff.

76. *Kitāb ᶜuqlat . . .*, p. 45.

it emerged in a Form [*ṣūra*]. And God created man as an exalted design by summarizing the ideas [*maᶜānī*] of the macrocosm, and made him a manuscript containing in miniature everything in the macrocosm... With regard to him the Prophet has said, God created Adam after His own image."[77] Now, "he who has his existence in the form of something, contains that something in his form so that by the very same act by which he perceives his own form he perceives also that in whose form he exists."[78] Hence, he who knows himself knows his Lord.[79] God, man, and world coincide. They are three aspects of the same entity, and man is the connecting link. Man who is created in the image of God is the throne upon which Allāh is seated, while the physical world is the throne on which the Merciful seats himself. The Merciful is the *Logos*, the Spirit of Allāh, the perfect man, Muḥammad, and ideally man as such.[80]

It is a long way from Plato's interpretation of the Delphic maxim to the complex pattern of al-Ghazālī's and Ibn al-ᶜArabī's mystical understanding of the *ḥadīth* formula. The Philonic *Logos*, the mythological *Adam Qadmon* motif, Neoplatonic elements, and Biblical notions as reflected in the Qurᵓān and the Ḥadīth have a share in it. The position is somewhat similar in medieval Jewish mysticism. Here too a variety of motifs, developed from Neoplatonic, Gnostic, and other late-Hellenistic sources, overlay the original Platonic theme of the soul's kinship with God, and enter into combination with the Biblical idea of man's creation in the image of God. But there is little stress here on self-knowledge, although—as we shall see—this aspect is not entirely missing and, in fact, somehow continues to loom in the background even where it is not articulated.

The *Sēfer Bahīr* (#55) sees in the seven (or six) limbs of the body of man an image of the seven (six) lower *Sefirot* or six mystical Days of Creation, and applies to this analogy the verse, "For in the image of God made He man" (Genesis 9:6). This passage is reflected in *Tiqqūnē Ha-Zohar* (130 b), where it is said: "The limbs of man are all arranged in the order of the Beginning [*ᶜal sidrē bĕrēshīt*]"—that is, of the mystical days of creation which are identical with the six lower *Sefirot*—"and man is therefore called a microcosm [*ᶜolam qatan*]."[81] The mystical interpretation of the

77. Cf. Nyberg's translation and discussion of this text, *Kleinere Schriften*, pp. 98ff.

78. Cf. *Kitāb ᵓinshaᵓ al-dawāᵓir*, p. 15 (quoted and discussed by Nyberg, *Kleinere Schriften*, pp. 99ff.).

79. *Kitāb ᵓinshāᵓ al-dawāᵓir*, p. 18; *Kitāb ᶜuqlat* . . ., p. 52; *Kitāb al-tadbīrāt*, p. 209. See Nyberg, *Kleinere Schriften*, p. 100.

80. Cf. Nyberg, *Kleinere Schriften*, p. 101.

81. It is interesting to note that the term is preserved in its Hebrew form, although the context is in Aramaic.

microcosm motif[82] becomes increasingly important and furnishes one of the decisive aspects for the kabbalistic exegesis of the Genesis passages speaking about man being made in the image of God. The most outspoken passage—which is significant also because of its clear reference to the theme of self-knowledge leading to the knowledge of God—is found in the *Sēfer Tĕmūnah* (Lemberg, 1892, fol. 25a–b): "The *Sefirot* which are the image [*dĕmūt*] of man—for man is a microcosm [*ᶜolam qatan*] according to 'Let us make man in our image, in our likeness'—are seven Forms, and the soul [*ha-nĕshamah*] is in the body and is the hidden light which is in his head. For in it [*scilicet*, the body] is the mystery of the 'small image' [*tĕmūnah qĕtanah*], for it is written, 'And from my flesh I behold God'; and the mystery of the 'supernal image' [*tĕmūnah ᶜelyōnah*]." The quotation of Job 19:26 (see above, Page 198) immediately links the kabbalistic notion expounded here with the philosophical tradition in medieval Judaism which uses this verse as *locus probans* for the concept of self-knowledge leading to the knowledge of God. The *Sēfer Tĕmūnah* thus implies that from the mystical understanding of the human body one may arrive at an understanding of the "supernal Image" which is the world of the *Sefirot*. In making the contemplation of the body the point of departure for the knowledge of the Sefirotic realm the *Sēfer Tĕmūnah* obviously follows the precedent of the *Sēfer Bahīr*. Other kabbalistic passages describe the totality of man (body and soul) as comprising both the supernal and lower grades of existence. Thus Isaac the Blind says in his *Commentary on Sefer Yeṣirah*[83] that "Man is a great seal in which the beginning and the end, the totality of all created things, are contained." Man is "composed of the supernal and the lower [forces], and he belongs to the world, the year and the soul [*ᶜolam*, *shanah*, *nefesh*]. For all that is in the world is in the year, and all that is in the world and in the year is in the soul."[84] There are also several *Zohar* passages which speak of man as a totality "comprising everything": that is, both the supernal and lower grades.[85] Likewise in Menaḥem Recanati's *Sēfer Taᶜamē Ha-Miṣwōt* (Basle, 1581, fol. 2b):

82. As distinct from its use in philosophical literature, which will be investigated below (Section 2).

83. MS. Hebrew Union College, Cincinnati, fols. 35, 36.

84. Quoted in part by J. Tishby, *Pērūsh Ha-Aggadōt Le-Rabbi ᶜAzriel* (Jerusalem, 1945), p. 5, n. 7, together with parallels from the writings of ᶜEzra ben Solomon,ᶜ Azriel of Gerona, and Naḥmanides; and by G. Scholem, *Rēshīt Ha-Qabbalah* (Tel-Aviv, 1948), p. 114. The analogy between *mundus* (*ᶜolam*), *annus* (*shanah*), *homo* (*nefesh*), which is one of the themes of *Sēfer Yeṣirah* (chap. iii), is a variant of the microcosm-macrocosm motif which has a parallel in Isidor of Seville, as J. G. Weiss has suggested (in a lecture at the Institute of Jewish Studies, Manchester, in 1959).

85. *Zohar*, II, 75b; III, 117a, 141b.

"All that exists of all created beings is in the image [*ᶜinyan dugmaʾ*] of the Ten Ineffable [*belīmah*][86] *Sefirot*, and when man below came to be created, he was made in the image of the supernal Form [*ha-ṣūrah ha-ᶜelyōnah*], the Ten *Sefirot* being formed (*meṣuyyar*] in him."[87] Yet other passages are content to leave it open as to whether the reference is to man as a totality of body and soul or to him *qua* soul alone. Thus, we hear simply that "God created man in His image, in the manner [*ke-gawna*] of the Ten *Sefirot*" (*Tiqqūnē Ha-Zohar*, 90b). Still another passage says distinctly that only the soul resembles the supernal world, while the body is not worthy of being united to the supernal, although the image of the body too is fashioned in the mystery of the supernal (*Zohar*, I, 140a).

A decidedly Platonic view is taken by Moses de Leon in his Hebrew writings and taken over into the *Zohar* when man is said to be identical with the soul.[88] An exposition of this view occurs in the *Sēfer Sheqel Ha-Qōdesh* (ed. Greenup, pages 33–34): "They said that He, blessed be His Name, created man in the 'image and likeness' and fashioned him in the supernal Form, as He says, 'And God created man in His image' . . . They said in [the exposition of] the mysteries of the Torah[89] that the intellectual Form [*ha-ṣūrah ha-sikhlīt*] which is in man is the one called 'man'; for skin, flesh and bones are but the garment of man. Therefore, they said, it is written (Job 10:11), 'Thou hast clothed me with skin and flesh, and knit me together with bones and sinews.' And if skin and flesh are the garment, consider who is the man." Similarly in the *Sēfer Ha-Mishqal* (Basle, 1608, fol. 1 Cd, 2 Cb): "One has to search and inquire

86. On the term *bělimah*, see G. Scholem, *Major Trends in Jewish Mysticism* (New York, 1946), p. 77.

87. Similarly in Recanati's *Pērūsh Ha-Tefilōt* (quoted from MS. Munich, 112 in M. Steinschneider's *Die Hebräischen Handschriften . . . München*, 1895, pp. 69ff.): "In all created beings is something (*ᶜinyan*) corresponding to the Ten *Sefirot*, like the shadow following the form."

88. Cf. *Zohar*, I, 20b, 22b; the main passage is *Zohar*, II, 75b–76a, which has striking parallels in the texts quoted above. The term "the inner man" goes back to Porphyry's *On "Know Thyself"* (see Note 24), ed. Meineke, i, 334: "Such is the precision of Plato who sought most eagerly to know himself above all other things . . . and again to know himself wholly in order that the immortal *inner man* might be known and the *outer man* which is an image might not be unknown, and that the things which make a difference to these might become well known. For an all-perfect mind makes a difference to the *inner part* of us, in which Man himself is, and of which each one of us is an image."

For Plotinus' discussion of Plato's view, see *Enn.*, I, 3, 3; VI, 7, 5; for his assertion that the soul is man, see *Enn.*, III, 5, 5; IV, 7, 1; for his use of the term "image" in this connection, see *Enn.*, VI, 4, 10, 16. Plotinus does not, however, use the term "inner man." It occurs in St. Augustine's *Confessiones*, X, 6, 9.

89. Clearly a reference to the *Zohar* passages quoted in the preceding Note.

as to who is the 'man,' whether it is the body or the Form. To say that of the body that comes from a fetid drop and which is flesh [destined to become] full of worms and maggots, it is said, 'In the image of God created He him,' is, Heaven forfend, something that will never occur to a wise man. And they said in [the exposition of] the mysteries of the Torah,[90] 'Thou hast clothed me with skin and flesh' etc.—If skin and flesh are the garment, consider who is the 'man.' He is what matters [*ha-ᶜiqqar*], and skin and flesh are but the garment and the covering accruing to man." The passage goes on to say that only the "inner man" is in the image of God. There is, however, a sequel to the former passage in which it is explained in terms of the most profound secrecy that the inner man is arranged in three distinct orders (*tiqqūnīm*)—that is, three souls: *nefesh* (appetitive soul), *rūaḥ* (vital spirit) and *neshamah* (intelligent soul)[91]—and that this threefold structure of the soul has its prototype in the Heavenly Man (*Adam Qadmon* or *Sefirot*) of whom it is said: "And upon the likeness of the throne was a likeness as the appearance of a man upon it above" (Ezekiel 1:26). This introduces the Ezekiel passage as an elaboration of the Genesis verses speaking of man as in the image of God. ᶜAzriel of Gerona too says in his *Pērūsh ᶜEser Sefirot* (ed. Goldberg, 4b) that the doctrine ascribing "a measure of limit and corporeality" to the *Sefirot* occurs in the Torah ("in our image, after our likeness"), in the Prophets ("and upon the likeness of the throne," et cetera) and in the words of the Sages, the latter being a reference to the *Shīᶜūr Qōmah.*[92] This aspect is, however, not touched upon in the *Sēfer Ha-Mishqal*, which is primarily concerned with the nature of the human soul and its fate after death. In posing the problems of the mystery of the soul (*sōd ha-neshamah*) it reveals a truly Platonic concern with self-knowledge, and in comparing the soul with God it stresses in rather homely fashion the kinship of God and the soul: "Even as God sees and is not seen, the soul sees and is not seen," et cetera.[93] It is with this Stoic-Talmudic aspect of the kinship between

90. See preceding Note.

91. For the psychology of the *Zohar*, see Scholem, *Major Trends*, pp. 240ff.; R. J. Z. Werblowsky, "Philo and the Zohar," *JJS* 10:38–44, 112–114 (1959).

92. The linking of the *Genesis* passage with the *Shīᶜūr Qōmah* mysticism shows the radical possibilities inherent in the *homo imago Dei* concept and throws into bold relief the reticence with which this notion is treated in classical Rabbinic sources. For the Rabbinic attitude, see A. Geiger's note on *ṣelem ᵓelohīm* in *Oṣar Neḥmad*, ed. I. Blumenfeld, III (Vienna, 1860), 4–6, 119. On the *Shīᶜūr Qōmah* see G. Scholem, *Jewish Gnosticism, Merkabah Mysticism, and Talmudic Tradition* (New York, 1960), pp. 36–42, and Saul Lieberman's Appendix, pp. 124–125.

93. *Sefer ha-Mishqal*, fol. 2 C 2.

the two in view that he finally interprets the Biblical notion of man being created in the image of God.[94]

We conclude this account by quoting the passage from the *Zohar Ḥadash* (Warsaw ed., 70b) on Canticles to which a fleeting reference has already been made (see above, Page 202) in connection with Origen's exegesis of Canticles 1:8. It presents a curious mixture of motifs and thereby shows the extent to which kabbalistic texts are prone to gather their material from a variety of sources: "The wisdom which man requires: Firstly to know and contemplate the mystery of his Lord [*rāza de-marē*], and, secondly, to know himself [*lĕ-mindaᶜ lē lĕ-gufē*]." This interprets the Biblical verse, Canticles 1:8 (*ᵓim lō tēdĕᶜī lakh ha-yafah ba-nashīm*, et cetera) in the same way in which Origen had understood *lakh* as an object in the reflexive sense, meaning the "self" or the "soul." The reference to God as "his Lord" recalls the *ḥadīth* use of *rabbahu*. Knowing oneself and knowing one's Lord are coupled together as in the *ḥadīth* formula. The text continues: "And to make himself aware who he is"—this is the question we met twice in Moses de Leon—"and how he was created; whence he comes and whither he goes"—quoting the well-known passage in *Abōt* 3, 1 which reflects Gnostic influence, as S. Lieberman has shown in his valuable paper published in this volume[95]—"and how his body has been arranged [*tiqqūna dĕ-gūfa hēᵓakh ittaqen*]"—This reflects a philosophical motif which will be more fully discussed below (Pages 214, 218, 221): from the arrangement of his body man can infer the wisdom of his Maker. The term *tiqqūna* used in our passage has a precedent in, for example, Samuel ben Nissim Masnūt's *Maᶜyan Ganīm* (twelfth century), where the meaning of Job 19:26, "From my flesh I behold God," is explained: "From the formation of my limbs and from the arrangement of my body [*we-taqqanat gūfī*]—contemplating them—I behold God" (ed. Buber, 61). The text goes on: "And how he is destined to appear in judgment before the King of the universe"—reverting to the *Abōt* passage ("and before Whom thou wilt render account and reckoning"). That the theme from *Abōt* and the philosophical motif are merely interjected becomes apparent from the resumption of the original subject of self-knowledge in what follows: "And, secondly, to know and contemplate the mysteries of the soul; what this soul in him is, and whence it comes, and why it entered this body, a fetid drop, which is here today and in the grave tomorrow. Moreover, to contemplate this and know the world in which he finds himself,

94. For this theme, see above, Page 200, and n. 33.
95. Pages 123–141.

and why it has been established. And afterward to contemplate the supernal mysteries [*bĕ-rāzīn ᶜilāʾīn*] of the supernal world to become aware of his Lord [*le-marē*]." One looks in vain in this entire passage for any development of the theme of self-knowledge as a road to the knowledge of God or the supernal world. The two kinds of knowledge are coordinated rather than causally related. But there is still vaguely discernible in this discussion the outline of the two-stage formula connecting man's self-knowledge with the knowledge of God.

2. *The Microcosm Motif.* In the Platonic tradition, which has just been analyzed, knowing God proceeds from knowing one's soul (or vice versa), and the "self" which the Delphic oracle bids us know is not the body nor the totality of soul and body but the soul alone. It is in the spirit of this tradition that St. Augustine could say: "Deum et animam scire cupio: Nihilne plus? Nihil omnino."[96] In tracing this line of thought in medieval Islam and Judaism we noticed the intrusion upon it of the Neoplatonic concept of the Intellect as the archetype of the truly divine soul. This development will be more fully discussed in the next section (3). We also came across the microcosm motif, which extends the base of the desired knowledge of God to include the body beside the soul. Jewish mysticism, we saw, wavers uneasily between the purely Platonic approach and an attempt to see in the totality of man as body plus soul an image of the Divine realm of the *Sefirot*. The microcosm motif is used here in a profoundly mystical sense, which completely annihilates any Gnostic disparagement of the body. This line of approach shall not be pursued further. We propose, instead, to investigate the microcosm idea as reflected in the philosophical literature of medieval Islam and Judaism and to do so only insofar as this idea is linked with the theme of self-knowledge and the knowledge of God.

Speaking about the microcosm-macrocosm motif, A.-J. Festugière says, "There is no more famous image in antiquity, amongst Christians and pagans, and it continued to be employed in the Middle Ages."[97] (He should have included "Jews" in the Hellenistic as well as medieval period, as will be shown below.) It is found in Democritus (fragment 34 Diels), Aristotle (*Physics*, VIII, 2, 252b, 26–27), and there is an allusion to it in Plato (*Timaeus*, 30 D; 44 D). According to the *Vita Anonymi* of

96. *Soliloquies*, 1, 7; *De ordine*, 2, 30, 44, 47; *De quantitate animae*, 24E, *et passim*.

97. A.-J. Festugière, *La Révélation d'Hermès Trismégiste*, 2nd ed. (Paris, 1949) I, 92.

Pythagoras,[98] "Man is called μικρὸς κόσμος not because he consists of the four elements—this applies also to each of the animals, even to the lowest—but because he possesses all potencies (δυνάμεις) of the cosmos. For in the cosmos are the gods and also the four elements, and [in it] are also the irrational animals and the plants. All these potencies man possesses. For he has the divine rational potency; he has the nature of the elements, the potency of nourishment, growth and reproduction." There existed, then, a tradition tracing this motif back to Pythagoras.[99] It is this tradition which underlies al-Shahrastānī's account of Pythagoras' doctrine: "He says that in his natural disposition man corresponds to the whole world, and is a microcosm, whereas the world is a Great Man."[100] Possibly Aristotle drew on that tradition when using the terms "small world" and "large world" as current concepts, and Philo distinctly re-echoes it when recording the opinion of "some" who "have ventured to affirm that the tiny animal man is equal to the whole world, because each consists of body and rational soul, and thus *they* declare that man is a small world and alternatively the world a great man."[101]

In the Hellenistic period the microcosm motif is strongly allied to astrological ideas. It is now "no longer a matter of imagery but one literally speaks of limbs of the world and finds relations between each part of the heaven and each member of the body."[102] We meet this new doctrine of

98. In *Photii Bibliotheca*, cod. 249, quoted by M. Joel in "Ibn-Gebirol's (Avicebrons) Bedeutung für die Geschichte der Philosophie" (first published in *MGWJ*, 1857, 386ff., 420ff.; 1858, 59ff.), *Beiträge zur Geschichte der Philosophie* (Breslau, 1878), Supplement, p. 30, n. 2.

99. According to H. Siebeck, *Geschichte der Psychologie* (1880–84), I, 43 (quoted by S. Horovitz, *Die Psychologie bei den jüdischen Religions-Philosophen des Mittelalters von Saadia bis Maimuni* [Breslau, 1898], p. 129, n. 110), the microcosm motif is first found in Heraclitus. Diels, *Vorsocratiker*, 4th ed., 55 B 34 traces it to Democritus, while G. P. Conger, *Theories of Macrocosms and Microcosms* (New York, 1922), p. 6, cites the passage in Aristotle's *Physics* as the first authentic occurrence of the term, though he admits that Aristotle draws on an earlier tradition. Cf. the note (b) in P. H. Wicksteed's and F. M. Cornford's edition of the *Physics* in the *Loeb Classical Library*, II, 286–287.

100. See al-Shahrastānī, *Kitāb al-milal wa-l-niḥal*, ed. Cureton, p. 275 (in T. Haarbrücker's German translation, *Religionspartheien und Philosophen-Schulen*, II, 106), quoted by J[acob] Guttmann, *Die Philosophie des Salomon ibn Gabirol* [Göttingen, 1889], p. 117, n. 3).

101. *Heres* 155; see also *Migr.* 39, 220; *Opif.* 82 (quoted by H. A. Wolfson, *Philo*, I, 424–425, n. 5). The notion that man is "equal" to the whole world may be indebted to Rabbinic sources (cf. *Abōt de-Rabbi Nathan*, ed. Schechter, Version A, chap. 31, p. 91). I. Heinemann, *Philons griechische und jüdische Bildung* (Breslau, 1932), is silent on this point.

102. Cf. Festugière, *Hermès Trismégiste*, 2nd ed., I, 92; on the influence of this motif, especially in its Stoic form of a "universal sympathy," see the note in S. van den Bergh, *Averroes' Tahafut al-Tahafut* (London, 1954), II, 90.

the microcosm in the astrological texts of Manilius, Firmicius, and of the *Corpus Hermeticum.* The principal work of "Egyptian" astrology by Nechepso and Petosiris bears testimony to it.[103] In Rabbinic literature too an echo of this doctrine is quite audible. Thus, *Abōt de-Rabbi Nathan* (ed. Schechter, Version A, chap. 31, pp. 91–92) contains a long description of analogies between man and the world, ending with the sentence: "Hence you learn that everything which the Holy One, blessed be He, created in His world He created in man."[104] The astrological concern plays some part in a late midrash published by A. Jellinek and entitled by him *Aggadat ᶜOlam Qatan.*[105] The *Sēfer Yeṣirah,* above all, employs the microcosm motif on the threefold level of *mundus-annus-homo* (see above, Page 209), and its commentators develop this scheme. In Shabbatai Donnolo's *Commentary* (*Sefer Ḥakmōni* in the Warsaw 1884 edition of *Sefer Yeṣirah,* pp. 121ff.) a large-scale account of the microcosm-macrocosm is offered in an exegesis of the Genesis verse, "Let us make man in our image" (edited and explained by Adolph Jellinek in *Pērūsh Naᶜaseh Adam . . .,* Leipzig, 1854).

The connection of the microcosm motif with the Delphic maxim is first attested in Porphyry's *On "Know Thyself"* (ed. Meineke, i. 332), as I have shown elsewhere.[106] The relevant passage reads: "Others who assert that man has been well described as a microcosm claim that the [Delphic] saying is an exhortation to know man, and that since man is a microcosm it commands him only to philosophize . . . proceeding from our own perception to the contemplation of the Whole." I suggested that this passage might be regarded as one of the sources for the definition of philosophy as self-knowledge which is found in al-Kindī and Isaac Israeli. It also underlies the combination of the theme of self-knowledge with the microcosm motif which we meet in the *Ikhwān al-Ṣafāᵓ.*[107] The salient point common to the *Ikhwān,* al-Kindī, and Israeli is that by knowing himself as a microcosm man knows himself "in both his spirituality and corporeality" and therefore knows "everything": that is, "the spiritual and

103. Cf. Albert Dieterich, *Eine Mithrasliturgie* (1923), pp. 55ff.

104. See also *Kohelet Rabba,* XII, 2, 1. For further references see A. Jellinek, *Der Mikrokosmos von R. Josef Ibn Zadik* (Leipzig, 1854), p. x; B. Beer (in a review of Jellinek's edition of Ibn Ṣaddiq's work), *MGWJ* 3:159–161 [1854]).

105. *Bet Ha-Midrash,* V, 57–59. In his Introduction (p. xxv) Jellinek makes it clear that the title *Aggadat ᶜOlam Qatan* was chosen by *him.* The term *ᶜolam qatan* for microcosm, he points out, does not occur in haggadic literature and was adopted into Hebrew literature only under the influence of Arabic philosophy.

106. Cf. Altmann-Stern, *Isaac Israeli,* p. 204.

107. *Ibid.*

corporeal substance." This point is neatly expressed by al-Masᶜūdī (d. 957/8), who attributes to Aristotle the saying: "Whosoever knows himself, knows thereby everything."[108] It should be noted that this interpretation of self-knowledge as leading to the knowledge of "everything" omits any reference to God as the ultimate goal of the quest for knowledge. Neither the *ḥadīth* formulae nor the Delphic exhortation in its two-stage form is quoted in this context, although the *Ikhwān* use the *ḥadīth* when interpreting self-knowledge as the knowledge of the soul.[109] Obviously, knowing the macrocosm is the be-all and end-all according to the tradition which is here followed. It is clear that the microcosm-macrocosm motif holds a great fascination for the *Ikhwān* in particular, as is evident from the ample treatment they accorded it in their writings.[110] When dealing with it, they are absorbed in the vistas it offers, and theology recedes into the background.

It is characteristic of medieval Jewish philosophy that it goes beyond the aspect of the macrocosm when employing the Delphic maxim in the sense of the microcosm-macrocosm motif. Isaac Israeli already moves in this direction. Explaining the definition of philosophy as meaning that one who knows himself knows "everything"—that is, "the spiritual and corporeal substance"—he adds: "and also knows the first substance which is created from the power of the Creator without mediator . . ."[111] This suggests that self-knowledge eventually leads to knowing the supernal wisdom, but not to the knowledge of God who, like Plotinus' "One," is unknowable.[112] Shorn of its Neoplatonic orientation which is implied in the notion of the supernal wisdom,[113] Israeli's reference to the ultimate goal of self-knowledge could be interpreted to mean that the contemplation of the macrocosm or totality of being (corporeal and spiritual) shows the wisdom

108. Quoted by F. Rosenthal, "On the Knowledge of Plato's Philosophy in the Islamic World" (see Note 6), p. 410. Rosenthal surmises that the saying is taken from the *Theology of Aristotle*, ed. Dieterici, p. 19. But there is nothing in that or any other passage of the *Theology* which could be considered the source of al-Masᶜūdī's quotation. Rosenthal (p. 409) also cites al-Masᶜūdī as reporting: "On the gates of the temple of the Sabians in Harrān there was written in Syriac language the saying of Plato, the translation of which is: Whosoever recognizes his essence is divine (*taᶜallaha*)."

109. Cf. F. Dieterici, *Die Philosophie der Araber im* X. *Jahrhundert n. Chr.*, II *Mikrokosmus* (Leipzig, 1879), p. 185; *idem, Die Philosophie der Araber, Achtes Buch* (1872), pp. 167–168.

110. Cf. the passages quoted by me in Altmann-Stern, *Isaac Israeli*, p. 203, n. 2, and the references given by G. Vajda, "La Philosophie et la théologie de Joseph ibn Çaddiq," *Archives*, 17:96–97 (1949).

111. Cf. Altmann-Stern, *Isaac Israeli*, p. 27, lines 104–108; pp. 28, 202–203.

112. *Ibid.*, pp. 207-208.

113. *Ibid.*, pp. 159–164.

of the Creator and proves His existence. This step is taken in Joseph ibn Ṣaddīq's *Sēfer ʿOlam Qatan.*[114] It quotes Israeli's definition of philosophy as self-knowledge by which man "knows everything" (that is, the corporeal world and the spiritual world), and adds: "And this is the science of philosophy, which is the science of sciences and their final purpose, because it is the preliminary step (*madregah*) and road (*shebhīl*) to the knowledge of the Creator and Initiator of everything, blessed and exalted be He."[115] In another passage, which once more quotes Israeli's definition of philosophy as self-knowledge, he adds: "and he will thence reach the knowledge of his Creator, as it is written in Job (19:26), 'And from my flesh I shall behold God.'"[116] This verse, we have already noted, represents the Jewish version, so to speak, of the *ḥadīth* formula, "He who knows himself, knows his Lord." Joseph ibn Ṣaddīq thus interprets this saying to mean that by knowing oneself as a microcosm one will eventually know God.[117] In portraying man as a microcosm he draws on such sources as Israeli's "Chapter on the Elements," which sees in man a balancing of the four elements;[118] and on "the Ancients"—probably a version of some Hellenistic text which compared the limbs of the human organism to the heavenly bodies (viz., the head to the [all-encompassing] sphere, the eyes to sun and moon, the ears to Saturn and Jupiter, the nostrils to Venus, the mouth to Mars, the tongue to Mercury, and the vertebrae of the spinal cord to the signs of the Zodiac); the arteries to the seas and rivers; the bones to the mountains; the hair to the plants; and the four temperaments to the four elements.[119]

While Ibn Ṣaddīq is content to develop the microcosm motif along traditional lines and link it but loosely with the theme of knowing God, one of his predecessors, Baḥya ibn Paqūdah,[120] treats it with much greater seriousness and independence. (The Neoplatonic outlook which determines his approach will be discussed in the next section [3].) He too quotes "some

114. The quotations which follow are from S. Horovitz' edition (Breslau, 1903).
115. Page 2.
116. Page 21.
117. Cf. Altmann-Stern, *Isaac Israeli*, p. 208. See also G. Vajda, "La Philosophie et la théologie de Joseph Ibn Çaddiq," in *Archives*, pp. 113ff.
118. The passage in *Microcosm*, p. 24, lines 14–19, is clearly based on Israeli's "Chapter on the Elements" (Altmann-Stern, p. 121, no. 3). For the sources of the passage in *Microcosm*, p. 24, lines 19–24, see Vajda, *Archives*, p. 114, n. 1.
119. This passage (p. 24, line 24, to p. 25, line 12) is introduced by a reference to "the Ancients" (*ha-rishonīm*). A pictorial presentation of the analogies mentioned by Joseph ibn Ṣaddīq is found in the microcosm drawing of Prüfening (1165) reproduced in F. Saxl, *Lectures*, II (London, 1957), Plate 37a.
120. In his *Al-Hidāya ʾilā Farāʾid al-Qulūb*, ed. A. S. Yahuda (1912).

philosophers" as saying that "philosophy is man's knowledge of himself," which he explains to mean that from the "traces of wisdom" exhibited in man as a microcosm we are able to recognize the Creator. Job 19:26 is cited as proof text.[121] The "philosophers" referred to are the *Ikhwān*[122] and, possibly, Israeli, but the context in which this passage occurs (*Hidāya*, II, 4–5) clearly shows the freshness of Baḥya's treatment of the theme. The dominant topic is a meditation on the "traces of wisdom" (*āthār al-ḥikma*) found in the "roots and elements" of the world, in man as a microcosm, in the construction of man and in the composition of his body as well as in the faculties of his soul and the light of intellect, in the entire animal world, in plants and metals, in the sciences, arts, and purposive actions of man, in the laying down of the Law (*al-sharāʾiʿ*) and the statutes (*al-suna*).[123] The microcosm idea is used here only as one among seven aspects serving the purpose of the discussion.

Abraham bar Ḥīyya[124] closely follows Baḥya in interpreting Job 19:26 to mean that "from the formation of your body [literally, "flesh"] and the arrangement of your limbs you can see and understand the wisdom of your Creator."[125] This theme becomes a popular topic in the twelfth and thirteenth centuries. Samuel ben Nissīm Masnūt,[126] who lived in twelfth-century Aleppo, quotes Job 19:26 as meaning to say that "From the formation of my limbs and from the arrangement of my body—contemplating them—I behold God (that is, the wonders of the Creator); for by seeing the created, man knows the wonders of the Creator, in the way in which it is said, 'The heavens declare . . .' (Psalm 19:2), which the *Targum* renders, 'Those who contemplate the heaven tell the glory of the Lord.'" Likewise, Joseph ben Jehudah[127] cites Job 19:26 as *locus probans* for the meritoriousness of studying medicine, for this verse means to say, "From

121. *Ibid.*, 106.

122. On Baḥya's indebtedness to the *Ikhwān*, see D. Kaufmann, "Die Theologie des Bachja Ibn Pakuda," *Gesammelte Schriften*, ed. M. Brann, II (Frankfort, 1910), 15–17; G. Vajda, *La Théologie ascétique de Baḥya Ibn Paquda* (Paris, 1947), p. 25, n. 3.

123. The exposition of this theme is given in a lengthy discussion (pp. 103–124). The term "traces of wisdom" occurs also in Ibn Gabirol (cf. Arab. Fragment 12.3, ed. S. Pines, *Tarbiṣ*, vol. XXVII [Scholem Jubilee Number], January 1958, p. 230: *al-āthār al-ḥikmīya*; in Falaqēra's *Liqqūtīm*, V, 65, ed. Munk: *rishūmē ha-ḥokmah*; *Fons Vitae*, ed. Baeumker, V, 41: *impressionibus Sapientiae*). It goes back to Plotinus' use of the term τύπος in *Enn.*, *passim* (see Bréhier, Index, *s.v.*). The *Hebrew Empedocles Fragments*, ed. Kaufmann, render it *rishūm* (as in Falaqēra's *Liqqūtīm*), whereas Jehudah ibn Tibbon's version of Baḥya's *Hidāya* has *simanē ha-ḥokmah*.

124. *Sēfer Hegyōn Ha-Nefesh* (Leipzig, 1865).

125. Fol. 1b.

126. Cf. above, Note 16, for references.

127. Cf. above, Note 16, for references.

the wondrous formation of my body I recognize the wisdom of my Creator as manifold and wondrous." As G. Vajda has pointed out, the Job verse figures in ninth and tenth century Karaite literature as proof text of a similar character.[128] But the texts at our disposal use this verse merely in the sense of clinching the cosmological argument. Thus Joseph al-Baṣīr says: "Since God is not visible, He can be known by us only through His works, because they—for example, our body—cannot be created by us. Job also declares: 'Out of my flesh I know God.' Now our method is prescribed: First we have to recognize the createdness of the bodies; then we can prove therefrom that they require a wise Creator."[129] The Job verse is used here in support of the Kalam method (later attacked by Maimonides) which seeks to prove the existence of God from His creation. From Baḥya onward it is employed in the sense of the teleological rather than cosmological argument. We have seen above (Page 212) that its traces can be found even in a kabbalistic text such as the *Zohar Ḥadash*. In Abraham ibn Ezra the microcosm motif is linked with the mystical notion of the Sanctuary as the "intermediate world" (*ᶜolam ᵓemṣaᶜī*) which, like the heart in the human body receiving the power of the soul in larger degree than any other organs, is the place in which the Divine power is most concentrated. "And if God has given you wisdom, you will understand the mystery of the Ark and the curtain and the Cherubim which spread their wings... And these things are the 'glory' of God... And he who knows the mystery of his soul [*sōd nishmatō*] and the arrangement of his body [*matkōnet gūfō*] is able to know the things of the supernal world. For man is in the image of a microcosm [*ki-dĕmūt ᶜolam qatan*]. He was the end of His creation on earth. This is alluded to in the verse (Genesis 44:12), 'beginning with the great and ending with the small.'"[130]

The sentence, "And *he who knows* ... is able to know the things of the supernal world" re-echoes both the *ḥadīth* ("*He who knows* himself knows his Lord") and Israeli's definition of philosophy as self-knowledge: "the mystery of the soul" and "the arrangement of the body" reflect Israeli's "spiritual and corporeal substance," and the "supernal world" described by Ibn Ezra as the goal of knowledge corresponds to Israeli's "First Substance" or "supernal Wisdom."[131] The doctrine interposing the "intermediate world" of the Sanctuary is quoted in the name of

128. See above, Page 198 and Note 15.
129. Cf. P. F. Frankl, *Ein mutazilitischer Kalam aus dem 10. Jahrhundert* (Vienna, 1872), p. 185.
130. *Commentary ad* Exodus 25:40, end.
131. It denotes, however, the entire world of Spiritual Substances or Angels.

"the Gaon": that is, Saadya Gaon, who in his *Commentary* on the *Sēfer Yeṣirah* (ed. Lambert, 67ff., 91) mentions eighteen analogies between the three worlds.[132] That the Sanctuary and its furniture mirror the cosmos is an old midrashic motif, particularly pronounced in *Midrash Tadsheh.*[133] The observation that creation began with the macrocosm and ended with the microcosm is already found in Philo (*Opif.* 82) and Abraham bar Ḥiyya (*Hegyōn Ha-Nefesh*, 1b).

There is a further reference to self-knowledge in Ibn Ezra. He links this theme also to that of the love of God which plays a cherished part in his thinking.[134] "It is the root-principle of the commandments that one should love God with all his soul and cleave unto Him. A man will not be perfect unless he recognizes the work of God in the supernal and lower worlds and knows His ways . . . and he will not be able to know God, unless he knows his own soul [*nefesh*] and his body and his intelligent soul [*nishmatō*]; for one who does not know the essence of his soul, what wisdom does he possess?"[135] This reflects the saying of the *Ikhwān* that one who regards the soul as a mere accident or mixture of the body "knows neither his soul not his true essence; how then should he know the true essence of things and their First Cause?"[136] But while the *Ikhwān* mention only the soul, Ibn Ezra—bearing in mind the microcosm motif—regards the knowledge of body *and* soul as a precondition for the knowledge of God.

Similarly, Netanᵓel Berab Fayūmī, a Yemenite scholar of the twelfth century, who was greatly influenced by the *Ikhwān al-Ṣafāᵓ* and by Baḥya ibn Paqudah, describes in his *Bustān al-ᶜUqūl* ("Garden of the Intelligences," edited and translated into Hebrew by Joseph ben David Qafaḥ, Jerusalem, 1954) the body and soul of man as a microcosm mirroring the macrocosm. The three worlds of (1) the Universal Intellect (*al-ᶜaql al-kullī*), (2) the spheres (*al-aflāq*), and (3) the coarse [*scilicet*, material] world (*al-ᶜālam al-kaṭīf*) are reflected in man's spirit, body, and three-

132. Cf. H. Malter, *Saadia Gaon, His Life and Works* (Philadelphia, 1942), pp. 186–187 and n. 436, where the references to the literature on the subject are given.

133. S. Z. Netter in his supercommentary on Ibn Ezra *ad loc.* offers a wealth of detail concerning these analogies.

134. Cf. G. Vajda, *L'Amour de Dieu dans la Théologie Juive du Moyen Age* (Paris, 1957), pp. 109–115.

135. Quoted from the recension of Ibn Ezra's *Commentary* in Cod. 53 of the Breslau Seminary, as reported in D. Rosin's valuable essay, "Die Religionsphilosophie Abraham ibn Esra's," *MGWJ* 43 (N.F. 7):231 (1899). This recension has a fuller text, but the last sentence is corrupt. It reads: *kī kol mī shelōᵓ lamad ḥokmah ḥokmah mā lō*. In our translation of the passage (see above) we have substituted the reading of the printed edition in the last sentence.

136. Cf. the passages in Altmann-Stern, *Isaac Israeli*, pp. 205–206.

dimensionality respectively. Hence it is said, "And out of my flesh I behold God" and "Thou hast made him but a little lower than the angels" (Psalms 8:6). "It thus befits us to consider and contemplate all his attributes of body and soul, the manifest and the hidden [*scilicet*, the corporeal and spiritual] in order to know the exaltedness of his Maker and Creator, blessed be He" (pp. 5, 13).

An interesting variation of our theme is offered in one of the interpretations of Genesis 1:26 recorded by Baḥya ben Asher in his *Commentary on the Torah* (9a, col. a–b): "Some explain 'in our image' as 'in the image which is ours but distinct from Us," i.e., the image of the world in its structure [*bi-tekhūnatō*], comprising the world of the angels, the world of the spheres, and the lower world. These three parts make up the totality of existence. Hence man is called a microcosm [*ᶜolam qatan*]; for he corresponds to the macrocosm [*ᶜolam gadōl*], and Job alluded to this when saying 'And out of my flesh I behold God.' He meant to say that from the three parts of his body one beholds the three parts of existence in creation, which is the work of God. For man's head, which receives the emanation of Intellect, corresponds to the supernal world in which the separate intelligences reside. The part from the neck to the loins is man's intermediate part . . . corresponding to the intermediate world which is the world of the spheres. . . From the loins downward is the third part . . . corresponding to this world of generation and corruption." In this account the body as such is conceived as a microcosm reflecting all stages of existence, including the supernal realm. The closeness of this view to the kabbalistic interpretation mentioned in a previous context (Pages 208ff.) is obvious.

The same is true of the interpretation of Genesis 1:26 offered by Joshuᶜa ibn Shuᶜeib (first half of the fourteenth century), who, like Baḥya ben Asher, was a disciple of Solomon ben Adret of Barcelona. In his *Sefer Dĕrashōt al Ha-Torah* (Constantinople, 1522, and Krakow, 1573, the latter edition being quoted here) he describes the body of man as made in the image (*ṣelem*) and archetype (*dugmā*) of everything found in the Ten *Sefirot* and in the Ten Heavens (symbolized by his ten fingers and ten toes respectively). His 248 limbs correspond to the 248 positive commandments and his 365 veins and sinews to the 365 negative commandments of the Torah. This is referred to in Job 19:26 and in Psalm 35:10 ("All my bones shall say: 'Lord, who is like unto Thee'"). The limbs of man, though resembling those of the animals, contain "something supernal mixed with them" and must therefore be guarded in their purity (fol. 60*v*, col. a). Genesis 1:26 teaches us "the rank of the creation of his body and of the form of his limbs" which have their counterpart in the world of the *Merkabah*, as known to the Kabbalists (fol. 2*v*, col. 1). It is interesting to note that both Ibn Shuᶜeib and Baḥya ben Asher, though steeped in Neoplatonic concepts and philosophically inclined, interpret the *homo imago Dei* motif by reference to the body of man as a microcosm.

3. *Soul and Intellect.* The third line of approach in interpreting the Delphic maxim is the Neoplatonic one. According to Plotinus (*Enn.*, V, 3, 3ff.), the soul has two modes of knowing intrinsic to her: sensation, which is turned toward the external things, and discursive reason which separates or combines the images presented by the senses, and judges them in the light of standards derived from intellect. In all these operations the soul is concerned with the external world, not with itself. In the act of judging the soul turns toward the intellect, but standing midway between sensation and intellect, it cannot wholly identify itself with intellect and know itself. Intellect is ours and is not ours. It is ours when we act by it. The sensitive principle is our "scout" (*angelos*); intellect is our king. But we too are kings, when we take our fill of intellect. Man becomes intellect when, ignoring all other phases of his being, he knows himself in the dual sense of knowing the nature of the discursive thinking of the soul and knowing its own conformity to intellect. Thus, essentially, the soul knows itself by looking upward to Intellect, not by looking merely into itself. The difference between soul and intellect is this: while the soul knows itself within something else (that is, intellect), the latter knows itself as self-depending and achieves its self-knowledge by simple introversion upon itself. In the act of self-contemplation the intellect and the intelligible are one. The precept, "Know thyself" addresses itself, therefore, only to those beings which are multiple and have to learn which of their parts is the dominant one and causes them to be "themselves" (*Enn.*, VI, 7, 41).

The salient points of this doctrine may be said to be the following. (1) The soul knows itself only by looking upward, not by looking upon itself. This tallies with Plotinus' theory of emanation which describes the emanant as becoming fully substance and reality at the second phase when it looks back to its source. (2) The act of self-knowledge implies a withdrawal from the sensible world. (3) The final goal of self-knowledge must lie beyond Intellect and can be found only in "union" with the One. There is no ecstasy in self-knowledge. Plotinus describes ecstasy in *Enneads*, VI, 9, 10–11, and in the famous passage IV, 8, 1, as a state in which the soul stands above the intelligible world. In this state the soul is divested of the body and it "enters into itself," but it reaches the end of the journey only when the image of the One takes shape in the soul. The desire for "contact" (ἁφή) is the keynote of this ultimate stage (V, 3, 17; VI, 9, 11). Here our concern is no longer the soul or self-knowledge. The soul is no longer itself. It becomes what it is in the very source of its being.[137]

In *Enneads*, V, 3, 7, Plotinus answers the view of the mystics who hold that by turning away from the sensible world we turn not to ourselves but to God. The view referred to is, as E. Bréhier remarks,[138] the Philonic doctrine according to which the exodus of the soul from the realm of sense leads not to self-knowledge but to the realization of the nothingness of the soul and of God as the only true Being. Philo had indeed interpreted the Delphic maxim as an exhortation to remember "thine own nothingness in all things" so as to remember the transcendence of God in all things (*Sacrif. Ab.*, 54). Socrates' quest for self-knowledge—represented in the Hebrew Scriptures by the character of Teraḥ—is not the ultimate end. "Abraham who gained much progress and improvement towards the acquisition of the highest knowledge" supersedes Teraḥ: "For when most he knew himself, then most did he despair of himself, in order that he might attain to an exact knowledge of Him Who in reality IS . . . And the man who has despaired of himself is beginning to know Him that IS" (*De Somniis*, 57–60).[139] Plotinus rejects this view because it ignores the fact that in knowing God the soul, at the same time, knows itself as derived from God. The tranquility (ἡσυχία) achieved in the act of knowing God is not "ecstatic" in the sense that the soul goes out of itself but means, on the contrary, that the soul rests entirely in itself: that is, in the self-knowledge of the intellect. This anticipates the critique medieval philosophers applied to the *Ṣūfī* doctrine of ecstasy as disregarding the essential role of intellect for the attainment of the ultimate stage of union.[140] For Plotinus, "knowing God"—he uses this term on this rare occasion—cannot be divorced from the self-possession of the soul in the pure act of intellect.

The Plotinian interpretation of the Delphic maxim is taken up in Porphyry's treatment of the theme in his *Sententiae*, in the *De abstinentia*,

137. Cf. Louis Gardet, *La Pensée religieuse d'Avicenne* (Paris, 1951), pp. 148–149, where the Plotinian view is compared and contrasted with Ibn Sīnā's.

138. Plotinus, *Ennéades*, ed. Bréhier, 2nd ed. V, 41–42.

139. Cf. also *Migr. Abr.* 8 (interpreting the Biblical *hishshamēr lekha* as "give heed to thyself": i.e., "know thyself"); *Migr. Abr.* 195 (moving from self-knowledge to the contemplation of Him who IS).

140. E.g., in Ibn Bājja's *Risālat al-wadāᶜ*, ed. M. Asín Palacios ("La Carta de Adiós de Avempace," *Al-Andalus*, vol. VIII, §8, pp. 21–22 [53–55]).

and in his large work *On "Know thyself."* "To them that are able to withdraw thinkingly into their own substance and to know their own substance by that very same knowledge, and to receive themselves back (αὑτοὺς ἀπολαμβάνειν) by the vision of this knowledge according to the unity of knower and known—to them, being present to themselves, Being too is present. But those who slip past their own being towards the other things are far from themselves and Being is far from them" (*Sententiae*, ed. Mombert, chap. 40, p. 38).[141] The characteristic phrase describing self-knowledge as a "receiving oneself back" corresponds to the phrase "returning to oneself" by which Proclus denotes the essential movement of intellect, and which also appears in the Arabic paraphrase of the Plotinus passage on ecstasy in the *Theology of Aristotle* (ed. Dieterici, p. 8). It is re-echoed in St. Augustine's *De ordine*, I, 3: "Ut se noscat magna opus habet consuetudine recedendi a sensibus et animum in se ipsum colligendi atque in se ipso retinendi . . . ita enim *animus sibi redditus* . . ." In turning inward, man finds not only himself but Being as such; he loses both when turning away from himself to the "other" which is non-being. He renounces his interior riches and becomes impoverished.[142] Porphyry is particularly emphatic about the need of practicing the virtues appropriate to the contemplative life. Only at the stage of the "paradigmatic virtues" may we expect the distance between soul and Intellect to be eliminated.[143]

In Proclus' scheme of the soul's ascent[144] self-knowledge is tacitly assumed to be identical with the first stage: that of "purification." "For whence else does it befit our self-purification and perfection to start than from the point where the Delphian god has commanded us? For to those entering the Eleusinian temple a notice was shown, 'Let none of the uninitiated and unexpiated enter here.' Indeed, the inscription 'Know thyself' upon the entrance to the Delphian temple likewise, I believe, indicated the manner of the ascent to the Divine and of the readiest way of purification, evidently as if to say to those capable of understanding that he who knows himself, starting as he does from the right beginning, can achieve union with God, the interpreter of all truth and leader of the purgative life."[145] The passage quoted shows clearly that the notion of self-knowledge merges here imperceptively with that of purification.

141. Cf. W. Theiler, *Porphyrios und Augustin* in *Schriften der Königsberger Gelehrten Gesellschaft*, vol. X, fasc. 1 (Halle [Saale], 1933), pp. 43ff., where this passage is discussed.

142. For the relevant passages in Porphyry and parallels in Hierocles, see Theiler, *Porphyrios und Augustin*, p. 44.

143. Cf. Theiler, *Porphyrios und Augustin*, p. 44, n. 1.

144. Cf. Altmann-Stern, *Isaac Israeli*, pp. 185ff.

145. Cf. Altmann-Stern, *Isaac Israeli*, p. 205.

The soul is capable of a true introversion only if it turns away from the things of the sensible, external world and, thus purified, rests entirely in the intellect from which it has its true being. There is an interesting parallel to the identification of self-knowledge and purification in Philo (*Leg. Spec.*, I, 263–264): "For he [Moses] holds that the most profitable form of purification is just this, that a man should know himself. . ."

The impact of this Neoplatonic view of self-knowledge upon medieval thought is very considerable. It is mediated in large measure by the Neoplatonic pseudepigrapha sailing under the flags of Aristotle, Empedocles and others.[146] We propose to trace some of the themes to which reference has been made in a number of medieval writings. In many instances these themes are explicitly connected neither with the Delphic maxim nor the *ḥadīth* or its Hebrew equivalent, but the pattern of the two-stage formula is always in the background.

The theme of the soul's withdrawal from the external world in order to find itself illumined by the Intellect occurs in the many medieval passages quoting the *Theology of Aristotle*'s paraphrase of Plotinus' portrayal of ecstasy. How closely the text of the *Theology* follows its protoype will be clear from a glance at the passages concerned in juxtaposition to each other:

Enneads, IV, 8,1:	*Theology*, p. 8:
Many times it has happened:	Sometimes,
Lifted out of the body	I was, as it were, alone with my soul: I divested myself of the body, put it
into myself becoming external to all other things and self-encentered	aside, and was as it were a simple substance without a body. Then I entered into my essence by returning into it free from all things. . .
beholding a marvellous beauty	I saw in my essence so much of beauty, loveliness and splendour. . .
then more than ever assured of community with the loftiest order, enacting the noblest life	I knew that I was a part of the exalted . . . divine upper world, and that I was endowed with an active life
acquiring identity with the divine	I rose in my essence . . . to the divine world and I was as it were placed there
stationing within it by having attained that activity, poised above whatsoever within the intellectual is less than the Supreme	and attached (*muta*ʾ*alliq*) to it. I was above the whole intelligible world. . .

146. Cf. Altmann-Stern, *Isaac Israeli*, pp. 149–150.

As I have shown elsewhere,[147] the passage from the *Theology* is quoted by al-Fārābī, Moses ibn Ezra (most probably from the *Epistles of the Ikhwān*), Shemtob ibn Falaqēra, and is reparaphrased by Solomon ibn Gabirol. The latter's chapter on ecstasy in his *Fons Vitae* (ed. Bäumker, III, 56–57)[148] is obviously based on the passage of the *Theology*, as already suggested by Jacob Guttmann.[149] To this list we should add Aaron ben Joseph's *Sēfer ha-Mibḥar* and al-Batalyawsi's "Imaginary Circles";[150] also Moses de Leon's *Mishkan ha-ᶜEdūth* (MS. Berlin, fol. 32a), where it is ascribed to the "true Teacher" (*mōreh ṣedeq*): "Regarding suchlike matters the true Teacher said, 'When I was alone with my soul and divested myself of my body and put it off and was like a soul without a body and contemplated the supernal world, I enjoyed a spiritual bliss like the bliss of the world-to-come such as mouths are unable to describe, and the image of which hearts are unable to contain. Hence a man must prepare himself with all his being before his God as if he were an altar of atonement prepared before Him.'"[151] A faint trace of the *Theology* passage is also found in ᶜObadyah's (grandson of Moses Maimonides) *Treatise of the Bowl*: "When thou remainest alone with thy soul after mastering thy moral qualities, a gate will open before thee through which thou wilt contemplate wonders. Indeed, with the suppression of thy five outward

147. Altmann-Stern, *Isaac Israeli*, pp. 191–192.

148. Also extant in the *Arabic Fragments*, ed. Pines, fragm. 2, pp. 221–222; Falaqēra's *Liqqūṭīm*, ed. Munk, III, 37.

149. *Die Philosophie des Salomon ibn Gabirol*, p. 165, n. 2.

150. See the reference in Guttmann, cited in Note 149.

151. G. Scholem was the first to notice Moses de Leon's use of the *Theology* passage in the *Mishkan ha-ᶜEdūt*. See *Major Trends in Jewish Mysticism*, p. 203 and p. 398, n. 155. The text of Moses de Leon's paraphrase does not, however, bear out Scholem's description of it as quoting Plotinus' account of the philosopher's "ecstatic ascent into the world of pure intelligence *and his vision of the One*" (p. 203). It is clear from the text that for Moses de Leon the highest stage is the contemplation of the supernal world, not the vision of the One. He says of this contemplation (*wa-etbōnēn ba-ᶜolam ha-ᶜelyōn*) that its bliss (*taᶜanūg rūḥanī*) is "like" (*dugmat*) the bliss of the world-to-come: i.e., like enjoying the splendor of the Shekhinah—if we interpret the phrase *taᶜanūg ᶜolam ha-bāᵓ* as a reference to the well-known passage in BT *Bĕrakhōt* 17a—but he does not indicate any ascent beyond the contemplation of the supernal world, i.e. beyond the spiritual substances. This interpretation is corroborated by another passage (fol. 2b) of the same work describing the highest stage (scil. that of prophecy) again as the vision, not of the One, but of the supernal Form: "For when the prophet enters into union, at the stage of his wisdom, so as to be attached (*lĕ-hiddabēq*) in his form to the supernal Form, he divests himself of all corporeal things and of all elements of this world." A parallel to the description of the vision of the supernal world of pure intellect occurs also in Moses de Leon's *Or zarūᶜa* (MS. Pococke 296.11, fol. 196a), where it becomes clear that the supernal Form is conceived in terms of the Spiritual Matter known from the Pseudo-Empedoclean Fragments (on which see Altmann-Stern, *Isaac Israeli*, pp. 159–164). For he speaks there of the *maᶜalat zohar ha-yesōd*, the vision of which "tongues cannot describe."

senses thy inner senses will awaken, and thou wilt be shown a dazzling light with the light of the Intellect."[152] The account given of the ecstatic experience is more in the Sūfī tradition but the Neoplatonic background is sufficiently attested by the opening phrase and the reference to the light of the Intellect. "When thou remainest alone with thy soul" is obviously a literal borrowing from the *Theology* ("I was as it were alone with my soul").

The theme of "looking upward" to the Intellect is predominant in the Hebrew Pseudo-Empedocles Fragments published by D. Kaufmann.[153] According to the ontological scheme of this text the hypostasis of (intelligible) Matter is interposed between God and the Intellect.[154] Hence Intellect loses its prerogative of being the ultimate goal of the soul's self-knowledge, short of her union with the One. But otherwise the mode of interpretation which we traced in Plotinus is fully preserved. "Likewise, the soul looks to Intellect beyond herself, and is lit up by looking to Intellect, and is raised and becomes truly soul and one with Intellect. When she looks to the things below which are caused by her, she becomes diffused and darkened. But in looking at herself, she looks at the part of herself which is Intellect in the same way in which Intellect looks at the part in itself which comes from (intelligible) Matter. She continues looking at Intellect until lit up by its light."[155] The equation of self-knowledge and purification which we met in Proclus is also much in evidence in the Pseudo-Empedocles Fragments. "It is *necessary* for us *to investigate* the soul which is within us [that is, to obey the precept, "Know thyself"] and to speculate as to her nature. Such investigation should not relate to the soul as existing in this body of ours, a soul full of passions and held in the grip of animal pleasures of an evil nature so that it is dominated by anger, injustice, violence, and similar vices. But we are *obliged* [that is, to obey the Delphic precept] to investigate the soul which has abandoned all this and which is cleansed of all filth. In her we shall know what she really is. . . For the soul which has abandoned those evils and is clean while still in the body is, as it were, no longer in it nor tied to it. Once we know what this soul is, what her essence and her attributes are, we shall not be mistaken in our statements nor in whatever we ascribe to her. . . When the soul receives the divine and exalted virtues . . . it becomes apparent without doubt that the

152. Cf. G. Vajda, "The Mystical Doctrine of Rabbi ᶜObadyah, Grandson of Moses Maimonides," *The Journal of Jewish Studies* 6:218 (1955).

153. In his *Studien über Salomon Ibn Gabirol* (Budapest, 1899), pp. 17–51.

154. Cf. Altmann-Stern, *Isaac Israeli*, pp. 162–164.

155. Cf. Kaufmann, *Studien*, p. 21.

soul is an exalted substance of the genus of the Upper World: spiritual, divine and simple . . . when she becomes one in us and we one in her, she puts us on the level of that exalted world."[156]

The influence of the Pseudo-Empedocles Fragments on Solomon ibn Gabirol cannot be gainsaid.[157] We propose to offer a detailed analysis of this influence elsewhere. It appears that amongst the Arab philosophers in Spain Ibn Bājja too succumbed to the spiritual temper of the Pseudo-Empedoclean tradition. His Neoplatonic leanings are pronounced, and his description of the ultimate stage of man's union with the Agent Intellect is wholly Neoplatonic. At that stage, he says, the unity of knower and known is complete and man truly knows himself.[158] It is highly significant that he explicitly links the theme of self-knowledge with that of union. From Proclus he borrows the notion of the intellect's "returning to itself," which was mediated to him by an Arabic version of some of Proclus' Propositions attributed to Alexander of Aphrodisias.[159] In following the trend of the Neoplatonic emphasis on purification, he makes the attainment of self-knowledge and union dependent upon a conversion from the world of the senses to the pure intelligibles. When saying that at the ultimate stage man is "simple, divine"[160] he literally quotes the Pseudo-Empedocles passage cited above. It may be noted in passing that Ibn Rushd's summary of Ibn Bājja's *Treatise on the Union of Intellect with Man* in his *Epitome* of Aristotle's *De anima* finds occasion to quote the two-stage formula in the form, "Know thyself, know thy Creator."[161]

156. *Ibid.*, p. 36.

157. The problems clustering around Falaqēra's allegation (in the Preface to his *Liqqūṭīm*) that Ibn Gabirol followed (Pseudo-) Empedocles' *Book of the Five Substances* have been briefly touched upon in my article, "Problems in Jewish-Neoplatonic Research," in *Tarbiṣ* 27:505 (July 1958).

158. Cf. *Risālat al-wadāʿ* (see Note 140), # 30, p. 39 [85].

159. See my article, "Ibn Bājja on Man's Ultimate Felicity" in *H. A. Wolfson Jubilee Volumes*, which are about to appear.

160. Cf. *Tadbīr al-mutawaḥḥid*, ed. M. Asín Palacios (*El Régimen del Solitario por Avempace*, Madrid-Granada, 1946), p. 61 [100–101].

161. Cf. *Talkhīs Kitāb al-Nafs*, ed. Ahwānī, p. 93. He makes the point that metaphysics deals with intelligibles which exist by themselves—i.e. are simple substances. (On this interpretation of the nature of metaphysics, see S. Pines, "Studies in Abul-Barakāt al-Baghdādī's Poetics and Metaphysics" in *Studies in Philosophy*, Scripta Hierosolymitana, VI (Jerusalem, 1960), 156, and n. 115.) Yet metaphysics deals with these abstract intelligibles only in relation to the material intelligibles. The "science of the soul," however, need not begin in the way metaphysics begins. Hence, it has been said: "Know thyself, and thou wilt know thy Creator." In his *Epitome* of the *Metaphysics* Ibn Rushd goes beyond this in suggesting that metaphysics presupposes what has been demonstrated in psychology. In other words, it starts out from psychology. Hence: "Know thyself, and thou wilt know thy Creator." Cf. van den Bergh, *Die Epitome* . . ., pp. 117, 250–251. For the notion that psychology is the beginning of the sciences, see Plotinus, *Enn.*, IV, 3, 1, and Alexander of Aphrodisias, *De anima*, ed. Bruns, p. 1.

In Baḥya ibn Paqūdah's *Hidāya* the Neoplatonic pattern of the treatment of self-knowledge is preserved but given a meditative and moralistic turn by the motif of the "scrutiny" (*muḥāsaba*) of the soul which is said to result in "all virtues" and in the "excellence, i.e. purity (*ṣafāʾ*)" of the substance of the soul from the "darkness" of ignorance.[162] This stage of the "scrutiny" of the soul corresponds to Proclus' stage (1) of self-knowledge, and as in Proclus it is identified with that of purification. This is followed up, again as in Proclus, by stage (2) of illumination: "For when you have done this . . . your intellect will be lit up . . . and you will be of the rank of the best friends of God, and there will arise within you a strange exalted power . . . then you will discern the glorious things and see the subtle mysteries by the purity of your soul and the cleanness of your heart."[163] To Proclus' stage (3) of union there corresponds in Baḥya the vision of the spiritual substances: "And the supernal and exalted Forms which you have no way of seeing with your eyes is the Wisdom of the Creator and His Power and the totality of the supernal world."[164]

Baḥya's dialogue between the soul and Intellect, described as the "admonition" (*tanbīh*) of Intellect and as an "inspiration" (*ilhām*) which comes from God to man through the intermediacy of Intellect, is also cast in the Neoplatonic mold and akin to the Delphic maxim. I. Heinemann suggested that the dialogue form and other features of this passage indicate Baḥya's dependence on a Hermetic source. This has been disputed by D. Z. Baneth[165] and G. Vajda.[166] The form of dialogue, Vajda has shown, is not unknown in the ascetic literature of Islam, and the term *tanbīh* is no proof for direct Hermetic influence, as it is a current term in totally un-Gnostic writings. We are not concerned here with the literary *Vorlage* of Baḥya's dialogue but may point out in this connection that the dialogue between soul and Intellect has a close parallel in the medieval "Streitgedicht" and in the Hebrew literary genre of *tōkhēḥah*.[167] The discussion between body, soul, and intellect in Jehudah al-Ḥarīzī's *Taḥkemōnī*[168] is a case in point. What interests us in particular is the description of the soul

162. *Hidāya*, III, 4, p. 349.
163. *Ibid.*, p. 350.
164. *Ibid.*, p. 351.
165. Cf. D. Z. Baneth, *Kiryat Sēfer*, 3:136.
166. G. Vajda, *REJ* 102:98–103 (1937); *idem*, *La Théologie Ascétique* . . ., pp. 57ff.
167. Cf. B. Sutorius, *Le Débat provençal de l'âme et du corps* (Freiburg, 1816); H. Walther, *Das Streitgedicht in der lateinischen Literatur des Mittelalters* (Munich, 1914) (quoted by José M. Millás Vallicrosa, *Šĕlomo Ibn Gabirol como Poeta y Filósofo*, Madrid-Barcelona, 1945, p. 101).
168. Ed. Paul de Lagarde (Hannover, 1924), pp. 67–71.

and her relationship to intellect offered in his text. The soul depicts herself as having once upon a time been "dwelling on high and occupying the first rank in the Kingdom," "like a dove nesting in the bosom of God" (4, 1–2); she had "descended from the ranks of the higher beings and become separated from the Divine world" (4, 3); she is now "held in bondage" by the body, "bitten by the serpent of the [evil] inclination," and "alone, desolate," "caught in their prison" (7, 3–4). Having been "in the palace of God like a burning candle," her light is now "dimmed in the darkness of the body" (7, 31). Intellect reminds the soul of her origin, and does so with certain Gnostic overtones: "Wake up, O soul, who art pure, hewn from the glory of God, and held captive in the prison of the body" (6, 4). It exalts the soul to purify herself (6, 6; 11) and to provide herself with food for her "long journey" (6, 14). Let her not be asleep while *intellect* is drowned in the sea of the passions (6, 15–16).

Intellect is here not the universal *Nous* of Neoplatonism but man's individual reason, "thy intellect" (6, 16). Intellect itself is "drowned in the sea of passions" owing to the forgetfulness of the soul. It depends on the soul's return to God for its own salvation (6, 28). Intellect is thus not entirely separate from the soul but involved in its spiritual fate. There is, nevertheless, an echo of the Neoplatonic *Nous* in this dialogue. The soul is admonished by Intellect. Hence the two are not identical, and it is only by rising to the level of intellect that the soul achieves her true essence.

In Ibn Gabirol's and Jehudah Hallevi's poetry we possess many examples of the Hebrew genre of *Zurechtweisungsgedicht* or admonitory poem (*tōkhēḥah*). The poet—not the Intellect—addresses his soul, but the Neoplatonic flavor is still discernible. In Ibn Gabirol, in particular, I. Heinemann was able to lay bare the Neoplatonic orientation toward the world of Intellect.[169] The soul is compared to a "king in captivity"[170] and the poet praises wisdom and exhorts her to seek wisdom and its Lord.[171] Gnostic motifs such as the image of the "pearl" for the soul reinforce the Neoplatonic trend.[172] A good example of this kind of poetry is the *tōkhēḥah* "Forget thy sorrow" (*shikhĕḥī yegōnēkh*), which Karl Dreyer has analyzed.[173] Jehudah Hallevi's poem, "If thy soul be precious in thine eyes, know thou her essence and seek her Creator," has already

169. Cf. his *Die Lehre von der Zweckbestimmung des Menschen* . . . (Breslau, 1926), p. 56.
170. Cf. Dukes, *Shirē Shĕlōmo*, I, 4.
171. *Ibid.*, poems nos. 7, 8, 9, 10, 12.
172. *Ibid.*, pp. 16, 35.
173. Cf. Karl Dreyer, *Die religiöse Gedankenwelt des Salomo ibn Gabirol* (Leipzig, 1930), p. 120. For the literature on this poem, see Dreyer, p. 120, n. 99.

been mentioned above (Page 199). The allegorical interpretation of Canticles as a dialogue between the soul and Intellect belongs essentially to the same category of *tōkhēḥah.* As A. S. Halkin has shown, Maimonides was the first to introduce this type of allegorization.[174] It is followed by Moses ibn Tibbon, Joseph ibn Kaspi, Gersonides, and Joseph ben Jehudah ibn ᶜAknin. The "lover" is the Agent Intellect and the rational soul is the "beloved."

We conclude this analytical survey with an account of the *homo imago Dei* motif as it appears at the very end of medieval Jewish history in Spain in Shemtob ben Joseph Shemtob's philosophical *Homilies* (*Dĕrashōt Ha-Torah*, Salonica, 1525, fol. 2a–b), where all the three variations of the theme we have traced—namely, the Platonic one of the soul's likeness to God, the microcosm idea, and the Neoplatonic notion of the upward way—occur together. Discoursing on Genesis 1:26, the author first points out that it is in the nature of all beings to produce their like (*she-yaᶜasu dĕmūtam*). Thus the elements assimilate whatever comes into contact with them to their own essence, fire making things fiery, water making them watery, and so on. If this be true of the lower ranks of existence, it applies a fortiori to the supernal world. Hence God, who is the archetypal pattern (*dĕmūt u-dĕfūs*) of all existing things, willed that there be in this world an image of the Divine Form: moreover, that there be found in it an image of the macrocosm (*ha-ᶜōlam bi-kĕlalō*): that is, man, who is a microcosm (*ᶜōlam qatan*). Obviously, two different motifs are placed here alongside each other. The idea that God willed to create his own image is formulated in the bold sentence that "God formed his own self (*et ᶜaṣmō*) in this matter," it being "in the Divine nature" which knows no envy to be desirous to create its like, seeing that even lower beings show the same propensity. In truly Platonic fashion the self or essence (*ᶜaṣmūt*) of man is identified with his soul, compared with which the body is but a "stranger and alien" (*zar we-nokhrī*). No motivation is offered for God's further desire to make man an image of the macrocosm. The author quotes Job 19:26 but discards the traditional interpretation according to which the contemplation of man as a microcosm leads to the knowledge of God. Instead he explains this verse as meaning that by knowing his true self—that is, his own high rank—man will pursue the intellectual virtues, "for it befits him who resembles a divine being [*lĕ-bar elōhīn*] to conduct himself in action and speech in perfect order so as to preserve his form."

174. A. S. Halkin, "Ibn ᶜAknīn's Commentary on the Song of Songs," in *Alexander Marx Jubilee Volume* (New York, 1950), pp. 396ff.

But "it is impossible for man to know the macrocosm by knowing himself, for he is neither in heaven nor beyond the seas to be able to comprehend the 'measure' of the Creator and thereby gain the bliss of the world-to-come," a reference to the statement of the Tannaitic *Shiʿūr Qōmah* Gnostics that "Whoever knows the measurements of our Creator and the Glory of the Holy One, praise be to Him, which are hidden from the creatures, is certain of his share in the world-to-come."[175] The contemplation of the microcosm is therefore abandoned as a way to the knowledge of God, except in the sense that on the analogy of soul and God as the hidden, incorporeal, guiding forces in the human body and in the cosmos respectively man becomes aware of God. Shemtob quotes the account of this analogy as offered by Maimonides (*Guide*, I, 71).

The Neoplatonic theme of ascent and union is developed by stressing man's endowment with intellect: "Since in his intellectual form man resembles the Holy One, blessed be He, and the separate intelligencies, the prophets called the Holy One, blessed be He, by the name of 'man,' as is said, 'And upon the likeness of the throne was a likeness as the appearance of a man upon it above' (Ezekiel 1:26), and as they said in *Genesis Rabba* (24:1), 'How great is the power of the prophets who liken the form to its Former.'" By actualizing his material or potential intellect man is able to rise to the angelic stage and achieve union with the separate (agent) intellect during his lifetime, a possibility which, we may note, had been advocated already by the author's father, Joseph ben Shemtob, in his *Commentary* on Averroes' *Epistle on the Possibility of Conjunction.* The angelic stage is also described as one of self-knowledge, which reflects the Neoplatonic notion of intellection as a return of the intellect upon itself as found in Proclus and Ibn Bājja (see above, Page 228). It cannot be said that Shemtob succeeded in making the three motifs completely consonant with one another, but his attempt highlights the significance which they had attained in the course of the development which we have traced.

175. Cf. Gershom G. Scholem, *Jewish Gnosticism, Merkabah Mysticism, and Talmudic Tradition* (New York, 1960), p. 40.

The Medieval Jewish Attitude Toward Hebrew

By A. S. HALKIN

During the Middle Ages Jews, as is well known, used as their vernacular the language of the territory they lived in.[1] This holds as true of the people living under Islam as of those in the domains of Christendom. However, among the many differences obtaining between the former and the latter,[2] the divergence in their attitude to Hebrew is far from being the least significant.

Owing to the dissimilarity in the relation to their environment of the Jews in the Christian and Islamic worlds, the primary question of the utilization of Hebrew in writing received distinct answers. In Christian lands, where it took a long time for the spoken languages to gain the status of literary media,[3] and where Latin was the language employed, the Jews could have recourse only to Hebrew, their own sacred language,[4] and consequently the literary output of the Jews under Christendom was uniformly in Hebrew.[5] In many instances their writings lack grace of

1. Occasionally, in conversation with a Jew from another land, or for purposes of secrecy, Hebrew was employed. See *Sefer Hasidim* (ed. Wistinetsky [Berlin, 1891–93]), pars. 739, 902, 1368, 1923. It is doubtful that in the Middle Ages or early modern times a group existed which spoke Hebrew normally, as is suggested by Eldad ha-Dani (ed. A. Epstein [Pressburg, 1891], I, 38) or by David ha-Reubeni. Abraham Abulafia notes the curious phenomenon of the survival of Arabic among Sicilian Jews, in addition to Greek and Italian (see *REJ* 9:149 [1884]).

2. See H. J. Zimmels, *Ashkenazim and Sephardim* (London, 1958), pp. 82–267.

3. Note the paucity of production in the vernacular in the Middle Ages compared with the large output in Latin.

4. Bernhard Blumenkranz, *Juifs et Chrétiens dans le monde occidental* (Paris, 1960), p. 5, maintains that "cultured Jews, particularly scholars and merchants," knew Latin. While the contention is plausible, it can hardly be extended to imply a knowledge adequate for literary composition, or its spread to the scholars interested in Jewish lore.

5. Works in Yiddish and other spoken idioms were generally justified as a service to uncultured men and to women. See I. Zinberg, *Toledot Sifrut Yisra'el* (Tel Aviv, 1958), IV, chap. i, *passim*; Ṣidkiyahu ben Abraham, *Shiboley ha-Leḳeṭ*, ed. S. Buber (New York, 1959), p. 78: ומצות הקורין בתורה להעמיד תורגמין לתרגם מה שקורין כדי להשמיע לנשים ולעמי הארץ. Jonah Gerondi, *Sefer ha-Yir'ah* (ed. Weiner, Dubnow, 1804), p. 99: ואם אין לו תרגום (כשהוא משלים פרשיותיו) יקרא שנים מקרא ואחד לעג וטוב יותר מלומר ג״פ המקרא, כי התרגום היה להבין המקרא למי שאינו בקי כ״ש לעז פירוש שהוא לשון הלעזות. In a letter published by S. Assaf, *Meḳorot*

style or even the rudiments of grammar;[6] yet their uninterrupted employment of the language contributed greatly to the growth of medieval Hebrew, which left a legacy to modern times. It was not so in Muslim lands. The closeness of literary Arabic to the spoken vernacular, naturally serving the Jews as well, and the prolific output of writing in that tongue induced the Jews to imitate their hosts. They did not abandon this practice in Spain until after the reconquest, and in the Arabic-speaking world until much later. Even authors who, as we shall presently see, spoke with grief and chagrin of the neglect of their own tongue, did not as a rule hesitate to resort to Arabic in their literary productions. The bulk of prose literature, including halakhic and religious works, were in that tongue from the second half of the ninth century.

It is significant that, unlike prose, poetry was generally composed in Hebrew. Undoubtedly the tradition established by liturgy, beginning with the Palestinian initiators who never entertained the thought of introducing a foreign language into the divine services,[7] played its part in deciding later poets to continue in Hebrew even for their secular compositions. But to my mind there is another, more immediate reason for the choice.[8] Poetry among the Arabs served the purpose of displaying the beauties of their language, and they strove to emulate one another in elegance of style and extravagance of metaphor. The finest example of style was believed by them—as a principle of faith rather than as a conviction, one feels certain—to exist in the Ḳurʾān. At this the Jews balked. Their pride in their own language and in their own Bible not only restrained them from displaying the beauties of Arabic and its masterwork, but also impelled them to do for Hebrew as their neighbors did for their tongue.

---

u-meḥḳarim (Jerusalem, 1946), pp. 250–251, a rabbi urges a friend to desist from composing a halakhic work in Yiddish for women, since it is likely to lead to error; they had better ask a rabbi. But he grants that many ignorant people (even *shoḥetim*) cannot benefit from Hebrew books.

6. Writers in lands with a tradition of correct Hebrew are critical or condescending in their evaluation of the literary and linguistic skills of the Franco-German Jews. See the chiding couplet of Abraham ibn Ezra in acknowledging verses by R. Jacob Tam: ומי הביא לצרפתי בבית שיר ועבר זר מקום קדש ורמס (David Kahana, *Abraham ibn Ezra* [Warsaw, 1894], p. 80); Abravanel's praise of Saul ha-Cohen (Zimmels, *Ashkenazim and Sephardim*, p. 273); and the comment of Joshua Soncino: וכל האשכנזים בטבעם הם עלגי שפה כבדי פה וכבדי לשון ואין כח בהם לבטא בשפתים ולא לכתוב בקולמוס העומק השוכן תוך לבם ולא יבינם אלא מי ששמע אותם וקבע בישיבותיהם עידן ועידנין (David Conforte, *Koreʾ ha-Dorot*, ed. D. Cassel, Berlin, 1846, p. 29a).

7. L. Zunz, *Synagogale Poesie des Mittelalters*, 2nd ed. (Frankfurt am Main, 1920), p. 8; *idem*, *Literaturgeschichte der Synagogalen Poesie* (Berlin, 1865), chap. ii.

8. The explanation offered by Jacob Simchoni (*Ha-Tekufah* 10:146 [1921]) that the poets were impelled by an awareness that only what was written in Hebrew would survive, and their desire of immortality, in addition to their fondness of the language, made them choose Hebrew, does not sound convincing.

This sentiment is voiced in the clearest terms in Judah al-Ḥarīzī's introduction to his *Taḥkemoni.*[9] He writes: "When I saw the work of al-Ḥarīrī[10] the heavens of my joy were rolled together and the rivulets of my mourning flowed, because every nation is concerned for its speech and avoids sinning against its tongue, whereas our tongue which was a delight to every eye is considered a brother of Cain. . .[11] Therefore I compiled this book in order to display the force of the sacred tongue to the holy people." He further informs us that he translated al-Ḥarīrī's work into Hebrew, but then realized that he had acted foolishly and sinfully by forsaking our book of eloquence and undertaking to translate a book belonging to others; hence he turned to the task of creating a similar composition in Hebrew.

Al-Ḥarīzī is deeply chagrined over the treatment of the sacred tongue at the hands of the Jews. He weeps over its neglect in favor of Arabic, and is saddened by the contemplation of its present low state compared with its ancient glories and high station. However, the twelfth-century author is in no wise the first to feel pained by this fact. One after the other we find Arabic-speaking and Arabic-writing men taking sorry note of the sad state of Hebrew. Some of them confess to a sense of guilt, taking upon themselves and their ancestors the blame for this failure. Saadia Gaon recounts the history of the development in these words: "In the year 101[12] after the ruin of the holy city, three years before the Greeks had their first king, we began to forsake the holy tongue and to converse in the languages of the alien peoples of the land. When Nehemiah saw us speaking Ashdodite he was grieved;[13] he scolded and quarreled with the people. We were subsequently scattered through the world, no nation existing which our exiles did not enter. There again we raised our children, studied their languages, so that their gibberish obscured the beauty of our speech. This is not proper. The eastern diaspora speaks Greek and Persian; Egypt expresses itself in Coptic, and the inhabitants of Christian and

9. Ed. P. de Lagarde (Hannover, 1924), 6. 35–37; 7.1.

10. C. Brockelmann, *Geschichte der arabischen Litteratur*, 2nd ed. (Leiden, 1943–49), I, 276–277; Supplement, I, 486–487.

11. = הבל, vanity.

12. He follows *Seder ʿOlam Rabbah*, chaps. 29 and 30 (ed. B. Ratner, Wilno, 1894–97, pp. 134ff.), according to which the Second Temple was started seventy years after the destruction of the First, and Persian rule lasted thirty-four years after that date, which yields a total of 104 years. It assumes that Darius and Artaxerxes are one individual who ruled thirty-six years. Since the Temple was built in his second year (Ezra 4:24), and Nehemiah rebuked the people of Judah on his second visit, which was after the thirty-second year of the Persian king (Neh. 13:6), Saadia's date is confirmed.

13. Neh. 13:23–27.

Andalusian countries use foreign tongues. Our heart bleeds and our spirit is low that the speech found in our sacred bastion is wanting in our mouths."[14]

Similarly the poet Solomon ibn Gabirol (1020–58) upbraids his contemporaries for employing different tongues and denying any acquaintance with Hebrew.[15] He even reports that his readers react to his Hebrew poetry with the demand that he address them in the vernacular, since they consider his medium a kind of Philistine.[16] Moses ibn Ezra (*ca.* 1055–1140) goes so far as to say: "Our ancients deserve a scolding for having been remiss in preserving their Hebrew and making no strenuous effort to hold on to it."[17] Three centuries later, the grammarian Profiat Duran (second half of the fifteenth century) shows a like inclination to accuse the Sages. "Those who exerted themselves in the study of Talmud," he says, "left the chosen language and employed Aramaic for their statements, which is only deteriorated Hebrew. Perhaps they did not do this by choice."[18] He further makes the rather startling declaration that "much damage and loss have resulted from the sloth and indolence in relation to the preservation of Hebrew, which is in the final analysis the result of the neglect of concentrated study of Scripture. I declare that this caused the destruction of Israel by the sword, and their dispersion, submission and humiliation, as well as the growth of new religions, because their ignorance of the language of Scripture led them to slander the Torah with the consequences which you know very well."[19]

In a less emotional if equally pathetic strain, Judah ha-Levi,[20] followed by the above-mentioned Duran who uses his language, links the relinquishment of Hebrew speech and its present lowliness to the sorry

14. He levels the same charge in his *Commentary* on the Pentateuch (M. Zucker, in *Sura*ʾ, ed. S. K. Mirsky [Jerusalem, 1955–56], II, 339). Contemporaries of his, Rabbanite as well as Ḳaraite, share his view. Samuel ben Ḥofni elaborates on the verse in Nehemiah that "this is the story of most of the people of our time, that they have abandoned their language, are ignorant of it, and occupy themselves with the books and the grammar of the Gentiles" (*PAAJR* 23:3–4 [1954]). The Ḳaraite Salomon ben Yeruḥim in his comment on Lam. 1:8 (ed. Feuerstein, p. lxx) includes among the many sins of the Jews our "efforts to learn their language [i.e., of the Gentiles] grammatically, and spending money to achieve it, and abandoning the knowledge of the sacred tongue . . ."

15. In his poem "Etten lĕ-ʾēlī" (ed. H. N. Bialik and J. H. Rawnitzky [Tel-Aviv, 1924–25], I, 173–180), lines 11–16.

16. In his poem "Niḥar be-korʾī geronī," (Bialik and Rawnitzky, I, 4–6), lines 26–27.

17. *Shirat Yisraʾel* (ed. Halper, Leipzig, 1924), p. 59.

18. *Maʿaseh Efod* (Vienna, 1865), chap. vii (pp. 39–40). He concludes the explanation with: אבל מה אתן התנצלות לראשונים.

19. *Maʿaseh Efod*, pp. 40–41.

20. *Kuzari*, II, 68 (ed. Cassel, Leipzig, 1869, p. 173); cf. *Maʿaseh Efod*, p. 39.

state of the Jewish people. "What happened to its bearers happened to it; it became impoverished." This is also the position of Judah ibn Tibbon, who records it without any show of personal participation.[21]

However, the subject of the elimination of Hebrew as a medium of speech is really separate from the problem of its disregard as a literary vehicle. Jews in Christian lands were evidently not troubled by the question why they were not speaking Hebrew. They encountered all around them a similar situation in which the vernacular of the country and the language employed in writing were different. And so they naturally turned to their own sacred tongue in their literary productions. But in Islamic lands, where, as indicated above, Arabic became the widely employed language in writing, the condition provoked a good deal of soul-searching and self-reproach, and impelled writers to take a position on it.

The most realistic evaluation—it might almost be called callous—is to be found in the analysis of the circumstances by the celebrated translator Judah ibn Tibbon (1120–*ca.* 1190). In the introductions to his versions of both Baḥya ibn Pakudah's *Duties of the Heart* and Ibn Janāḥ's grammar, *Sefer ha-Riḳmah*, especially in the former, he writes at length on the issue of Arabic and Hebrew. He traces the history of Jewish writing in Arabic back to "the majority of the Geonim in Islamic lands who spoke Arabic as did the Jews of the time, so that their explanations, responses and independent works were therefore in Arabic."[22] He also finds no difficulty in explaining and justifying their action. "They did it," he writes, "because it is the language people understood, and also because it is an adequate and rich language for every subject and for every need, for every speaker and every author; its expression is direct, lucid, and capable of saying just what is wanted much better than can be done in Hebrew, of which we possess only what has been preserved in Scripture and [which] is insufficient for the needs of a speaker. It is simply impossible to express the thoughts of our hearts succinctly and eloquently in Hebrew as we can in Arabic, which is adequate, elegant and available to those who know it."[23] We feel, as we read these words, that he regarded the conversion into Hebrew of the works which he translated an arduous task which he

21. See his preface to the Hebrew translation of Baḥya's *Duties of the Heart* (ed. Ẓifroni [Jerusalem, 1928]), p. 2. However, see his opening remarks in the introduction to his translation of Ibn Janāḥ's *Sefer ha-Riḳmah* (ed. Wilensky, 2 vols. [Berlin, 1928–30] p. 2).

22. *Duties of the Heart*, p. 2; *Sefer ha-Riḳmah*, pp. 4–6. His son Samuel was similarly obsessed with the inadequacies of Hebrew; cf. the prefatory remarks to his glossary of "foreign words" in his translation of Maimonides' *Guide*.

23. *Duties of the Heart*, p. 2; *Sefer ha-Riḳmah*, pp. 4–6.

undertook only as a public service. "The exiles in France and in the other Christian lands," he writes, "do not know Arabic, and works in that language are like closed books to them." Himself a refugee in Provence from the persecutions of the Almohades,[24] he was yet incapable of grasping the large problem of writing in an alien tongue in its full depth and implication. It is a need which must be filled, this task of translation,[25] but one might almost hear him say between the lines that it would be much simpler if everybody knew Arabic. Perhaps a partial explanation of this stand can be found in his awareness of the very rich diversity of subject matter cultivated by the Spanish-Jewish community, compared with the limited world of the Franco-German Jews, and the irrepressible first feeling that Hebrew cannot possibly prove equal to the challenge which the new situation presented.

Maimonides, whom one would hardly classify as a romantic, is much more personal in his relation to the subject of language. He utilizes several occasions to give expression to his sentiments. In his response to the people of Tyre[26] on the enumeration of the precepts, he refers to his own *Sefer ha-Mizwot*, and declares that he regrets having written it in Arabic because everybody has to read it,[27] and he is now hoping to translate it into the holy tongue.[28] And when Joseph ibn Jabbār asks him about the likelihood of getting the *Mishneh Torah* in Arabic, he responds that he will under no circumstances consent to this eventuality "because all of its loveliness will be lost. I am looking for an opportunity to restore my commentary on the Mishna and my *Sefer ha-Mizwot* to the holy tongue, and I shall certainly not render this work in Arabic. Do not ever ask this of me again."[29] He becomes truly lyrical in a confession he makes to the Lunel community in a letter in which he informs them that he sent them the third part of the *Guide* in Arabic.[30] He feels compelled to decline their request that he himself translate it into Hebrew, and adds: "Would I were again young enough to do what you ask for this book and the other

24. A Berber religious body which seized Spain in 1146. On their persecution see Ibn Aḳnin's *Ṭibb al-Nufūs*, chap. vii (ed. Halkin, *Conference on Jewish Relations: The Joshua Starr Memorial Volume* [New York, 1953], pp. 101–110).

25. *Duties of the Heart*, p. 4: כי לא מלבי ולא ברצוני נכנסתי בענין זה וכי לא נסתר מנגד עיני כל אשר זכרתי.

26. Maimonides' *Responsa* (ed. Freimann [Jerusalem, 1937]), 368 (pp. 334–335).

27. The passage וניחמתי הרבה על שחברתיו בלשון ערבי מפני שהכל צריכין לקרותו is somewhat ambiguous, but probably the explanation offers the reason why it is in Arabic.

28. *Responsa*, 335.

29. *Ḳobeẓ Teshubot Ha-Rambam Ve-Iggerotav* (Leipzig ed., 1859), II, 15d.

30. 44a–b.

books which I composed in the tongue of Kedar which has darkened my sun because I dwell in the tents of Ham. It would be a source of deep joy to me to salvage the precious from the cheap and to restore the theft to its rightful owners." It is not easy to determine whether such utterances were dictated by a sense of personal guilt or by an understanding of the large import of the whole complexity of Israel's checkered political and linguistic history. It may well be that his experiences as a victim of persecution and the knowledge of the precarious situation of the Jews in the world and particularly under Islam, which he analyzes most acutely in his *Iggeret Teman*, offer the key to an evaluation of his sentiments.

The difficulty of the limited vocabularly in Hebrew was noted by several scholars. Samuel ibn Tibbon, the translator of the *Moreh Nebukhim*, whom Maimonides praises for his fluency in Arabic, explains that he was compelled to use foreign words "because our language is limited, and works on demonstrated sciences do not exist among our people, so that those foreign words are not found in our language which those who possess the particular sciences employ."[31] His father Judah also apologizes for his recourse to foreignisms because of the special problems which Hebrew presents.[32]

The philosopher and grammarian Profiat Duran does not dispute the assertion regarding the inadequacy of Hebrew. But he goes into a lengthy argument to demonstrate that it is not an intrinsic failing in the language; it is rather the product of the neglect by its bearers. He points to the reported existence of a *Sefer Refūʾōt* which undoubtedly contained in Hebrew all the terms of which medicine avails itself, and to the work of constructing the Tabernacle and the Temple, which predicates a vocabulary ample enough to provide the needs of that activity, and so with others. He is deeply grieved by this serious loss, for which even the supplementary material in the Mishnaic orders of *Zeraᶜim* and of *Tohorot* compensate in only small measure.[33]

Such views, whether uttered with an air of equanimity or spoken in

31. Introduction to the glossary (see Note 22). Abraham ibn Ezra writes at the conclusion of his commentary on Canticles (*ad* 8:11 בפעם הראשונה): והעומד על זה החבור אולי יתמה למה אומר כאן בלשון ישמעאל בעבור קוצר דעתנו כי לא נדע מלשון הקדש כי אם הכתוב במקרא שהוצרכו הנביאים לדבר ומה שלא הוצרכו לא נדע שמו ובעבור היות לשון ישמעאל קרוב מאוד ללשון הקודש כי בנייניו ואותיות יהוא והמשרתים ונפעל והתפעל והסמיכות דרך אחת לשתיהן וכן בחשבון ויותר מחצי הלשון ימצא כמוהו בלשון הקדש על כן כל מלה שלא נמצא לה חבר במקרא ויש דומה בלשון ישמעאל נאמר אולי פירושה כן אע״פ שהדבר בספק.

32. *Duties of the Heart*, p. 4 bottom.

33. 41; Maimonides, *Guide*, I, 67, says: עם דעתנו שאנחנו היום בלתי יודעים לשוננו (Wilno ed., p. 99a), and in chap. 67 he adds: ואפשר שיורה כפי הלשון אשר אין אתנו היום ממנה אלא דבר מועט (92a); *Kuzari* II, 68 (ed. Cassel, p. 176): כאשר תחסר לנו היום בעבור שאבד ממנו.

grief, are not shared by Judah al-Ḥarīzī. He rejects the contention that Hebrew cannot meet the demands of his society, and he states bluntly that those who hold these views do not realize that the fault lies with them and not with the language, inasmuch as they do not understand its words and do not appreciate its qualities. "Like a sick person who suffers from an eye-infection and is unable to see the sun and believes the sun to be at fault, not realizing the defect in himself, so most of our fellow-Jews scorn the sacred tongue because its virtues are beyond them, and cannot see the the light even if they have eyes."[34] Nor can it be argued that al-Ḥarīzī speaks in this fashion only in connection with belles-lettres, in view of the fact that the preceding passage is taken from his introduction to the *Taḥkemoni*, in which he presses the thesis that Hebrew is very much able to serve as a vehicle for eloquence and elegance. We find him a much less timid translator than the Tibbonids. It is noteworthy that in the prefatory statement to his version of the *Guide* not a word is found reminiscent of the fears and the hesitation which are so prominent in Samuel ibn Tibbon's preface to his translation. And in the introduction to his rendering of the Sage's *Commentary to the Mishnah* he boasts triumphantly of his achievement.[35] "In response to a request by the leaders of the Jewish community of Marseilles," he writes, "I have rendered this great commentary from Arabic into Hebrew, transferring its lights from west to east. I have restored to our precious rich penetrating language the outer language of his extremely learned composition. I have transmitted it from the black tongue of Kedar to the tongue of gold and of riches. For I am filled with zeal for the commentaries which the Torah has engendered and they have precedence, yet they were born upon the knees of Hagar, maid of Sarah, and Sarah was barren. In amazement I said to myself: 'How can the holy and the profane be joined, and how can the light and darkness dwell together? But it was the aim of the Sage to offer wisdom to the fools, and he compiled it only for those who know not Hebrew but Arabic' . . . Therefore I exerted myself, and removed the sacred treatises from alien tongue, so that from its imprisonment it would go forth to reign." Not a word is said about the difficulties confronting him owing to the shortcomings of

34. *Maʿaseh Efod*, p. 6 bottom. In a similar vein, if not with the same sense of adequacy, Saadia emphasizes that in the Hebrew which has survived as many as seven synonyms may be available for one Arabic word (cf. A. Harkavy, "Liqquṭim me-Rav Saadya Gaon," *Ha-Goren* 1:89–91 [1898]). But he qualifies this with the admission: "This is what we encounter within the limits of the superficial knowledge of this language among the people of our age."

35. Wilno ed., 53a.

Hebrew, although he goes into some detail regarding his procedure and discusses hurdles which he had to make. The difference in attitude between him and his fellow translators may stem as much from his personal sense of self-confidence as from a zeal and determination to attain a goal, which minimized the magnitude of the obstacles. One cannot think of Maimonides' masterly Hebrew in his *Mishneh Torah* without reflecting that had he been stirred by a similar zeal he himself would have produced an incomparably more readable and more elegant Hebrew commentary on the Mishnah or *Moreh Nebukhim* than either of the two scholars who accomplished these tasks.

Turning from the practical application of the sacred tongue in literary works to views and doctrines regarding it, we find both unity and diversity among scholars. It was uniformly believed—at least among people in Islamic lands[36]—that Hebrew was the first tongue, and that it was only after the incident of the Tower of Babel that the multiplicity of languages developed.[37] This doctrine is established by both tradition and reason. Tradition has preserved the proof of the primacy of Hebrew in the etymologies and in the origin of things.[38] Reason also confirms the claim of Hebrew. As the language employed for revelation, for prophecy, and for divine services it must necessarily be superior and primary in eloquence and pedigree.[39] Other assertions, however, did not win everybody's approval. The relation between Hebrew and what we know as its cognate languages

36. In the Franco-German tradition this position is not maintained uniformly. Although Rashi, in his commentary on שפה אחת (Gen. 11:1) says: לשון הקדש, R. Joseph Bekhor Shor, *ibid.*, explains it to mean that every one knew all the seventy languages, and justifies this, along with חזקוני (*ad* Gen. 11:7) by arguing that it is difficult to grant that languages were formed in a special creation subsequent to the creation of the world.

37. *Kuzari*, II, 68 (ed. D. C. Cassel, p. 173); Yaᶜaḳob ben Asher (Baᶜal ha-Turim) *ad* Gen. 11:1 points out that numerically שפה אחת=לשון הקדש. The Ḳaraites also adhere to this view; see Aaron ben Joseph's *Sefer ha-Mibḥar* (the supercommentary *Ṭirat Kesef* gives the above-mentioned gematria); Aaron ben Elijah's *Keter Torah*, *ad* Gen. 11:1; J. Mann, *Texts and Studies in Jewish History and Literature*, 2 vols. (Cincinnati, 1931–35), II, 107.

38. *Cf. Kuzari*, II, 68 (ed. Cassel, pp. 173–174); David Kimḥi *ad* Gen. 2:20; Ibn Ezra on Gen. 11:1; see also his *Safah Berurah*, p. 1, n. 5, and also pp. 2–5; Naḥmanides (see next note); Joshua ibn Shuᶜaib, *Derashot*, 5b. Ibn Shuᶜaib, after explaining that at the Tower of Babel the seventy languages developed, continues: ונשאר לשון הקדש בישראל ובזרעם ואבדנו ממנו הרבה ונשאר ממנו קצת בפי האומות וזהו אמרם ז״ל. . . טט בכתפי שתים פת באפריקי שתים כי הוא לשון הקדש וכן בראש השנה שכן בערביא קורין לדכרא יובלא כי חלילה שנלמוד מצותינו הקדושות מלשונות הגוים ושנביא ראיה מלשונם הגרוע אבל הוא לשון הקדש נשאר בידם.

39. *Kuzari*, II, 68 (ed. Cassel, p. 176); Naḥmanides, in his comment on Exodus 30:3 takes issue with Maimonides who explains (*Guide*, III, chap. viii, end) that the name לשון הקדש is applied to Hebrew because of its avoidance of vulgar language. He accounts for it by pointing to its being the language of Torah, prophecy and all holy matters. It contains the divine names, particularly the Tetragrammaton, and is the language of creation.

was not universally recognized. In all likelihood many felt that it did not redound to the honor of the language of Torah to have parallels with languages like Aramaic and Arabic, much less to lose its uniqueness by being treated as one of a family. If we find that Judah ha-Levi does not hesitate to speak of Hebrew, Aramaic, and Arabic as related and similar languages,[40] and if Maimonides declares unqualifiedly that Arabic "is certainly Hebrew somewhat corrupted,"[41] and many other scholars take this position, we also know of men who did not care to admit this relationship. Menaḥem ben Sarūk (tenth century), the first European grammarian of Hebrew, abstained from drawing conclusions from similarities to other languages.[42] His disciples do not maintain any opposition in principle to the suggestion of parallels; they cite evidence from Arabic for the replacement of *tau* by *daleth* and *teth* under certain conditions, for example.[43] Nevertheless they are wary of too ready a disposition to point to the close relation among the three languages. In answer to the objection by Dunash ben Labrat, Menaḥem's contemporary and critic, that the latter could not relate ולמוח (Psalm 109:19) to יזח (Exodus 28:28), and that it has to be interpreted like Arabic *zḥḥ*, they assert that it is sheer nonsense; "it is incorrect to compare Hebrew to Arabic."[44] To Dunash's explanation of פגרו (I Samuel 30:10) as *they collapsed*, on the basis of Aramaic, in place of Menaḥem's *they remained*, they remonstrate by proclaiming: "What do Hebrew and Aramaic do together? If we said of every Hebrew *hapax legomenon* that it finds a parallel in Aramaic and Arabic, then the languages would be identical, and we could supply all the unknown and missing Hebrew vocabulary from them, but this cannot possibly be."[45]

Opposition to comparative linguistics was certainly raised by the devout Talmudic scholars and the mystically inclined pietists who were generally

40. *Kuzari*, II, 68 (Cassel, pp. 175–176). He is consistent enough to suggest that Abraham's mother-tongue was Aramaic, but solves the difficulty arising from this suggestion by adding that Abraham knew Hebrew as a sacred language.

41. In his letter to Samuel ben Tibbon, *Ḳobeẓ*, II, 27c: והוספתי תימה היאך יהיה טבע בן שנולד בין העלגים כך וירדוף אחרי החכמות ויהיה מהיר כל כך בלשון ערבי שהוא ודאי לשון עברית שנשתבשה מעט. In *Pirḳe Mosheh* (23a): ואמנם לשון עברי וערבי הנה נתאמת לכל מי שיודע ב׳ לשונות שהם לשון אחד בלתי ספק והארמי קרוב מהם קצת הקורבה.

42. The famous grammarian Judah Ḥayyūj, who wrote his original work on weak and geminative verbs in Arabic (ed. Jastrow), cites a parallel from Arabic only to the final *aleph* in ההלכוא (Josh. 10:24; Arab. 20) and אבוא (Isaiah 28:12; Arab. *ibid.*, the Hebrew [12] and English [14] do not make this clear at all), but ibn Janāḥ calls it unfounded (*Lumāᶜ*, 203; *Riḳmah*, 306).

43. Stern, *Liber responsionum*, p. 40. Cf. also p. 38.

44. *Ibid.*, p. 62: כי לא יתכן לדמות לשון עברית אל לשון הערב.

45. *Ibid.*, pp. 96–97. Cf. also their criticism of Dunash in the opening verses (15, lines 76–77).

averse to a humanistic treatment of Hebrew. They were irritated to see the language of the Bible, replete with mysteries and inner meaning, subjected to laws and principles governing other human languages.[46] Ibn Janāḥ is very vehement in his disgust with them. He characterizes them as weak-minded individuals with little understanding who put up a front of orthodoxy and adorn themselves with piety when in fact they possess a very limited appreciation of the true situation.[47] He confronts them not only with the numerous examples from the Talmud of Rabbis who did not hesitate to seek aid from foreign languages in the understanding of Hebrew words, but also with celebrities of post-Talmudic times like the Geonim Saadia, Sherira, Hai, and Samuel ben Ḥofni, all of whom recognized properly the value of comparative study.[48] But one cannot escape the feeling that despite the vigor of the attack this protagonist of progress betrays an insecurity and an anxiety not to be charged with heretical tendencies. It shows in his collection of evidence from Talmudic authorities to justify his interest, and in an impassioned refutation which follows a comparison with Arabic which he has drawn: "Do not suspect me of bringing Arabic words and usages in this and other books of mine as proofs to strengthen my statements regarding the ways and manners of Hebrew. I do it merely to show the fools and those who think they are wise and believe they know, although they are stripped of knowledge, that what I regard as permissible in Hebrew has its parallels in other languages."[49]

Opinions were also divided on the requirement to study Hebrew grammar. There were undoubtedly many in the Middle Ages, generally recruited from the ranks of those who dismissed every subject except Halakha as a waste of time, who discounted the inquiry into the structure and the laws

46. In discussing the position of the pious, Duran (*Maᶜaseh Efod*, 13) reports that some of them reject the need of Biblical grammar and say: והוא טוב למאמינים אשר באמונתם יחיו ולא יבקשו ראיה עליה. He characterizes their attitude to grammar as negative and adds: וקרה להם זה למיעוט ערך חכמת הלשון בעיניהם וכמעט שהיא בעיני רב החכמים רצוני המפורסמים בחכמה מותר ודבר שאין צורך לו. Apologetically, Ḥayyim ben Beẓalel in the introduction to his Grammar (quoted by S. Assaf, *Meḳorot le-Toledot ha-Ḥinukh be-Yisrᵓael* [Tel-Aviv-Jerusalem, 1925–42], I, 43) refutes as untrue a Gentile accusation that: היהודים האומללים האלה. . . לשונם לשון הקדש היה נחלת אבות ועתה נשכח מפיהם. . . ויחפאו דברים על בני ישראל אשר לא כן. . . כל העם הזה. . . עשו זאת חוק ומשפט מן היום שלא ללמד נערי ישראל דקדוק לה״ק לפי שידעו שהורס את מצב משפט התלמוד שלהם.

47. Introd. to *Riḳmah* (ed. Wilensky, p. 11); ואשר הקל מהם בחכמה הזאת . . . הנוטים מהם אל מעט מחכמת התלמוד בעבור גאותם במזער אשר יבינו אבל חכמת השמוש והדבור היא להם מן הדברים אשר מנחשים בהם וכמעט שלא ישימוה מן האפיקורוסות. Similarly, קונטרס בדקדוק שפת עבר (ed. Poznanski), 19: יש קצת מן התלמידים הלומדים קצת בתלמוד ומתלוצצים בזאת המלאכה . . . וכל מי שידעו שהוא משתמש בה כמעט שלא יחשדוהו בעיניהם בחוקת אפיקורוס.

48. *Riḳmah* (ed. Wilensky), p. 12.

49. *Lumāᶜ*, 217; *Riḳmah*, 235–236.

of the language.[50] In Germany and Poland a literary medium developed over the centuries which, apart from stylistic crudities, is usually distinguished by a lack of regard for the rules of grammar. Among the Jews in Islamic lands voices of opposition were also heard. This is evident from the lengthy introduction of Ibn Janāḥ to his grammatical work, in which he takes issue with this attitude. He is vehement in his denunciation of their opposition. He points out that such negativism was condemned by the Rabbis of the Talmud who castigated the Galileans as forgetting their learning because they were lax in their treatment of their language, which he explains to mean that they paid no attention to grammar.[51] He reminds his readers of the truly great Talmudic scholars such as Saadia Gaon and Samuel ben Ḥofni, who were very much concerned about the proper forms and who urged the importance of study and investigation.[52] He emphasizes that it is essential for the study of Halakha to take note of grammatical matters, and that our great Rabbis left much evidence in the Talmud bearing witness to their interest in, and occupation with, the linguistic problems.[53] He tells of his embarrassment over the fact that the Muslims are extremely conscious of their language,[54] and says that the attitude of his negatively-oriented coreligionists is in reality the product of a disrespect for the language and of a lack of concern for its proper usage.

Some four centuries later, the philologist Profiat Duran again engages in a discussion of the legitimacy of grammatical studies. In the spirit of his age, which is marked by a general decline of the freedom of inquiry and of secular and semisecular learning and by a triumphant march of Talmudism,[55] he adopts a conciliatory tone, granting that the study of Torah is of paramount importance as the one comprehensive pursuit which achieves the goal that man ought to set before him. At the same time, however, he voices his disagreement with the extremists who maintain that even the study of the Bible is a waste of time, and recalls that the Rabbis

50. *Riḳmah*, 11: עד אשר הגיעני על אחד מגדוליהם שהוא אומר על חכמת הלשון שהיא דבר שאין לה טעם והעסק בה אין בו תועלת ולא הנאה.

51. *Riḳmah*, 14, lines 5–13.

52. *Ibid.*, 12, lines 4–13, 1.3.

53. *Ibid.*, 14, lines 14–16, 1.5.

54. *Ibid.*, 11, lines 6–8: וראיתי את העם אשר אנחנו עומדים בתוכם מתחזקים להגיע אל תכלית חכמת לשונם כאשר זכרנו ממה שמחייב אותו העיון וגוזרת בו האמת.

55. Examples of the severe judgments on philosophy and other secular studies can be found in Shelomo Alami's *Iggeret Musar* (ed. Haberman [Jerusalem, 1946], p. 16); Isaac Arama's *Ḥazut Ḳashah* (18a); Joseph Jabez's *Or Ha-Ḥayyim* (Ferrara, 1554), 2a. See also F. Baer, *Toledot ha-Yehudim be-Sefarad* (Tel-Aviv, 1945), 2, 145.

recommended giving a third of one's time to the learning of the Scriptures.[56] He also finds justification for an interest in "Greek Wisdom,"[57] contending that the Sages were certainly well versed in it. Bible, however, cannot be properly acquired without a true knowledge of Hebrew, contrary to the view of those who consider it an unnecessary diversion.[58]

What are the written sources of Hebrew? This query, which even in our day has scholars divided, evidently disturbed medieval students. The Talmudic statement, in a halakhic context, that "the language of the Sages is different from the language of the Bible"[59] may have served as the basis for a divergence of opinion on a linguistic issue. The attitude of the Ḳaraites to post-Biblical literature, with its corollary judgment on the language in which it was edited, probably also played a part in a scholar's position on the problem. This may certainly be said of Saadia Gaon, whose polemics with the Ḳaraites have given him the status of their bitterest enemy. In his preface to the little tract on Biblical *hapax legomena*[60] he states: "I have met Jewish people who deny the commandments and ordinances transmitted in the name of the prophets but not written in Scripture, and others who deny the language which they hear from the religious community but do not find it in the Torah." As the late Benjamin Klar, the editor of the Arabic original, and others after him have recognized,[61] this short study, in which Saadia frequently succeeds in giving the meaning of an isolated Biblical word from a Rabbinic parallel, is definitely polemical in its purport. Its author declares in explicit terms that he will cite proof-texts from the prosaic language of the Mishnah which was the popular speech of the time. Undoubtedly, he continues, the Mishnaic and Talmudic authorities were much more familiar with the language since they were chronologically closer to the prophets and

56. He reports (*Ma^caseh Efod*, 5) that they rely on Rashi's comment on מנעו בניכם מן ההגיון (BT *Berakhot* 28b): לא תרגילום במקרא יותר מדאי משום דמשכא but refutes it by the Rabbinic statement (BT *Kiddushin* 30a) לעולם ישלש אדם שנותיו שליש במקרא שליש במשנה שליש בתלמוד and explains Rashi's יותר מדאי to mean in excess of one third.

57. See his long discussion, *Ma^caseh Efod*, 6–9.

58. *Ibid.*, 16.

59. לשון תורה לעצמה ולשון חכמים לעצמה, BT *Hullin* 137b; BT *Abodah Zarah* 58b.

60. Ed. Nehemiah Alony, "Kitāb al-sab^cīn lafṭa," in *Ignace Goldziher Memorial Volume*, II (ed. S. Löwinger, A. Scheiber, J. Somogyi, Jerusalem, 1958), 14–47. See also *idem*, ישעיהו בשבעים מלים בודדות לרס"ג in *Tur-Sinai Jubilee Volume*, pp. 282–283.

61. הנוסח המקורי של פתרון שבעים מלים בודדות (in *Meḥḳarim we-^cIyyunim*), pp. 258, 263ff. Klar gives Geiger credit for this understanding of the character of the tract; cf. p. 263, n. 22.

employed those difficult words when they conversed with their students, and spoke them naturally and freely.[62]

But there were also men of letters among the Rabbanites who had their reservations with respect to the range of the language and the justice of utilizing the Mishnah and other Rabbinic texts as freely as the Bible in writing Hebrew. Moses ibn Ezra speaks sorrowfully of the small remnant which has remained of Hebrew, although he approves of the occasional use of Mishnaic "because its words are in pure Hebrew."[63] Judah ibn Tibbon apologizes to his readers for using Rabbinic Hebrew along with Biblical, as well as for occasionally selecting the Rabbinic instead of the Biblical word.[64] His plea "let not the reader consider me a sinner because I mixed the language of the Bible with the language of our Rabbis in places" indicates his conviction that the latter is not Hebrew, and rouses the feeling that he is addressing himself to other people who may take exception to this practice. And Profiat Duran, although he cites the Mishnaic Order of *Tohorot* in evidence of his claim that Hebrew once possessed an adequate terminology for utensils and tools, of which only a fraction has been preserved in it, and the Order of *Zeraᶜim* to prove the same for drugs and medicine, he adds significantly, in both instances, the qualification "and it is not all the sacred tongue."

On the other hand, staunch defenders of the genuineness of Mishnaic Hebrew provide us not only with some of the reason for the position of the opponents but also with the answers to them. Ibn Janāḥ, for example, condemns certain people as ignorant fools for attacking him because of his readiness to bring testimony from the Mishnah.[65] According to them

62. *Tur-Sinai Jubilee Volume*, pp. 282–283.

63. In his *Shirat Yisraᵓel* (ed. Halper), he says, p. 59: ולא נשאר לנו מן השפה העברית שום שריד ופליט לבד מעשרים וארבעה הספרים המקודשים שאינם כוללים מן הלשון אלא אותן המלים הדרושות לענינים שהספרים האלו דנים בהם. . . . מן הספרים הללו לקחה אומתנו את היסודות לחבר תפלות ובקשות . . . ואם נסתייע לפעמים בשפת המשנה יפה משום שמלותיה עברית טהורה. This passage sheds light on Abraham ibn Ezra's celebrated outburst against Eleᶜazar Kalir in his comment *ad Kohelet* 5, 1: . . . והדבר השני שפיוטיו מעורבים בלשון תלמוד וידוע כי יש כמה לשונות בתלמוד ואינמו לשון הקדש וכן אמרו לשון מקרא לחוד ולשון תלמוד לחוד . . . ולמה לא נלמד מן התפלה שהיא כל דברי צחות בלשון הקדש. . . . So also Ibn Janāḥ: ולשון הקדש אין בידינו ממנה כי אם הנמצא בספרי המקרא. (Introduction to *Riḳmah*, 3.)

64. Introduction to *Duties of the Heart* (ed. Zifroni), p. 5: ואל יחטיאני מפני שערבתי לשון המקרא ולשון רבותינו במקומות ושהבאתי לשון רבותינו במקום שהייתי מוצא לשון המקרא כי אחזתי בלשון הקרוב וכפי שנזדמן לי בשעת ההעתקה. His son also, in listing the "foreignisms" which he employed in his translation of the *Guide*, includes: והמין השני מלות נמצאות במשנה או בתלמוד אינם ידועים אך לקצת חכמים כמילת אסטוס וסוג.

65. Introduction to *Riḳmah* (ed. Wilensky), 19: ויותר נפלא ומגונה מזה ממעשיהם ונגלה מסכלותם מה שהם תופשים עלינו עדת המפרשים ספרי האלהים, בהביאנו עד מן המשנה בעבור שהם מגנים אותה במה שנמצא בה ממלות זרות יוצאות חוץ להקשת הלשון. The editor (*Riḳmah*, n. 8) identifies these as the Ḳaraites, who are not otherwise mentioned by ibn Janāḥ.

it is not qualified to serve that purpose since its word formation is not "regular." He insists that such an argument is untenable and that the coinage of new forms like תרם and התחיל can certainly not be called erroneous.[66]

This view is defended more vigorously and in greater detail by the thirteenth-century exegete and lexicographer Tanḥūm ben Joseph Yerushalmi. He prefaces his glossary to the *Mishneh Torah* of Maimonides, whom he admires exceedingly,[67] with a discussion of the valid reasons for the treatment of Mishnaic Hebrew as genuine. In the course of his remarks he declares:[68] "There are words in the Mishnah, nouns and verbs, which are formed contrary to the known usage of the roots of the language. They are exceptions and depart from analogy with the usual formations which followed true models and clear patterns. The same method is followed in other books of law, and the words have been adopted by the community. Some modern philologians, however, reject it and call this practice an inadmissible error. For example, they point to תרם, which was converted by them into a verb by treating the *tau* as a radical, or to יתחיל, התחיל, which they constructed from תחלה . . . All this, however, is sound and is formed in accordance with the rules of inflection of words derived from their roots conforming to the correct analogies which are found in Scripture. But the clinching reply to these arguments and to similar objections is to say that the Hebrew language was not encompassed in its entirety in the available Biblical texts, nor did those whose words are recorded in these texts intend to expound the principles of the language and to list its legitimate practices; no, they said what was needed at the time. If more words were recorded we might perhaps find in them what we have today. Since we find these forms used by our ancients, who were nearer than we to the time of the development of the language and the spread of its practices, and the increase in the knowledge of its grammar, we know for sure that it was permissible; hence they utilized it in their speech. Such forms are not erroneous, as the obstinate people think who develop their own opinions." He then proceeds to prove that the forms to which they

66. ואנחנו מרוממים מעלת המשנה ממה שחרפוה בו מהטעות במלות האלה. Cf. Parḥon, *Maḥberet he-ᶜArukh*, XXII: וכל מה שהוא דומה ללשון המקרא בין מן התרגום בין מן המשנה בין מן התלמוד אביאנו.

67. Cf. his tribute to him in his introduction (see next note), 5, lines 16–24.

68. *Kitāb al-Murshid al-Kāfi* (described and edited in part by W. Bacher, *Aus dem Wörterbuche Tanchum Jeruschalmi's* [Strassburg, 1903]), Arabic section, pp. 13–14. The general argument was stated by Ibn Janāḥ before him, but he is more explicit in the theses he propounds. (Part 1 of the Glossary has now appeared with Hebrew translation by B. Toledano [Tel Aviv, 1961].)

raise objections have their parallels in the Bible.[69] Clearly he, like his distinguished predecessor Ibn Janāḥ, is progressive enough to recognize the validity of unsupported patterns of language as genuine Hebrew, but maintains that in the case of Mishnaic Hebrew it is not even necessary.

69. *Aus dem Wörterbuche Tanchum Jeruschalmi's*, 141, 9ff.

INDEX OF SCRIPTURAL QUOTATIONS

INDEX OF NAMES

INDEX OF SUBJECTS

Index of Scriptural Quotations

Index of Names

Index of Subjects